MARKET COMPLICITY AND CHRISTIAN ETHICS

The marketplace is a remarkable social institution that has greatly extended our reach, so shoppers in the West can now buy fresh-cut flowers, vegetables, and tropical fruits grown halfway across the globe, even in the depths of winter. However, these expanded choices have also come with considerable moral responsibilities as our economic decisions can have far-reaching effects by either ennobling or debasing human lives. Albino Barrera examines our own moral responsibilities for the distant harms of our market transactions from a Christian viewpoint, identifying how the market's division of labor makes us unwitting collaborators in others' wrongdoing and in collective ills. His important account covers a range of different subjects, including law, economics, philosophy, and theology, in order to identify the injurious ripple effects of our market activities.

ALBINO BARRERA is Professor of Economics and Theology at Providence College in Rhode Island. His previous publications include *Globalization and Economic Ethics* (2007), *Economic Compulsion and Christian Ethics* (Cambridge, 2005), *God and the Evil of Scarcity* (2005), and *Modern Catholic Social Documents and Political Economy* (2001).

NEW STUDIES IN CHRISTIAN ETHICS

General Editor
ROBIN GILL

Editorial Board
STEPHEN R. L. CLARK, STANLEY HAUERWAS, ROBIN W. LOVIN

Christian ethics has increasingly assumed a central place within academic theology. At the same time the growing power and ambiguity of modern science and the rising dissatisfaction within the social sciences about claims to value-neutrality have prompted renewed interest in ethics within the secular academic world. There is, therefore, a need for studies in Christian ethics which, as well as being concerned with the relevance of Christian ethics to the present-day secular debate, are well informed about parallel discussions in recent philosophy, science or social science. *New Studies in Christian Ethics* aims to provide books that do this at the highest intellectual level and demonstrate that Christian ethics can make a distinctive contribution to this debate – either in moral substance or in terms of underlying moral justifications.

MARKET COMPLICITY AND CHRISTIAN ETHICS

ALBINO BARRERA

CAMBRIDGE
UNIVERSITY PRESS

CAMBRIDGE UNIVERSITY PRESS
Cambridge, New York, Melbourne, Madrid, Cape Town, Singapore,
São Paulo, Delhi, Dubai, Tokyo, Mexico City

Cambridge University Press
The Edinburgh Building, Cambridge CB2 8RU, UK

Published in the United States of America by Cambridge University Press, New York

www.cambridge.org
Information on this title: www.cambridge.org/9781107003156

First published 2011

Printed in the United Kingdom at the University Press, Cambridge

A catalogue record for this publication is available from the British Library

Library of Congress Cataloguing in Publication data
Barrera, Albino.
Market complicity and Christian ethics / Albino Barrera.
p.   cm. – (New studies in Christian ethics)
ISBN 978-1-107-00315-6 (hardback)
1. Christian ethics.   I. Title.
BJ1251.B346   2010
241′.64–dc22
2010030375

ISBN 978-1-107-00315-6 Hardback

For the street kids of Maláte and the children of Ortol – so joyful and eager to learn more about God.

Contents

General editor's preface

After the near-collapse of the global financial system in 2008 this new addition to *New Studies in Christian Ethics* is very timely indeed and is written with great wisdom and clarity. Albino Barrera's previous contribution, *Economic Compulsion and Christian Ethics* (Cambridge, 2005), attracted some very fine reviews. His rigorous training in both economics and theology really has given him an extraordinarily authoritative voice (that and an ability to write clear prose), matching so exactly the aims of the series: namely, to promote studies in Christian ethics which engage centrally with the present secular moral debate at the highest possible intellectual level and, second, to encourage contributors to demonstrate that Christian ethics can make a distinctive contribution to this debate.

Economic Compulsion and Christian Ethics was a top-down book, looking at the way in which markets can create economic hardships for some individuals and communities (so-called pecuniary externalities), whereas *Market Complicity and Christian Ethics* is more a bottom-up book, examining the various ways in which we are all complicit in the harmful effects of our market choices (including, but certainly not exhausted by, pecuniary externalities). Together the two books offer an unparalleled account of current market economics from a perspective within Christian ethics to which all those engaging in this area responsibly in the future will need to respond.

Albino Barrera's new book is particularly helpful for those concerned with untangling what the complex and multilayered moral concepts of complicity, accountability, and responsibility entail in relation to modern market economies. Theologians and ethicists looking for easy answers will not find them here. Instead what they will soon discover is one of the most thoughtful and gifted Christian ethicists currently writing about these crucial economic issues.

It is a privilege and delight to be able to welcome this unique and important new contribution to the series.

ROBIN GILL

Acknowledgments

I owe a debt of gratitude to many who helped me in the course of this project. Ernest Bartell provided insights and encouragement on the key chapters. The two anonymous readers and Robin Gill, series editor, were extremely generous with their time in carefully pointing out problematic areas and in offering a wealth of materials for incorporation. They clearly improved the final output with their excellent suggestions and critique. I cannot thank them enough. Of course, any mistakes that remain are my sole responsibility. Laura Morris, Joanna Garbutt, and Joanna Breeze of Cambridge University Press were very helpful and professional in shepherding the project through production. Carol Fellingham Webb provided excellent copy-editing services. Kate Mertes furnished a superb comprehensive index. I am truly grateful for these friends and colleagues.

Introduction

Are we morally responsible for the distant harms spawned by our market transactions? If so, what are the grounds for these non-contractual obligations? How strong are their claims and what are their limits?

For all its genuine benefits, the market, unfortunately, also magnifies the harmful ripple effects of economic activity. In fostering specialization and division of labor, the market gives us a much wider selection of goods and services than would have otherwise been the case, but it also makes us unwitting collaborators in the wrongdoing of others. We inadvertently facilitate the misdeeds of unscrupulous market participants or perpetrate collective wrongs.

For example, the higher returns of investors in tobacco stocks come at the expense of the premature death of millions, especially in the developing world where tobacco firms have taken advantage of lax regulations and non-existent health education to promote smoking aggressively. US chicken farmers and livestock owners heavily use antibiotics in their feeds for better animal growth, but the overuse of antimicrobials has increasingly rendered lifesaving antibiotics ineffective against bacteria that have mutated with a stronger resistance to these drugs. The market for ivory objets d'art and jewelry makes it even more difficult to save endangered elephant herds from being decimated further by poachers. Hedge funds invest in commodities like oil, but their speculative trading causes greater volatility and unwarranted price increases that drive nations into deeper poverty. And, of course, as consumers, we stretch our incomes by demanding cut-rate prices for our fruits, vegetables, coffee, chocolate, meats, and apparel, but often at the cost of low wages and poor working conditions for the laborers who toil to keep our pantries and closets well stocked.

These are instances of material cooperation in economic wrongdoing or in collective harms. Clearly, the marketplace is a remarkable social institution that has greatly extended our reach. As ordinary shoppers, we can enjoy fresh-cut flowers, vegetables, and tropical fruits grown halfway across the globe, even in the depths of winter. But these expanded choices also come with considerable moral responsibilities. Our buying and selling decisions take even greater moral significance because they now have more extensive and more consequential spillover effects that either ennoble or debase human lives. As proof, we only have to look at the subprime lenders and financial institutions whose excesses precipitated the 2008–2009 global financial meltdown that brought economic chaos and suffering to many.

The problem of how we unwittingly aid and abet evildoing through our economic choices has been long acknowledged in Christian faith and practice. John Chrysostom stressed emphatically to his congregants not to engage in trades or occupations that beget turpitude or illiberality in the human heart or that produce useless goods or luxuries. To do so is to live on disgraceful gains. Toward the end of her married life, St. Elizabeth of Hungary often went hungry rather than partake of food and drink that were unjustly appropriated from peasants. In preaching on the proper use of money, John Wesley urged caution that even as we should gain as much as we could in our work, we should do so without harming our neighbors' livelihoods or bodily and spiritual health. Abolitionists urged the English public to spurn slave-grown sugar during the bitter struggle to outlaw the slave trade at the turn of the nineteenth century. Our own generation has seen many consumer boycotts aimed at redressing economic injustice. Indeed, Christian theologians, saints, preachers, ethicists, and reformers have been well aware of the problem of blameworthy economic material cooperation in others' wrongdoing.

However, to my knowledge, there is no systematic treatment of the problem of economic complicity in Christian ethics to date. Knowing where to draw the line between permissible and blameworthy material cooperation is one of the more vexing problems in moral theology. Clearly, our interest in this book is to examine what Christian ethics has to offer in dealing with moral complicity in market harms. How might we apply scholastic "cooperation with evil" and the principle of double effect in evaluating contemporary economic wrongdoing? Can we give an adequate account of economic complicity using the resources of Christian ethics alone? If not, what methods and insights could we adopt from economics, social philosophy, and law in the attribution of individual responsibility for distant harms or collective ills? What can we learn from the legal doctrine of complicity and its theory of causation?

Unfortunately, before we can get to these questions, it is important that we first understand the nature of the problem. What moral issues are raised by the phenomenon of economic complicity? What are its defining formal characteristics? How common is this problem? In philosophy, complicity is viewed as a specialized topic, one of its least explored subjects. There is little scholarship on moral complicity, and not surprisingly, there is even less work on economic complicity. Thus, we have to add a second goal to our study by necessity. We first have to examine the nature of economic complicity itself and the moral issues it raises. This includes identifying the most prevalent instances of market-mediated complicity and then assessing the economic, philosophical, and theological warrants for why they deserve censure. These will then become the bases for our work in appraising what Christian ethics has to offer in dealing with economic complicity.

CHALLENGES

To what extent are we culpable for the unintended consequences of our actions? Is there a half-life to these duties over space and time, or are we responsible even for the most distant ills indirectly caused by our moral choices? Common sense tells us that we cannot be held to account for everything. But where do we draw the limits of our moral obligations and why?

To compound this dilemma even further, these unintended consequences unfold in a complex economic terrain. Assessing material cooperation in economic wrongdoing is made even more challenging by the market's labyrinthine web of causes and effects, simultaneous harms and benefits, and interdependent economic agencies. Moreover, we often have to deal with accumulative harms in which acts that seem benign at the individual level become terribly injurious at an aggregated level (e.g., speculative investments).

TIMELINESS

Despite these conceptual hurdles and the paucity of materials, it is well worth the effort to grapple with the problem of faulty economic material cooperation because of the urgency of the issue. We are the generation that ushered in the post-industrial era. Globalization is a major shift in socio-economic life, as significant as the Industrial Revolution was in shaping the modern age. Global economic integration is a paradox: it creates new and more demanding economic obligations, even as it greatly expands the occasion for our complicity in or indifference to one another's economic misconduct.

On the one hand, globalization has made us ever more interdependent, better informed, and more capable of providing mutual assistance – all the necessary ingredients for weightier moral obligations for one another's well-being. We are ever more potent in enriching or diminishing others. More than ever, the marketplace calls for integrity, restraint, and virtue at the individual level if it is to function properly.

On the other hand, while globalization has made it even more pressing to sensitize the public to the issue of moral complicity, it has also made it far more difficult to tackle the problem in practice. Global economic integration has made the chain of causation much more intricate. And as ever larger circles of people are needed to get things done, moral hazard becomes even more of a problem as market participants refuse to take personal responsibility for collective outcomes, choosing instead to hide behind the anonymity of group membership. It has become increasingly difficult to individuate culpability for communal faults. And as ever more of our interpersonal relationships unfold through the marketplace, our shared ethos is increasingly marked by a hardened competitive individualism and an acquisitive consumerism. Greater marketization has made it so much easier to walk away from our mutual responsibilities and to watch out only for our own interests.

We could mitigate this paradox through clear thinking and discourse about economic complicity. We have to make people understand the phenomenon so well and make the case for addressing it so compelling that they voluntarily internalize their responsibilities for distant harms and communal wrongs. Moreover, providing a theoretical framework would go a long way toward a more comprehensive and systematic approach to rectifying the market's ill effects.

CONTENT

Chapter 1 surveys the conceptual tools currently available in the literature and examines similarities and differences between the scholastic notion of material cooperation with evil and the philosophical understanding of complicity. The legal doctrine of complicity, various accountability-limiting principles from social philosophy, and the principle of double effect can be combined into a single overarching framework that highlights their complementarity. Part I of the book sets out to do just that.

Chapter 2 examines the problem of accumulative harms whereby activities that are innocuous at the individual level turn out to be ruinous when aggregated with others' similar actions. Consequently, the ascription of individual responsibility for collective harms is made much more difficult because of a superfluity of causes and interlocking economic agencies.

Chapter 3 deals with the problem of overdetermination. How do we impute individual culpability for market outcomes that arise from a multiplicity of causes? In particular, is the individual's causal contribution to the accumulative harm too minuscule or redundant to be morally significant? Philosophical and theological arguments, ranging from rule utilitarianism to the familial view of community, converge on the same conclusion: despite their duplicative and minute causal contribution to ultimate harms, individuals are nonetheless still morally accountable.

Chapter 4 grapples with the problem of interdependent agencies. Tort jurisprudence provides a wealth of ideas on disentangling causes and effects. Many of these legal formal and informal rules of thumb can be adapted for use in the attribution of personal responsibility for collective economic ills. Tort scholarship amplifies scholastic cooperation with evil because both face the same task of determining who is morally liable in the chain of causation.

Part II applies the preceding conceptual tools to four types of market-mediated complicity. It proposes a typology that differentiates "hard" from "soft" complicity. The former entails a direct, unjustifiable entanglement with the wrongdoing, while the latter involves roundabout, unavoidable causation through accumulative harms. Each type of faulty material cooperation is examined according to its object of accountability (complicity in what?), its basis for accountability (why culpable?), and its subject of accountability (who is complicit?).

The topic of chapter 5 is what most people commonly associate with economic complicity – benefitting from and enabling wrongdoing. This kind of material cooperation can be shown to be blameworthy using the Christian understanding of the divine order of creation or John Stuart Mill's notion of "harm to others." Among the practical problems we address are: How do we determine what constitutes wrongdoing? How do we deal with activities that produce simultaneous beneficial and baleful effects? Is it moral to appropriate benefits from past wrongs? As an illustration, we assess the case of the Saipan apparel sweatshops using the framework of analysis from Part I.

Chapter 6 examines economic conduct that precipitates gratuitous harms. Such behavior is blameworthy because its ensuing damages are completely avertible. Thus, the wasteful use of oil, speculative investments in vital commodities, and inappropriate production methods generate terribly injurious consequences for unsuspecting third parties downstream. These activities are legal, but market participants who engage in them are nonetheless morally culpable for precipitating the resulting ills. This claim can be justified using the just-use obligation from Christian ethics and the notion of undue risk creation from tort law.

Chapter 7 also deals with collective harms, but unlike in the preceding chapter, these injuries are unavoidable by the nature of market operations. Economic life is in a constant state of flux as people exchange goods and services. The resulting price changes benefit some, but at the expense of others. The latter adverse effects can be particularly severe. The community as a whole is not blameworthy for these, but it is nonetheless liable for mitigating the more grievous instances of such spillover effects. Rawls's justice as fairness and the notion of economic security as a divine gift are among the philosophical and theological grounds for this liability.

In chapter 8, we generalize the preceding chapter's findings by extending the analysis to non-pecuniary accumulative harms. On the surface, the smooth operations of the market seem to be the spontaneous result of people coming together to trade with one another. In reality, the market is undergirded by customs, law, and usage slowly accumulated and refined over time through our individual buying and selling decisions. Unfortunately, some of these underlying institutions and practices are unjust or harmful to segments of the population. The notions of bounded rationality, path dependence, and network externalities from economics, and the idea of social sin from Christian ethics are helpful on this issue. They provide arguments for why there is a moral duty to rectify these detrimental structures that we unavoidably reinforce through our participation in market exchange.

Responsibility is the corollary of complicity. Thus, chapter 9 lays the groundwork for a theology of economic responsibility using ontology, Sacred Scripture, and Christian social thought. Such theology must examine the relationship between power, responsibility, and freedom, given the nature of market operations. Responsibility is theocentric, not anthropocentric. It is God who provides the grounds for the moral agent's relationships and response to others.

We conclude the book in chapter 10 with a comparison of what secular philosophy and Christian ethics have to offer on the problem of economic complicity. There is a substantial overlap between the two, no doubt partly due to the use of both faith and reason in Christian ethics. Nevertheless, moral theology has a much "thicker" notion of the good. It is distinctly dissimilar from many secular, liberal philosophies in terms of the wider range of activities it deems to be morally wrong, the weightier obligations it embraces, and the importance it accords to the integrity of relationships and the virtue of the person.

Written for social ethicists, moral theologians, economists, policymakers, business ethicists, and students of market morality, this book advances the literature on economic complicity in the following ways. First, it identifies some of the key issues that have to be addressed in any reasonable account of blameworthy material cooperation in economic life. This study examines the nature of market-mediated complicity, a task that has not been undertaken in economic, philosophical, or theological literature to date. Second, it outlines what Christian ethics has to offer on this phenomenon. Moreover, this study embeds the scholastic principles of legitimate cooperation with evil and double effect within a much richer conceptual framework that facilitates their application to economic problems.

Third, the book identifies those occasions on which we might be complicit to misconduct in the marketplace; it also presents the moral grounds for such culpability. In particular, it proposes a typology of market complicity. Fourth, we gain a better appreciation for the nature of accumulative economic harms and the special problems they pose for social ethics. Fifth, business ethicists can use the proposed framework of analysis in their assessment of corporate complicity.

Sixth, we see an example of the use of faith and reason in moral reflection. The book highlights the points of convergence and divergence between social philosophy, economics, law, and Christian ethics in their ascription of individual responsibility for distant harms and communal wrongs. Interdisciplinary work makes a big difference.

Finally, this study is a timely contribution to public discourse. The near-collapse of the global financial system in 2008 clearly demonstrated the unintended damage individuals can wreak in the marketplace and the swiftness with which they can inflict such harms. These recent events also underscore the need to sharpen our moral reasoning in dealing with blameworthy material cooperation in economic wrongdoing.

According to development economics, sustained economic growth expands people's opportunities. They have many more choices available to them. Thus, those who have benefitted from globalization now enjoy a much broader freedom of action. But as mentioned earlier, global economic integration has also led to an increased marketization of our common life. This means that our economic choices are less private and more social than ever before, because they have much wider and more consequential spillover effects on others. Indeed, greater economic liberties come with correspondingly greater social responsibilities. Unfortunately, many wholeheartedly embrace the former but conveniently ignore the latter. Thus, there is urgent need to sensitize the winners from globalization to both the potency and the duties of their newfound economic autonomy. I hope this study will be a modest contribution to that end.

PART I

Theory: material cooperation in economic life

Conscientious shoppers willingly pay a much higher price for tuna caught in dolphin- and turtle-free nets. Environmentalists voluntarily embrace a simple lifestyle to minimize their footprint on the ecology. Socially responsible investing is a growing segment of capital markets, covering 11 percent of all funds under professional management in the United States in 2007. Indeed, people intuitively acknowledge their obligations for the harmful ripple effects of their economic transactions. Unfortunately, the academic literature has yet to provide a rigorous theoretical foundation for our moral intuitions on the residual duties we know we owe one another in the marketplace.

The first half of this book lays the groundwork for a theory of economic complicity in wrongdoing or in collective harms. Chapter 1 outlines the scholastic principles of legitimate material cooperation with evil and double effect, the legal doctrine of complicity, and insights from social philosophy on moral complicity. The next three chapters break down the phenomenon of complicity into its three constituent issues. Chapter 2 examines the object of accountability (complicity in what?) and its attendant problem of accumulative harms. Chapter 3 is an account of the basis for accountability (why culpable?) and its concomitant problem of overdetermination. Chapter 4 grapples with the subject of accountability (who is complicit?) and the problem of interdependent economic agencies.

CHAPTER I

The nature of material cooperation and moral complicity

COOPERATION WITH EVIL

For Christian ethicists, the scholastic notion of "cooperation with evil" (also known as the principle of legitimate material cooperation) is the logical starting point in evaluating our moral responsibility for inadvertently facilitating others' wrongdoing. Our actions that are appropriated and used by others for their misconduct can be described as merely "the occasion (but not the cause) of the sinful deed."[1] In fact, our actions may yet be morally licit even if we foresee their subsequent misuse by others. Alphonsus Liguori (1696–1787) is credited with formulating this principle in his *Theologia Moralis*:

That [cooperation] is formal which concurs in the bad will of the other, and it cannot be without sin; that [cooperation] is material which concurs only in the bad action of the other, apart from the cooperator's intention. But the latter [material cooperation] is licit when the action is good or indifferent in itself; and when one has reason for doing it that is both just and proportioned to the gravity of the other's sin and to the closeness of the assistance which is given to the carrying out of that sin. (Grisez 1997, 873, 876)[2]

This principle has been developed even further, and there is wide agreement among commentators on its key distinctions.[3]

Coordinate agent (co-principal) versus a mere cooperator

A coordinate agent or a co-principal is one who has the same wrongful intent as the principal and who performs part of the wrongful act itself. Thus, a coordinate agent (co-principal) is always guilty. On the other hand,

---

[1] Griese (1987, 389).   [2] Translated from Liguori (1905–1912, I:357).
[3] I draw the following distinctions from Gonsalves (1990), Griese (1987), Häring (1964, 494–519), Kaveny (2000, 285), Keenan and Kopfensteiner (1995), and Oderberg (2004).

a cooperator merely provides some assistance to the principal in the latter's commission of the wrongdoing and may even be guiltless depending on the particulars of the case. Such cooperation can be evaluated according to the nature of the intention and the nature of the act. Moreover, the nature of the act can be examined further in terms of its degree of influence and its level of responsibility.

Nature of the intention: formal cooperation versus material cooperation

The formal cooperator intends the wrong committed by the principal; the formal cooperator endeavors to make the principal succeed in the wrongdoing. For example, unscrupulous offshore banks are in formal cooperation when they assist their clients to avoid taxes in their home countries or launder money from criminal activities. During the 2005–2008 US housing bubble, dishonest mortgage brokers were in formal cooperation when they aided and abetted unqualified borrowers in falsely certifying their annual income or assets. The material cooperator has no such intention. Formal cooperation is always morally wrong and blameworthy. The material cooperator need not be morally culpable, depending on the facts of the situation.[4]

Nature of the act: degree of influence

Immediate versus mediate cooperation: Immediate cooperators share in part of the principal's commission of the wrongdoing to the point where the principal's act becomes their own. One can no longer distinguish between the cooperator's and the wrongdoer's acts. This is always blameworthy, just like formal cooperation. For example, Wall Street banks were in immediate cooperation as they helped Enron manipulate its financial statements and mislead investors.[5] The mediate cooperator, on the other hand, performs tasks before or after the principal's wrongdoing. Examples of mediate cooperators are the office personnel supporting top Enron executives with

---

[4] We can further differentiate formal and material cooperation in terms of whether they are implicit or explicit, positive or negative (omission), and physical or moral.

[5] The Enron scandal was a massive accounting fraud to inflate the stock price of the company. This Houston-based firm filed for bankruptcy in 2001, resulting in enormous losses for its investors and workers. In July 2003, J. P. Morgan Chase and Citigroup paid a fine of $300 million for their role in the accounting fraud. In September 2003, Merrill Lynch acknowledged the complicity of its employees. Four former Merrill Lynch executives were subsequently convicted of fraud and conspiracy in November 2004. See www.latimes.com/sns-ap-enron-trial-glance,0,267898.story?page=1 (last accessed March 7, 2010).

clerical, accounting, and secretarial services. Such mediate cooperators are not necessarily blameworthy, depending on the circumstances of each case.

Indispensable versus dispensable cooperation (aka *necessary versus contingent cooperation*): This distinction pertains to the causal necessity of the cooperator for the wrongdoing. "But for" the indispensable cooperator, the harm would not have been inflicted by the principal. Thus, Enron's accounting fraud should have been flagged much earlier and the public damage contained, but for the negligence of its auditor, Arthur Anderson, LLP.[6] In contrast, the dispensable agent cannot satisfy the "but for" test. For example, even without the mid-level managers and executives, the Enron fraud would have still been perpetrated. They were merely dispensable, contingent cooperators.[7] The indispensable cooperator exercises relatively greater moral and practical leverage in determining whether or not the wrongdoing succeeds and is, consequently, more culpable than the dispensable cooperator.

Proximate versus remote cooperation: This distinction pertains either to the causal importance or to the "moral connection" of the cooperator with the principal wrongdoing, or both.[8] Thus, Enron accountants were causally much more significant for the fraud (proximate cooperators) compared with other office staff doing clerical work (remote cooperators). Examples of a "moral connection" to the wrongdoing itself were the mid-level Enron executives who were aware of the fraud but who kept quiet out of fear of jeopardizing their own holdings of Enron stocks in their retirement investment accounts.[9] In contrast, there is no moral connection between the Enron fraud and Enron suppliers.

Nature of the act: level of responsibility

Unjust versus unlawful cooperation:[10] Unjust cooperation entails injury to a third party while an unlawful cooperation does not. An example of an unlawful (but not unjust) cooperation is the case of the person who brings

---

[6] Arthur Andersen, LLP was the largest of the Big Five public accounting firms prior to its dissolution in the wake of its role in the Enron scandal.

[7] Of course, there is the separate issue of their duty to alert authorities. We will examine the issue of failure by omission in a later chapter.

[8] To this, one can also add temporal and geographical proximity (Kaveny 2000, 285).

[9] Another example of a moral connection in the wrongdoing itself is the case of the owners of US retail chains and distribution outlets for sweatshops. These proprietors are at least proximate cooperators because their interests overlap those of their overseas sweatshop suppliers – keeping labor costs down. In contrast, there is a minimal "moral connection," if at all, between these retail chains' employees and the overseas sweatshop operations.

[10] I draw this distinction from Oderberg (2004, 205–209).

drugs to an addict.[11] No third party is involved besides the cooperator and the principal. The cases we examine in Part II of our study involve injury to third parties.

In sum, Alphonsus Liguori identifies three conditions that have to be satisfied if material cooperation[12] is to be morally licit.

1 The cooperator's act must not be evil in itself.
2 The cooperator is motivated by a good intention.
3 The cooperator's reason is proportioned to:
   a the gravity of the perpetrator's wrongdoing;
   b his or her proximity to the wrongdoing.[13]

Principle of double effect

Of Liguori's three conditions, the proportionality between the cooperator's reason for acting and the ensuing collateral harm is the most demanding and the most open-ended criterion. In particular, there are problems associated with disentangling, measuring, and comparing interlocking harms and benefits. This is not even to mention the difficulty of identifying the key consequences we have to consider.

For this third condition, moral culpability hinges on whether or not the cooperation was justified to begin with. There may be overwhelming benefits relative to the ensuing harms that warrant such cooperation. Are there mitigating circumstances or gains that negate the cooperator's culpability? In effect, our task of assessing varying types and degrees of licit material cooperation ultimately becomes an exercise in the use of the principle of double effect.

Thomas Aquinas's (1225–1274) exposition on whether or not it is lawful to kill in self-defense is considered to be the *locus classicus*[14] of the principle of double effect (PDE), sometimes known as the doctrine of double effect or double-effect reasoning.[15]

---

[11] Oderberg (2004, 207).
[12] Kaveny (2000) argues that some issues are better described in terms of "appropriation of evil" instead of the traditional "cooperation with evil." For example, we have the case of benefitting from scientific research from aborted fetuses or from embryonic stem cell research.
[13] This last condition is related to our earlier differentiation between *immediate versus mediate* material cooperation and *proximate versus remote* material cooperation.
[14] Cavanaugh (2006, 2). See also Kissell (1996).
[15] Cavanaugh (2003, 149) is emphatic that we should not call this a "principle" or a "doctrine" because it gives the wrong impression that it is an authoritative religious teaching rather than a philosophical way of thinking. Hence, he suggests using "double-effect reasoning." For this study, I will call it the principle of double effect in line with common usage.

Nothing hinders one act from having two effects, only one of which is intended, while the other is beside the intention. Now moral acts take their species according to what is intended, and not according to what is beside the intention … Therefore this act, since one's intention is to save one's own life, is not unlawful, seeing that it is natural to everything to keep itself in *being*, as far as possible. And yet, though proceeding from a good intention, an act may be rendered unlawful, if it be out of proportion to the end. Wherefore if a man, in self-defense, uses more than necessary violence, it will be unlawful … (Aquinas, 1947–1948, II–II, q. 64, a. 7, reply, emphasis original)

By the seventeenth century, this reasoning was recognized to be a general principle that can be applied in all areas of moral theology.[16] Since then, the principle has seen further development and use from the late Scholastics onward.[17] The principle can be stated in its most general and concise formulation as follows:

One may state double-effect reasoning as permitting an act causing good and evil when it meets the following conditions:
1　The act considered independently of its evil effect is not in itself wrong;
2　The agent intends the good and does not intend the evil either as an end or as a means; and,
3　The agent has proportionately grave reasons for acting, addressing his relevant obligations, comparing the consequences, and, considering the necessity of the evil, exercising due care to eliminate or mitigate it.

(Cavanaugh, 2006, 36)

Business ethicists find the requirement of due care (no. 3) to be extremely important. The most common paradigm for the application of PDE is the case of the just war. However, business ethicists and philosophers are quick to note that there are disanalogies between war and business operations that make PDE incomplete and unsatisfactory in dealing with the harmful side-effects of modern corporate activity. In particular, the analogy with war is inappropriate because of the following differences. Business is primarily engaged in value creation rather than the destruction of life and property. Furthermore, it can engage in constructive dialogue and consultation with all stakeholders both *ex ante* and *ex post*. Moreover, business has some leeway in staving off or at least minimizing the harmful side-effects of its operations.[18]

---

[16] Mangan (1949, 56).
[17] See Mangan (1949) and Cavanaugh (2006, 1–26) for the history of the development of this principle.
[18] Rossouw (2003).

For example, multinational companies can be good corporate citizens by being sensitive to their impact on the local community, its environment, and its social ecology. And in the case of odious host governments that abuse the human rights of their own citizens, such multinationals could exert moral suasion through both formal and informal channels so as not to be complicit in such abuses. Thus, business ethicists suggest that PDE's third requirement of due care can be made even more explicit when it comes to business and economic cases:

- That ongoing consultation and conversation are conducted with stake-holders, especially those who are adversely affected.
- That ongoing measures are taken to prevent or at least minimize negative side-effects.
- That the ill effects are unavoidable with no other alternative means available to achieve the positive benefits of the business operations.[19]

The principle of double effect resolves two issues at the same time: (1) whether or not cooperation with evil is justified and (2) how far such permissible cooperation should go. In other words, not only can we use the principle to establish whether or not there is complicity, but we can also employ it to "grade" the degree of such complicity. To implement this principle, we have to assign relative weights to the good and ill effects of the act under consideration. The proportionality condition of the principle of double effect requires prudential judgment in the absence of a more detailed set of criteria.[20]

Many have proposed intuitively appealing rules of thumb in applying the principles of double effect and legitimate material cooperation, such as:

- The greater the harm[21] inflicted, the more compelling the reason must be to cooperate with the wrongdoer.[22]

---

[19] Bomann-Larsen (2004); Bomann-Larsen and Wiggen (2004, 99).
[20] The principle of double effect is not without its problems and controversies. In particular, philos-ophers have been debating whether or not we can conflate "intending" and "foreseeing." If a person can already foresee the harmful unintended consequences, but nonetheless proceeds with the act, might we not then simply say that the foreseen harmful consequences are de facto intended? Is there a difference between foreseen side-effects and intended consequences? This debate is beyond the scope of this book. For purposes of this study, we will simply adopt the most common interpretation of the principle that makes such a distinction. See Cavanaugh (2006, 73–163) and Bennett (2001) for the debate over the "I/F distinction." See also Kaveny (2000, 299–304) for a brief explanation of the difference between intending and foreseeing.
[21] I define "harm" in this case and for all the following rules in terms of Feinberg's (1984, 31–64) three criteria: the act itself is wrong, it sets back vital welfare interests, and it violates rights.
[22] Häring (1964, 499); Oderberg (2004, 215).

- The greater the wrongdoing of the principal, the more compelling the reason must be to cooperate with the wrongdoer.[23]
- The closer one is to the wrongdoing in the chain of causation, the more compelling the reason must be to cooperate with the wrongdoer.[24]
- The more indispensable one's contribution is to the wrongdoing, the more compelling the reason must be to cooperate with the wrongdoer.[25]
- The more certain is the occurrence of the harm, the more compelling the reason must be to cooperate with the wrongdoer.[26]
- The greater one's obligation is to avoid cooperating with the wrongdoing or to prevent the harm, the more compelling the reason must be to cooperate with the wrongdoer.[27]
- The greater is the risk of scandal to others, the more compelling the reason must be to cooperate with the wrongdoer.[28]
- The greater the danger of adversely affecting our own character and virtue, the more compelling the reason must be to cooperate with the wrongdoer.[29]

A word of caution: some believe that the principle of double effect should not be used in economic ethics.[30] It might lead people to acquiesce to harms simply because such injuries can always be compensated as part of the third condition on mitigating the ill effects. Moreover, there is the danger of weighing market consequences in monetary terms alone since this is the common denominator used for comparison. This reinforces even further the market's reductionist tendency of assessing everything in quantitative, monetary terms to the exclusion of non-pecuniary considerations, such as the unintended consequences on morals and human flourishing. For example, no amount of compensation or punitive damage can make up

---

[23] This condition is different from the first one (on the gravity of harm) in that this pertains to the gravity of the principal's wrongdoing. This is the third condition of Liguori's (1905–1912, I:357) formulation of the principle of material cooperation. See also Häring (1964, 499). Moore (1999, 27) has a similar formulation but states it in a slightly different manner: "The greater the culpability with which an act is done, the greater the causal power of that act."

[24] This is also the third condition of Liguori's (1905–1912, I:357) formulation of the principle of material cooperation. See also Häring (1964, 499) and Oderberg (2004, 215). As we will see in chapter 4, the direct causation principle states that accountability diminishes with intervening events (Kutz 2000, 262). Recall the notion of proximate material cooperation.

[25] Häring (1964, 499); Oderberg (2004, 215). Compare this with the "but for" (*sine qua non*) standard in legal and social philosophy. Recall the notion of indispensable material cooperation.

[26] Feinberg (1984, 216); Häring (1964, 499); Oderberg (2004, 215); Parfit (1984, 73–75).

[27] Oderberg (2004, 215–216). The proximity principle states that one is more accountable for harms (or failure to prevent such harms) for the people who are socially, physically, or temporally closer to us than to the more distant ones (Kutz 2000, 262). Interpersonal bonds and ties are also important determinants of moral responsibility.

[28] Grisez (1997, 880); Häring (1964, 499).   [29] Grisez (1997); Kaveny (2000).

[30] For example, see Gowri (2004).

for the ruined health or lost lives in communities adversely affected by pollution. Similarly, monetary restitution or new jobs created can never restore the natural beauty of the land ruined by mining.

These criticisms have a point. Nevertheless, in the absence of an alternative method, the principle of double effect is by far one of the most useful conceptual tools we have in sorting through moral dilemmas in economic life. We just have to use the principle with appropriate caution and safeguards.

COMPLICITY IN LAW AND PHILOSOPHY

Besides the scholastic principles of material cooperation and double effect, another set of conceptual tools that is useful for our study is the notion of complicity from law and social philosophy.

Kadish

In a substantial article entitled "Complicity, Cause and Blame: A Study in the Interpretation of Doctrine," Sanford Kadish surveys the Anglo-American common-law account of the legal doctrine of complicity. This work examines complicity in criminal law in terms of its nature, the actions that bring it about, the agent's intention, and its outcomes. First, by its nature, complicity is always in reference to the unlawfulness of the principal's action. As a result, complicity liability (accomplice liability, accessorial liability, secondary party liability) is merely derivative liability. If the principal's action is not unlawful, then there is no complicity liability. Furthermore, accomplice liability cannot be greater than the primary party's liability. However, secondary parties are guilty not because of the principal's unlawful act (for which the latter alone is responsible), but for what they had contributed to the principal's actions that ultimately led to the violation of the law. Thus, secondary parties cannot be held liable for the violation of the law itself.[31]

Second, there is complicity whenever secondary parties intentionally influence or assist the principal to commit an unlawful act. Actions that constitute influencing the principal include advising, persuading, commanding, encouraging, inducing, instigating, inciting, provoking, and soliciting. Assistance includes providing the means, opportunity, information, or any other contribution to the preparation or commission of the

---

[31] Kadish (1985, 337–342).

unlawful act.[32] However, there is a threshold beyond which such actions are no longer mere assistance (complicity liability) but co-conspiracy. This is when one commits part or all of the crime's *actus reus* (the wrongful act or omission that actualizes the crime). Thus, one becomes a co-principal of the crime instead of being merely an accomplice in any of the following instances: when both parties commit all (or part) of the acts constituting the crime or when each of the parties commits some of the acts that jointly constitute the crime.[33]

Third, the secondary party must have intended to influence or assist the principal actor in the commission of the crime. Intention is a necessary element for complicity liability.[34] Thus, the legal doctrine of complicity has a much higher bar than the doctrine of causation, because the latter does not require intention in order to incur liability (e.g., negligence).[35]

Kutz

In his book *Complicity: Ethics and Law for a Collective Age*, Christopher Kutz goes beyond the legal doctrine of complicity and the traditional principles of individual accountability to propose his own method for dealing with complicity in a collective setting. He claims that economic complicity arises in at least three ways: through a substantial individual causal contribution, through participatory intent, and through quasi-participatory intent in an unstructured harm. We examine each of these in what follows.

Complicity through a significant causal contribution

The traditional legal approach to complicity has revolved around three principles that guide most people's thinking on individual accountability, namely:

The *Individual Difference Principle* holds that I am only accountable for a harm if something I did made a difference to its occurrence. If substantially the same harm would have occurred regardless of what I have done, I cannot be accountable for it.

---

[32] Kadish (1985, 342–346).
[33] Kadish (1985, 344) gives the example of two parties robbing a victim at gunpoint. Regardless of how they divide the *actus reus* between them (holding the gun and taking the person's wallet), both are co-principals of the crime.
[34] Kadish (1985, 346–355).
[35] We will examine the doctrine of causality in greater depth in chapter 4. Kadish's fourth point pertains to how complicity arises if the secondary party's action could have possibly been a *sine qua non* ("but for") condition for the principal's criminal act.

The *Control Principle* holds that I am only accountable for events over which I have control, and whose occurrence I could have prevented. Finally, the *Autonomy Principle* holds that I am not accountable for the harm another agent causes, unless I have induced or coerced that agent into performing an act. (Kutz 2000, 3, emphasis added)

These principles are widely used in the ascription of individual responsibility because they are intuitively appealing. That we should be held responsible only for what we have caused or could have prevented seems to be both commonsensical and fair to most people.

Complicity in organized collective harms

Kutz finds the preceding principles inadequate for many contemporary moral issues in which harms are incurred collectively. He uses the case of the Dresden bombers to illustrate his point. Dresden was completely destroyed and more than 35,000 people were killed in the firestorm wrought by the Allies' strategic bombing campaign during February 13–15, 1945. There were more than a thousand planes and eight thousand crew directly involved in this "area (carpet) bombing" as pilots, gunners, navigators, and bombers, not counting the ground crews that serviced and prepared the planes.[36]

To what extent is an individual crew member complicit in such a massive loss of civilian lives? Is he even personally culpable at all? To begin with, the contribution of each crew member was infinitesimal; tens of thousands were involved in planning and carrying out this three-day raid. Furthermore, each crew member's contribution was redundant because the city would still have been destroyed and the civilian lives lost even without his participation. Others would have filled his place. Moreover, the cause of the city's destruction was overdetermined in that a fraction of the thousand planes dropping incendiary bombs would have been sufficient to wipe out Dresden. There was a superfluity of causes, each of which would have made no individual difference to the ultimate outcome and each of which could not have controlled the final outcome. None of the planes could have singlehandedly destroyed the city or killed so many people on its own, but taken together, the thousand planes were sufficient to ensure that Dresden was reduced to rubble. By the three aforesaid commonsensical principles (autonomy, individual difference, and control) none of these crews could be held individually accountable for the Dresden firestorm bombing.

---

[36] Kutz (2000, 116–124).

Thus, we have an *I–We problem* "in which I participate in a harm we do [together], but I am not personally accountable for that harm, because of the insignificance of my contribution."[37] Kutz argues that at the root of *I–We problems* is the solipsistic nature of the three aforementioned commonsensical principles. These principles are individualistic in their world-view whereby people are held accountable only on the basis of what they had done and what they had caused[38] without regard to other considerations, such as their sociohistorical location, relationship to the victim(s), or other perpetrators acting similarly. A possible solution to *I–We problems* is to adopt a communitarian approach. Kutz does not take this path but simply expands the scope of individual responsibility to include collective outcomes in which the individual has a stake through intentional participation. Thus, he suggests another principle:

The Complicity Principle (Basis) I am accountable for what others do when I intentionally participate in the wrong they do or harm they cause. (Object) I am accountable for the harm or wrong we do together, independently of the causal difference I make. (Kutz 2000, 122)

Obviously, each individual crew member bears a share of the moral responsibility for the Dresden bombing by virtue of his participative intent in fulfilling his part of the bombing mission. Later in his book, Kutz applies this principle to shareholders and goes so far as to criticize current corporate limited-liability laws. He argues that in the event that a corporation's assets are not sufficient to compensate the victims of its corporate misdeeds (or those of its officers), then shareholders should be held personally liable to make whole the obligation. His rationale for this proposition is that by staying vested in the corporation, each shareholder demonstrates participative intent and contributes toward furthering the aims and operations of the corporation. They should, therefore, bear responsibility for its corporate misdeeds.[39]

Unintended market outcomes and complicity

The examples presented earlier in the Introduction are cases of unintended but foreseen market harms. People who facilitate or contribute to these ills are in material cooperation. However, is it proper to use the term "complicity" to describe these cases? After all, in the legal doctrine of

---

[37] Kutz (2000, 5).   [38] Kutz (2000, 4) calls these relational and causal solipsism respectively.
[39] Kutz (2000, 204–253).

complicity, the secondary agent – the accessory – must intend to promote or facilitate the wrongdoing of the principal. Intention is an important requirement of complicity. Some would even go so far as to claim that no material cooperation is the same as complicity because the latter requires sharing in the wrongdoer's intent.[40] And, indeed, sharing in the wrongful intent constitutes formal, not material, cooperation.

Kutz himself acknowledges that the complicity principle is applicable only to structured harms, as in the case of corporations, organized groups, or coordinated activities in which there is a shared intention (e.g., Dresden bombing, Mafia). Consequently, his complicity principle fails in the case of unstructured harms in which there is no coordination or a shared goal on the part of the parties involved. For example, air pollution results from the uncoordinated, spontaneous individual actions of drivers, farmers, factory managers, and power plant operators. One cannot ascribe a participative intent to any of these economic actors for the resulting harm (cancer-causing pollution) as they intend merely to go about their respective work. Unstructured harms are important for our study because most economic ills are of this type. Furthermore, the market is widely viewed as an unstructured social entity.

Nevertheless, I propose that we can properly use the term "complicity" to describe the subject matter of our study, for at least two reasons. In the first place, the use of the term is not univocal. Second, the market is not entirely "unstructured." We briefly examine each of these arguments.

Popular usage
The requirement of intention on the part of the cooperator in the legal doctrine of complicity is understandable, particularly in criminal law. Given the severity of the resulting penalties imposed, accomplice liability must necessarily show intent. However, for this study, we are talking of moral, not legal, responsibility. Their respective standards of blameworthiness are clearly different, with the latter requiring a much higher bar.

Furthermore, complicity is not a univocal term, not among social philosophers or the general public. For example, using the language of ordinary discourse and wide-ranging literature, Kissell (1996; 1998; 1999) has shown that toleration of evil is also an instance of complicity. For the public, complicity is not limited only to positive acts that bring about harms. Instead, complicity also includes acts of omission, such as not speaking up against wrongs or doing nothing to change grave systemic

---

[40] Oderberg (2004, 217–218).

evil. Unlike traditional, casuistic approaches to complicity, a fuller account of complicity must necessarily view the moral agent within the context of the community. This entails paying heed to the individual's responsibilities toward the group. Thus, our deepest moral intuitions censure people who, by failing to confront wrongdoing, "diminish important values and debase the [community's] moral climate."[41] Public morality frowns on individual or collective failure to live up to our better and noble selves.

Parker (2003) expands moral complicity even further to include conduct in which one expressively affirms another's wrongdoing. For him, the threshold for what constitutes complicity is much lower in that no causal contribution is even necessary. All it takes for such "expressive alignment" with someone else's misconduct is to manifest publicly one's desire, belief, or attitude in support of such misdeed. This behavior is blameworthy because it distorts moral law. Parker's expressive account of moral complicity is not entirely new. Moral theologians have long argued that the risk of scandal to others is an important factor to consider as we weigh the proportion of harms and benefits in the principles of double effect and material cooperation.[42] What is new in Parker's formulation, however, is his description of such behavior as "moral complicity."

Complicity in unstructured collective harms

There is a second reason why we can use the term "complicity" in our study of economic harms. Kutz extends further his earlier analysis. He argues that even if a moral agent does not have a determinative causal impact in effecting the harm or even if the agent is not part of a concerted action to inflict the harm, the person may nonetheless still be culpable. He cites the example of a merchant who knowingly sells tools that may be used in a wrongdoing. The merchant is only one of many other vendors selling such tools and is interested only in making a sale, not in fostering a criminal enterprise. Using the standards we have seen thus far, we cannot hold the merchant culpable for the subsequent lawbreaking in which the tool was used because he made no causal difference to the commission of the crime. (The criminal would have secured the tool from other merchants anyway.) Moreover, the merchant was definitely not part of a concerted action. Nonetheless, Kutz (2000, 166–203) asserts that the merchant should be held morally liable for the resulting harm. He argues in favor of individual responsibility for such unstructured harms, for two reasons.

[41] Kissell (1998, 267).
[42] See, for example, Grisez (1997, 880), Häring (1964, 499), and Keenan and Kopfensteiner (1995, 26).

First, the marketplace does not arise in a vacuum but is in fact undergirded by structures, institutions, and practices built up over time through economic activity. Individual economic choices ultimately gel into a collective whole. The economic actor is, in fact, a partaker of and a contributor to a way of life. The market and its participants are part of a culture.[43] The market may not be considered concerted action, as in the case of a corporation or of the Dresden bombers, but it is not entirely uncoordinated or unstructured either. Economic agents reinforce and perpetuate formal and informal societal rules through their conduct in the marketplace.[44] Thus, market participants can be said to have a quasi-participatory intent.[45]

A second reason for holding individuals accountable for unstructured harms is simple and straightforward: character formation.[46] Many are keenly aware of their responsibility to correct collective harms even if there is no legal basis for such duty. People simply take it upon themselves to do their share in ameliorating collective harms because of their character and virtue. We have recent examples of such voluntary behavior in the proliferation of NGOs, the emergence of social entrepreneurship, the Fair Trade and anti-sweatshop movements, and the carbon offset programs.

For this study, I subscribe to Kutz's position on unstructured harms because, as I will argue in chapter 8, the marketplace is, in fact, undergirded by societal norms and institutions. It may seem to be unstructured on the surface, but in reality, it is governed by formal and informal rules compiled over time from customs, law, and usage. Market participants both sustain these underlying structures and benefit from them through their buying and selling activities. They are fully cognizant of both the good and harmful outcomes of market processes. One could ascribe a "virtual" or presumed intention to market participants. Thus, Kutz's notion of a quasi-participatory intent in "unstructured" harms is both reasonable and an accurate description of socioeconomic phenomena.

We can further justify Kutz's expanded notion of individual participation by recalling the importance of context. To assess fully the morality of an individual act, we have to consider it in the context of the collective act to which it contributes and in which it participates.[47] This applies whether the

---

[43] Furthermore, most of these economic agents are also citizens and, thus, they have a role in shaping their nations' political economy. Passive acquiescence is in itself a choice – keeping the status quo. We will come back to this phenomenon in chapter 8 when we examine its underlying economics: bounded rationality, network externality, and path dependence.

[44] For example, by giving out-sized bonuses, banks and financial institutions are reinforcing the informal market ethos (especially in the USA) of tolerating large pay inequalities.

[45] Kutz (2000, 186).   [46] Kutz (2000, 17–65, 167).

[47] This point and the following examples come from Isaacs (2006, 65).

collective is organized or unstructured. Running a marathon takes a different moral quality if it is done as part of a fundraiser for a worthy cause. Murder is viewed in a different light if it is committed within the context of genocide. It is a mistake to evaluate individual acts in isolation from the larger collective context of which they are but a part and to which they contribute. Such moral assessment will be grossly inadequate and incomplete. The collective context can and often does change the moral quality of the individual act. For our study, this means that we cannot weigh fully the moral import of market participants' individual choices in isolation from the praiseworthiness or blameworthiness of market processes and outcomes.

Finally, besides Kutz's two reasons, we can add a third argument. An act that is intended either as an end or as a means is called "directly" voluntary. The unintended but foreseen consequences of such directly voluntary acts are called "indirectly" voluntary.[48] Even as they are unintended, they have been accepted nonetheless by the moral agent. Thus, the moral agent can still be held responsible for indirectly voluntary acts. After all, the moral agent could have averted these unintended but foreseen consequences but did not. The indirectly voluntary moral agent is not blameworthy for the harm, but may nevertheless still be held liable for mitigating the resulting injury depending on the context of the situation (the third condition of PDE). Failure to fulfill such liabilities, if any, constitutes grounds for censure.

In sum, for this study, we will go beyond the narrow definition of the legal doctrine of complicity and adopt philosophers' more expansive notion of "moral complicity." In the first place, there are strong reasons to sub-scribe to Kutz's expansion of individual responsibility to include "unstru-ctured" harms. There is indeed quasi-participatory intent as we causally contribute to reinforcing social structures and as we accept the unintended but foreseen consequences of our actions. Second, the expansive scope of moral complicity is more in line with the public's moral intuition of what constitutes blameworthy cooperation than is the legal doctrine of complicity.

Complicity and material cooperation

Moral complicity is not identical to material cooperation. On the one hand, moral complicity also encompasses formal cooperation. On the other hand,

---

[48] Fagothey (1972, 31–34).

material cooperation includes excused or justified acts.[49] These are not blameworthy and do not constitute moral complicity. Despite these differences, there is a substantial overlap between complicity and material cooperation. In particular, moral complicity includes the blameworthy instances of material cooperation. For this study, I use "moral complicity" or "complicity" as shorthand for blameworthy material cooperation.

Why not simply stick with the language of material cooperation? What do we gain by using the language of complicity in this study? We can enrich both concepts by using them together. Let us first examine how the language of complicity supplements the scholastic notion of material cooperation. First, not all forms of material cooperation deserve censure. In using "complicity" we immediately focus on that subset of material cooperation that is faulty. Second, we can adopt insights and methods from the legal doctrine of complicity. It teaches us much about the subjective conditions that determine the cooperator's blameworthiness[50] and the nature of the relationship between the cooperator and the principal.[51] This is not to say that many of these insights are missing in the principle of material cooperation. It is just that the legal literature brings a different and enriching perspective, as we will see in the following chapters.

Third, in imputing individual responsibility for harmful market outcomes, we have to deal first with collective harms. There is not much in the literature on material cooperation in economic life, much less on the problem of market accumulative harms, since the interest has largely been on questions of war and bioethics.[52] In contrast, social and legal philosophers have paid relatively more attention to using the notion of complicity in assessing economic problems, including the phenomena of accumulative harms and collective responsibility.[53]

Fourth, "complicity" is a much simpler concept that the public will immediately recognize, understand, and associate with blameworthy activities. People will straightaway know that we are referring to acts that deserve censure. Not so with "material cooperation." Few would understand what the term is, much less its implications.

---

[49] For example, deforestation is often aggravated by poor rural families who are driven to cut down trees as fuel for cooking and heat. The material cooperation of these families in the denudation of the land is excusable and non-liable because of the economic compulsion involved.
[50] For example, we have knowledge, intent, voluntariness, and personal capacity.
[51] Kissell (1998, 264). For example, we have derivativeness and asymmetry to the harm.
[52] For examples of the use of material cooperation in assessing economic issues, see Grisez (1997) and Häring (1964, 494–519).
[53] For example, see Feinberg (1970; 1984) and Kutz (2000).

For its part, material cooperation also adds to the language of complicity. In the first place, the various distinctions we examined earlier in this chapter provide different degrees of culpability for harms. Material cooperation greatly enriches the lexicon of complicity, especially when it comes to describing the nature of the accomplice's act and its resulting responsibilities. Second, material cooperation's three conditions provide a ready framework with which to assess complicity. Finally, most people associate the term "complicity" only with illicit activities. Material cooperation expands this usage to many more cases as we will see in Part II.

DEFICIENCIES

The scholastic principles of cooperation with evil and double effect help us greatly in the attribution of individual responsibility for harmful market processes and outcomes. Unfortunately, despite the many distinctions we examined earlier in the chapter, these principles are still insufficient for our study, for a number of reasons.

First, in the ascription of individual responsibility for collective harms, we have to evaluate whether the material cooperation involved is proximate or remote. Recall that this distinction refers to the causal or moral connection between the principal's wrongdoing and the cooperator's act. This requires further elucidation of what constitutes causal nearness or definiteness. Unfortunately, the principles of material cooperation and double effect do not have a theory of causality. They do not have the lexicon or the framework with which to disentangle and assess causes and effects.

Second, both principles require weighing proportions between harmful and beneficial outcomes, in the case of double effect, and between the harm and the cooperator's reason for acting, in the case of material cooperation. Such comparisons require multiple sets of criteria in determining which consequences to consider, how we assess commensurability, how to prioritize competing ends, and what metric to use in reducing outcomes to a common denominator for comparison. Furthermore, we can make such comparisons only within the context of specific cases. But which contextual factors do we consider, how much attention do we devote to each, and why? The principles of material cooperation and double effect are unable to address these issues on their own.

Third, for this study, we have to deal with socioeconomic accumulative harms. Neither of these principles provides a straightforward method for disentangling interlocking market harms and benefits and unraveling interdependent economic agencies. These are unavoidable tasks in the imputation of individual responsibility. We cannot transplant directly methods and insights from law, social philosophy, and moral theology to issues of economic harms. We have to modify and adapt these conceptual tools in light of the nature and dynamics of the marketplace.

Fourth, recall that the first conditions of both the principles of legitimate material cooperation and double effect require that the act in question (of the cooperator or the moral agent) is not intrinsically evil. Ascertaining whether or not an act is morally wrong in itself is beyond the scope of these two principles. We need a separate moral standard for that. After all, these two principles are just methods and nothing more. They do not propose an anthropology or an overarching vision of the good. Thus, both principles can operate only within a much larger theological or ethical schema.

Given these limitations, both scholastic principles need to be complemented by moral standards, premises, and methods drawn from both within and beyond Christian ethics. We have to embed the principles of material cooperation and double effect within a much larger framework that can deal with the richness and complexity of social life. Such a framework of analysis should also take into account the special problems that arise given the distinctive nature of market processes.

SCOPE OF THIS STUDY

What kind of economic complicity are we assessing in this study? Consider the choices we face in defining the scope of this project.

- Complicity can refer either to a co-principal/co-conspirator or to a mere accessory who provides material assistance to a wrongdoing. This study is about the complicity of accessories. We are interested in material, rather than formal, cooperation.
- Complicity can involve either an individual's direct material assistance to a particular wrongdoing or an individual's roundabout material assistance to a collective, accumulative harm. We will be dealing with both types of complicity later in Part II.
- The notion of complicity can be restricted only to those instances where there is a specific intent to commit the wrongdoing, or it can be more expansive by including participation in foreseen but unintended harms. We will take the broader and more inclusive approach and adopt Kutz's (2000) position that there can be individual complicity even in "unstructured" collective wrongs. Quasi-participatory intent is

good enough to constitute grounds for complicity in accumulative socioeconomic harms.

- The ascription of individual responsibility for communal wrongs can be based either on group membership or on the individual's causal contribution to the harm. We take the latter approach and require individual contributory fault as a condition of complicity.

All the four choices we have made above in setting the scope of this study are the more difficult positions to take. In return, we get a more robust study of economic complicity. We can apply or extend our findings to many more areas and problems of economic life beyond the four types of market-mediated complicity we examine in the second half of this book.

SUMMARY AND CONCLUSIONS

The scholastic principles of legitimate material cooperation and double effect provide intuitively appealing rules of thumb and useful conceptual distinctions. However, these principles' distinctions cannot be applied as though we had an absolute, mathematical sliding scale with which to grade complicity.[54] Far from it. As we will see in the next chapters, many factors must be considered before we can ascertain whether a particular cooperator is in immediate or mediate, indispensable or dispensable, and proximate or remote material cooperation. To make matters worse, some of these factors may not even be commensurable to each other. Furthermore, we cannot make blanket judgments; we have to consider the specific context of cases. Moreover, even within the concrete particularities of each case, evaluators will assign different weights to these manifold considerations. In other words, we cannot make these moral evaluations in cookbook fashion.

Nevertheless, these difficulties do not excuse us from being precise and rigorous in our moral deliberations, to the extent possible. Consequently, it is all the more important to have a tightly argued, but open-ended, framework within which to apply the scholastic notions of material cooperation and double effect.

The next three chapters examine conceptual tools from law, social philosophy, and economics that can be modified and adapted for use in Christian ethics. We will also examine the nature of markets and identify their peculiar features and problems that make the study of economic complicity that much more demanding.

---

[54] Oderberg (2004, 208–209).

CHAPTER 2

Complicity in what? The problem of accumulative harms

Since the cooperator's blameworthiness is merely derivative, we must first establish the nature of the principal's wrongdoing and why it deserves censure. What is the economic harm we have facilitated (the object of accountability)? This chapter undertakes two tasks. First, it briefly examines criteria from Christian ethics and liberal social philosophy on what constitutes economic wrongdoing. Second, it outlines the considerable difficulties we face in the attribution of individual responsibility for market harms because these economic ills are accumulative in nature and are mediated by the "invisible hand."

COMPLICITY IN WHAT?

Christian ethics: telos

For Christian theology, a wrongdoing is that which goes against the divine order of creation. Creation is not a random event. God always acts for a purpose. There is an end (*telos*) for which everything has been created, including economic activity. Economic life is about facilitating the human quest to requite divine love through the reasoned use of freedom. The intellect and will enable humans to live up to the fullness of their creation in the image and likeness of God.

Christian ethics has an extensive literature on what constitutes economic wrongdoing. Since these works are well covered by both scholars and commentators, we will only briefly sketch their main features and how they might help our study of economic complicity. One approach to summarizing Christian economic ethics is to examine the official statements on economic life by the various Christian traditions. These church teachings, theological reflections, or pronouncements articulate what they believe are the requisite features of a truly functional economy in God's order of creation.

The differences between the Roman Catholic and Protestant churches on matters of faith, morals, and church discipline are wide, despite their common core beliefs in the essentials of the faith, such as the Blessed Trinity and the salvation won for us by Jesus Christ on Calvary. Even the various Protestant denominations themselves differ widely, especially in their social thought and praxis. In fact, in the United States, the Protestant traditions are often categorized into two groups based on their position on social issues. On the one hand, the mainline Protestant churches are proactive in addressing social ills. These mainline traditions include the United Church of Christ, the Reformed Church in America, the Unitarian Congregationalists, and the Episcopalian, Methodist, Presbyterian, and Lutheran churches. Because each of these traditions has a central structure and functions as a single entity whenever necessary, these mainline churches have issued, on occasion, official statements on contemporary economic injustice. On the whole, they are practically indistinguishable in their assessment and proposed solutions to the ills of the economy. They stand on the liberal end of the spectrum of political philosophy. For all their differences in theology and church discipline, the Roman Catholic Church and the mainline Protestant denominations take fundamentally similar positions on questions of economic justice. In fact, bishops from these different traditions laud, support, and cite each other's official declarations on the economy. There is unity in their socioeconomic vision amidst their theological and ecclesiological diversity.[1] Differences in their economic teachings lie more in tone and degree rather than substance.

On the other hand, evangelicals and fundamentalists stand to the right of the political spectrum, are pro-market in their stance, and are relatively less concerned with socioeconomic problems such as poverty and inequality. However, even this characterization is not entirely accurate because there are also wide variations even among evangelicals and fundamentalists. In fact, some have been extremely generous in working on behalf of the poor and are more proactive on social issues than others.[2] The difficulty with assessing the socioeconomic stance of evangelicals and fundamentalists is that they are governed as independent churches or as denominations centered on preachers such as Jerry Falwell, Pat Robertson, and the teleevangelists. Thus, we do not have a single official church statement on economics from the group as a whole. However, we do have close

---

[1] De Vries (1998, 213–234).
[2] See De Vries (1998, 213–254) for a more extended discussion of the differences between these congregations.

substitutes. Forty conservative groups active in mission, relief, and development work gathered in the Swiss town of Villars in 1987 and issued *The Villars Statement on Relief and Development*. Similarly, about a hundred evangelicals with a wide variety of expertise as theologians, business practitioners, economists, development workers, and church leaders met in Oxford, England in 1990 and promulgated the *Oxford Declaration on Christian Faith and Economics*. This was subsequently revisited and reaffirmed at Agra, India in 1995 by Christians from forty-two countries in what has come to be known as the *Agra Affirmations on Christian Faith, Market Economics and the Poor*. These three declarations are important for our study because despite lingering disagreements among evangelicals, these conference statements are, for the most part, descriptive of their most commonly held views regarding a just economic life.[3] It is as close as we can get to something comparable to the official pronouncements of the mainline Protestant churches.

The Protestant traditions differ in their views on the proper relationship between the Church and society. On one end of the spectrum, we have the primitive communism of some Anabaptist communities that believe in a complete separation from the secular world. At the other end of the spectrum is the Calvinism of Max Weber and his well-known attribution of the rise of modern capitalism to the values and virtues of Protestantism.[4] Of course, there are also variations within the Roman Catholic Church itself that span the entire political spectrum, from staunch anti-capitalist critics to liberation theologians to the pro-market advocates. Despite these differences, however, there is a distinction between magisterial teachings and mere commentaries in Catholic social thought.

Most of these church documents or pronouncements begin with an examination of the biblical foundations of an ideal economic life. They then use these as criteria in gauging how far we have fallen short of God's expectations. This is followed by an acknowledgment of human sinfulness and a call to action in rectifying economic injustice.

Despite their profound disagreements over fundamental theology, ecclesiology, church discipline, and even political philosophy, the various Christian traditions agree on many key issues of economic justice. Of course, there are differences, mostly in terms of what they include and

---

[3] The *Agra Affirmations* were said to have been endorsed by an overwhelming majority of participants at the conference. However, there were a few attendees who wanted changes in some of the affirmations, but the conference ran out of time. See Third International Conference on Christian Faith and Economics (1995).

[4] Schweiker (2009, 410).

exclude. For example, the *Villars Statement* and the *Oxford Declaration* of the evangelicals and fundamentalists accentuate the importance of incentives for production and are critical of the self-inflicted problems of many poor countries. More liberal traditions like the United Church of Christ, however, underscore the need for affirmative action, progressive taxation, less military spending, and greater economic democracy, such as co-ownership and co-management of the means of production.

The fault-line that divides the more liberal mainline Protestant churches and Roman Catholicism, on the one hand, and the more conservative fundamentalists and evangelicals, on the other hand, is the degree to which markets ought to be left to operate on their own. Given their fierce disagreements on political economy, it is remarkable that they even agree on many issues of economic morality.[5] This is probably due to their common acknowledgment of the privileged role of Sacred Scripture in theological reflection.

There are at least four points of convergence in the declarations of Christian churches on economic life.[6] First, they share a common understanding of the nature of the person.

- Humans are created in the image and likeness of God.
- Humans enjoy genuine moral agency given their reason and authentic freedom; they are consequently accountable for their actions both as individuals and as a community.
- Humans are sinful, but they have been redeemed by Christ.
- Human accomplishments are not in competition with God's since humans merely participate in God's ongoing act of creation.
- All are brothers and sisters in the one family of God regardless of race, gender, nationality, or accomplishments.
- All creatures reflect the goodness and love of God.
- The human experience of Creation–Sin–Redemption is eloquent testimony to the unmerited nature of the grace that envelops human existence and history.

Second, these churches have a common understanding of the nature of the human community. As family of the one and the same God, we

---

[5] In his comparison of the various Christian traditions, De Vries (1998) also comes to the same finding that for all their theological differences, these churches arrive at very similar assessments and conclusions on contemporary economic injustice.

[6] These official statements include: American Lutheran Church (1980), Lutheran Church in America (1980), National Conference of Catholic Bishops (1986), Perkinson (1988), Pontifical Council for Peace and Justice (2004), Presbyterian Church (1984; 1985), Reformed Church in America (1984, 1990), Smock (1987), United Church of Christ (1989), United Methodist Church (2000), Villars Statement (1991), and the Second and Third International Conferences on Christian Faith and Economics (1990 and 1995 respectively) [*Oxford Declaration* and *Agra Affirmations*].

exercise our moral agency with the goal of achieving the good of all according to God's intended order. How this common good looks or works in practice is difficult to define completely, if at all possible. However, this does not mean that the common good is an impracticable concept. We can still use this notion to good effect by limiting ourselves to the barest minimum conditions any reasonable Christian would accept as necessary for the common good to be truly present. At a minimum, we would expect this one family of God to be imbued with biblical *sedeq* (righteousness), a perennial theme highlighted in both the Old and the New Testament. *Sedeq* entails living up to the demands of our manifold relationships especially in five critical areas:[7]

- between God and the human person
- between human persons
- between the community and those who are marginalized
- between the community and every member in its ranks
- between the human community and the earth.

Economic life contributes to the common good by strengthening these foundational relationships.

Third, the Christian use of human rights is different from liberal rights language because most Christian traditions embed rights within a much larger framework of obligations stemming from the common good. In particular, the first relationship (God and the human person) is the primary relationship that defines the nature and requirements of the other four. We enjoy rights only that we might have the means to discharge our obligations. These duties flow from the relationships comprising the common good. This inseparability between rights and duties is best illustrated in the various Christian traditions' view of private property ownership. While these churches acknowledge the importance and legitimacy of the right to private property ownership, they are also quick to observe that this right carries a correlative obligation of using such possessions for the benefit of others, especially for the poor and the destitute. This common teaching stems from the Christian churches' shared reading and understanding of Sacred Scripture as designating the earth as a divine gift meant for all. Moreover, these traditions also share the common belief that we should use the fruits of the earth with a humble attitude of stewardship, knowing full well that we have to render an account someday before God on how we used these gifts entrusted to our care. The right to private property ownership, far from being absolute in its claims, is in fact

---

[7] Achtemeier (1962a; 1962b); Donahue (1977).

saddled with significant duties. Even the more conservative Christian traditions hold this position, as we find in the *Oxford Declaration* (nos. 2–8) and the *Agra Affirmations* (no. 3).

Fourth, there will be inevitable trade-offs among human goods. Resolving such clashing claims is ultimately about maintaining the biblical notion of *sedeq* (righteousness), that is, getting relationships right by satisfying their respective requirements. These churches' lists of social principles and duties specify concretely what constitutes rectitude in economic life.[8]

- The person's development has to be integral – body, mind, and spirit (integral human development).
- The earth is a gift of God meant for all; material sufficiency is a divine bequest for all (economic security as divine gift; just-use obligation; stewardship; universal destination of the goods of the earth).
- People ought to do what they can and should be doing for themselves (subsidiarity).
- Extending assistance to those in need is an obligation of justice and charity and is not supererogatory (socialization).
- We have a genuine and active concern for the welfare of others because we see in them a fellow child of God (solidarity).
- The poor deserve an extra measure of care, attention, and love from us (preferential option for the poor).
- Human work deserves respect and adequate remuneration. It should not be treated as a commodity, and the worker should be viewed as a person and a worthy, dignified contributor to the common productive effort (primacy of labor).
- We have been entrusted by God to care for the threefold gifts of the self, of each other, and of the earth. We are interdependent and share a finite earth (stewardship).
- As moral agents, we are accountable for our choices and their consequences (accountability).
- People should be able to partake of socioeconomic life without fear, discrimination, or great difficulty (inclusive participation).

Furthermore, according to many of these church social teachings, an economy that is consistent with the will of God as found in Sacred Scripture must exhibit the following characteristics: full employment; economic rights and universal basic needs satisfaction in food, clothing, shelter, education, and health care; equality of opportunity; relative equality; mutual respect;

---

[8] I have put the names of these principles in parentheses for ease of reference.

efficiency and the judicious use of resources; and individual freedom. The economy serves the human person and not the other way around.

The marketplace's much-touted division of labor and specialization should be an affirmation of our co-humanity. They have to result in vibrant and harmonious communities – local, national, and international. Industry, government, and private voluntary organizations ought to work together seamlessly since extra-market mechanisms improve market operations. The ideal economy is a school for developing virtue, such as hard work, industriousness, thrift, honesty, and truthfulness. These virtues, in their own turn, shape the other spheres of life, such as politics, culture, and social life. Such an economy is conducive to personal growth and development. It builds up vibrant communities, affirms human dignity and the sanctity of life, and facilitates the attainment of life's purpose – love of God and neighbor. Most of all, the Christian churches believe that such a just and compassionate economy is testimony to the reign and love of God in our midst. In the final analysis, the soundness of an economy is a function of its spiritual vibrancy and fidelity to God.

In sum, the various official statements of the Christian churches offer a detailed understanding of what they believe is God's order of creation for socioeconomic life. While they do not agree on the practical policies that should govern market operations, these disparate Christian traditions share many similar ideals and principles that help us identify instances of economic wrongdoing. Whether as producers, consumers, or civil servants in the marketplace, we have the following rough guide in ascertaining whether or not an activity is morally permissible:

Here then is the norm for human activity – to harmonize with the authentic interests of the human race, in accordance with God's will and design, and to enable people as individuals and as members of society to pursue and fulfil their total vocation. (Vatican II 1965, no. 35)

Philosophy: harm to others

From philosophy, we can use "harm to others" as a criterion for determining what constitutes economic wrongdoing. We start from the most generous position, the liberal presumptive case for liberty. Individuals ought to have the most wide-ranging liberties that are consistent with everybody else enjoying the same freedoms. These liberties are restricted only when they injure others.

[T]he only purpose for which power can be rightfully exercised over any member of a civilized community against his will, is to prevent *harm to others*. (Mill 1859 [1974], 68, emphasis added)

But what constitutes "harm" in this "liberty-limiting principle"? Three conditions must be satisfied before one can invoke this liberty-limiting harm principle. First, the action in question is a wrongful act (or omission). This precludes accidents, excused conduct, or justified actions that are not wrongs.[9] Second, the act in question must set back vital welfare interests. Welfare interests are the means by which people pursue their ulterior interests, that is, their ultimate goals and aspirations (e.g., raising a family, pursuing a successful career). Examples of welfare interests include bodily integrity, physical health, financial stability, and social relationships. One could be even more expansive than this and include among welfare interests the necessary means, options, and opportunities to exercise one's autonomy in a meaningful manner.[10] Third, the act in question must be in violation of rights. The victim has been wronged and not merely injured.[11] These three criteria were originally proposed for use in evaluating whether or not there is cause to enact liberty-limiting legislation to avert harm. Nonetheless, I propose that these criteria can be adapted for our use in identifying what constitutes economic wrongdoing.

The harm principle pertains not only to personal conduct but also to accumulative harms.[12] Pollution is a classic example of an accumulative harm. An individual factory's emission of greenhouse gasses may be harmless by itself, but not when considered together with other polluting plants. Their collective discharge of effluents will overwhelm the ecology's capacity to process waste. Many economic problems are similarly cumulative in their dynamics. Thus, lone investors betting against the US dollar may not cause harm on their own, but this is not the case when millions of other speculators are wagering similarly that the US dollar will lose value. Together, these speculative short-sellers will precipitate a self-fulfilling run against the US dollar. Accumulative harms can and often do satisfy the preceding three conditions on what constitutes liberty-limiting harm to others. These accumulative harms are frequently the result of wrongful action (or omission), they set back vital interests, and they frequently violate rights.[13]

---

[9] For example, an excused conduct is when one is coerced. An example of a justified damage to property is when a fireman breaks down a door to save a child from a burning building.

[10] Raz (1986, 413). This is very much along the lines of Sen's (1992) "functionings and capabilities" approach to development.

[11] These three conditions come from Feinberg (1984, 31–64, 215).   [12] Kernohan (1993).

[13] Excessive consumption, inappropriate production methods, and speculative commodity investments are good examples. We will examine these in chapter 6.

ASCRIPTION OF INDIVIDUAL RESPONSIBILITY
FOR ACCUMULATIVE HARMS

The bulk of this study is about blameworthy material cooperation (moral complicity) in accumulative harms. Who is morally responsible for these communal wrongs? This is ultimately a question of how to impute individual responsibility for collective outcomes. Philosophers are still debating whether or not collectives can be held morally responsible since they cannot have an intention of their own. On the one hand, the *individualist* sense of collective responsibility claims that only individuals can bear moral responsibility. On the other hand, the *substantive* sense of collective responsibility argues that some collectives can be held morally accountable as a group, separate from the moral duties of its individual members.[14]

We will not delve into this debate as this would take us too far from our study. Instead, I will take the more restrictive position and impute individual moral responsibility, not on account of people's group membership, but by virtue of their individual causal contribution to the accumulative harm.[15] This is the more general position to take because it does not preclude the possibility that the collective itself may have additional moral duties separate from its constituent members' obligations. Besides, it is much more intuitively appealing to commonsense morality that complicity must at least entail contributory fault. It makes a much stronger case for holding people to account. Unfortunately, this comes at a price since it is the more difficult position to take, given the need to establish the individual agent's causal contribution to the collective harm. This is not a straightforward task because of the nature of the marketplace.[16]

THE ECONOMICS OF MARKET-MEDIATED
ACCUMULATIVE HARMS

Most of the harms we examine in this study are accumulative in nature. The rest of this chapter will be devoted to explaining why the individual

[14] Isaacs (2006, 61). See also Gilbert (2002) and Graham (2006, 258).
[15] Thus, the liabilities we ascribe to economic agents in this study are not vicarious liabilities but personal liabilities. A vicarious liability is one in which the person is held liable (for damages, ameliorative action, etc.) even if the person did not causally contribute to the harm. For example, employers are vicariously liable for the conduct of their workers. The same is true for parents vis-à-vis their underage children. In contrast, personal liability requires contributory fault.
[16] There would have been no need to do this if we had simply justified individual responsibility on the basis of group membership.

difference, control, autonomy, and complicity principles from chapter 1 cannot be used in the case of accumulative harms. Recall that for these principles, individuals can be held to account only for their own actions, if they are part of an organized effort, or if they are able to control or make a difference in the events that produce such harm. As we will see in this section, the economics of accumulative harms do not satisfy these conditions. In fact, only Kutz's (2000) notion of accountability based on quasi-participatory intent in "unstructured harms" can deal with accumulative harms. The aforesaid more popular, commonsensical principles fail because of the peculiar features of market operations. In what follows, we examine briefly the economics of accumulative harms in three broad areas: market processes, the individual economic agent, and market outcomes.[17]

Market processes

*Market transactions that are innocuous at the individual level can
be harmful when aggregated with other similar activities*
Accumulative harms have a peculiar feature in that activities pursued at the individual level are harmless but become injurious at the aggregate level when lumped together with other similar acts.[18] For example, a New Yorker's purchase of a shirt made in Bangladesh in order to save money does not injure anyone when taken as a single event. It may in fact be lauded as an act of frugality. However, tens of millions of other US residents buying cheaper apparel from overseas rather than from local manufacturers will hurt the interests of US apparel workers who will most likely see a decline in their wages, if not lose their employment altogether.

Adam Smith (1776) is often cited for his observation on how self-interested individual actions are somehow transformed by the market's "invisible hand" to produce social benefits.[19] Thus, the butcher, the baker, and the brewer, by pursuing their respective interests, end up promoting the larger societal good

---

[17] In what follows, we examine only competitive markets in which no economic agent can single-handedly control market processes or outcomes. Thus, we exclude monopolists, monopsonists, cartels, and other instances of market control.

[18] Lichtenberg (2008, 6) calls these "new harms."

[19] It is important to make a distinction between what Adam Smith actually meant and what subsequent commentators and scholars (Smithian school) attribute to him. Adam Smith used the image of the "invisible hand" merely to illustrate his point on how the pursuit of private initiatives produces an unintended, positive social effect. Subsequent commentators, however, employed the "invisible hand" normatively, as shorthand for either the dynamics or the benefits of unfettered market operations. This Smithian use of the "invisible hand" is the common usage and understanding of this term.

through the provisions and services they make available to the entire community.[20] However, this "invisible hand" is double-edged. It can also inflict damage at an aggregated level just as it produces much collective good. At the heart of accumulative harms is the dynamic by which benign individual acts are transformed into a malign aggregated outcome. This is the defining formal characteristic of an accumulative harm.

It is difficult, if at all possible, to dissect accumulative economic harms and to trace them back to their particular causes in the marketplace

Commonsense morality requires that we clearly prove the causal connection between the harm and the person being held responsible for it. We must be able to trace back a particular harm to its distinct cause(s) before we can make a judgment as to who is accountable for such injury.

The Smithian "invisible hand" can be described as a "black box" because its inner workings are not always clearly understood. Disparate individual acts simply end up as collective outcomes. We cannot definitively identify which parts of market outcomes are due to which specific individual contributions. The "invisible hand" cannot be reverse-engineered to reveal specific cause-and-effect linkages. Moreover, these linkages are further obscured by many intervening activities in the marketplace, in addition to the chance and contingencies of economic life. Consequently, socioeconomic accumulative harms cannot be taken apart and attributed to particular individual acts.

For example, who is causally or morally responsible for the low prices farmers obtain for their coffee beans? Consumers who shop for the best prices? Middlemen, consolidators, food processors, or wholesalers who maximize their profit margins? New entrants to the industry who add more acreage to coffee production? How do we factor in the vagaries of weather and shifts in consumer preferences for alternative drinks?

The marketplace suffers from a problem of overdetermination in that economic outcomes have a superfluity of particular causes

Market processes and outcomes are the end results of the interaction of innumerable households and business enterprises.[21] The individual market

---

[20] Waterman (2002) proposes that the *Wealth of Nations* can in fact be read as a natural theology, similar in style to Newton's *Principia*. This may account for why some mainstream economists see economic life as governed by an immutable set of laws just like physics. This is in sharp contrast to a more evolutionary view of economic life along the lines of Darwin.

[21] By "market outcomes" I am referring not only to macroeconomic results like inflation or unemployment, but to something as simple as being able to obtain a chocolate bar from the corner shop.

participant is merely one of a great multitude of economic agents. Thus, the lone economic actor is neither sufficient nor even necessary to bring about market outcomes. This is the problem of overdetermination (1) in which there is a superfluity of potential causes and (2) in which single causes are not sufficient to produce the requisite results. They can only do so collectively. In the preceding example, there are many causes behind the weakness in the global price of coffee beans.

Individual economic agency is heavily mediated by intervening events, institutions, and other market participants

The contribution of a particular individual to a specific market outcome passes through an entire chain of socioeconomic structures, formal and informal rules, chance and contingencies, and the economic decisions of other market participants. Thus, the precise causal contribution of an economic agent to an accumulative harm is difficult to establish, if at all possible. Moreover, these collective wrongs are "distant" harms in the sense that there are many intervening events and market actors between the agent and the ulterior harms.

Market exchange is the outcome of a mutually beneficial division of labor among its participants

Individuals, or even households of extended families, are unable to produce all their needs or wants by themselves. As a consequence, they trade their surplus goods or endowments for goods or services they are unable to produce on their own. The modern economy has taken specialization and division of labor to a whole new level since Adam Smith's treatment of the subject matter in his *Wealth of Nations*. Contemporary globalization has intensified this division of labor because more advanced information and communication technologies permit easier cross-border collaboration in production.[22]

The corollary of specialization and division of labor is market exchange because the more people specialize in their particular comparative advantage, the more they have to rely on the marketplace both to sell their output and to procure their other needs. Consequently, the marketplace is inevitably a web of interlocking economic agencies.

---

[22] Examples of this are the electronics, car, and aircraft industries. Parts are manufactured in different sites across the globe and then assembled at a single location.

Individual economic agents

Ordinary market participants do not intend to inflict harm on anyone in their economic choices

Intent to harm is a necessary condition to be a co-conspirator in criminal law. In the *Uniform Commercial Code*, the moral agent who acts with intent is more culpable than one who is merely knowledgeable or negligent.[23] In the scholastic distinctions governing cooperation with evil, to intend harm or to share the intention of the principal wrongdoer is to be in formal, rather than material, cooperation with the wrongdoing. In law, moral philosophy, and religious thought, intent to harm is a critical factor in establishing fault or in determining the degree of its blameworthiness.

We have examples of market transactions that are clearly intended to inflict harm, such as human trafficking, drug pushing, price gouging, fraud, price-fixing, predatory pricing, smuggling, and many other criminal activities.[24] Participating in and sustaining these repugnant activities are among the most grievous instances of economic wrongdoing. However, these are the exceptions rather than the norm in the marketplace. Our study is primarily concerned with economic complicity in unintended injuries. These are the more interesting cases that involve the average market participant.

Ordinary economic actors do not engage in market exchange with the intention of harming anyone. They do not even have participatory intent to engage in a hurtful collective action.[25] Instead, average market participants are merely concerned with procuring their needs through market exchange or with selling their goods or services to earn a livelihood. They do not intend the resulting accumulative harms from such economic transactions. At best, these harms may have been foreseen and accepted, but not intended. Thus, shoppers go to Wal-Mart, not because they intend to put neighborhood mom-and-pop stores out of business, but because they find the selection of goods and services to be much wider and cheaper.

Ordinary market participants are price-takers

Average economic agents are unable to change singlehandedly market outcomes with their buying or selling decisions. In the theory of the perfectly competitive market, *Homo oeconomicus* is "atomized" because the economic

---

[23] Phillips (1982). The *Uniform Commercial Code* is a set of laws that are partially adopted by all the US states to ensure uniformity in adjudicating conflicting business claims.
[24] See, for example, Nordstrom (2007) and Schendel and Abraham (2005).
[25] Recall Kutz's (2000) example of the Dresden bombing crews.

actor is only one among a large number of buyers and sellers in the marketplace. Consequently, individual economic decisions are infinitesimal relative to the total size of the market. From a strictly economic point of view, they are insignificant and inconsequential to overall market outcomes, *ceteris paribus*. The quip "It does not matter whether I do it or not" is aptly descriptive of the atomized market participant.

Market participation is a necessity

Moral philosophy and law require voluntariness as a necessary condition of moral responsibility. Accomplices must have participated voluntarily if they are to be held jointly and severally liable for their group's criminal wrong-doing. Thus, coercion or fear, or both, are grounds for mitigating, if not completely negating, a moral agent's culpability for a particular harm that was inflicted only under duress.[26]

As already mentioned, modern economic life is characterized by special-ization and a division of labor. To procure their other needs, modern economic agents have to trade for them in the marketplace. Thus, market participation is a necessity for the vast majority of people. Very few, if any, can thrive as a Robinson Crusoe in our era. Consequently, most market participants cannot completely opt out of or hermetically seal themselves off from the marketplace, no matter how dissatisfied they might be with the market's systemic injustices.

Market participants reap what they sow, but only to a certain extent

The marketplace constantly redistributes burdens and benefits across eco-nomic agents. Who reaps gains or bears losses is determined by socio-economic structures, laws, public morality, and sheer luck. However, such market gains or losses are not completely exogenous to individual economic actors because they play a significant role in determining the extent to which they reap these benefits or bear these burdens. After all, the distribution of market outcomes is also in large part a function of people's work ethic, the ongoing development of their skills and training, the relationships they have painstakingly cultivated over the years, the produc-tive assets they have accumulated, and their prudential choices in the preceding rounds of economic activity. Their earlier moral and economic choices partly determine the mix of burdens and benefits they receive later in economic life. In other words, the distribution of market burdens and

---

[26] See Fagothey (1972, 25–30) for a brief description of factors that modify moral responsibility, such as ignorance, passion, fear, force, and habit.

benefits is determined by factors that are both exogenous and endogenous to individual market participants. Economic actors reap what they sow, but only to a certain extent. In many cases, they have no control over what they receive from the marketplace because of their disadvantaged sociohistorical location and many other factors beyond their control, such as poverty traps.

Market outcomes

The market is a collaborative effort: responsibility for its outcomes cannot be attributed to any particular individual

The market is, by its nature, a joint effort because it requires more than one party to consummate an exchange. Given the ever finer divisions of labor as part of economic growth, market exchange has expanded exponentially. Outcomes in economic life have increasingly required ever larger circles of people working together. Thus, responsibility for many socioeconomic communal wrongs cannot be imputed to a single or even a handful of economic actors. One could analogically describe the sum of all market participants as the "principal" behind socioeconomic accumulative harms. Individuals are merely the "secondary" parties. Their individual moral culpability is derivative from the principal's (the collective) blameworthiness.

The market is synergistic in nature: its outcomes are larger than the sum of their constituent parts

For many economic activities, there are increasing returns to collective action. For example, specialization and division of labor produce gains that would not have been possible without such collaboration. Or, consider the larger social good produced by Adam Smith's butcher, baker, and brewer under the "invisible hand." This is an example of a synergistic benefit. Note that such a synergistic dynamic works both ways. The market can readily produce synergistic harms just as it can easily bring forth synergistic benefits. Socioeconomic accumulative harms can be and often are greater than the sum of their individual contributory causes. Global warming and the 2008–2009 global economic fiasco are examples of synergistic harms.

The market produces an interlocking stream of burdens and benefits

The market produces simultaneous burdens and benefits for economic agents. For example, the general public benefits from the manifold gains from international trade at the expense of domestic manufacturing workers who lose their jobs as a result of cheaper manufactured imports. This cross-border trade also benefits future generations by moving nations to their respective comparative advantage, thereby pushing the global economy closer to allocative efficiency. Thus, the cumulative harm suffered by displaced manufacturing workers must also be weighed against the communal benefits reaped.

Implications for complicity

We cannot easily impute market accumulative harms to ordinary[27] market participants using the commonsensical accountability-limiting principles from chapter 1 because:

- individual acts considered singly by themselves are harmless;
- cumulative harms cannot be traced back to their individual particular causes;[28]
- individual market participants fail the "but for" test because the accumulative harms would still have occurred with or without their respective participation;
- many intervening events and causes come between individual causal contributions and the final accumulative harms;
- market exchange is, by its nature, a cooperative endeavor, thereby making it tautological to talk of economic complicity;
- market participants have no individual or collective intent to harm;
- collective wrongs are merely the unintended consequences of market transactions;
- individual actors are price-takers and cannot control or change flawed market processes or outcomes by themselves;
- the vast majority of people cannot opt out of market participation no matter how appalled they might be by unjust market processes;
- the market produces intertwined harms and benefits;
- accountability for market harms is diminished to the degree that victims had contributed to their own harms through their own negligence.[29]

---

[27] I use the qualifier "ordinary" or "average" to distinguish them from economic actors who have some market power and are able to affect singlehandedly market processes and outcomes. Examples are monopolists, monopsonists, colluding actors, and oligopolists.

[28] Zanardi (1990) argues that it is difficult to link particular causes to their particular effects in a system as complex as the economy.

[29] One additional and more technical reason: some would argue that individuals cannot be held to account for the increment in the total harm due to the market's synergistic dynamic. Why should the individual be held to account for increasing returns to scale (i.e., resulting outcomes are much larger

In other words, no one is morally at fault for market ills by the individual difference, control, autonomy, and complicity principles.[30] These widely used commonsensical principles fail in the case of most market ills. As we will see in chapter 8, only Kutz's (2000) notion of quasi-participatory intent can deal with accumulative harms.

Christian ethics, moral philosophy, and economics have their respective contribution to make when it comes to determining the object of accountability (complicity in what?). From Christian ethics, we have its vision of the divine order of creation and the end (*telos*) of economic activity. Economic life is a means to actualizing the fullness of human dignity. Anything that impedes or goes against this end is most likely an instance of economic wrongdoing. For liberal social philosophy, harm to others is the basis for determining what constitutes wrongdoing. Of course, there are varying degrees of such wrongdoing.

The discipline of economics has a completely different contribution to make on the question of the object of accountability. By examining the nature of the market, it highlights the formidable hurdles we face in imputing individual moral responsibility for market outcomes. Analyzing complicity in market harms is extremely complicated because of their accumulative nature. We cannot reverse-engineer economic outcomes to their respective particular causes (economic agents' choices) because of the black-box nature of the Smithian "invisible hand." No single economic decision can be identified as indispensable for the resulting market outcomes (the "but for" test). Besides, some would claim that there can be no complicity without wrongful intent, and economic agents do not participate in the market jointly with a shared purpose, much less an intention to inflict harm. Even Adam Smith's famous quip on the butcher, the baker,

---

than the sum of their individual parts)? The market's synergistic harm is an example of Feinberg's (1970, 233–251) fourth type of collective responsibility: a group contributory fault that is collective but non-distributive.

[30] Because it claims that we are responsible only for our own actions and not for those of others, the autonomy principle is intuitively appealing and widely perceived as fair. Proponents of the autonomy principle can use the aforesaid market features to extend this principle even further, namely: *We can be held to account only for the nature of our acts at the time of their commission.* This means that we cannot be held responsible for the changes wrought in our original action by subsequent intervening events, superseding causes, or others' concurrent action, as in the case of accumulative harms. However, critics will respond by noting that the morality of individual acts can only be gauged in the larger context of which they are a part and to which they contribute. Recall the preceding chapter's example of murder within the context of genocide (Isaacs 2006, 65).

and the brewer reminds us that the much-touted allocative efficiency that the "invisible hand" brings forth is an unintended consequence. Thus, by the individual difference, control, autonomy, and complicity principles, we are faced with the result that no one can be individually held responsible for market ills. Not surprisingly, moral complicity is hardly a concern in economic theory, policy, or practice.

Nonetheless, there can be complicity even in a seemingly "unstructured" setting such as the marketplace. All that is needed is a quasi-participatory intent whereby people contribute to, draw benefits from, and perpetuate underlying social structures and institutions through their participation in the marketplace.[31] To this we might add that such complicity in unstructured harms turns out to be the norm rather than the exception in everyday life. In fact, this is the most common kind of economic complicity given the nature of life in community.

In conclusion, if we were to rely solely on the widely accepted individual difference, control, autonomy, and complicity principles, then we face an awkward situation in which no one is morally responsible for market harms no matter how severe or horrific they might be. The attribution of individual responsibility for injurious market outcomes is made much more difficult because of the nature and dynamics of the marketplace in which:

1 There is a problem of overdetermination. Cumulative market wrongs are the result of a multitude of economic decisions, each of which is neither sufficient nor necessary on its own to bring about deleterious market processes and outcomes. Furthermore, the ordinary individual agent's causal contribution is not merely superfluous, it is also minute!

2 There is a problem of conjointness. First, economic transactions are a cooperative venture by the nature of the market exchange. Second, market outcomes come as a blend of interlocking harms and benefits. We must sort through this dual web of interdependency before we can impute individual responsibility for communal economic wrongs.

The next two chapters address each of these problems.

---

[31] Kutz (2000, 166–203).

CHAPTER 3

Too small and morally insignificant?
The problem of overdetermination

To what extent am I morally culpable for global warming if I purchase a gas-guzzling sport utility vehicle (SUV) despite what we now know about the damaging effects of fossil fuels? To what degree am I morally responsible for the overfishing of bluefin tuna if I persist in eating gourmet sushi despite the well-documented abuses of tuna-fishing fleets? Even if I replace my SUV with a hybrid or even if I curb my appetite for bluefin tuna, climate change will continue unabated, and bluefin tuna stocks will still be depleted to the point of extinction. After all, I am only one among a multitude of people who sustain the SUV or the bluefin-tuna markets. My individual behavior neither makes a difference in changing the final outcomes nor does it control any of the social dynamics harming the environment or global fish stocks. As the saying goes, "It makes no difference whether or not I do it." By the autonomy, individual difference, control, and complicity principles, I am not accountable for global warming or the imminent extinction of bluefin tuna.

Moreover, even if we were to assume, for the sake of argument, that I am nevertheless still morally culpable for climate change and overfishing, my actual contribution to these market ills is minute relative to the magnitude of these problems and the mass of people who act similarly. My blameworthiness will be correspondingly minuscule. Some would say that my accountability is inversely proportional to the number of people, both past and present, engaged in the same activities.[1] Given the numbers involved, my accountability diminishes to a vanishing point! Common sense tells us that there has to be proportionality between a person's causal contribution to an injury and culpability for that harm. In fact, in the case of

---

[1] According to the dispersion principle, accountability diminishes as the aggregate harm is divided up among more people or over time. Furthermore, the parallel acts principle states that accountability diminishes if other agents act similarly. See Kutz (2000, 262) for a list of some of the widely used accountability-limiting principles.

accumulative harms such as pollution, it has even been claimed in tort law "that to be liable the defendant must have 'contributed substantially' rather than infinitesimally – a clear application of the substantial factor test of causation."[2]

Or recall the longstanding legal maxim "The law does not concern itself with trifles."[3] The law may inadvertently cause even more damage by wasting scarce legal resources or by unnecessarily and disproportionately restricting people's liberties to avert trivial harms.[4] Such injuries should simply be considered inconsequential. Moreover, in law, to be held liable as a legal cause, one must have more than a tiny causal contribution to the injury in question.[5]

Both of these issues (duplicative causation and minuscule causal contribution) stem from the same problem of overdetermination in which there is a superfluity of causes, none of which is individually sufficient or even necessary for the occurrence of the harm. Can an individual contributory fault ever be so minute or redundant as to be morally insignificant? We examine each of these issues in this chapter.

CHRISTIAN ETHICS

For Christian ethics, neither superfluous causation nor minuscule causal contribution negates moral culpability. This position comes from at least three sets of arguments: (1) virtue theory and the teleological dimension of Christian morality, (2) its familial view of community, and (3) its underlying Aristotelean–Thomistic metaphysics.

Virtue theory

In Aristotelean–Thomistic virtue theory, the human act has a reflexive dimension to it: our actions come back to define and form who we are. Our moral choices shape the kind of person we become. Thus, people who have a knack for maligning others, who think only of their own interests, or who maltreat others make life very unpleasant for the people around them. But they hurt themselves the most because through their repeated moral choices, it becomes second nature to them to be mean-spirited and

---

[2] Prosser (1971, 323).   [3] Feinberg (1984, 189).   [4] Feinberg (1984,188–190, 216).
[5] Smith (1911–1912, 110). To be sure, I am not suggesting that legal liability is identical to moral responsibility. Nevertheless, jurisprudence is often a source of insights on how to deal with culpability, legal or moral. All I am highlighting here is the law as an analog for establishing degree of moral responsibility.

self-absorbed. Maligning and maltreating others become constitutive of their character and personality. We choose the kind of person we become through our moral acts over time.[6]

Thus, for people who are virtuous, the issue is not whether they are a cause or a mere condition of the harm. The issue is not whether their causal contribution to the harm is minute enough to be morally insignificant. Rather, the right question for them is whether or not their actions are ultimately and needlessly injurious to others or to themselves. Is their injury-causing conduct justifiable using the principle of double effect? Are there viable alternatives to avoid these harms? The measure of their behavior is not the remoteness of the damage they inflict or their superfluity in the face of others' similar actions. Rather, the measure of their moral choices is whether or not each of these acts is consistent with their self-understanding of who they are as persons and as a human community.

Closely related to this, of course, is the notion of sin, understood as "missing the mark." There is a scalar quality to sin in that it comes in varying degrees of gravity. Nonetheless, no matter how slight the sin may be, it is still "off the mark." With the aid of divine grace, the goal of Christian moral life, indeed, its ultimate destiny is perfection – union with God. Not surprisingly, Christian life is about loving God with our whole heart, soul, and mind, and about loving our neighbor as ourselves (Mt 22:37–39). It is total in its commitment and it settles for nothing less than this. As a result, it has no room even for "slight" sin. A contributory fault is never too minute to be morally significant.

We can explain this dynamic in Christian life by highlighting the difference between a deontological versus a teleological approach to ethical thinking. Law, by its nature, is concerned with conformity to norms and standards. This is reflected in the measures it uses: "but for" necessity, cause versus a mere condition, substantial contribution, remoteness of damage, and many other standards we will see in the next chapter. Law has to be precise not only in establishing culpability but in "grading" the varying degrees of liability. Law is deontological by the nature of its tasks and methods.

In Christian life, duty and conformity are likewise essential. They are constitutive of moral life. Thus, living up to moral precepts, such as the Ten Commandments, is a must. However, such deontological conformity is understood to be merely the ground floor, the entry point to another even

---

[6] See, for example, Cessario (1991) and Porter (1995) on the nature of moral action, virtue, and character formation.

more vibrant dynamic to which all are invited: the pursuit of true and full humanity.[7] Jesus Christ is the measure of what it is to be truly and fully human. The Incarnation revealed to us who we truly are as persons and who we are as a human community. With this self-understanding, we emulate Jesus Christ and follow in his footsteps, not out of fear of failing to live up to a standard, but out of a deep yearning to be who we truly are. This is a teleological yearning so vividly and accurately captured by St. Augustine's "our heart is restless until it rests in you."[8]

Far from being compelled by some external impetus (such as the fear of punishment for violating laws), Christians are in fact impelled from within – in a restless longing to be who they truly are. Within such a teleological dynamic, the focus is not the remoteness or the superfluity of one's contributory fault. Rather, a better gauge of one's moral choices is whether or not they impede one's journey to moral perfection. In the end, the various tests of causation to assess remoteness of damage are not needed by virtuous people. In their quest for perfection, they are guided by an internal moral compass in their choices. They will be self-policing and will be their own harshest critic when it comes to inflicting injury on others (no matter how distant) or on themselves because of their economic conduct. After all, this is what being virtuous is all about.

Familial treatment of each other

From a Christian perspective, there are no limits to the scope of our moral responsibility for one another. The Genesis accounts of creation are clear in the shared responsibility we exercise not only over the earth, but even more importantly, for each other's well-being. This is repeatedly affirmed in both the Old and New Testament. Despite their keen appreciation for their corporate identity as the Chosen People of God, the Hebrews nevertheless understood that even the aliens and strangers in their midst were supposed to be accorded respect and assistance in YHWH's vision of an Israel different from all the other nations. Moreover, as they matured in their faith and in their understanding of their covenant relationship with YHWH, they realized that they were to be the vessels of grace for the salvation extended to many other nations and peoples in the New Jerusalem.[9]

---

[7] Mark 10:17–27 is an excellent illustration. The rich young man who had observed the commandments all his life was still searching for eternal life. He was invited to greater perfection by selling all his possessions, giving to the poor, and then following Christ.
[8] Augustine (1960, book 1, chapter 1, no. 1). [9] See Verhey (1984, 12–13).

National borders, race, gender, or class are irrelevant for the disciples of
Christ when it comes to mutual obligations. Despite the disagreements on
whether or not the Johannine "new commandment" of love is reserved only
for those within their faith community, the overwhelming evidence from
the New Testament itself and the predominant view of scholars point to
the universal scope of the Gospel.[10] We can do no less than Jesus Christ
who, in his practice of "table fellowship" in his public ministry, extended an
unconditional welcome to one and all. Jesus had no qualms associating with
or assisting the unclean, the sinners, and even the hated Roman occupiers or
their collaborators.[11]

Paul describes this solidarity when he notes that with baptism in Christ,
there is "neither Jew nor Greek, slave nor free, male nor female" (Gal 3:27–29).
This is once again affirmed in the public ministry of Paul, an apostle sent to
the Gentiles, and in the subsequent ministry of the other apostles to the non-
Jews. After all, they were to preach the Gospel to the ends of the earth. Paul's
collection from the Gentile churches for the poor of Jerusalem is a concrete
affirmation that there are no divisions either in the one Body of Christ or in the
Kingdom of God that we are all engaged in building.

Limits to our mutual obligations of solicitude, especially when it is the
poor who are at risk, are incompatible with the radical selflessness required
by the Gospel of Christ. Thus, disciples are to give up even their tunic after
having to give up their cloaks, turn the other cheek, give to all who ask, and
even love the very enemies who abuse them (Lk 6:27–35). In both the Old
and the New Testament, alleviating the plight of the poor is incumbent not
only on the king or the temple; it is a duty of every community member. It
does not matter whether or not one is causally responsible or blameworthy
for the poor's destitution. It is sufficient that the poor are one's neighbors
and that one has the means to provide some assistance.

The New Testament provides two of the most clear-cut and conclusive
responses to whether or not there are racial, class, gender, or geographic
boundaries to our moral duties for one another's well-being. First is
Jesus' response to the scribe's question "Who is my neighbor?" The Good
Samaritan could only see the need of the man who fell in with the robbers
(Lk 10:29–37). Everything else was irrelevant, including the man's Jewish
faith and the inconvenience, delay, and expense of having to go out of his
way to bind the man's wounds, bring him to an inn, and come back to the

---

[10] See Matera (1996, 115–116), Schrage (1988, 295–319), and Verhey (1984, 143–144) for a concise
discussion of the arguments and counter-arguments on the restrictive nature of Johannine love.
[11] See, for example, Burridge (2007).

inn at a later time to pay for whatever else may have been incurred for the man's care.

Second, we have the even more powerful example of Jesus Christ laying down his life and dying on the Cross in a most gruesome manner for others' sins, for the undeserving, and even for the very people who had brutalized him. Bonhoeffer uses this as the basis for his claim that there are no limits to the scope of Christian responsibility. In particular, he argues that "Jesus took upon Himself the guilt of all men, and for that reason every man who acts responsibly becomes guilty."[12] Clearly, this goes beyond vicarious liability because there is in fact no basis for imputing such liability.[13] Jesus simply voluntarily atones for humanity's sin. Bonhoeffer expects the Christian to do likewise – to take the liability even when neither legally nor morally obligated to do so, except for our desire to imitate Christ. If the Cross is indeed the paradigm of Christian responsibility in which we willingly accept liability even when we are faultless, then how much stronger are our obligations in those instances when we in fact contribute to the harm? Given such high standards, the minuteness or the redundancy of our contributory fault does not absolve us from our moral duties.

Taken as paradigms for Christian discipleship, both the Cross and the parable of the Good Samaritan provide a succinct but unmistakable response to the question of how far-reaching are the moral obligations we owe one another. Christ invites us to be as heroic and as ready to pour out ourselves, our time, and our substance for those who are in need, without pause or questions asked. There are no boundaries when it comes to mutual solicitude because all are brothers and sisters of the same family of God.

People's mutual concern for one another does not depend on whether or not they are the "but for" cause, a redundant cause, or merely a "trivial" cause of socioeconomic harms. It is sufficient to know that we run the risk of harming a brother or a sister, a fellow child of God, and that we could prevent or mitigate such injury. Imputing personal accountability in the face of overdetermination is not a problem because of the familial spirit that characterizes Christian discipleship. We care for one another because we see ourselves in each other.

---

[12] Bonhoeffer (1964, 210). Schliesser (2006, 66–68) notes that there is a difference between guilt that is non-actively incurred (as in the case of Christ's atonement for our sins) and guilt that is actively incurred (as in the case of Bonhoeffer's political activism and involvement in the plot against Hitler). Hence, one must be extremely careful with the statement that "every person who acts responsibly is guilty." See also Schliesser (2008).

[13] Recall that in vicarious liability, faultless agents may nonetheless still be held liable by virtue of their social role or relationship to the party at fault (e.g., employers for their workers' misdeeds).

Aristotelean–Thomistic metaphysics

Aristotelean–Thomistic metaphysics can also be used to arrive at the preceding arguments of both virtue theory and the familial view of the human community. In particular, one can use Aquinas's notion of the twofold order of creation: the external and the internal order of the universe. On the one hand, the external order of the universe describes the manner by which all creation, as a single entity, finds its end in God, the Final Cause. On the other hand, the internal order of the universe is about each constituent member of the universe contributing its share in moving the whole external order to its Final End.

Each member of the universe has its specific role to play according to the mode of its being and operation. Thus, no individual causal contribution is ever deemed to be so trivial as to be morally insignificant. Moreover, there are no redundant or superfluous causes because in the grand scheme of God's order of creation, every creature is unique, with its particular contribution to make in communicating and reflecting the perfection and the goodness of God. The difficulties raised by overdetermination are non-issues if we employ Aristotelean–Thomistic metaphysics in assessing the question.[14]

LAW AND PHILOSOPHY

In the next two sections, we will examine insights from law and social philosophy regarding the culpability of redundant causes or minuscule causal contributions to injuries. Are these morally insignificant given their superfluity or minimal contributory fault?

Redundant causation

The superfluity of causes in the problem of overdetermination poses difficulties for the ascription of individual culpability. In particular, none of these simultaneous causes can pass the "but for" test. None of these overlapping causes can be said to be necessary for the occurrence of the harm. Since none of them can be properly called a *sine qua non* cause, some will claim that we cannot impute responsibility for the harm to any of these causes.

---

[14] See Wright (1957) for a further examination of Aquinas's twofold order of the universe. See Barrera (2005b, 19–40, 209–37) for an application of Aristotelean–Thomistic metaphysics to economic life.

We can present many philosophical arguments against such claims. Intuitively appealing as it may be, the "but for" (*sine qua non*) test is flawed because it does not discriminate causes from mere conditions. Neither does it differentiate the relative importance of various causes. Moreover, the "but for" test leads to absurd results in cases of simultaneous causation.

Mill's "cause"

John Stuart Mill's notion of "cause" is a good starting point in addressing the problems raised by overdetermination.[15] Mill argues that it is the whole ensemble of conditions that are jointly sufficient in bringing about an event that should properly be called "the cause" of the event. We ought not single out one of these conditions and call it "the cause." Equally important for our study of accumulative harms, Mill's approach to causation acknowledges that there are, in fact, multiple sets of such jointly sufficient conditions that can bring about the same occurrence. Outcomes are not the result merely of one unique set of jointly sufficient conditions. Other similarly jointly sufficient sets may have been at work, but were preempted before they could take effect. Mill's insight is important for our study because economic life is the spontaneous outcome of innumerable sets of jointly sufficient conditions. His notion of causation can account for the condition of overdetermination.

NESS

We can sharpen Mill's notion of causation even further by overlaying it with the "necessary element in a set of jointly sufficient conditions" test (NESS). The value of NESS comes to the fore whenever we deal with cases entailing a surfeit of causes and sets of conditions that can bring about the same event. Take the case of two separate forest fires, X and Y, each of which would have been sufficient to burn down a house at the edge of a clearing.[16] In the first scenario, both fires reach the house at the same time and burn it down. In the second scenario, fire X arrives at the house first and then burns it down before fire Y reaches it. Note that in both scenarios, fire X is not a necessary condition because even if there were no fire X, fire Y would have burned down the house. The same can be said for fire Y because even without fire Y, fire X would have been sufficient to burn down the house. Thus, in both

---

[15] Mill (1843 [1973], 327–334, book III, chapter 5, section 3).

[16] Wright (1988, nos. 1019–1023) expands Hart and Honoré's (1985) notion of jointly sufficient conditions and presents a succinct exposition on the properties of NESS and how it is a vast improvement over the "but for" test. I take the following case from him.

cases we have the absurd case in which neither fire X nor Y can be properly called a cause of the house burning down because they fail the "but-for" test. NESS, however, is an effective test to apply in this case of concurrent or "duplicative" causes.

Fire X is a necessary element in the set of conditions (wind, oxygen, etc.) that were jointly sufficient to burn down the house in both scenarios 1 and 2. Fire Y is likewise a necessary element in its own set of conditions (wind, oxygen, etc.) that were jointly sufficient to burn down the house in scenario 1. The same would have been true for scenario 2 had it not been for fire X having burned the house first. Thus, in scenario 2, since there is no longer a house to burn down, fire Y is not a NESS, but is merely a preempted NESS. The important point is that even in this case of redundant causes, it is still possible to single out one of the concurrent causes as *the* or at least *a* cause responsible for the harm unlike the "but for" test.

Consequentialism and moral mathematics

We can also examine the problem of overdetermination using consequentialism. There are said to be "five mistakes in moral mathematics."[17] Among these is the error of "ignoring the effects of sets of acts." The fallacy in this error is to argue that the only relevant results are the effects of individual acts alone. This error arises in two instances: overdetermination and coordination problems (also known as collective-action problems).

If we embed cases of overdetermination within the framework of utilitarianism, it would be a mistake to consider only the effects of one particular act in isolation from other similar actions. We fail to consider its synergy with these other actions in producing benefits or minimizing harms. Thus, the rule of thumb for consequentialism ought to be reformulated[18] as:

Even if an act harms no one, this act may be wrong because it is one of a *set* of acts that *together* harm other people. Similarly, even if some act benefits no one, it can be what someone ought to do, because it is one of a set of acts that *together* benefit other people. (Parfit 1984, 70, emphases added)

Thus, from a consequentialist point of view, redundant causes cannot exonerate themselves of culpability because their individual effects cannot be viewed in isolation from the entire set of ultimate outcomes to which they contribute and of which they are a part.

---

[17] Parfit (1984, 67–86).
[18] Utilitarianism's more popular rule of thumb is "An act benefits someone if its consequence is that someone is benefitted more" (Parfit 1984, 69).

The other possible scenario is the collective-action problem. This is best illustrated in the prisoners' dilemma. This is the case in which prisoners unwittingly produce a suboptimal outcome for themselves (both individually and as a group) by pursuing the seemingly "rational" path of promoting only their respective individual interests. In fact, the optimal solution is paradoxically to have all the players sacrifice their individual interests and, in the process, produce the right maximization solution. The "irrational" strategy turns out to be the right approach.

Thus, *collective consequentialism* is superior to its more popular variant, individualistic consequentialism. In collective consequentialism, the interests of the whole rather than the individual take precedence and, as a result, better outcomes are obtained than would have otherwise been the case.[19] From a consequentialist point of view it is a mistake to focus our attention only on the effects of single acts to the exclusion of the larger milieu in which such action produces its outcomes.

Put another way, there is a distinction between act and rule utilitarianism. In act utilitarianism, the maximization exercise is concerned only with each particular act and how it might promote the social utility. In contrast, under rule utilitarianism, we have a two-step process. In the first instance, we identify the right moral rules that optimize social utility under different conditions. These moral rules maximize social utility only if everybody follows them. The second step is to weigh each particular act in question against these social-utility maximizing moral rules.[20]

For example, in major urban centers plagued by traffic congestion, special highway lanes are reserved for the exclusive use of public buses and private vehicles with more than two passengers. This is partly an effort to encourage people to use public transportation or to car-pool as a way of reducing the number of vehicles on the road. Act utilitarians could free-ride on everybody else by ignoring the restrictions (or having inflatable dummies in the car) and driving on these specially designated and smoothly flowing lanes. As a result, they reap the windfall of not becoming stuck in traffic and reaching their destination sooner. They gain in terms of savings in time and gas (if they are not ticketed by the police). However, this imposes costs on everybody else because it makes these special lanes less effective, especially if there are many other act utilitarians. In contrast, rule utilitarians will reason

---

[19] Parfit (1984, 30–31). In the preceding case of the prisoners' dilemma, individual players end up with much larger gains by working together than if they were to work only for their own respective interests. Public goods (e.g., defense, public health, roads, etc.) provide enormous benefits for all, but they would not have been produced to begin with had it not been for collaborative work.

[20] Harsanyi (1979, 311, 316, fn 8).

that even if they can reap personal advantage by cheating the system, they will not do so because this laudable traffic initiative will fail if everybody else ignores the restrictions. Unlike act utilitarians, rule utilitarians consider not only the consequences of their actions but also the consequences of others behaving similarly.

Rule utilitarianism is superior to act utilitarianism as an ethical theory because it is much more effective in coordinating joint action in pursuing social goals.[21] Besides, rule utilitarianism has more desirable effects than act utilitarianism in shaping people's expectations and the incentives they face. These findings can be readily applied to our case of redundant causation. Overdetermination does not matter under rule utilitarianism because everyone is expected to follow the moral rules that have been identified to be optimal for the whole community (e.g., preserving the ecology). In contrast, there is no similar expectation or mechanism to coordinate joint action in act utilitarianism given its narrow focus on particular acts in isolation from each other.[22]

Tort law and apportionment of damages
William Prosser's (1971) *Law of Torts* deals with the problem of accumulative harms in the section on joint tortfeasors.[23] Unlike many other cases of torts, an accumulative harm is in a class by itself because single acts, while harmless in themselves, become injurious only in conjunction with other similar acts. Prosser uses the classic example of pollution and argues that even a very slight pollution is unreasonable and wrongful in cases where others' similar pollution, no matter how minimal, will jointly create a dangerous situation. Polluters should have known better and should have gauged their conduct according to how they might "concur with that of others to cause damage" (323). It is incumbent upon people to know that their decisions will interact with others' similar actions, and it will be negligent of them not even to check how their own acts might work together with others' conduct. And this applies even for a slight pollution. In terms of liability, all parties to the ensuing pollution will have to bear a part of the total damages.

---

[21] Harsanyi (1979).
[22] For our study, rule utilitarianism is convergent with Christian ethics in their common concern that the moral agent think always in terms of the entire group rather than only of the agent's own interest. However, Christian ethics is not entirely compatible with rule utilitarianism. The most significant difference is that utilitarianism does not acknowledge that there are intrinsically evil acts. Any means employed are morally acceptable for as long as they produce the desired results. Christian ethics does not accept the reasoning that the end justifies the means.
[23] Torts pertain to damages and restitution for injuries to person or property.

This shared liability with its division of the damages among the joint tortfeasors is the norm in many of the other "duplicative" cases considered by Prosser (1971, 313–323). In other words, redundancy in causation does not excuse one of culpability or liability.

Quasi-participatory intent in unstructured harms

We can impute individual responsibility even with overdetermination using Kutz's quasi-participatory intent in unstructured harms (chapter 1), for at least two reasons. First, whether or not an individual is merely a superfluous cause of the harm is immaterial when it comes to character formation. What is more important is the commission of the act itself (or its omission). The impact of the individual act on the person's virtue is just as important as the harm inflicted on others.[24] This effect on personal character does not depend solely or entirely on the person's actual causal contribution to the ultimate harm. What is morally relevant is that the individual did in fact commit the act. Thus, even if one's excessive consumption cannot be proved to be causally responsible for raising food prices in poor nations, the indulgent lifestyle alone mars that person's moral integrity. It is the same argument we saw earlier from virtue theory in Christian ethics.

Second, Kutz underscores the impact of one's behavior on others' choices. Other market participants are much more willing to join in ameliorative collective action that mitigates or prevents accumulative harms if there is a perceived high rate of compliance from others. This is the standard problem of the commons or the prisoners' dilemma.[25]

Individual action within its collective context

As we have seen earlier, the moral import of an individual's actions can be satisfactorily evaluated only within the larger context of the collective outcome to which it contributes and in which it participates. Recall Isaacs's (2006) examples of murder in the context of genocide or running a marathon in the context of a fundraising event. Individual acts are part of something much larger than themselves and, consequently, an overly individualized assessment of moral acts not only fails to capture the entire picture, but it is also more likely to be inaccurate. The deficiency of such a

---

[24] Kutz (2000, 17–65). Kaveny (2000) makes a similar argument but for a different purpose – making the case for "appropriating benefits from evil" as a new category.

[25] See Kutz (2000, 180) for a brief application of the "assurance games" to the problem of overdetermination. This is the exact opposite of giving scandal in material cooperation. In this case, instead of scandalizing others, our good example prompts others to follow suit.

narrow account of moral agency becomes even more serious in light of the synergies in economic life (e.g., accumulative harms).

Summary

Accumulative harms, by their nature, arise from a superfluity of causes. The redundancy of such concurrent causation means that none of them can be properly called a "but for" cause. Not one of them is, strictly speaking, necessary for the occurrence of the harm. Individual agents could claim that "whether or not I do it makes no difference for the outcome." Thus, by the solipsistic standards of the autonomy, individual difference, and control principles, none of these duplicative causes can be held morally culpable as a cause, much less as *the* cause. We end up with an odd case in which there is a harm but no responsible cause(s).

We have examined these claims from different angles in law and social philosophy using a wide variety of conceptual tools ranging from Mill's notion of cause, to causation theory's "necessary element in a set of jointly sufficient conditions" (NESS), to Parfit's collective consequentialism and Harsanyi's rule utilitarianism, to Prosser's apportionment of damages in torts, and to Kutz's quasi-participatory intent in unstructured harms. All these bring us to the same conclusion: whether or not a particular act makes a difference to the outcome by itself is not the right criterion to use. Instead, such individual acts must be considered in the context of the collective outcome to which it contributes. After all, going back to Mill, it is in fact a whole ensemble of conditions, often complex, that brings about an effect. Thus, it is this whole ensemble that should properly be called *the* cause of the effect. Redundant causes may not excuse themselves from moral culpability no matter how superfluous their causal contribution might appear. The right question to ask is "Will my act be one of a set of acts that will *together* harm other people?"[26]

Minuscule effects

We come now to the second problem posed by overdetermination: is an infinitesimal causal contribution morally significant? By their nature, economic accumulative harms are the spontaneous outcomes of innumerable households and business enterprises, each pursuing its own interests. The sheer numbers involved translate to a minuscule causal contribution on the

---

[26] Parfit (1984, 86, emphasis original).

part of each market participant. Is this reason enough not to hold these individual economic agents morally culpable?

Moral mathematics

The moral significance of minute contributions is also taken up by Parfit (1984, 75–86) in his account of the "five mistakes in moral mathematics." In particular, he argues that it is an error to think that we may ignore very small or imperceptible effects on very large numbers of people. Using consequentialism, Parfit argues that there can be no such thing as a very small or an imperceptible impact because if taken in conjunction with other similarly minuscule or imperceptible effects, they will eventually become collectively large and will be perceptible if enough people act in a similar fashion. Again, the error lies in considering the results only of one particular act taken in isolation by itself without considering its joint impact with others.

Parfit's point on very small and imperceptible effects dovetails the case of accumulative harms perfectly. The market is an effective social institution in coordinating a multitude of disparate decisions into a coherent common economic life. Economic agents are price-takers and cannot change market processes singlehandedly through their individual buying or selling decisions. However, they are price-makers when considered as a group: their economic choices jointly determine market outcomes. For example, family A's decision to tighten its belt and not purchase a new car during the 2008–2009 recession did not by itself make a dent in the Big Three automakers' revenues. It would have been accurate to call it an infinitesimal effect, hardly perceptible, if at all, to the auto giants. But, with enough families in similar straits who have forgone purchasing new or used vehicles, we have an economic disaster for the Big Three.

Of course, an even better illustration is the well-known paradox in macroeconomics. Thrift is a virtue and should be encouraged at a personal and household level. But taken together for the whole economy, a surge in savings rates leads to a recession and perhaps even a deflation. Indeed, Parfit has a point in claiming that there are no such very small or imperceptible effects when there are enough people who engage in the same activity. It is particularly descriptive of economic life.

Absolute responsibility

The notion of absolute responsibility is a powerful argument against treating minute causal contributions as morally insignificant. Addressing the link between responsibility and complicity, Aronson (1990) uses the Holocaust as an analog for apartheid. The Final Solution was not merely the work of a handful of men like Hitler and Himmler, nor was it limited to a few thousand SS officers bent on carrying out orders, nor was it confined to the tens of thousands of camp guards and railroad workers who kept the murder machine running smoothly. It also included both the fifty million Germans who acquiesced passively to the murderous brutality of their state and the Allied leadership who could have done much more to stop the mass murders. The Holocaust was the outcome of the complicity of many, all of whom shared moral responsibility.

Aronson (1990, 64–65) acknowledges that there are varying degrees of responsibility. The ordinary "good" German citizen was not as responsible as Himmler. Thus, he distinguishes between:
- those who gave the command,
- those who carried out the command,
- those who were actively complicit,
- those who were passively complicit (e.g., good German citizens who could have actively opposed their government), and
- those who were negatively complicit (e.g., Allied leadership who could have done more).

Millions were responsible for the Holocaust, each in their own way and in varying degrees. Aronson describes this as the spiral of responsibility, with Hitler at the very center and the culpability spreading outwards in ever wider circles, coopting people into participating in this orchestrated genocide.

Even while acknowledging variations in the degree of responsibility, Aronson is emphatic that "less responsible" does not mean being excused: "They remain responsible, even if to a lesser degree . . . [E]ach is absolutely responsible. In other words, *even when partial, responsibility is absolute*" (Aronson 1990, 66–67, emphasis added). Responsibility is absolute no matter how small it might be because the Final Solution could not have been pulled off unless "each of those responsible contributed in a specific and definite way" (65) to prop up and make the entire system work. And in contributing in a "specific and definite way," each is necessarily also responsible in a "specific and definite way." This is the same point that Kutz (2000, 166–203) makes to justify his extension of individual participation to include those in "unstructured" harms. What may appear to be spontaneous and uncoordinated on the surface is often undergirded by socioeconomic structures and institutions. Thus, in participating in such "unstructured" harms, one is in effect perpetuating and further strengthening the ills of their underlying foundations in a "specific and definite way." Similarly, recall the point of Isaacs (2006) on how important it is to evaluate individual acts, not in isolation by themselves, but within the larger context of the collective to which they contribute and in which they participate.

Aronson's argument of how responsibility is absolute even when partial because of the specific and definite way by which people contribute to wrongdoing is capped off with a potent example: the refusal of tens of thousands of Danes to follow orders when the Final Solution reached the shores of Denmark. As a result, the killing machine ground to a halt and Danish Jewry was saved (67). This incident is not merely convincing but is conclusive in making the point that complicity can never be so minuscule as to be morally insignificant. In fact, the Danish response is actually more common than most people think.

Recall, for example, Dietrich Bonhoeffer who avoided complicity in Hitler's madness by joining the resistance. Unfortunately, in Bonhoeffer's case, he was presented with an unpalatable choice of being complicit in Hitler's evil or being complicit in the plot to assassinate Hitler. Franz Jägerstätter is another example of singular courage. An Austrian, he was the only citizen in his community to vote against the *Anschluss*, the annexation of Austria by Germany. And when he was called up for service in the German army in 1943, he made known his conscientious objection to Hitler's war and asked to be put instead in a non-violent service. His request was denied and Jägerstätter was tried for sedition and executed.[27]

Or note, for example, the successful grassroots movements against Nestlé's unethical infant-formula marketing practices, against inhumane agricultural working conditions in the grape and tomato industries, and against college apparel sweatshop subcontracting. Or recall consumer initiatives on Fair Trade and voluntary carbon offset programs. These recent examples suggest that the notion of absolute responsibility is intuitively appealing and widely held. People simply know that no matter how seemingly small or remote their part in wrongdoing might be, they are nonetheless still morally responsible for such causal contribution.

Aronson (1990, 56–57) strengthens his point by raising Sartre's notion of ethical subjectivity. Sartre argues that "I was merely obeying orders" is not an acceptable excuse, much less does it relieve one of culpability. In following an order, one interiorizes it, makes it one's own, and then "re-exteriorizes" it as one's own project. For Sartre (1948, 12), "to exist is always to assume its being; that is, to be responsible for it instead of receiving it from outside like a stone." People never lose their ethical subjectivity; they retain responsibility for themselves and their moral choices.[28] There is no excuse, whether for the guards who were merely following orders, or even for the millions of good Germans who were cowed into quiet, passive acquiescence.

There is a remarkable convergence between Aronson's and Sartre's notion of absolute responsibility, Parfit's moral mathematics of very small or imperceptible effects, Harsanyi's rule utilitarianism as a superior ethical theory to act utilitarianism, Kutz's quasi-participatory intent in unstructured harms, and Isaacs's moral evaluation of individual acts within their larger collective context. They all come to the same conclusion that individual causal contribution and responsibility can never be so minute as to be morally unimportant.[29] These "very small or imperceptible effects" have a reach that extends way beyond their immediate circle. They are much more consequential than people often think.

ECONOMICS

In the neoclassical economic theory's formulation of the perfectly competitive market, *Homo oeconomicus* is a price-taker and cannot singlehandedly affect market outcomes and prices.[30] Thus, some would argue that the individual "atomized" agent can be absolved of moral culpability for accumulative harms using the individual difference, control, and autonomy principles. I disagree. This atomization of *Homo oeconomicus* must be understood in the context of its accompanying qualifier – *ceteris paribus*, that is, everything else held constant or unchanged. In practice, not everything stays unchanged because the market consists of more than just one economic actor. It is an economic terrain with many individual parts moving simultaneously. Taken together, these disparate, minute economic choices collectively determine market processes and outcomes. It is what Adam Smith's "invisible hand" is all about. The baker's, brewer's, and butcher's actions, insignificant and atomized when taken individually, combine together to bring about the social good of provisioning the entire community with their respective goods or services.

---

[28] Sartre takes a more demanding position in the ascription of responsibility than Aronson by not even making distinctions with respect to degrees of responsibility. Aronson (1990, 70) describes "Sartre's sweeping absolutism" in the following manner: "everyone is born into it, living within it, benefitting from it, is responsible for it." Aronson accounts for Sartre's absolutism as "verbal extravagance" in order to move people to guilt and action (59).

[29] One could describe it as asymptotic in that it approaches zero but is never equal to zero.

[30] In a perfectly competitive market, there are no monopolies or monopsonies, and the ordinary economic agent faces infinitely elastic demand or supply curves.

Far from being excused, the individual atomized economic agent has, in fact, even stronger obligations for taking responsibility for collective wrongs. Consider the following arguments based on empirical evidence and the minimal effort required. First, note the success of grassroots actions in recent decades: the César Chávez grape boycott, the Nestlé infant-formula protest, the South African apartheid divestment, the entire field of socially responsible investing, the anti-sweatshop campaign for college apparel, Fair Trade, carbon offset programs, micro-lending, and many other private initiatives. Or note the stunning proliferation in the number and variety of NGOs and the emergence of social entrepreneurship as a vehicle for applying business solutions and methods to alleviating socio-economic ills. Collective actions do not arise on their own. Individual action and private initiative give rise to and fuel what eventually balloons into a concerted effort.

Individual economic decisions cut both ways – they can contribute to cumulative harms or to cumulative benefits. Atomized economic actors are, in fact, not helpless at all. Their actions, even at the individual level, can be effective if properly channeled. This is particularly true in the age of information and communication technologies like Twitter, Facebook, etc. that have greatly empowered the individual, in addition to making it so much easier to organize joint action.

A second argument for even stronger obligations at the individual level is the likely minimal effort required. The call for acquitting people of their moral culpability stems from either the redundancy or the minuteness, or both, of their causal contributions to the accumulative harm. Both arguments can, in fact, be used to call for even stronger moral duties for the individual. It is very likely that liability is assigned proportionately to causal contribution or contributory fault in the vast majority of cases. If so, the redundancy and the individual's infinitesimal causal contribution would also mean that the share of the ordinary economic actor in the liability would be correspondingly minuscule. Given this minimal effort or cost to individuals, their moral obligation to contribute toward averting or miti-gating communal wrongs becomes even stronger.

Finally, the absence of any organized effort to remedy socioeconomic harms is not an excuse for individuals to be unconcerned about these collective ills. Many have voluntarily owned up to their share of the responsibility. A good recent example of this is the carbon offset market. While awaiting a more organized multilateral effort to address climate change, individuals have taken the initiative of offsetting their own carbon footprint. The same is true for many other market harms from our everyday consumption.[31] And, of course, as citizens, they could also lobby for governmental action.

MORAL BLAMEWORTHINESS VERSUS MORAL LIABILITY

Before we conclude this chapter on overdetermination, it is important to highlight the difference between blameworthiness and liability. Let us revisit the legal maxim "The law does not concern itself with trifles."[32] This legal maxim is completely understandable if we remember that jurisprudence has to enforce the law in a cost-efficient manner. As we will see in the next chapter, proximate cause is an artificial line drawn by the courts to delimit how far it will look for liable parties. Tort law is not interested in tracking down every single cause-in-fact in order to make each of them bear their share of the damages. Instead, courts identify the parties who in the eyes of the law are best suited to bear the cost of the damages according to established social and legal policy or practice.[33]

The legal maxim "The law does not concern itself with trifles" can also be explained in terms of cost-efficiency in deciding whether or not to limit people's liberties.[34] Legislation that proscribes activities limits people's freedom of action and, consequently, there must be a compelling case for such laws. After all, the presumption is in favor of granting everyone as wide a range of freedoms, to the extent possible. As noted earlier, to limit people's liberties in order to avert merely trivial harms is to cause even more damage than good. One might inflict even more injuries by needlessly enacting legislation or by being overintrusive.

Furthermore, the law and the courts are concerned with more than just dispensing justice; they are keenly aware of trade-offs in community life. For example, the law sometimes limits the extent of liability because the risk of potentially excessive liabilities can paralyze people into inaction or excessive caution, with nothing getting accomplished in social life as a result. Or courts simplify what would have otherwise been a tedious, complicated case of sorting through the causal contributions of multiple tortfeasors by designating one, among many causes, as *the* cause responsible for the damages.[35]

The law has pragmatic reasons for ignoring trivial harms or minuscule contributory faults. There are no such constraints when it comes to moral responsibility. The secular philosophies we examined and Christian ethics

[31] See, for example, Clawson (2009).   [32] Feinberg (1984, 189).   [33] Calabresi (1975).
[34] Feinberg (1984, 189–190).   [35] Shavell (1980, 499–500).

converge in their stance on overdetermination: redundancy or minute causal contributions do not negate moral culpability. Unlike law, they are not concerned with cost-efficiency in their moral query, and they can afford to be exacting and uncompromising in their requirements. After all, moral responsibility is enforced primarily in the internal forum.[36] It is self-enforced, from the human heart and mind. There are minimal transaction costs in its enforcement, if any at all. Furthermore, Christian ethics and social philosophy can limit their discourse to moral responsibility and not even impute liability. In contrast, law, by its nature, is enforced in the external forum. It has to mete out liabilities. Moreover, the law has to deter future wrongdoing. Furthermore, the law has to adjudicate and balance conflicting legitimate claims. Thus, courts and legislators do not enjoy the luxury of simply dispensing justice in their decisions; they also have to be pragmatic.

Having said this, we must, however, acknowledge that there are limits to the uncompromising stance of Christian ethics and the philosophers we examined. They can afford to be rigorous in the internal forum, but not in the external forum, not where the proverbial tire hits the road. Thus, for example, in cases in which there is material cooperation with evil as a side-effect of business operations, they employ the principle of double effect in sorting through the interlocking web of simultaneous benefits and harms. Moral culpability is never so minute as to be morally insignificant. However, the corresponding liability for such moral culpability may be too minuscule to enforce in practice or might cause even more or greater injuries. In such cases, the liability is better left unenforced. In other words, in moral discourse concerning overdetermination, it is important to distinguish whether one is talking of blameworthiness or liability. Each requires a different set of considerations.

SUMMARY AND CONCLUSIONS

Two ethical questions arise because of the problem of overdetermination in accumulative harms. First, is a minuscule causal contribution morally significant? Second, is there moral culpability in cases of superfluous causation in which the cause is neither necessary nor sufficient for the harm's occurrence? This is the classic defense "It makes no difference whether I do it or not." (The shark population would have been depleted anyway regardless of whether or not I curb my appetite for shark-fin soup.) By

---

[36] Feinberg (1970, 33).

the autonomy, individual difference, and control principles, the redundant or minute cause is not morally culpable for such collective wrongs.

Both questions can be answered in the affirmative using various arguments from social philosophy, Christian ethics, and economics. There is moral responsibility even if one was merely a superfluous cause or a tiny bit player in a huge ensemble of causes responsible for the harm. Various thinkers in secular philosophy and Christian ethics converge on this conclusion, but for different reasons.

For the philosophers and legal scholars we considered, the key consideration is not the impact of a particular conduct taken in isolation by itself, but the ultimate outcome of such an individual act working jointly with other similar acts. For Christian ethics, the main consideration is not the minuteness or the redundancy of one's causal contribution, but whether or not such injury-causing acts can be avoided or rectified for their deleterious consequences. Superfluity or diminutive causation, or both, are not the decisive factors. Rather, it is the familial nature of the human community and its concomitant mutual obligations that are paramount. Some philosophers and Christian ethics also point to the importance of moral choices on virtue and character formation regardless of whether they are merely duplicative or trivial causes in the ensuing harms.

Disagreements regarding the degree of individual culpability in the face of overdetermination can be traced ultimately to differences in the evaluators' value commitments. For example, the autonomy, individual difference, and control principles are solipsistic in nature.[37] As a result, these principles argue that the individual has minimal moral responsibility, if any at all, for accumulative harms. In contrast, at the other end of the spectrum, Christian ethics claims that the person can flourish only within a community. The right focus is not the individual, but the person with all her bonds and ties to the rest of the community.[38] Divergent underlying philosophical commitments account for much of the difference on this issue.

Finally, the economics of overdetermination requires collective action if the community is to be cost-effective and timely in attending to socio-economic accumulative harms. For the atomized economic agent, not to do anything at all in the face of a collective injury is in fact a choice – staying with the status quo. It is the default position, and the easier choice for the vast majority. Hence, non-governmental organizations, social entrepreneurs, and other private initiatives become even more important as catalysts in initiating action at both the individual and communal levels. Ultimately,

[37] Kutz (2000, 3–5).   [38] Maritain (1947).

however, even with collective action, we still have to motivate atomized people at the individual level. Collective action is only as good as the commitment of its constituent members. In the final analysis, the battle is really won or lost not in the external forum, but in people's hearts and minds. Thus, it becomes even more important to make a compelling case in the internal forum that blameworthy material cooperation (moral complicity) in socioeconomic accumulative harms ought to be taken seriously and addressed.

CHAPTER 4

Who is morally responsible in the chain of causation? The problem of interdependence

Who is complicit? This chapter deals with identifying the subject of accountability. It looks to tort jurisprudence for insights and methods in the attribution of individual responsibility for distant harms or collective ills.

DISENTANGLING THE WEB OF CAUSATION

One of the more demanding issues to resolve in blameworthy material cooperation (moral complicity) is the question of where to draw the limits of moral responsibility for collective or distant harms. Consider the following difficulty posed for moral theory and practice by the nature of the market.

The first principle of morality is indeed to do good and avoid evil ... But [the person] cannot be obliged to avoid any and every bringing about of evil at his own hands, even if unintended, for the simple reason that there is very little people do in the ordinary course of their lives which does *not* involve their bringing about evil effects, even as a consequence of wholly good actions. Hence, if morality is not to reduce people to virtual inaction, it has to permit the bringing about of evil effects in some circumstances ... (Oderberg 2004, 210, emphasis original)

This dilemma is particularly acute for the marketplace. As already noted in chapter 2, division of labor is at the heart of economic life. And with this comes a tight web of economic interdependence.[1] The circular flow of economic life accentuates the complexity of economic complicity as an issue largely because people are linked to each other across space and even across time through interlocking transactions in input and output markets. Our buying and selling decisions precipitate ripple effects of varying magnitude and significance throughout the entire circular flow and even down to the next generations.

---

[1] The literature on this phenomenon is vast. See Dicken (2007, 137–172) for a brief overview.

To compound this even further, market processes often produce a mix of harms and benefits at the same time. These salutary and ill effects are so intertwined as to be inseparable. And to top it all, there are many instances of misconduct in the marketplace that ordinary economic actors unwittingly sustain. In fact, by participating in the marketplace, we might as well resign ourselves to supporting wrongdoing somewhere along the circular flow.

However, if we claim that we are culpable for each of these collateral effects, then the notion of economic complicity, indeed of economic responsibility itself, becomes vacuous. It has been said that "if we are all responsible for everything . . . then we are equally responsible for nothing."[2] Our moral sensibilities alert us to the ill effects of our economic choices. But at the same time, our common sense counsels us that there are limits to our responsibility for these spillover effects. We have to draw the line somewhere. Recall the nursery rhyme:

> For want of a nail the shoe was lost.
> For want of a shoe the horse was lost.
> For want of a horse the rider was lost.
> For want of a rider the battle was lost.
> For want of a battle the kingdom was lost.
> And all for the want of a horseshoe nail.[3]

The dilemma lies in knowing where to set the limits of one's duties. We have to be able to identify that point at which economic interdependence turns into economic complicity.

The notion of economic complicity will be taken seriously only if we are able to delineate the scope of individual responsibility in a coherent and non-arbitrary fashion.[4] At a minimum, we have to be able to differentiate various types and degrees of market responsibilities and then justify the criteria we employ. The method and standards we use in identifying the limits of our moral responsibility can also be used to "grade" the degree of complicity.

Economic accumulative harms pose additional challenges because we have to impute personal culpability under the following conditions:

---

[2] Aronson (1990, 59).

[3] See www.rhymes.org.uk/for_want_of_a_nail.htm (last accessed February 16, 2010).

[4] Otherwise, it may share the same fate as economic rights. Many are skeptical of economic rights because even as they may be conceptually valid and morally appealing, they cannot be implemented because they give rise to many unanswered issues, such as who pays for them, the scope and duration of the entitlements, and the conditions that would have to be attached in order to prevent free-ridership. See Trimiew (1997, 115–126) for a discussion of these problems.

1 the individual is only one of a multitude of other agents, each causally contributing to the ultimate harm, albeit in an infinitesimal manner (problem of overdetermination);

2 the individual's act is not injurious in itself but becomes harmful only beyond a certain threshold in combination with others' actions (problem of accumulative harms);

3 the ultimate harm is merely the unintended result of a positive benefit sought by the market participant (problem of double effect); and

4 market outcomes are the joint result of innumerable individual decisions (problem of interdependence).

Disentangling individual responsibilities for accumulative harms under these conditions is still possible, but we need conceptual tools that can make distinctions with the precision of a surgeon's scalpel. In chapter 1, we saw that the scholastic principles of cooperation with evil and double effect are helpful tools for such a task. Nonetheless, these scholastic principles merely provide a method. They say little about the many other factors we must consider as we grapple with different types of material cooperation. Moreover, they have no theory of causation. Given these deficiencies, we need to supplement the principles of material cooperation and double effect. The Anglo-Saxon common-law tradition has much to offer in this regard.

VALUE OF TORT JURISPRUDENCE AS A STARTING POINT

Tort law deals with providing relief, recovery, or compensation for damages sustained from wrongful injuries.[5] Tort jurisprudence has much to contribute to a theory of economic complicity, for a number of reasons. First, tort law is about determining (1) whether or not there is wrongful injury to begin with, and if there is, (2) who is legally responsible, and (3) to what extent the offending party is liable for damages.[6] Identifying the limits of responsibility is important for torts. Its only injunction is not to act unreasonably so as to cause others harm.[7] These are the same tasks and concerns that any theory of economic complicity faces: articulating a method for determining who is

---

[5] Prosser (1971, 1–7) claims that there is no satisfactory definition of a tort and presents instead some of the characteristics common to torts.

[6] Jeremiah Smith (1911–1912, 103–104) breaks down the inquiry into two questions: was the defendant's tortious act in fact the cause of the plaintiff's damage? If so, is there any "arbitrary rule of law that absolves the defendant from liability for such a tortious act?" See Hart and Honoré (1985, xliv) and Wright (1988, no. 1004) for variations in the formulation of these questions in establishing tort liability.

[7] Moore (2002, 151).

responsible for economic harms, why they are at fault, and to what degree they can be held to account. Both tort law and the notion of economic complicity are engaged in the same exercise and grapple with the same problems that come with the attribution of individual responsibility for harms. Of course, economic complicity is much more difficult than torts because it involves accumulative harms rather than direct or straightforward injuries.

Second, law requires clarity, precision, and consistency. Thus, its legal thinking and methods in the ascription of individual responsibility have to be rigorous in articulating the bases for resolving conflicting claims. Law has a practical end to it that requires exactitude. These are the same qualities we would want to have in any practicable theory of economic complicity.

Third, tort jurisprudence provides a wealth of insights on the conceptual and practical difficulties of imputing individual culpability. Courts have produced an enormous body of case law. In fact, criminal law "borrows" heavily from tort law on methods pertaining to causation.[8] A theory of economic complicity requires a theory of causation, and we can learn much from tort law.

Fourth, courts do not adjudicate tort cases in an arbitrary fashion or by simply following case precedents in cookbook fashion. Instead, courts are ever attentive to the commonsensical practices and intuitions of ordinary, reasonable people regarding responsibility. It is this belief that has led numerous legal scholars on the quest for the "holy grail" of tort law: a conceptual superstructure of rules and principles that describes and systematizes courts' reasoning in assigning responsibility for damages.[9] Legal scholars have worked hard over the years to distill useful rules and principles in their attempts to formulate such an overarching theory of torts.

Fifth, tort scholars are candid about the value-laden nature of their task. They acknowledge that social policy, rather than some objective measure of causation, is often the ultimate determinant of who is liable for damages. This up-front admission is helpful because it warns us of the philosophical commitments underlying some of the rules and principles from tort law that we might incorporate or adapt in a theory of economic complicity. Moreover, it brings home the point that the ascription of individual

[8] Moore (2002, 151).
[9] See, for example, the massive work of Hart and Honoré (1985) and the magisterial survey of Honoré (1973). See also Coleman (1982; 1983). Hart and Honoré (1985) are valuable for our study because (1) they attempt to separate causal questions from policy choices, and (2) they glean principles of causation used by courts based on commonsensical notions of causation and responsibility.

culpability for harms is unavoidably value-laden. Any theory of economic complicity must also be transparent about its value premises.

Finally, many cases in tort law match the complexity we encounter in dealing with economic harms. As the preceding chapters show, accumulative harms are, by their nature, difficult to disentangle into separate individual components, if this is at all possible. Tort law provides insights on how to sort through such complications. The manner by which it deals with apportioning damage among joint tortfeasors is one such example.[10]

To illustrate the aforesaid points of convergence between tort law and the problem of economic complicity, consider the classic case of *Palsgraf* v. *Long Island Railroad Company*.[11] The plaintiff was on the platform of the Long Island Railroad Company waiting for her train to Rockaway Beach. Another train stopped on her platform, took on passengers, and started on its way. A man, carrying a package, raced to catch the moving train, got on board (albeit unsteadily) with the help of two railway guards: one on the train who held the door open and lent a hand to steady the boarding passenger, and another guard on the platform helping from behind. In the process, the boarding passenger's package was dislodged, fell on the rails, and exploded. The package had fireworks in it. There was nothing on the package or in its appearance to indicate that it contained fireworks. The shock waves of the explosion caused weighing scales at the other end of the platform to fall, injuring the plaintiff, for which she sued the railroad.

Was the railroad responsible for the plaintiff's injuries since the package was dislodged and fell on the rails as two of its guards helped the boarding passenger? The New York Court of Appeals had a split decision with the majority ruling against the plaintiff. They noted that the crux of the case was not the causal connection: from the assistance rendered the boarding passenger by the railroad guards, to the accidental jostling of the passenger's package, to its falling on the rails and exploding, and ultimately to the resulting concussion that caused weighing scales at the other end of the platform to fall and injure the plaintiff. Instead of hinging on the issue of causation, the case revolved around the question of the scope of the law of negligence. The majority judged that the entire chain of events was outside the scope of the law of negligence and ruled in favor of the railroad company.[12] The guards did not act negligently in relation to the plaintiff,

---

[10] See, for example, Prosser (1971, 313–323).

[11] (1928), 248 N.Y. 339, 162 N.E. 99, 59 ALR (American Law Reports annotated) 1253. Reprinted in Morris (1961, 285–291).

[12] Hart and Honoré (1985, 174). Hart and Honoré concur with this decision based on commonsense causal principles.

standing quite a distance away. There was nothing on the package to warn them of its dangerous contents. The series of events could not have been foreseen by the railroad guards by any reasonable standard.

The dissenting minority argued otherwise and concluded that the plaintiff's injuries were the proximate result of negligence:

The act upon which defendant's liability rests is knocking an apparently harmless package onto the platform. The act was negligent. For its proximate consequences the defendant is liable ... Except for the explosion, she [Mrs. Palsgraf] would not have been injured ... So it was a substantial factor in producing the result – there was here a natural and continuous sequence – direct connection ... There was no remoteness in time, little in space. (Morris 1961, 291)

Note how the adjudication of the case depended on the Court's assessment of the extent to which the guards' inadvertent role in jostling the package loose was a direct or substantial cause of the subsequent injury. Neither side offered any objective basis for their judgment on the remoteness of the guards' actions; it was ultimately a subjective call. In fact, the dissenting opinion openly acknowledged this.

What do we mean by the word "proximate" is that because of convenience, of public policy, of a rough sense of justice, the law arbitrarily declines to trace a series of events beyond a certain point. This is not logic. It is practical politics. (Morris 1961, 290)

This much-quoted description of the true nature of "proximate" cause underscores the formidable task facing legal scholars and philosophers who have long sought an overarching theory of torts. We face the same dilemma and challenge as we grapple with the phenomenon of economic complicity. Indeed, *Palsgraf* v. *Long Island Railroad Company* (1928) illustrates how both tort law and a theory of economic complicity face the same difficult question: where do we draw the limits of responsibility for the unintended ripple effects of people's actions?

CAUSATION IN TORT JURISPRUDENCE

Causality is an essential consideration in any adequate account of complicity. Unfortunately, causality is also one of the more difficult concepts to define and pin down, whether in law or in the social sciences.[13] Fortunately, legal scholarship provides a large body of literature on causality. Unlike academic discourse that can afford the luxury of indeterminacy and

[13] See, for example, Hicks (1979).

interminable discussion, law has a pressing practical requirement it must fulfill: it has to adjudicate conflicting claims. As mentioned earlier, it cannot be indeterminate since it has to make a ruling. Moreover, courts have to be precise in their judgments, and they often justify and articulate their reasons for these decisions. As a consequence, we can learn and borrow much from jurisprudence on the conceptual and practical ways of imputing causation.

Admissible causes

What kinds of acts do we treat as admissible causes? Law has a much broader understanding of the term "cause" compared with its popular usage. While most people employ the term "cause" to refer only to the antecedent that brings about the outcome, law uses the term to include "any and all antecedents, active or passive, creative or receptive, which were factors involved in the occurrence of the consequence."[14] For example, bartenders and homeowners are held legally liable for serving excessive amounts of alcohol to inebriated patrons or guests who subsequently cause harm through drunk-driving. The law's more expansive use of the term "cause" is better suited for dealing with the complexities of economic life. We will follow the legal rather than the popular notion of "cause."

The legal literature has at least four types of actions that qualify as causes. The first is the most common type: our actions bring about particular effects. For example, the top executives of Lehman Brothers who over-exposed the firm to real-estate securities can be aptly described as having caused the company's 2008 bankruptcy.

The second type of causation is that of inducing others to commit the harm-producing act. Such inducement includes enticing, influencing, compelling, or coercing others to engage in such wrongful behavior.[15] Occasioning subsequent harm is a third type of causation. It is an action that creates or substantially contributes to a dangerous situation. For example, we have the case of a house-sitter who unintentionally leaves the doors of the house unlocked. If the house is subsequently burgled, this careless person can be aptly described as a cause in having occasioned the ensuing intrusion and loss of property.[16] This type of causation is prospective in the sense that it is concerned with action that increases the likelihood of a future occurrence.[17] One could also view it as "risk creation." Another

---

[14] Carpenter (1932a, 229).   [15] Hart and Honoré (1985, 51–53).   [16] Hart and Honoré (1985, 59).
[17] In contrast, the first type of causation is retrospective in that we examine the cause of an effect, *ex post* (Shavell 1980, 466).

feature of this kind of causation is "cause as causal link." There is a causal link if there is known evidence to forewarn the moral agent that a particular action greatly increases the probability of injury. Thus, this notion of causation has a "predictive and empirical" dimension to it.[18]

Omission is the fourth type of cause. Failure to perform a lawful duty that subsequently leads to injury can be faulted for the ensuing harm.[19] There is a legal obligation to prevent harm to others whenever we are able to do so at no danger or at minimal cost to ourselves.[20] Thus, we have Good Samaritan laws.[21] However, even if there were no lawful duties, social norms alone can also make acts of omission blameworthy.

Causation and responsibility

An important first step in the ascription of responsibility for harms is the identification of the factual cause(s). However, this is easier said than done. To appreciate both the nature and the difficulty of determining the cause-in-fact, consider the metaphors that have often been used by courts. Metaphors are important in jurisprudence because in the absence of definite rules and principles of causation, courts have had to rely on analogies to explain their decisions. For example, we have the popular image of the ever expanding ripple effects of a stone dropped in the stillness of a pond. "Cone of causation" depicts every event as merely the tip of a whole series of causes fanning out behind it in time, forming an ever widening cone as we move further into the past.[22] Related to this is the more common metaphor of "chain of causation." Every cause is itself the effect of some other cause which itself is the effect of some cause, and so on in an infinite regress of cause and effect. And as if these were not complicated enough, every effect is the joint result of multiple causes operating simultaneously – multiple causes that are themselves each the joint outcome of earlier multiple causes, and so on in another infinite regress. And so, what we have here is not

---

[18] Calabresi (1975, 71, fn 4) cautions that his use of the term "causal linkage" does not claim a definitive causal relationship in the philosophical sense between the action and the harm. He is only referring to an empirical relationship. It is not clear, however, whether or not he requires this empirical evidence to show a definitive causal relationship that moves from the action to the effect or if all the law requires is empirical evidence of correlation between the two. Establishing correlation in empirical work is much easier than establishing causality. Moreover, correlation does not mean causation. It is very likely that only correlation needs to be established. If so, this is a much lower bar to satisfy.

[19] Hart and Honoré (1985, 138–141).   [20] Feinberg (1984, 126–186).

[21] See Rudzinski (1966) for a survey of such legislation across countries. Europeans have been more amenable to such laws, the earliest being in Portugal in the mid-nineteenth century. Anglo-Saxon common law, however, has also enacted similar, though less stringent and less punitive, laws.

[22] Hart and Honoré (1985, 69) citing Williams (1951, 239).

merely one "cone of causation" or one "chain of causation," but a whole
cluster of cones of causation or a whole series of chains inextricably webbed
together.[23] And, of course, we have the metaphor used in the dissenting
opinion in *Palsgraf* v. *Long Island Railroad Company*: the image of a stream
joining many other tributaries to form a river flowing into the ocean. There
in the river and in the ocean, one can no longer distinguish the source of
each drop of water.[24] This metaphor of the streams ultimately forming a
river and then an ocean is particularly apt for economic accumulative harms
that are themselves the results of a multitude of individual market decisions.

   The key problem of courts in adjudicating torts and our problem in the
ascription of economic responsibility is the search for objective rules in
determining how far back we go in looking for the cause of an outcome, or
how far down into the future we are responsible for the ripple effects of our
actions today. Are there tests that can objectively select one out of a complex
set of conditions as *the* cause of an event? How far removed do we have to be
from the harm to be absolved of accountability for its occurrence? Consider
some of the following proposed solutions in legal scholarship.

"But for" or sine qua non *test*

The most intuitively appealing rule is the "but for (but for which)" test or
the "*causa sine qua non*" test, also known as the necessary condition test: the
event or harm would not have happened but for the cause. A genuine cause
is therefore unique and stands out among all the other conditions behind an
event because it is *the condition* that brings about the harm or the event. In
other words, a true cause has to be an indispensable condition. It must have
made a difference in the occurrence of the ensuing harm. This is the
"scientific" notion of causation.[25] It is a demanding test that unambiguously
identifies the factual cause, also known as the "cause-in-fact," "material
cause," "*causa sine qua non*," "*conditio sine qua non*," and "but for cause."[26]
Not surprisingly, the "but for" condition is used in criminal law in establishing guilt beyond a reasonable doubt.[27]

   Unfortunately, there are both conceptual and practical problems associated with the "but for" test.[28] First, the notion of a necessary condition is

---

[23] Another image is Aronson's (1990, 63–65) "spiral of responsibility" from the preceding chapter.
[24] Morris (1961, 290).   [25] Moore (2002, 152).
[26] Hart and Honoré (1985, 90); Shavell (1980, 467); Smith (1911–1912, 109–111).
[27] Note the importance of the "but for" test for the autonomy, individual difference, and control
   principles.
[28] Hart and Honoré (1985, 109–129) discuss the technical conditions and qualifications that determine
   when it is appropriate to use the "but for" test and when it is not. See Hart and Honoré (1985, 338–341)
   and Moore (2002, 153–156) for in-depth discussion of the problems surrounding the "but for" test.

vague and can cover an entire range of antecedents to the point of being meaningless. Any one of the acts-events in the "chain of causation" is strictly speaking a "but for" condition because were it not for that particular act-event, the "chain of causation" would have been broken and would have most likely not unfolded in the manner we receive it today. In effect, one can pick a "but for" cause from the "entire infinitude of past events"[29] and end up with nonsensical results. The test is unable to account for time or space in the chain of causation, nor does it discriminate among different types of necessary conditions.[30] Thus, for example, the twenty-first century would not have had to deal with climate change and depleted oil stocks "but for" Henry Ford's assembly-line innovation that made cars cheap enough to be an item of mass consumption. Other possible culprits under the "but for" test are: Richard Arkwright for inventing the spinning frame and inaugurating the age of mechanization; Thomas Savery, Thomas Newcomen, and James Watt for developing the steam engine; Sir Henry Bessemer for mass producing steel. "But for" any of these people, we would not have had to endure the ills of the Industrial Age. Which "but for" cause do we blame for global warming?

Second, even if we were to limit ourselves to current causes and eliminate past antecedents, there is still the practical problem of implementing the test. We look for the blameworthy cause-in-fact, *ex post*, that is, only after the event or after the damage had already been incurred. In applying this test, we then ask the counterfactual question, "But for this or that antecedent, would the event or the damage have transpired?" This works well in simple tort cases, such as "*but for* his reckless driving, the accident would not have occurred." Unfortunately, anything slightly more complex than this poses problems. There are both speculative and arbitrary elements to counterfactual exercises in choosing what counts as a normal course of events. There are endless scenarios or antecedents we could include in our counterfactual exercise, each with a different outcome. Besides this indeterminacy, there is also an interpretative problem in that the results we obtain depend on how we pose the counterfactual question. Thus, the test has been called "the hopelessly promiscuous counterfactual cause-in-fact test."[31]

The test uses no controlling principles to ensure that we respond objectively to our counterfactual "but for" test. And then, there is also the problem of concurrent causes. For example, commentators, politicians, academics, and the common person on the street have observed that the

---

[29] Feinberg (1984, 120).   [30] See Smith (1911–1912, 109–111) for a critique along these lines.
[31] Moore (2002, 158).

2008–2009 global economic slump could not have happened "but for" the subprime mortgage lenders who lowered the standards to dispense more loans; the Wall Street bankers who bundled and securitized home mortgages; the rating agencies that gave Triple A marks on many of these financial instruments in the absence of empirical data; the banks for highly leveraging themselves and aggravating the housing bubble; Alan Greenspan and Ben Bernanke as Federal Reserve chairs who kept interest rates so low as to fuel the bubble even further; the US Congress for having deregulated investment banking and loosened regulatory oversight; the Chinese for saving too much and snapping up US Treasury bills, bonds, and notes that enabled US consumers to spend freely beyond their means. We could go on with our list.

The test is deficient because it is unable to answer the "but for" counterfactual query in a conclusive manner; it is unable to discriminate among potential causes. This is particularly important in the more complicated cases such as accumulative harms. We have to supplement it with other tests and know its limitations and the conditions for its valid use. The "but for" or *sine qua non* rule helps in identifying the factual cause, the cause-in-fact, but only if the test is conducted and interpreted properly.

Substantial factor test

In his lengthy three-part work, Jeremiah Smith examines what constitutes a legal cause and what is the legal test for establishing the existence of a causal relationship. Critical of past efforts to set definitive criteria for legal cause, he notes that the most that can be achieved is to specify a "general rule" as follows:

To constitute such causal relations between defendant's tort and plaintiff's damage as will suffice to maintain an action of tort, the defendant's tort must have been a substantial factor in producing the damage complained of. (Smith 1911–1912, 310)

Smith explains that a "substantial factor" does not necessarily mean that it is the sole or even the predominant factor causing the harm. It is sufficient that it is distinctly "one of the substantial efficient antecedents" (109), "a substantial part of the causative antecedents," or "one of several substantial factors" (311). Furthermore, Smith notes that to be considered as having caused the damage, the substantial factor's effect must have been active all the way up to the very moment of the injury or at least active in setting in motion the factor that ultimately produced the damage.[32]

---

[32] Smith calls the latter condition a "practically active cause" in contrast to being the "active cause" in the first instance. See Smith (1911–1912, 312–314) for a brief survey of cases to illustrate his points.

While intuitively appealing and self-evident, the "substantial factor" rule is silent on what constitutes "substantial." What standards should we use and who sets the criteria? Left in its current formulation, the "substantial factor" test hardly improves the rough guideline we already have in the distinction between remote and proximate material cooperation. What is considered "substantial" requires further explanation and justification.

"Active force" test

Joseph Beale (1920) proposes two requirements for a defendant to be considered the proximate cause of a harm. First, the defendant must have unleashed a "force" by acting or failing to act according to a lawful duty. Second, (1) such "force" must have either brought about the harmful result itself or created another force that ultimately caused the harm; or (2) such "force" created or increased the risk of another force bringing about the harm. This is a case in which a metaphor is employed in the absence of clear, descriptive, and definite rules. Beale uses the language of physics in describing causation in terms of mechanics. Unfortunately, no criteria are provided on what qualifies as an active force. Moreover, it does not take the potency of such a force into account for purposes of imputing varying degrees of accountability.

"A cause or a mere condition?" test

The legal usage of "cause" differs in a fundamental way from the scientific or philosophic use of the term. The legal use seeks to identify a specific and restricted set of antecedents as *the* cause of a particular outcome. In contrast, the scientific and philosophical understanding of the term encompasses a much broader sweep. John Stuart Mill is representative of such a position. As we have seen earlier, Mill identifies the whole ensemble of conditions that are jointly sufficient to bring about the outcome as the cause of the event.[33] From a legal point of view, this means that every necessary element of the set of jointly sufficient conditions is a cause.[34] This all-inclusive definition is obviously problematic for the law and the courts that have

---

[33] Mill (1843 [1973], book III, chapter v, s.3). A conceptual and practical difficulty with Mill's approach is similar to the one we encounter in the "but for" test. How can we be certain that we have accurately included only the necessary elements in the set of jointly sufficient conditions? Even tiny changes in past events or in one's assumptions about past causes and events alter the subsequent composition of necessary elements in the set of jointly sufficient conditions (Honoré 1973, 7–54 [28]). See also Hart and Honoré (1985, 13–25) for an extended critique of Mill.

[34] Every *conditio sine qua non* is a cause and every cause is a *conditio sine qua non* (Honoré 1973, 7–53 [27]).

the duty of sifting through a whole set of antecedents to a tort and then determining who ought to be held liable for the consequent harms.[35]

One solution to get out of this bind is to distinguish a cause from a mere condition in Mill's all-inclusive set of antecedents. This effort to differentiate a cause from a mere condition has been criticized as arbitrary and meaningless unless we have objective criteria to carry out such a differentiation.[36] Hart and Honoré (1985, 33–44) propose just such a solution.

> Mere conditions ... are simply "part of the background," whereas causes stand out. Conditions are part of the "normal" course of events or state of affairs, whereas causes are abnormal, unusual events or stages that make the difference between a particular unexpected result and things going on as usual. (Howarth, 1987, 1398)

For example, a man throws a lighted cigarette into a wastepaper basket and starts a fire that burns down the house. What was the cause of the house's destruction? The oxygen that fed the fire? The trash in the waste-basket that caught fire from the cigarette? The winds that fanned the flames? The humidity for that day? The wooden structure of the house? All these are necessary antecedents in a set of conditions that together were sufficient to burn down the house. Using Mill's all-inclusive notion of cause, this entire set of jointly sufficient conditions would have been the cause of the event. Under Hart and Honoré's distinction, only the person who threw the lighted cigarette into the wastebasket is properly the cause of the house fire. To be sure, the oxygen, the humidity for the day, the winds, and the wooden structure were necessary conditions for the house to burn down. But left on their own, this set of conditions would not have resulted in the house burning down. But today was different because it was not a normal day. Somebody threw a lighted cigarette into the wastebasket. This was the abnormal occurrence that interrupted the normal state of affairs. It is the antecedent that injected something "abnormal" in the usual state of affairs in the joint set of conditions. Thus, the careless smoker can be aptly called the cause of the house fire. All the other factors are mere conditions.[37]

---

[35] Hart and Honoré (1985, 23–25) note that this divergence is due to the difference in the nature of the tasks facing scientists and philosophers, on the one hand, compared with lawyers, on the other hand. The former are engaged in an explanatory query in accounting for how things came to be. The latter are engaged in an evaluative exercise in looking for who is at fault.
[36] Carpenter (1932a, 237–238); Smith (1911–1912, 108–109).
[37] This example is taken from Hart and Honoré (1985, 336).

"Necessary element in a set of jointly sufficient conditions" (NESS) test
Besides the preceding distinction between a cause and a mere background condition, another useful idea is the notion of a complex set of conditions that are jointly sufficient to bring about an event. Thus, in the preceding example, the oxygen, the humidity for the day, the winds, the wooden structure of the house, the wastebasket full of papers, the lighted cigarette, and the careless man constitute a set of conditions that together were sufficient to burn down the house. Any element that is essential to make the whole set of conditions sufficient to burn down the house (such as the oxygen, the lighted cigarette, the careless smoker, etc.) is called a necessary element in a set of jointly sufficient conditions (NESS). Unlike much of the literature on torts and causation, NESS focuses not on the cause but on the background conditions and their role in facilitating the harm inflicted by the cause. This is a much more robust formulation and a much more useful framework for our study because economic complicity often deals with the attendant conditions of the harm rather than with the primary cause of the harm.[38]

Intervening events

One of the earliest and most misunderstood legal maxims is that from Francis Bacon: "In law, not the remote but the near (proximate) cause is sought for."[39] In this legal maxim, Francis Bacon argues that courts do not have to go back to an infinite regress in search of the "causes of causes."[40] It is sufficient for courts to look only at the immediate cause and to look no further than this. In fact, a flaw of the "but for" rule is its failure to recognize that not all necessary conditions are equal. Those that are "remote in time or space may have practically spent [their] force" and would most likely have been no longer operative at the time of the harm, or may have had just an infinitesimal causal contribution.[41]

Despite its intuitive appeal, the rule is fraught with problems, the most obvious of which is the absence of objective criteria in determining what constitutes proximity (temporal, spatial, functional contribution, etc.?). Legal scholars have been critical of the vagueness of this maxim and its consequent misuse over time.[42]

---

[38] See Wright (1988) for further distinctions on different versions of NESS.   [39] Feinberg (1984, 121).
[40] Smith (1911–1912, 106).   [41] Smith (1911–1912, 109–110). See also Moore (2002, 157, 159).
[42] For some of these criticisms, see Smith (1911–1912, 106–108).

Causal contribution (and therefore responsibility) diminishes with intervening events, particularly those that are human acts, abnormal natural events, or preemptive causes.[43] Take the earlier case of the careless smoker who had burned down the house. Imagine a different scenario in which person B deliberately douses the wastebasket with lighter fluid after person A carelessly tossed in the lighted cigarette. B's action sets the wastebasket fiercely ablaze and this then burns down the house. In this case, the careless smoker is not the cause of the fire because person B had broken the "chain of causation" by dousing the wastebasket with lighter fluid.[44] The causal link between the careless smoker and the burning of the house ceases with the intervention of another human act.

This "chain of causation" can also be broken by freak accidents of nature. Let us say that in the original case of the carelessly tossed cigarette, strong gusts of wind suddenly blow through the open windows, topple the wastebasket over on its side and spill its burning contents all over the rug, which then catches fire and sets the whole house ablaze. In this third scenario, the careless smoker is not the cause of the house burning because of the intervening, abnormal natural event.

Preemptive causes also break the "chain of causation." Going back to the original example, let us say that the careless smoker drops his lighted cigarette into the wastebasket and sets off a fire that would have eventually burned down the house. However, before the flames in the wastebasket could spread to the rest of the room, workers welding pipes in the yard rupture a gas line and set off an explosion that destroys the house. Again, in this case, the careless smoker is not the cause of the destruction of the house.

These three scenarios illustrate how intervening human acts, freak accidents of nature, and preemptive causes break the "chain of causation" between the careless smoker's act and the subsequent destruction of the house. The smoker's tossing of a lighted cigarette is relegated to a mere background condition. This conclusion is consistent with the reasoning we saw earlier regarding the distinction between a cause and a mere condition.

The notion that accountability diminishes with intervening events[45] is also seen in criminal law. In the legal doctrine of complicity, the secondary party's liability is understood to be merely derivative from that of the principal. Consequently, the accomplice's liability could not exceed that

---

[43] Moore (1999, 44).   [44] This example is from Hart and Honoré (1985, 336–338).
[45] This has been called the direct causation principle.

of the primary party. This is the conventional derivative liability principle of the legal theory of complicity.[46]

Intervening events are important for our study because accumulative harms are heavily mediated by social structures, economic actors, and contingencies. There are many causal factors standing between individual agents and market ills.

IMPORTANCE OF NON-CAUSAL CONSIDERATIONS: PROXIMATE (LEGAL) CAUSE

Both the metaphor of the "cone (chain) of causation" and Mill's notion of "cause" give us an idea of how difficult it is to identify *the* cause(s) that should be held responsible for outcomes. As already mentioned, the law faces a practical constraint. Courts cannot go backward or forward indefinitely in an infinite chain of causation. They have to draw the line somewhere and determine who ought to bear the cost of the damages. Consequently, they have had to adopt a second-best solution, a legal device called "proximate cause," also known as "legal cause."

To understand the nature of proximate or legal cause, we first have to appreciate the difference between an explanatory query and an attributive (evaluative) query. On the one hand, an *explanatory query* is about identifying the cause-in-fact of the event in question. It is a positive exercise of describing "what is or what had transpired" in its search for the factual cause of an occurrence. An *attributive query*, on the other hand, is about finding who is to blame for the particular event in question. It is an evaluative exercise in imputing fault.[47] The latter is a normative exercise of describing "what ought to be" as it seeks to fix responsibility for the event in the eyes of the law. *Cause-in-fact is to an explanatory query, as proximate (legal) cause is to an attributive query.* The two queries need not be coincident, nor need they be mutually exclusive either. In fact, an attributive exercise would most likely begin with an explanatory query in ascertaining factual causes before it assigns culpability.[48]

---

[46] Kadish (1985, 339–340).

[47] See Hart and Honoré (1985, 24) for a brief explanation of the difference between an explanatory and an attributive query.

[48] Moore (2002, 158) argues that despite repeated attempts by legal scholars, there is no "unitary conception of causation" to date that is capable of satisfying both the explanatory and attributive queries simultaneously. See Moore (2002, 158–159) for four examples of such unsuccessful proposals. The other difficulty is that it is not always easy to distinguish one type of query from the other (Golding 1961, 90). In fact, Wright (1988, no. 1004) ascribes much of the confusion surrounding legal causation in the last century to the mistaken conflation of these two types of inquiries.

Many legal scholars and practitioners acknowledge the difficulty of establishing cause-in-fact and consequently conclude that it is best to leave such questions of causation to the intuitive judgment of juries of reasonable people. And they openly admit that this is neither a scientific nor a precise exercise.[49] It is not any easier when it comes to determining legal cause. Consider the various tests that have been employed over the years to establish proximate cause:

- "ad hoc test" that promotes or balances competing social goals,
- "rules-based tests" that are essentially rules-of-thumb courts have devised,[50]
- "harm within the risk test" that checks whether or not the likelihood of the harm is among the reasons for holding the act negligent,[51] and
- "foreseeability test" that examines whether or not the defendant could have or should have foreseen the ensuing harm at the time of the act.[52]

Observe how all these tests are ultimately based on policy rather than on objective standards of factual causation. These tests are evaluative in nature as is proximate (legal) cause.

In short, in contrast to cause-in-fact, a proximate cause is simply the court's determination that, in the eyes of the law, it is *this* cause and not that cause or any other cause that ought to bear the cost of the damages. The selection of this one cause to be designated as *the* cause, among all the other equally necessary causes, is a matter of preference on the part of the court.[53] Proximate cause is a policy-laden, preference-driven legal device. As we have seen earlier in the quote from the dissenting opinion of Judge Andrews in *Palsgraf* v. *Long Island Railroad*, proximate cause is merely about the court drawing an arbitrary line in a series of events beyond which it will not go any further in its evaluation.[54] It is a line that is ultimately based on expediency and politics rather than on facts.[55]

---

[49] Carpenter (1932b, 399).

[50] For example, we have the "last wrongdoer rule" in which the last (or the nearest) voluntary act in the chain of antecedents bears responsibility for the harm (Smith 1911–1912, 111–113). Or note the "first house rule" in New York. In the event that a negligently caused fire spreads to other buildings, damages may be recovered from the negligent party only for the first structure destroyed (Golding 1961, 91).

[51] Hart and Honoré (1985, 208). For example, teenage drivers with learner's permits are not supposed to drive beyond a certain time nor are they permitted to drive by themselves without an accompanying adult with a valid driver's license. If they get into a collision with another vehicle under these circumstances and end up injured, they may be deemed to be partly at fault (contributory negligence), even if the other vehicle caused the accident.

[52] Moore (2002, 152).   [53] Hart and Honoré (1985, 326).   [54] Morris (1961, 290).

[55] See Feinberg (1984, 121–125) for a further description and critique of proximate cause.

Relevance for economic complicity

The extensive literature on proximate cause is a reflection of the long struggle of the legal profession in linking causal contribution with legal responsibility. Identifying the cause-in-fact and then determining the blameworthiness of such factual cause in an objective manner are critical tasks because the law requires an objective basis for the ascription of legal responsibility and liability for damages, to the extent possible. After all, this is about determining who bears the cost of the damages. There is much at stake. Satisfying these requirements has turned out to be extremely difficult. Courts and legal scholars have been compelled to resort to proximate cause as a legal "universal solvent." For them to do so, despite the need for factual precision, only goes to underscore the formidable hurdles to establishing factual causation. If judges and legal scholars have been unable to come up with definite rules and principles that establish factual causation, how much more difficult would it be for us who are interested in moral, not legal, responsibility? And even if we were to assume, for the sake of argument, that there were such definite rules that establish factual causation, we still have the problem that causation does not necessarily or automatically imply fault. For example, we have cases of justified causation (e.g., blowing up a dam to prevent catastrophic flooding) or excusable causation (e.g., coercion or illness).[56] In these two cases, non-causal considerations determine whether there is faulty action or not.

Economic complicity requires establishing not only factual causation but also faulty action.[57] Fault is measured against a particular moral standard. Consequently, both causal and non-causal factors are essential for a theory of economic complicity. Causal contribution matters in the ascription of responsibility, but so do non-causal factors.

LESSONS LEARNED FROM TORT SCHOLARSHIP

Any workable theory of blameworthy economic material cooperation must have a method for grading varying degrees of complicity. Tort jurisprudence has a wealth of conceptual tools, distinctions, philosophical warrants, and principles in the attribution of individual responsibility for wrongful injuries in socioeconomic life. A review of tort scholarship teaches us much about legal thinking and methods, but more importantly, it gives us an idea of what is or is not possible when it comes to imputing individual

---

[56] Coleman (1982, 381).   [57] Recall the three conditions of contributory fault (chapter 2).

responsibility for accumulative harms. We are alerted to which debates are fruitful and which are pointless.

What is possible

It is possible to come up with a much richer specification of scholastic material cooperation beyond its traditional distinctions of immediate versus mediate, proximate versus remote, and dispensable versus indispensable cooperation. Not only are we able to have a much richer lexicon, but we can also have a much more robust and general model that includes a wide array of causal and non-causal considerations. How people mix these causal and non-causal factors in their deliberations is dependent on their underlying values. Thus, a further advantage to providing more structure to the notion of material cooperation in Christian ethics is that it helps us trace the source of people's differences over what constitutes complicity to their philosophical commitments.

We have also learned that it is possible to anchor our attributive (evaluative) query on commonsensical rules and principles. Reasonable people are not arbitrary in how they impute individual culpability. Their deliberations and decisions are rooted in their sense of decency and fairness and in their intuitive understanding of causation and responsibility. For this reason, it has been argued that it is best to leave questions of causation and responsibility to juries. Courts and legal scholars have long tried to distill people's commonsensical intuitions regarding blameworthiness into general rules and principles.

What is not possible

Tort literature has also taught us much about what seems to be not possible. First, it does not seem possible to have a closed set of rules and principles that can be generalized for all tort cases. There is no consensus when it comes to the doctrine of causation or to an overarching theory of torts. In fact, if there is anything that comes close to an agreement among tort scholars, it is the conclusion that there is no single, overarching moral theory undergirding torts.[58] Legal scholars and philosophers agree that the essence of causation is difficult to pin down. The most that can be accomplished is to offer a lexicon and a set of conceptual tools, rules, and

---

[58] See, for example, Coleman (1982; 1983), Edgerton (1924a, 211, 218, 241; 1924b, 372), Golding (1961, 93–94), and Smith (1911–1912, 317–319).

principles that can be used for a wide variety of cases as needed. Torts are highly contextual. Each case has its own particular and often complex set of circumstances. Assigning blame cannot be done at an abstract level. It requires an actual examination of the concrete particularities of the case, *ex post*. Thus, there are no definite, universal rules and principles in the ascription of individual culpability that apply to all situations. It is the same case for economic complicity.

Second, it does not seem possible to limit ourselves to issues of causation in imputing responsibility. Establishing different parties' causal contribution to a harm is an important step in determining who ought to be blamed for such injury. Common sense and people's notion of fairness call for nothing less than this. However, this is just a first step. Causation is neither a necessary nor a sufficient condition for legal culpability. Non-causal factors also matter and are often decisive in determining who is at fault and the degree to which they are liable. Non-causal factors may in fact trump or even render causal considerations irrelevant in assigning legal blame for harms.[59]

Third, it does not seem possible to be completely value-free in imputing individual responsibility. Policy is among the non-causal factors that have to be considered, and in many cases, it is policy that drives the entire process of deciding who is at fault and who is liable. Ideology and value commitments determine which factors are considered in the attribution of blame and what relative weights to assign them.[60]

Fourth, we cannot simply transplant tort philosophy, methodology, rules, and principles in a straightforward manner into a theory of economic complicity. They need to be adapted further to deal with the peculiar features of market accumulative harms. While tort jurisprudence and the notion of economic complicity overlap in their tasks, they nonetheless differ in many important respects.[61] In particular, as we have seen earlier, courts are concerned with cost-efficiency in prosecution, enforcement, recovery, or damage prevention. Unlike a moral query that can be inconclusive in its deliberations, the law must decide and adjudicate between competing claims. It does not have the luxury of being indeterminate.[62] In fact, the law often limits liability for the sake of not overburdening the

---

[59] Moore (1999, 44–45).
[60] See Wright (1988, nos. 1004–1010) for a succinct description of the various schools of legal thought and their positions regarding the relative importance of causal and non-causal factors.
[61] See Hart and Honoré (1985, 66–67) and Feinberg (1970, 30–33) for a comparison of a legal versus a moral query.
[62] Borgo (1979, 419); Hart and Honoré (1985, 67).

courts with having to expend time and effort in tracking down every single cause of a harm.

As mentioned earlier, courts resort to the convenient legal device called "proximate cause." To expedite their work, they simply identify one cause among many possible candidates as *the* cause of the harm in the eyes of the law. The entire liability for damages may be assigned to a single party (the legal/proximate cause) instead of the court having to locate and divide up the damages across all contributory causes. This proximate cause need not even be the cause-in-fact. Legal economists (Law and Economics school of thought) argue that courts have, in fact, assigned legal liability for damages to the parties that are in the best position to bear the cost ("deep pockets" argument) or to the parties best able to undertake least-cost preventative measures to avert such harms in the future.[63] Furthermore, the scope of liability is also sometimes delimited so as not to let potentially crushing liabilities discourage people from pursuing socially useful activities.[64] Such compromises are, of course, not a good model to follow in our efforts to impute moral responsibility for economic harms.

Moral query is not bound by constraints of cost-efficiency in enforcement or prosecution. It is interested in identifying who is morally at fault, and enforcement occurs mostly in the internal forum. We can cast as wide a net as necessary, and we can even employ Mill's notion of "cause" as the whole complex set of conditions surrounding an event. Mill's idea of "cause" is far more applicable to accumulative harms than the law's legal device of proximate cause.

The law is said to be interested in assigning individual legal responsibility or liability in a cost-efficient manner. In contrast, our moral query is concerned with the full and accurate ascription of individual moral culpability. Thus, we could say that law is seeking "attributive cost-efficiency" while the moral inquiry of Christian ethics desires "attributive precision." Nevertheless, even without being constrained by the need for attributive cost-efficiency just like the courts, we still have to draw the line somewhere in separating those who are morally at fault for accumulative harms and those who are not. Moreover, we also have to distinguish varying degrees of moral culpability.

We have to adjust standards as we adapt insights from jurisprudence. Law sets a much higher bar before it imposes liabilities because the court's judgment triggers consequential official action, such as the curtailment of

---

[63] Calabresi (1975).
[64] Beale (1920); Carpenter (1932a, 232–233); Feinberg (1984, 123–124); Shavell (1980, 499–500).

life or liberty in the case of criminal law, or burdensome monetary compensation in the case of civil law. Thus, note the differences in the standards used even within law itself. Criminal law, for example, requires "proof beyond a reasonable doubt." It requires criminal intent and fault. In contrast, torts only require a preponderance of evidence, with neither fault nor intent even being necessary to incur liability (e.g., strict or vicarious liability).[65] We can afford a relatively much lower bar (compared with law) for the attribution of moral responsibility or liability in Christian ethics because its enforcement is not as intrusive, as punitive, or as publicly ruinous as legal judgments often are.

In sum, tort jurisprudence provides many insights on how to impute individual responsibility for wrongful injuries in a relatively more thorough manner that is also intuitively appealing. Our next task is to adapt these ideas in the attribution of individual responsibility for market harms.

SUMMARY OF PART I

The preceding chapters have identified both the conceptual tools and the difficulties involved in determining moral complicity in economic wrong-doing. These difficulties include:

- the accumulative nature of many economic ills (innocuous individual acts that become injurious when aggregated),
- the problem of overdetermination (redundant and minute causation), and
- the problem of interlocking economic agencies (interdependent causes).

The key conceptual tools from Christian ethics are the scholastic principles of double effect and legitimate material cooperation with evil. However, these are insufficient on their own. We can cite at least two deficiencies. First, the distinction between remote and proximate material cooperation requires an assessment of causality. The principle of legitimate material cooperation does not have a theory of causation. Second, both scholastic principles require a weighing of the intended goods vis-à-vis the unintended harms. How do we compare these goods and harms, what metric do we use, and why? These two principles are just methods and have to be embedded within a much larger moral framework. They need to be supplemented further by tools and methods from both within and beyond Christian ethics. Law and social philosophy can augment these scholastic principles

---

[65] Carpenter (1932b, 399).

with a theory of causation and with insights on weighing the proportionality of the intended good with its harmful unintended consequences.

Blameworthiness can be properly characterized as a continuum: from people who are completely guiltless, to those who bear some responsibility, to those who are blameworthy. In other words, moral culpability for economic wrongdoing comes in varying degrees and is not binary in the sense of either being culpable or not (0, 1) with no other categories in between.

To facilitate our assessment of actual cases in Part II and to provide readers with a ready reference, herewith is a diagnostic framework of analysis for evaluating cases of economic complicity. It is a synthesis of the preceding chapters' insights and methods from law, social philosophy, economics, and moral theology.

DIAGNOSTIC FRAMEWORK OF ANALYSIS

A Key questions to be addressed in the following order:
  1 In terms of moral responsibility:
    a Is the action permissible or blameworthy material cooperation?
    b If blameworthy, what is the degree of such culpability?
      [Conceptual tools: principle of material cooperation and its distinctions]
  2 In terms of liability: What are the liabilities, if any, of the moral agent for the resulting harm?[66]
B Inquiries to be pursued in the following order:
  1 Explanatory query: identifying the cause(s)-in-fact and the causal contributions of various parties. This is a descriptive exercise in reporting what actually happened.
  2 Attributive query: attribution of individual moral responsibility for harms incurred. This is an evaluative, normative exercise in fixing blame for the injury.
    a The attributive query takes into account the following:
      i causality (results from the explanatory query above);
      ii non-causal factors (to be discussed below).
    b Conceptual tools for attributive query: principles of double effect and material cooperation

---

[66] Liability pertains to mitigating or rectifying the damage. It is different from moral responsibility which pertains to blameworthiness. Note that permissible material cooperation can nevertheless still be liable for the resulting injury (e.g., chapters 7 and 8).

  i 1st condition: act is not intrinsically evil
  ii 2nd condition:
   1) moral agent does not intend the harm
   2) harm cannot be intended as a means to achieve the good intended
  iii 3rd condition:
   1) Is the intended good proportionate to the unintended harm?
   2) due care:
    a) Is the harm avertible? Are there alternatives to get to the good intended?
    b) If not, could the harm be minimized or mitigated?
C Factors to be considered in both the explanatory and attributive queries:
 1 Causal relations and admissible causes
  a direct act
  b inducing harm
  c occasioning harm
  d failure to prevent harms (omission).[67]
 2 Nature and severity of the harm
  a How vital are the interests at risk?
  b What other private or public interests are dependent on the interests at risk?
  c What is the inherent moral worth of the interests at risk?[68]
 3 Character and capacity of actors
  a knowledge and intention
  b voluntariness and capacity to act
  c bonds, ties, and social role.
 4 Nature of the economy
  a type of economic harm: direct or accumulative?
  b which feature of market involved (e.g., see market features in chapter 2).
 5 Moral standards used (e.g., religious or secular, teleological or deontological, etc.)
D Principles and rules of thumb
Some accountability-limiting principles proposed in the literature are as follows:[69]

---

[67] Hart and Honoré (1985, 51–53).   [68] Feinberg (1984, 202–206).
[69] I am not endorsing all these principles. I am merely reporting what has been suggested in the literature. Some of these are problematic such as the solipsistic principles criticized by Kutz (individual difference, autonomy, and control) and the parallel acts principle. Evaluating the grounds and the claims of all of these principles is beyond the scope of this work.

- Individual difference principle: moral agents are accountable for harms *only* if these would not have occurred but for the agents' action (or omission).
- Control principle: moral agents are accountable *only* for events they could control.
- Autonomy principle: moral agents are not accountable for others' wrongdoing unless the former coerced or induced the latter to do so.
- Complicity principle: moral agents' intentional participation in a collective wrongdoing makes them accountable for the entire harm regardless of the causal difference they made.
- Expanded complicity principle: moral agents are accountable even for "unstructured" harms (e.g., market harms) through their quasi-participatory intent in societal institutions and practices.
- Direct causation principle: accountability for harms diminishes with intervening events.
- Dispersion principle: accountability diminishes as the aggregate harm is divided up among more people or over time.
- Extended dispersion principle: accountability *may* diminish as it is spread among more moral agents.
- Proximity principle: moral agents are more accountable for harms to people who are socially, physically, or temporally close to them.
- Positive acts principle: moral agents are more accountable for the harm they cause than for the harm they fail to prevent.
- Parallel acts principle: accountability diminishes if other people act similarly.[70]

Other rules of thumb we can infer from the preceding chapters are as follows:

- Accountability is directly proportional to moral agents' causal contribution and to the immediacy, proximity, and indispensability of their material cooperation.
- Accountability is directly proportional to moral agents' intention, knowledge, voluntariness, contributory fault, and capacity to act otherwise or to avert the harm.
- Accountability increases proportionately with the likelihood or the gravity of the ensuing harms, or both.

---

[70] Kutz (2000) merely lists but does not argue for or against these commonly held accountability-limiting principles: proximity principle, positive acts principle, direct causation principle, dispersion principle, and parallel acts principle (262). He argues against the individual difference, control, and autonomy principles (3). He proposes his own complicity principle (122) and an expanded version that includes quasi-participatory intent in unstructured harms (166–203). The extended dispersion principle is my own extension of the dispersion principle.

- Accountability diminishes if the injured parties contributed to their own harm (contributory negligence).
- Accountability is greater in cases of material cooperation in recurring wrongdoing.

The weights assigned to each of these determinants or rules of thumb are determined by the evaluator's underlying value commitments and the context of every case. Clearly, prudential judgment is important in evaluating the individual's blameworthiness for distant harms or collective ills.

PART II

Application: a typology of market-mediated complicity

Using our findings and conceptual tools from Part I, the second half of this book examines four types of market-mediated complicity: enabling wrong-doing (e.g., buying sweatshop apparel), precipitating gratuitous harms (e.g., financial speculation), leaving severe pecuniary externalities unattended (e.g., indifference to displaced workers), and reinforcing unjust or harmful socioeconomic institutions or practices (e.g., regressive credit allocation).

All four types of complicity share at least two common features. First, the resulting harm is completely unintended but foreseen. Unlike most tort cases, economic accumulative harms are not one-time events, but ongoing side-effects incurred in the course of market exchange. Hence, the causal links between individual economic choices and their ensuing harmful ripple effects are fairly well documented and widely known in the empirical literature. Second, all four cases entail a contributory fault: there is a causal contribution to the harm, the causally contributory act is faulty, and there is a link between the faulty act and the subsequent harm.[1]

Despite their similarities, these instances of blameworthy material coop-eration have significant differences. In particular, we should differentiate "hard complicity" (the first two cases) from "soft complicity" (the last two cases). First, hard complicity is preventable while the occasions for soft complicity are much more difficult to avoid. People's buying and selling decisions precipitate price changes. This is inevitable by the nature of the market. Unfortunately, such price changes reshuffle burdens and benefits within the community (pecuniary externalities), often to the further dis-advantage of those who are already struggling. This unintended but fore-seen harm is unavoidable since people have no choice but to participate in the marketplace in order to procure their needs (e.g., getting a job in order to be able to buy groceries and pay rent). Moreover, such pecuniary

---

[1] Recall that these are the three conditions for what constitutes "harm to others" (Feinberg 1970, 222). See chapter 2.

97

externalities ensure long-term allocative efficiency (i.e., putting the community's scarce resources to their most valued uses). Consequently, instances of soft complicity are permissible by the principle of double effect, given the importance of the gains pursued. In contrast, cases of hard complicity are avertible because there are many alternative courses of action available. Thus, for most people, there is no need to buy sweatshop apparel or to engage in harmful speculative investing given the availability of many other clothing lines and investment vehicles. These are unnecessary harms by the third condition of the principle of double effect.

Second, since hard complicity involves preventable harm, the moral obligation is to cease and desist from such activities (a negative duty). Failure to do so results in a contributory fault to the ensuing injury. In other words, hard complicity arises from a direct, blameworthy act.[2] In contrast, soft complicity's contributory fault stems from an act of omission, that is, the failure to prevent or attenuate harm. For most people, there is a moral obligation to mitigate the severe unintended consequences of their economic activities (a positive duty). The principle of double effect relieves moral agents of blameworthiness for the harm, but not from the liability of ameliorating the ensuing injury (blameless but liable). It is the failure to fulfill this liability that deserves censure in soft complicity. Hence, the contributory fault in soft complicity arises from acts of omission, that is, in the failure to attend to the liability of redressing the injury. This difference between hard and soft complicity is important because some people subscribe to the positive acts principle which states that we are more accountable for the harm we cause than for the harm we fail to prevent.[3] In short, hard complicity pertains to avertible material cooperation and is always faulty. In contrast, soft complicity falls under material cooperation that is permissible but liable for attenuating the resulting harm. Blameworthiness arises only if the cooperator fails to satisfy the attendant liability.

A third difference stems from the nature of the act. Many of the acts of hard complicity are wrong in themselves (*malum in se*).[4] For example, we have the wasteful consumption of oil or commodity speculation in food. These acts are faulty in themselves, and people should cease and desist from such behavior. In contrast, the individual act in soft complicity is not wrong in itself but inflicts harm only in an accumulative manner, that is, only in

---

[2] This refers to the first three of the admissible causes we examined in chapter 4: effecting, inducing, or occasioning harm (Hart and Honoré 1985, 2–3).
[3] See, for example, Moore (1999).   [4] I draw this distinction from Lichtenberg (2008, 15).

conjunction with others' similar acts. For example, as more local consumers shift to cheaper foreign imports, domestic manufacturing workers will ultimately find themselves unemployed.

Finally, the negative duty in hard complicity can be easily discharged by simply refraining from such unacceptable conduct. In contrast, living up to the positive duty in soft complicity requires collective action in order to ameliorate the ensuing harm. This is due to the aforesaid accumulative dynamic of soft complicity.

This fourfold typology is neither an exhaustive nor a definitive account of marketplace complicity. There are surely many other ways of classifying blameworthy material cooperation in economic life, depending on one's worldview. Each of the following chapters is organized under three major headings: the *object of accountability* (the wrongdoing for which the subject is culpable), the *basis for accountability* (the grounds for holding the subject culpable), and finally, the *subject of accountability* (the moral agents deemed to be culpable).[5]

---

[5] This threefold division is from Kutz (2000, 4).

CHAPTER 5

Hard complicity I: Benefitting from and enabling wrongdoing

Most people associate economic complicity only with criminal activities. For them, it is clearly immoral to facilitate money laundering, human or drug trafficking, arms smuggling, or child pornography and prostitution.[1] However, as we will see shortly, moral complicity extends to many more cases besides illicit activities. In what follows, we examine the basis, the object, and the subject of accountability when it comes to benefitting from and enabling wrongdoing.

BASIS FOR ACCOUNTABILITY: WHY CULPABLE?

Why is it morally blameworthy to benefit from and enable wrongdoing? The theological, philosophical, and economic arguments of chapter 3 on the problem of overdetermination apply just as well to this section's concerns. This section extends those earlier insights even further, in addition to examining the economics of facilitating misconduct.

Christian ethics

Benefitting from and enabling wrongdoing goes against the divine order of creation. It impedes the appropriator's moral life.[2] To benefit from and enable wrongdoing knowingly and intentionally, despite the availability of alternatives, is to harm our own virtue and character formation.[3] To be human is to reflect and to communicate the goodness and perfection of God using our signal faculties of reason and freedom. To appropriate the fruits of

---

[1] Nordstrom (2007); Schendel and Abraham (2005).
[2] For an extended treatment of virtue theory, see Cessario (1991) and Porter (1995; 2005).
[3] This is one of the reasons why Kaveny (2000) insists that it is important to supplement our language of "cooperation with evil" with its mirror image: "appropriation of evil." The latter better underscores the "intention-based, agent-centered morality" undergirding economic complicity.

wrongdoing when we could have avoided doing so is to damage our capacity to communicate and reflect such divine goodness and perfection.

Kaveny (2000, 305) argues that "intimacy with evil" poses dangers to character formation. There is a great likelihood of "contamination" from "seepage" and "self-deception" given the close proximity to evil. Such contamination occurs when appropriators unwittingly allow the evil intentions of the wrongdoer to reshape their own moral thinking and attitudes or to dim their own sensitivity to or intolerance for the wrongdoing. To use a biological analogy, one could describe this as a process of osmosis. For example, office workers who routinely process predatory subprime or payday loans may eventually lose their moral revulsion for such immoral loans.

Serious problems arise when the appropriation of evil becomes routine in economic life. Sociological evidence shows that character formation is influenced by people's work environment. For example, the increasing use of short-term contracts in the labor market has led to greater alienation, insecurity, and a diminution of trust and loyalty in society. In other words, economic activity can either enhance or corrode character.[4] Besides these deleterious direct effects, there are also harmful secondary consequences that may not be immediately obvious. In particular, the community ethos and narrative are important determinants in shaping personal virtue and character. Individuals often understand their moral world from what they have learned and adopted from the larger community.[5] Thus, a community that tolerates the appropriation of evil in its economic life runs the risk of desensitizing its members to the gravity and serious consequences of evil.

The issue of benefitting from and enabling wrongdoing is not merely a modern concern. In the last two years of her husband's life, St. Elizabeth of Hungary refused to eat or drink anything served on their table or by their hosts without first ascertaining that these provisions did not come from either unjust expropriation or theft from the peasants. Consequently, on many occasions, not only did she go hungry, but she also earned the ire of the other nobles who felt rebuked by her fastidious abstinence.[6] It was an indictment of the feudal system and all who benefitted from it.

In his *Euboean Discourse*, John Chrysostom expounds on inappropriate trades and occupations.

All which ... engender in the soul either turpitude or illiberality or, in general, are useless and good for nothing since they owe their origin to the silly luxury of the

---

[4] Sennett (1998).   [5] Hauerwas (1981).

[6] Her husband was the Landgrave of Thuringia, one of the powerful princes of the early thirteenth century. She was advised to avoid such moral complicity by her spiritual director (Robeck 1953, 78–79, 158).

cities – these cannot properly be called trades or occupations at all … [No] evil or disgraceful thing was entitled to that name. (Chrysostom 1971, nos. 110–111 [346–349])

Later in the same discourse, he severely criticizes the wealthy for their perfumery and cosmetics "to counterfeit youthfulness" and for the lavish adornment of their houses with gold, precious stones, ivory, and decorative paints. He argues that trades and occupations that supply these ought to be banned by the city and are not appropriate for his congregants.[7]

Even more significant for our study is his blunt language in criticizing those who aid and abet such cupidity and other economic activities that are injurious to the soul and body.

So where any of these evils … is attached to these activities, no self-respecting and honourable man should himself have anything to do with them or know anything about them or teach them to his sons … [H]e will incur the shameful reproach of being an idler living on disgraceful gains[8] and hear himself bluntly called sordid, good for nothing, and wicked. (Chrysostom 1971, nos. 111–112 [348–349]).

Note the unavoidable subjective element in determining what constitutes economic wrongdoing. For John Chrysostom, trades and occupations supplying the rich with luxuries and facilitating their sinful overindulgence are blameworthy. It is beyond the scope of our study to examine how his teaching might stand in the modern economy. However, it only goes to illustrate the time- and culturally conditioned nature of what constitutes economic wrongdoing.

Philosophy

Liberal social philosophy begins with the presumption of according individuals the maximum amount of freedom that is consistent with everybody else enjoying the same liberties. The burden of proof lies with those who want to encumber such private autonomy of action. They must present a compelling reason for imposing restrictions. As we have seen in chapter 2, "harm to others" is one such compelling reason.[9] "Harm to others" becomes a liberty-limiting principle when the act itself is blameworthy to

---

[7] Chrysostom (1971, nos. 117–118 [352–353]).
[8] The editor goes so far as to add that such disgraceful gain is the equivalent of what we might call today "a parasite living on tainted wealth" (Chrysostom 1971, 348).
[9] Mill (1859 [1974], 68).

begin with, when it sets back others' welfare interests, and when it violates rights.[10]

A second liberal reason for restricting individual freedoms is the moral obligation to treat human beings as ends in themselves and never as means. We can perhaps even go so far as to claim that violating Kant's imperative to respect every rational being "as an end in himself and not merely as a means to be arbitrarily used by this or that will"[11] is sufficient cause for censure. In other words, it is morally wrong for us to facilitate harm to others or to enable the treatment of others as means rather than as ends in themselves.

Economics

To appreciate better what is at stake, let us examine the economics of enabling wrongdoing. While benefitting from and enabling evildoing are clearly distinct from each other, both are in fact inseparable in the vast majority of market activities. Economic agents voluntarily exchange goods and services with one another in order to improve their pre-trade welfare.[12] All parties benefit from such consummated transactions, and everyone is better off than would have otherwise been the case in the absence of the market.[13] Hence, even as they themselves benefit from such exchanges, market participants can be said to enable their trading partners (including wrongdoers). For the rest of this chapter, I conflate benefitting from and enabling wrongdoing.[14]

Economic theory and evidence shed light on the manner and the extent to which individual agents causally contribute to economic wrongdoing. At the heart of economic life is the marketplace through which the disparate

---

[10] Feinberg (1984, 31–64, 105–125). Recall that welfare interests are the essential means for people's pursuit of their ultimate interests (their hopes and dreams). The most commonly accepted examples of such welfare interests are food, clothing, shelter, medical care, education, and other basic needs that are critical for human flourishing.

[11] Kant (1785 [1990], 45, second section, no. 428).

[12] Voluntariness is an essential condition for these transactions to be mutually beneficial. Market exchange is sometimes coerced. For example, governments may require their residents to sell their foreign currency earnings to the central bank (at unfavorable rates), or farmers may be compelled to sell their export crops to a marketing board that acts as a monopolistic exporter. In these cases, the exchanges may not necessarily be welfare improving.

[13] Market participants need not always benefit from such exchanges as in the case of having to sell property at fire-sale prices. However, despite losses from such a compelled transaction, the fire sale may in fact head off even worse damage or losses. In such cases, one could say that the market participant is still in a much better position, post-trade, than would have otherwise been the case. For example, recall the fire sale of Bear Sterns in 2008.

[14] One exception to this, of course, is the case of past wrongdoing. Current transactions do not abet wrongs that had already occurred and are not ongoing.

decisions of innumerable households and businesses are coordinated. Two common instances of material cooperation in economic misconduct are (1) facilitating the perpetrator's use of the marketplace for wrongdoing and (2) strengthening the wrongdoer's economic viability.

Enabling the wrongful use of the marketplace
The marketplace has a continuous circular flow. Picture the entire economy as a single system composed of three major groups of economic actors: households, businesses, and government. Businesses produce goods and services using labor, land, and capital bought from households via the input markets. Businesses pay for these supplies from the revenues they earn from selling their finished goods and services in the output markets. For their part, households earn their livelihood from renting out their labor, land, or capital to businesses in the input markets. With this earned income, these households procure their needs from the business sector via the output markets. Thus, the marketplace has been aptly described as a circular flow of goods, services, and payments flowing ceaselessly between households and businesses. Government is the third major actor. It is itself a major buyer and supplier in both the input and output markets.[15] It is also directly linked to both households and businesses via taxes, subsidies, and transfers.

People have to participate in the marketplace as a result of the modern division of labor. Economic agents specialize in the production of particular goods or services and then sell these in order to earn the necessary purchasing power to procure their other needs. Most people earn a livelihood by selling their labor in the input markets. They then use such wage earnings to buy their necessities from the output markets.

Mutual reinforcement is important in sustaining this circular flow. Buyers get to procure what they need only if they can find counterparties willing to sell them the particular good or service they require at the particular time, place, quality, and quantity needed, and at the right price. The reverse is also true. Sellers get to vend their goods or services only as there are willing buyers to be found. These voluntary exchanges can only be consummated if there are parties willing to engage in such trades. In other words, all the markets and parties must be in place for goods and services to flow smoothly. And herein lies the factual basis for market-mediated complicity.

---

[15] For example, in OECD countries, the share of government revenues or spending as a proportion of gross domestic product (GDP) ranged anywhere from 30 to even as much as 60 percent for the year 2005. See OECD (2006, 58–59).

The output and input markets are critical social institutions because of their much-touted ability to put scarce resources to their most valued uses. In particular, the price signals from these two markets convey a vast amount of ever changing information to widely dispersed economic agents, and in a timely and cost-effective manner. Nonetheless, it is also through these two markets that individual market participants are unwittingly caught up in others' economic misdeeds either through their direct or indirect causal contribution.

For example, in the output markets, households and consumers support criminal business enterprises by patronizing their illicit goods (e.g., sweatshop apparel) or services (e.g., brothels). Alternatively, legitimate business enterprises aid malefactors by readily providing them the means for evildoing (e.g., arms sale to tyrannical governments). Examples in the input markets include those instances of households providing businesses with cheap financing for their injurious enterprises (cf., socially responsible investing). Or we also have material cooperation moving in the other direction in which businesses enable individual misconduct by furnishing the necessary inputs (e.g., credit-card loans to fiscally irresponsible consumers). An economic agent that completes a wrongdoer's circular flow in the marketplace can be said to have a *prima facie* causal contribution to such wrongdoing.

Strengthening wrongdoer's economic viability
A second occasion for market complicity is the strengthening of the wrongdoer's economic viability. This occurs either by lowering the costs of such injurious conduct or by increasing the demand for the wrongful activity.

Supply
On the supply side, complicity occurs by facilitating a reduction in the cost of producing the said products or services. For example, cable companies, wholesalers, and retail shops are instrumental in lowering the cost of pornographers by providing a ready distribution outlet for their wrongful products. Without such willing distributors, these pornographers would have incurred much higher marketing costs.[16]

Demand
On the demand side, material cooperation occurs through the continued patronage of a known problematic good or service.[17] In the first place, there

---

[16] In graphical terms, this is a downward (rightward) shift of the supply curve.
[17] In graphical terms, one could view this as an outward (rightward) shift in the demand curve thereby leading to higher prices and larger quantities sold of the questionable good or service.

is a minimum threshold of sales that must be attained to warrant a business enterprise's continued operation. To be an ongoing entity, even wrongdoers must be able to cover both their fixed and variable costs. The incremental demand furnished by customers willing to buy such illicit goods or services directly assists these problematic firms by pushing them toward and beyond their shutdown point.[18] Every sale matters in a fledgling undertaking. Moreover, the revenues from these incremental sales will be critical in bolstering the firm's financial resources for further expansion.

A second mechanism by which consumer demand directly assists these firms is in helping them achieve economies of scale. Reaching the breakeven point is just the beginning. Expanding that revenue base is vital. Sales volume is important for business enterprises not only because of the correspondingly larger revenues it generates but also because of the need to reach economies of scale in production. There is a technologically determined optimum size of operation that produces the least unit cost. Making it to such economies of scale in production is critical because it maximizes the firm's economic rents (profits). It is often a struggle to reach these economies of scale in production. Under these conditions, individual buying decisions can potentially be the tipping point in bringing the firm "over the top" to its optimum scale of production.[19]

By helping these firms attain their economies of scale, consumers inadvertently strengthen wrongdoers by lowering the price they are able to charge, thereby expanding their sales, their reach, their market share, and their operations further than would have otherwise been the case. Consequently, the socioeconomic wrongs spawned by these firms multiply.

Related to economies of scale is the phenomenon of decreasing-cost industries. Different technologies have their respective economies of scale. There are a few industries (e.g., utilities) whose economies of scale are huge

---

[18] Recall from microeconomics that this is the point at which the marginal cost curve intersects the average variable cost curve at its lowest point. In other words, this is the point at which the firm is just able to cover its variable costs.

[19] The importance of market demand and market size cannot be overemphasized. Recall, for example, the classic infant-industry argument. Most neoclassical economists subscribe to the tenet that international trade is mutually beneficial for all trading partners, *ceteris paribus*. Thus, trade barriers are normally discouraged. However, there are a few occasions when such trade barriers are not merely legitimate, but in fact even encouraged, as in the case of the infant industry. This is the case in which a country has a comparative advantage in a particular industry. However, it may be difficult to get such an industry established locally either because the requisite economies of scale to be globally competitive are large or because of stiff competition from long-established foreign firms. The infant-industry argument calls for assistance to such nascent enterprises until such time that they can effectively compete on their own in the global marketplace. Attaining a sales volume that matches the requisite economies of scale is an imperative.

relative to the available market demand or whose technology is such that unit costs keep declining as quantity sold increases.[20] Obviously, incremental demand in these decreasing-cost industries lowers the unit costs even further for the next rounds of economic activity. Consumers' patronage becomes even more consequential.

Finally, demand is important, particularly in small markets that are crowded with too many competing firms. In such cases, individual buying decisions determine which firms survive and which do not. By competing for the same revenue base and by tapping the same limited pool of industry resources, wrongdoers are, in effect, crowding out legitimate firms that contribute positively to society. In the case of the Saipan factories, many apparel operations that adhered to labor standards were adversely affected and had to scale back or close down altogether because they were outpriced by these sweatshops.

Empirical evidence

Despite the atomization of the ordinary economic actor in the marketplace, theorists nonetheless stress the potency of individual economic agency. By refusing to support wrongdoing even at great personal sacrifice, the individual economic agent may produce powerful indirect effects, such as enticing others to behave similarly. It may be a teaching moment in instructing other market participants on the ills of the economy that must be avoided or rectified.[21] Giving scandal to others is one of the key concerns in the scholastic notion of cooperation with evil and the principle of double effect. But while human conduct can scandalize others and prompt them to misbehave similarly, it can also inspire. It can provide an edifying example that can take a life of its own and launch an entire movement. Muhammad Yunus's Grameen Bank is a recent illustration. From its humble beginnings in the 1970s, it has blossomed into a worldwide microfinancing phenomenon.

The power of consumer sovereignty is confirmed by both anecdotal accounts and hard empirical evidence. The *New York Times* columnist Nicholas Kristof (2009) describes the economics of prostitution and human trafficking in Cambodia. By their own admission, brothel operators acknowledge that low margins and poor demand are among the reasons that

---

[20] These are the natural monopolies.

[21] This is one of Kutz's (2000, 180–181) justifications for expanding his notion of individual participation to include unstructured harms. People are more likely to spurn free-riding if there is a high rate of compliance from other participants (cf., assurance games). It is also the reasoning used by Lichtenberg (2008, 14) in stressing the importance of addressing "new harms" (accumulative harms).

have led some to consider shutting down their operations. Managing a rice shop is said to be more profitable than running a brothel. Kristof argues that one way of curtailing human trafficking and prostitution is by treating these like any other business, that is, by raising their operating costs relative to alternative beneficial, less stressful, or less harmful enterprises.

Kristof's claim is an illustration of our earlier discussion of how complicity in economic wrongdoing occurs by shifting either the demand curve upward and to the right (higher demand) or the supply curve downward and to the right (lower cost), or both. In either or both cases, there is an increase in producer surplus, thereby strengthening the continued economic viability of the unlawful enterprise.

Another illustration of the power of individual market participants is no less than the turnaround of Wal-Mart. It has recently been vigorously selling itself as a green business in response to criticisms of its unethical and callous business practices, from its poor labor relations, to its paltry health care benefits for workers, to its environmentally damaging products and services, to its insensitivity to the needs of the local communities in which it operates. A decisive point was reached in the aftermath of a confidential 2004 McKinsey study it commissioned. The study found that 2–8 percent of Wal-Mart customers surveyed had stopped shopping at the mega-retailer because of its perceived lapses in corporate social responsibility. This led to a change of heart and a 180-degree turnaround for the firm. Wal-Mart's board of directors pressured its CEO to pay attention to good corporate citizenship and to repair the firm's sagging public image.[22] Indeed, solitary economic decisions do make a difference, especially when aggregated as a whole, even in a large industry such as retailing. The sudden "greening" of Wal-Mart is evidence of the power of consumers at the margins.

Of course, this is not the first time we have witnessed the power of consumer sovereignty when it comes to disputed goods or services. As we have seen in chapter 3, grassroots campaigns have forced changes in business practices, ranging from the marketing of baby formula, to the treatment of tomato and grape farm workers, to the subcontracting of college and brand name apparel manufacturing. Equally important, these initiatives have also transformed consumer thinking. Individual market participants can and do shape market processes and outcomes.

Finally, note that contemporary globalization has greatly empowered consumers. Consumer sovereignty has become even more important than

---

[22] Rosenbloom and Barbaro (2009).

ever because of two factors: the shift from a production-driven to a consumer-centric business model and the virtual market created by the Internet. The "balance of power" has shifted from producers to consumers in the Digital Age. In the Industrial Age of the nineteenth and twentieth centuries, the key to competitiveness and market share was producing goods and services at the lowest cost. Thus, note the importance of the Fordist and Taylorist innovations that led to mass production. Goods and services that used to be luxuries and well beyond the reach of ordinary citizens became items of mass consumption. Not surprisingly, the over-riding importance of cost gave rise to production-centric, production-driven business models.

Least-cost production is still important today as seen in the practice of international vertical specialization whereby parts are outsourced all over the world and then assembled at a single location. Nevertheless, consumer preferences and satisfaction have emerged to be just as important as product price, if not more. We find evidence of this in the brand consciousness of a new generation of consumers, in the endless stream of electronic gadgets and services with ever new features and uses, and in the intense pressure on firms to be nimble in adapting to changing market demand. Thus, the "new competition" is no longer about least-cost production, but about short changeover times in correctly anticipating and then satisfying consumer wants. For example, note the consumer-driven production networks in the apparel and car industries in which suppliers locate themselves close to their final markets in order to be even more responsive to market conditions.[23] Consumption has emerged as a major driving force shaping production networks and management practices in contemporary globalization.[24]

In addition to this shift, the microelectronics revolution has led to a wired world in which news and information are disseminated instantaneously, 24/7. Information barriers have come down and more than at any time in history, people are ever more aware of how others in far-flung places live. The Digital Age has made the "demonstration effect" even more potent. People imitate each other in what they consume, in how they live, in how they earn a livelihood, and, more important for our study, in their notions of right or wrong, justice, and fairness. The power of this demonstration effect is evident in the brand-consciousness of the past two decades and in the wildly successful export of US pop culture (fast foods, movies, clothes, lifestyles, music, etc.) all over the world, even in nations that are

[23] Barrera (2007, 62–66).   [24] Dicken (2007, 19–21).

politically hostile to US foreign policy. This demonstration effect cuts both ways. In the same way that it can be used to sell goods and services, the microelectronics infrastructure can also be used effectively to shame reprehensible economic practices and alert people to unethical products or services. The Internet has lowered the transaction costs of organizing joint action[25] and has been an effective vehicle for social networking. In fact, in many cases, there is even no need for people to organize or to encourage others to act. All that is needed is to get the information out on the Internet and like-minded people will spontaneously act accordingly, as is most likely the case in the 2–8 percent of respondents in the McKinsey survey who had stopped shopping at Wal-Mart.[26]

As further proof of the greater power of individual consumers in the wake of the electronic age, note the greater care with which Nike, Gap, and other major brands vet their subcontractors. These firms are keen to avoid the bad press from the anti-sweatshop movements that can undo their enormous investment in building goodwill for their brand names.[27] Indeed, individual consumer choices have gained even greater leverage in our wired global economy. But with such enhanced power comes greater moral responsibility. It is not an exaggeration to claim that the rapid spread and popularity of carbon offset programs and the growing worldwide sensitivity to global warming and ecological damage are in large part due to the demonstration effect facilitated by the Internet.

In sum, from an economic point of view, one enables wrongdoers in their injurious activities either by providing increased demand or by lowering their cost of production. Market participants are price-takers in that they cannot singlehandedly change market processes and outcomes with their buying or selling decisions. Nevertheless, despite their atomization, individuals collectively shape market outcomes. The individual's ultimate causal contribution to market outcomes is not at all trivial. Moreover, such causal contribution is made even more potent in the Information Age given its demonstration effect in spawning like causal contributions from other agents who are inspired to act similarly. These causal contributions are the bases for why individual market participants can be held culpable for benefitting from and enabling wrongdoing.

---

[25] Recall, for example, the grassroots protests in the aftermath of the 2009 Iranian presidential elections.

[26] Thus, the Internet can be said to mimic the same function as market price in that it disseminates ever changing information in a timely and cost-effective manner across widely dispersed agents and then elicits action.

[27] Skeptics note that these businesses probably do good only because it helps their profit margins.

OBJECT OF ACCOUNTABILITY: COMPLICITY IN WHAT?

The object of accountability pertains to the wrongdoing for which moral agents are held to account whether as principals or as cooperators. There are at least three relevant issues involved. First, what constitutes economic wrongdoing and why? Second, how do we deal with economic activities with interlocking beneficial and deleterious outcomes? Third, is it morally permissible to appropriate benefits from past evildoing?

Issue no. 1: What constitutes economic wrongdoing?

Chapter 2 has already dealt with the question of what constitutes economic wrongdoing from the point of view of Christian ethics and philosophy. The criteria offered are clear and straightforward. For Christian ethics, economic activity is meant to facilitate the attainment of the end (*telos*) for which creatures have been created. Economic life is about contributing to the preservation and maintenance of the divine order of creation. In the case of liberal social philosophy, "harm to others" constitutes grounds for wrongdoing.

For example, in the case of the Saipan apparel sweatshops, the object of complicity was the violation of human rights and internationally accepted labor standards in light of these factories' inhumane employment conditions. Workers' welfare interests were harmed; their well-being and safety were jeopardized. Not only were the welfare interests of workers set back and their human rights violated, but the act of exploitation itself was intrinsically wrong. Moreover, workers were used as means rather than as ends in themselves, and Kant's categorical imperative can be invoked to claim that there was, in fact, wrongdoing. Thus, from a theoretical standpoint, we ought to be able to identify readily what constituted economic wrongdoing in this case.

Unfortunately, this is easier said than done in practice. "Harm to others" and the violation of the *telos* in the divine order of creation undoubtedly provide helpful criteria in differentiating right from wrong in economic life. Nevertheless, they are insufficient for our study because they are still too abstract. For example, what will constitute the basket of the all-important welfare interests and rights that determine whether or not harm to others has occurred?[28] Who chooses these and on what basis? What do we do when

---

[28] The fierce debates over US health care reform in 2009–2010 illustrate the difficulty of reaching consensus even on something as basic as access to medical care.

people's welfare interests and rights conflict with each other? Not even the Christian notion of *telos* in the divine order of creation is spared such ambiguity and disagreement. For example, note the opposite positions taken by liberation theologians versus conservative evangelicals regarding the strengths and the weaknesses of market operations.[29]

Clearly, the underlying moral standard employed determines the scope of what constitutes morally unacceptable behavior. It is probably best to distinguish three types of economic conduct:

- economic activities that elicit near universal opprobrium,
- harmful economic activities that are socially tolerated, and
- economic activities that produce a mix of both intended benefits and unintended harms.

Unequivocal economic wrongdoing

Many will most likely agree that certain economic activities are so reprehensible as to have no place in the marketplace. For example, we can cite the human trafficking of sex slaves, child labor, and child prostitution; the sale of babies; money laundering; child pornography; trade in human organs; illegal arms sale; grossly destructive mining methods; unsafe and inhumane working conditions in sweatshops, mines, agriculture, and industrial plants. Reasonable people would find these practices unconscionable as to elicit near universal condemnation.

Harmful activities but socially tolerated

There are some economic activities that many people personally censure but will nevertheless still tolerate because of the greater value accorded to personal choice in a pluralistic society. For them, it would be paternalistic for the community to restrict such conduct. Moreover, banning such activities would be unacceptably intrusive for individual autonomy or national sovereignty and, consequently, cause even more damage. Examples of such blameworthy but socially tolerated activities are prostitution; pornography; violent video, e-games, and music; Internet dating websites that encourage adultery; finning[30] and whaling; overfishing; animal fighting (dog-fighting, cockfights, etc.); fox hunting; animal testing in the cosmetics and pharmaceutical industries; restaurants and stores selling

---

[29] The same clash can be found within the same traditions. For example, see Finn (2005, 458–462) for the reaction of both ends of the political spectrum to *Centesimus Annus*.

[30] Finning is the practice of catching sharks, slicing off their fins, and then dumping the live finless sharks back into the ocean to die. The fins are then used for shark fin soup.

body parts and organs from endangered species as aphrodisiacs, exotic food, or medicine; the use of prison labor; offshore banks that encourage tax avoidance or capital flight from poor nations; the use of sex and the degradation of women in advertising. Or consider intellectual property patent/copyright violations (software, music, medicines, and books), especially in developing nations. What may be piracy in the view of the developed world may be a matter of economic survival for poor nations unable to afford the necessary royalties. And then there are the black markets in foreign currencies and smuggled goods; the trade in ivory; Internet gambling; lobbyists for harmful products such as tobacco.

It is also important to note the whole range of issues that fall under commodification, such as commercial surrogacy, genetic engineering of a baby's physical attributes, and the trade in human eggs and sperm. We also have the question of harmful products that have attracted legislative scrutiny such as tobacco, liquor, trans fats, and high-sodium processed foods. Trans fat restrictions have been enacted in the entire state of California and in cities like New York, Boston, Philadelphia, and Baltimore, while the UK has pressed food processors to reduce the sodium content of their products.[31] And, of course, we have corn fructose and fast foods and their causal link to diabetes and obesity. New York State had considered an 18 percent "obesity tax" on sugary sodas and juice drinks.[32]

The list could go on. Labeling any of these as morally unacceptable will surely provoke heated debate. What may be a faulty, reprehensible choice for some is merely recreational or the exercise of consumer (or national) sovereignty for others. It is the classic problem in mainstream economic theory in which no distinction is made between a need and a want. To differentiate these is to "launder" consumer preferences according to an ideal. And if so, who gets to set this ideal set of preferences, what criteria will be used, and why? The search for an objective method in determining what constitutes blameworthy acts only painfully underscores our lack of a shared notion of the good.

This seeming indeterminacy should not come as a surprise because of what we have already seen in jurisprudence. Adjudicating who is at fault, who has to bear the damages, whether or not the injury is remote, and to what extent people are at fault, is to a large degree ultimately determined by the value commitments of judges and juries (chapter 4). Recall, too, how proximate cause is based not on causation but on social policy, on what is perceived to be just. Even the law's use of the "reasonable-person standard"

---

[31] BBC (2004); Black (2008).   [32] Chan (2008).

presupposes an underlying, unarticulable, but understood popular morality at work.

In sum, except for the most egregious forms of injurious economic conduct, there is no consensus on what constitutes market wrongdoing. Political dialogue and compromise ultimately determine what constitutes legal harms. Arriving at what constitutes moral wrongdoing in economic life, however, is a completely different story and a far more difficult task because it requires grounding on a common moral theory – unlikely in a secular, pluralistic community. Not even a field as narrowly defined as tort law and within the confines of a particular tradition (Anglo-Saxon common law) could come up with a single overarching moral theory on who ought to bear damages from harms.[33] We expect disagreements to be deeper and to be even more contentious in dealing with economic harms and in moving from legal to moral responsibility. Since Christian ethics has a much "thicker" and stricter notion of the good than secular philosophy, we expect it to proscribe a much broader range of economic activities as morally unacceptable.[34]

Issue no. 2: Interlocking harms and benefits

A second issue in weighing the object of accountability (complicity in what?) pertains to the unintentional enabling of wrongdoing. Consider the conceptual and practical difficulties posed by market transactions that produce interlocking harms and benefits. Many of the activities listed in the preceding section are intrinsically problematic by the nature of the goods or services they offer. For example, we have tax evasion in the case of offshore tax havens; titillating prurient desires in the cases of pornography, violent video, and lurid music lyrics; and easy but unconscionable profits from prison labor and organ harvesting from executions.

However, unlike these activities, most market exchanges are pursued for proximate ends that most people will agree are benign. For example, people buy jewelry as accessories or for gift giving, use a search engine on the Internet to find information, enjoy bluefin-tuna sushi, or stretch their income by buying cheaper imported goods. Unfortunately, there are unintended harms in the wake of these activities pursued with the best of intentions. There are collateral ill effects that come with the benefits we reap from such market transactions. In effect, we benefit from such

[33] Coleman (1982; 1983).
[34] Recall, for example, John Chrysostom's views regarding trades and occupations producing luxuries.

exchanges even as we unwittingly enable wrongdoing. Consider the following cases.

The revenues from coltan (an essential input in cell phones) and diamond mines have been documented to be fueling terribly destructive civil wars in Africa.[35] Poachers are able to move their ivory through the market because of the difficulty of distinguishing legitimately obtained ivory from poached ivory. To what extent are direct and indirect end users of ivory, diamonds, and coltan culpable for the collateral ill effects of these industries?

The increased demand for palm oil has led to deforestation in Indonesia. Similar pressure for economic development has led to the stepped-up destruction of the Amazon rainforest. And, of course, there has been the perennial problem of desperate migrants subjected to dangerous working conditions and exploitative wages in their host nations by unscrupulous employers. Similar problems with unsafe and inhumane working conditions and pay have been reported for coffee, banana, and cocoa plantations. To what extent are consumers of these agricultural goods complicit in these disreputable employment practices?[36]

Are clients of banks, insurance firms, mortgage brokers, and financial institutions complicit in numerous incidents of redlining, racial discrimination in setting interest rates, and predatory credit card practices? Are patrons of McDonald's and other fast food outlets complicit in the ill effects of obesity and diabetes associated with these types of food service?

Is it morally permissible for opponents of abortion to avail of drugs that were developed from aborted fetuses? It is the same question in the case of embryonic stem cell research. One cannot say that these merely involve appropriating benefits from a past wrong because research using aborted fetuses and embryonic stem cells is ongoing, and increased revenues from these new drugs will fund even more of such research and entice others to follow suit. For that matter, are we complicit in the ongoing unethical marketing and business practices of some pharmaceutical and health-insurance firms if we avail of their products or services?

These cases vividly illustrate one of the major hurdles to the notion of economic complicity: how do we identify the object of complicity if such harms turn out to be inextricably tied in with important benefits? In all the

---

[35] Essick (2001); Schendel and Abraham (2005).
[36] See Clawson (2009) for a further elaboration of the unintended consequences of our consumption choices. Kenner (2009) and Weber (2009) are also good recent resources on the ethical problems spawned by industrial farming.

cases mentioned, the resulting injury to others is merely the unintended consequence of pursuing legitimate benefits – diamonds and ivory for one's enjoyment, cell phone for work and safety, agricultural goods for nutrition, and banking and credit card use for market participation. The ill effects are merely incidental by-products resulting from the abuses of some economic agents, but not all.[37] If people are held culpable for the unintended collateral ill effects of their economic conduct, should they not also be given credit for the unintended collateral good effects? Is there wrongdoing at all considering these collateral positive benefits? Do these negative and beneficial outcomes merely balance out each other? Or is such calculus even the proper way of determining moral responsibility for activities with both good and deleterious side-effects? If not, what alternative method is there?

The principle of double effect is an important tool in sorting through our moral obligations in these cases with interlocking beneficial and baleful consequences. As we have seen in Part I, we have to consider the nature of the harm to others: its gravity and scope, whether or not it was avertible, and its proportion relative to the intended good that gave rise to such collateral injury to begin with. The question of whether or not the damage was preventable and the relative proportion of good and ill effects can only be considered together with many other factors, such as the capabilities and the sociohistorical location of all the parties involved.

In sum, determining the object of complicity in cases of mixed harms and benefits has to be done in conjunction with the bigger task of establishing who is complicit and where to draw the limits of such complicity. We have to deal with such activities within their concrete particularities. Context is essential.

Issue no. 3: Is it morally permissible to benefit from past wrongdoing?

This chapter is entitled "Benefitting from and enabling wrongdoing." To benefit from a particular misconduct in the marketplace is to enable it by providing the wrongdoer with greater revenues or inputs to persist in such

---

[37] For example, pay-day lending, auto-title loans, pawn-brokers, and subprime lenders arguably have a legitimate role to play in providing finance to those with poor or non-existent credit histories. These activities should not be outrightly dismissed as wrongdoing per se despite numerous anecdotal accounts of exploitative practices. It may perhaps ultimately be a question of whether or not a whole industry should be restricted or banned for the sins of some, at the expense of the rest who are innocent. It is interesting to note that in his sermon *The Use of Money*, John Wesley (1872) explicitly cites pawn-broking as an example of an activity that should be avoided because whatever good it may accomplish is outweighed by an abundance of evils. Besides, Wesley notes that one should not accomplish good with evil means (the charging of usurious interest).

behavior. "Benefitting from" and "enabling" are inseparable in the case of ongoing harms. Not so in the case of past wrongs. Obviously we are able to benefit from a past misdeed without enabling it. This being the case, is it moral to benefit from past wrongs?

This question is not a mere idle academic exercise because we are daily confronted with such cases. For example, do we avail of drugs that have been field-tested by pharmaceutical companies in poor countries using unethical protocols? The US space program and the subsequent commercial satellite industry it spawned benefitted from the experience and data acquired from the Nazi V-2 rocket program in Peenemünde and Mittelwerk, the Nazi underground rocket facility, where slave labor was used. In particular, Wernher von Braun, recruited at the end of World War II, was instrumental in building the US rocket program that culminated with the development of the Saturn V rocket for the Apollo moon missions. No doubt, satellite technology has been vital for everyday economic life, from GPS navigation to credit card use.

Companies that supplied Zyklon-B hydrogen cyanide gas pellets for the Nazi extermination camps and Swiss banks that facilitated the Nazi war effort continue to thrive today.[38] Vast amounts of gold and silver extracted from the colonies in the New World benefitted many European nations – gold and silver that are sorely needed today by impoverished Latin American nations. Many argue that the poverty of many nations today was due to their colonial exploitation.

How about the displacement and the destruction of the cultures of native peoples in all of the Americas and Australia? And, of course, we have the case of the Atlantic triangular slave trade from the seventeenth to the nineteenth century, the ruinous consequences of which continue to shadow and marginalize many African-Americans today. Brown University was established partly with the revenues from the slave trade of a past age. We visit many great museums for their wonderful collections of art and ancient artifacts, many of which were plundered during wars or the colonial era. Are we complicit in visiting and providing revenues to these museums?

There are many more cases that can be cited. Is it morally right to benefit from past wrongdoing? Can one be complicit in past misconduct? This is an

---

[38] Degussa AG had initially been tapped to supply anti-graffiti chemicals for a Holocaust museum. However, overseers of the project rescinded the offer when it was learned that Degussa's parent company is Degesch of Frankfurt am Main, the firm that had supplied Zyklon-B in the Nazi's final solution. See BBC (2003).

issue beyond the scope of this project.[39] However, we can provide a very tentative and partial response. In the first place, there can be no causal contribution and no contributory fault from contemporary economic agents for past misdeeds. Thus, there can be no complicity or blameworthiness for past evildoing.

Second, there may be consequent liabilities in some of these past wrongs. These liabilities would most likely be collective rather than individual.[40] Third, we can be complicit in the sense of not living up to our collective liability to assist or compensate those who have been adversely affected or disadvantaged to this day as a result of these past iniquities. One is not blameworthy for complicity in the past wrongdoing itself, but one may be faulted in failing to fulfill the consequent communal, contemporary liability, if any, from such misconduct. Fourth, in an agent-centric morality, appropriating benefits from a past wrongdoing is not completely costless because it may harm the appropriators' virtue and character formation.[41]

SUBJECT OF ACCOUNTABILITY: WHO IS COMPLICIT?

Our third and final task is determining the subject of accountability. Who is complicit in benefitting from and enabling wrongdoing? Given the circular flow of the marketplace, identifying who is complicit is, in effect, identical to both (1) knowing where to draw the limits of moral responsibility for economic harms and (2) "grading" the strength of such obligations (the degree of complicity). These are distinct yet inseparable issues. Determining the subject of accountability and the extent of material cooperation involved cannot be determined at an abstract, general level. We need the specific context.

As an illustration, let us examine who was complicit in the case of the Saipan apparel sweatshops. At its height, there were thirty-four garment factories on the island of Saipan employing tens of thousands of overseas workers. However, with the end of apparel import quotas in 2005 and with the admission of China into the World Trade Organization (WTO), the Saipan garment industry lost its comparative advantage. The last factories closed down in early 2010. We take the Saipan garment industry as a case

[39] See Kaveny (2000, 308–309) for a brief and well-argued exposition on the morality of using Nazi data in scientific research.
[40] Of course, the exceptions to this are the heirs of previous wrongdoers who have benefitted from the misdeeds of their ancestors. Nations and family-held corporations that were involved in past grievous wrongs come to mind.
[41] Kaveny (2000).

study in assessing the nature of complicity in sweatshops. To do so, we will first examine the nature of the harm, its economic terrain, the web of causation, and finally, the moral responsibility of the various parties that directly or indirectly sustained these factories.

Nature of the harm

Saipan is part of the Commonwealth of the Northern Mariana Islands (CNMI), which has a lower minimum wage than the US mainland. It enjoys duty- and quota-free access to the USA, is governed by less restrictive immigration laws on the number of guest workers permitted, and may use the "Made in the USA" label.[42] Clearly, US retail chains and brand owners had purchased their apparel from Saipan because of its cost and marketing advantages.

Reports indicated appalling working conditions in the Saipan factories, such as seventy- to eighty-hour work weeks, unpaid overtime, unsafe equipment, poor ventilation and extreme heat in work areas, and air filled with dust and textile fibers. Workers were housed in company-owned dormitories that were overcrowded and infested with vermin and insects. Food was said to be of poor quality and insufficient.[43] Based on our earlier discussion of liberty-limiting principles and the divine order of creation, it would appear that the Saipan apparel operations were a clear harm to others.

In January 1999, Saipan apparel workers and unions filed suits in US courts asking for relief and damages for their unlawful working conditions. What was unusual about the case was that the suits were filed against eighteen major US designers and retailers for the wrongful acts of their Saipan subcontractors in maltreating thousands of workers over ten years. The suits were eventually settled out of court with nearly all of the plaintiffs collectively putting together a $20 million fund.[44] While not an admission of guilt, such out-of-court settlements were an implicit acknowledgment of US retail chains' and brand owners' moral responsibility for the employment practices of their suppliers.

Let us set aside legal responsibility and talk only of moral responsibility. Who else ought to have been held accountable for sustaining sweatshop conditions in Saipan besides the subcontractors and the retail chains?

---

[42] Ross (2004, 140).
[43] Ross (2004, 141). Given our space constraint, we cannot examine the empirical evidence firsthand on whether or not the Saipan apparel manufacturers were indeed operating under sweatshop conditions. We have to rely on others' work and assume, for purposes of this study alone, that these operations were in violation of international labor standards and human rights.
[44] CBS News (1999). See also Associated Press (2002).

Economic terrain

We use the circular flow of the marketplace to identify the relevant parties and their relative proximity to the Saipan apparel sweatshops. These sweatshops were active in the output markets, transacting with a string of other businesses that de facto served as their distribution network: the aggregators, importers, wholesalers, brand owners, and retail chains. Brand owners commissioned subcontractors in Saipan to manufacture their product lines, which were then sold as brand-name products (e.g., Tommy Hilfiger) in retail chains (e.g., J. C. Penney) and independent stores. At the end of this distribution chain were the consumers, that is, the shoppers at the retail chains and loyal brand-conscious buyers.

These apparel sweatshops also transacted in the input markets to procure their machinery (equipment manufacturers), capital (bankers, investors, bondholders), labor (recruiters, accountants, staff), technology (engineering firms), managerial expertise, production site (real estate brokers, construction firms), raw materials (textile mills, button/zipper manufacturers), and government access (lobbyists). In addition to the output and input markets, these sweatshops' dealings with local, state, and federal agencies also materially affected these firms' economic viability (e.g., tax breaks, labor-law exemptions).

Given the interlocking nature of market transactions, who should have been held to account for the working conditions in Saipan's apparel industry? Moreover, to what degree were these parties culpable for these factories' misdeeds? Each of the economic agents constituting and completing these manufacturers' circular flow had a *prima facie* causal contribution to sustaining these sweatshop operations. Our next tasks, then, are to determine the causal contribution (explanatory query) and the moral culpability (attributive query) of all the parties involved.

Explanatory query: disentangling causal contributions

Recall that explanatory queries are about establishing the cause-in-fact, while attributive queries are about establishing blameworthiness for the ensuing harm.[45] This section is explanatory in nature in that we are assessing merely the causal contributions of key market participants. We examine culpability in the next section.

Should each of the aforementioned market participants be called necessary causes of the harm inflicted on Saipan's workers? Recall from chapter 4

---

[45] Hart and Honoré (1985).

that to be a necessary cause, one must be able to satisfy the "but for" test. For example, can we say that *but for* Target and J. C. Penney's retail stores, the exploitation of workers in Saipan would not have occurred? No, we cannot. Target and J. C. Penney stores were not necessary conditions for these sweatshops because they were not the only possible distribution outlets. There were many other retail chains and independent stores that carried Saipan-manufactured apparel. The abuse of Saipan workers was not contingent on the existence of Target and J. C. Penney stores. Such exploitation would still have occurred because there was nothing intrinsic to sweatshop apparel that required them to be marketed by Target or J. C. Penney stores. Other retail outlets would have done just as well. Hence, Target and J. C. Penney retail chains, or any other store for that matter, were not *sine qua non* conditions for the maltreatment of Saipan workers. However, by the sheer size of their market share, major retail chains and brand owners can each be considered a NESS (a necessary element in a set of jointly sufficient conditions). Any one of these chains and brand owners may not have been able to shut down the entire Saipan sweatshop industry, but each was capable of shutting down a factory or two just by the size of their purchases. Hence, each of them was a NESS, a concurrent cause in sustaining sweatshop operations. The same can be said of major suppliers (e.g., textile manufacturers, bankers, etc.) that were critical for the viability of the sweatshops.

A different argument has to be made in examining the causal contribution of consumers. Consumer A, an end user of branded apparel made by Saipan producers, was not a necessary condition for the economic viability of these sweatshops because these factories would still have operated even without consumer A's patronage. However, consumer A and other similar end users of Saipan apparel formed a set of conditions that were jointly sufficient to ensure a steady revenue stream for these sweatshop operations. Since A's impact was fully felt only in conjunction with other similar consumers, we can describe consumer A not in terms of a NESS, but in terms of collective consequentialism or rule utilitarianism (chapter 3). Each consumer's causal contribution was significant because of its joint (accumulative) impact with other like consumers.

Similarly, all the other parties directly or indirectly transacting with the sweatshops were either a NESS (direct impact on the viability of offending operations) or subject to collective consequentialism (indirect via accumulative effect). By transacting with the Saipan apparel manufacturers in the input and output markets, these blocks of distributors, end users, and suppliers collectively completed the circular flow that permitted the sweatshops to be viable, ongoing operations. After all, any business under-taking has to be able to move its final goods in the product market in order to raise revenues and accumulate profits, which the firm then uses to pay for the supplies it procures from the input markets. The circular flow is a seamless operation, with the firm transacting simultaneously with all the relevant parties (wholesalers, customers, suppliers, etc.) in both the input and output markets. Thus, even if there were retail chain outlets willing and ready to buy and distribute their output, Saipan apparel firms would have nevertheless been unable to operate if they had trouble procuring their needs from the input markets, such as raw materials, capital, equipment, technology, labor, and other services.

Take any piece away from this *particular* set of jointly sufficient con-ditions (NESS) (or from this *particular* circular flow), and the sweatshop operations would have ground to a halt. The major distribution outlets and major suppliers were individually and collectively necessary to complete this *particular* set of jointly sufficient conditions for the sweatshops' operations, but they were not necessary conditions for *all* possible sets of jointly sufficient conditions.[46] Recall Mill's insight on the multiplicity of ensem-bles of conditions, any of which would have been sufficient to bring about an effect. Using chapter 4's language of causation, we can say that all the aforementioned major parties and the input and output markets in the circular flow were necessary elements of a set of jointly sufficient conditions (NESS) that brought about the Saipan sweatshops.

Different degrees of causal contributions
Even if the aforesaid economic agents were equally a part of NESS (the sweatshops' circular flow), this did not mean that they had equal causal contributions to the harm. After all, not all conditions are equal in their importance for the occurrence of the harm since they may play different roles. Some are more immediate and indispensable than others. Moreover, different products and services face dissimilar requirements for success. For example, the key to the microelectronics industry is creativity in churning out ever more advanced applications and new products or services. High-tech designers and programmers are the linchpins in the e-industry. Banking institutions and Wall Street firms are heavily reliant on finance experts, investment analysts, and brokers. The automotive industry requires quality and cost-effective engineering.

---

[46] If they were necessary conditions for *all possible sets of jointly sufficient conditions*, then they would be necessary conditions for the occurrence of the sweatshops. They would satisfy the "but for" test.

In the case of apparel sweatshop operations, the crucial element is marketing, that is, the ability to move these common items of consumption (apparel) through extremely competitive global markets. As a business, apparel sweatshops require volume since their only selling point or comparative advantage, so to speak, is their low-cost manufacturing (at the expense of their workers). Thus, brand owners and retail chains are among the most important market participants that ultimately determine the economic viability of apparel sweatshops. Their causal contribution as a block (as a NESS of distributors) is much more substantial than most of the other economic agents in this circular flow. For example, brand owners and retail chains have a far more substantive material causal contribution to the sweatshops' wrongdoing than, say, the sweatshops' equipment and textile suppliers, or its real estate brokers. After all, marketing is at the heart of the apparel industry's business, and the retail chain stores and brand owners are its key gatekeepers. Using our earlier distinctions from chapter 1, we could say that these retail outlets are indispensable material cooperators.

However, having said this, we can only provide a rough approximation of the relative importance of various causal contributions as there is no systematic or objective method for grading these in a precise mathematical manner. For example, how do we quantitatively rank the importance of the retail chains' causal contribution relative to the contribution of the sweatshops' bankers, investors, and bondholders? Financing, after all, is just as important as marketing the output. Their material cooperation could also be described as indispensable. Thus, there is a limit to how far we can compare the relative importance of specific causal contributions. In some cases, we have to content ourselves with noting that many of these causal contributions may not even be comparable to each other in the absence of a common denominator or of an adequate metric. Nonetheless, despite this caveat, we should still be able to identify the key causal contributions for particular industries or lines of business.

Relative size of causal contributions
An indicator of the relative size of causal contributions is the size of the NESS. The greater the number of elements constituting a particular NESS, the more diffused are the causal contributions likely to be.[47] Going back to our example, the respective causal contributions of Target and J. C. Penney would have been much greater had they been the only firms subcontracting Saipan sweatshops.

---

[47] Recall the dispersion principle from the diagnostic framework in chapter 4.

In one sense, economic complicity is relatively easier to measure compared with other kinds of moral complicity. After all, economic causal contributions can often be approximated. For example, the retail chains' respective market shares in Saipan apparel revenues could be used as a proxy for their causal contribution to the wrongdoing. The same is true for the other economic agents. We can measure the causal contribution of suppliers by using, as a proxy, their market share in the total cost of production. Using this measure, we would most likely identify textile manufacturers as key causal contributors.

Second-order causality and transitivity

Going further upstream and downstream, who else can be said to have had a substantial contribution in the chain of causation? In order to make our assessment more realistic and interesting, we examine the next level of causes. We could refer to these as second-order causes to distinguish them from the earlier first-order NESS within which we find the sweatshops. Think back to chapter 4's image of the cone of causation with each point of that cone having its own respective cone of causation – an explosion of cones of causation within cones of causation in an infinite regress.

Each of the parties in the original NESS has its own respective cone of causation connecting it to its own circle of suppliers and customers. We can call these the second-order or higher-order cones of causation. Thus, for example, the Target and J. C. Penney chains were part of the first-order circular flow that sustained the Saipan apparel industry. However, these retail chains sold many other products (Revlon, Gucci, etc.) and procured equipment, materials, and goods from many suppliers (e.g., bankers, real estate brokers, insurers, and shippers). These formed Target and J. C. Penney chains' own cone of causation (their own first-order NESS). However, these were merely second-order causes in relation to the Saipan sweatshops.[48] Elements in this second-order cone of causation were remotely and indirectly associated with the Saipan sweatshops through their support of and association with the Target and J. C. Penney stores.

---

[48] The exceptions to this were the Target and J. C. Penney shoppers who bought sweatshop apparel. These sweatshop end users were part of the first-order NESS of the Saipan apparel industry; they contributed directly to the Saipan wrongdoing. After all, these end users ultimately provided the needed revenues (via the Target and J. C. Penney shops) that sustained the Saipan sweatshops in continued operations. Hence, there was an overlap in that end users of Saipan apparel were in both Target's and J. C. Penney's first-order NESS (circular flow) just as they were part of the first-order NESS (circular flow) of the Saipan sweatshops.

Obviously, their material cooperation (in the Saipan sweatshops) can be described as mediate, remote, and dispensable.

Second-order causes were one step further removed from the wrong-doing. All of them were mere conditions and not causes of the Saipan wrongdoing. Standing between them and the harm itself were two layers of intervening moral agents – the sweatshop operators and Target and J. C. Penney management. However, the more significant was the role of Target and J. C. Penney in sustaining Saipan sweatshops, the greater was the potential indirect causal contribution of these second-order causes to the Saipan exploitation. There is transitivity to causal contributions. If A causally contributes to bringing about B, and B causally contributes to effecting C, then we can say that A causally contributes to C's occurrence. Moreover, if B has a particularly important causal contribution to C, then A would also have a correspondingly greater indirect contribution to C's occurrence than would have otherwise been the case.

We could repeat the same exercise for the third-order causes (cones of causation) for each of the economic agents that sustained Target and J. C. Penney operations. Thus, we are able to build a series of causes in an infinite regress – the proverbial chain (or cone) of causation or spiral of responsibility. It is in fact better described as a web of causation.

In sum, relative causal contribution to wrongdoing is determined by (1) the functional importance of the causal contribution given the nature of the industry or business, (2) the remoteness of the cause from the actual wrongdoing (e.g., first-order, higher-order causality), and (3) the size of the causal contribution. Moreover, the more toxic is the harm, the more consequential and the more culpable are these causal contributions. In our example, the retail chains, brand owners, and the ultimate consumers (as a collective) were substantial causal contributors to the wrongdoing because of their importance in the Saipan sweatshops' circular flow – they provided the revenue stream that sustained these factories' operations.

Thus far we have been talking only of relative causal contributions rather than moral responsibility. Many more factors have to be weighed in addition to causality. It is to this that we now turn our attention.

Attributive query: imputing individual moral responsibility

Let us now examine the blameworthiness of the parties involved in the Saipan apparel industry. To be complicit in the Saipan wrongdoing, market participants must have been aware that the factory working conditions were substandard, had adversely set back the welfare interests of workers, and were in violation of human rights and international labor standards. They must have known that there was wrongdoing in the Saipan operations. To facilitate our exposition, we assume this to have been the case for all the economic agents we discuss in this section.[49]

We will further assume that none of them intended to exploit the Saipan apparel workers. If they did, then they would be subject to Kutz's (2000) complicity principle. Such shared intentionality in a common task with the wrongdoers would have made them morally responsible not only for their own acts, but also for all the consequences of the Saipan manufacturers' misdeeds. In moral theology, this is formal, and not merely material, cooperation.

Unless otherwise noted, it is unlikely that market participants had intended to harm Saipan workers. Instead, their causal contribution to the Saipan wrongdoing was merely the foreseen but unintended consequence either of doing business with the sweatshops (as in the case of suppliers, retail chains, etc.) or of procuring needed goods from these factories (e.g., end users of apparel). Double-effect reasoning will be important in weighing the moral culpability of these economic agents.

Output market
Retail chains and brand owners
Let us begin with the strongest possible allegation. Were the retail chains and brand owners co-conspirators in the maltreatment of workers? For our purposes, what was interesting about the 1999 law suits was the use of the Federal Racketeer Influenced and Corrupt Organizations Act.[50] Were the retail chains and brand owners merely accessories or were they, in fact, co-principals or co-conspirators with the sweatshop operators? As we have seen from chapter 1, to make the case for co-conspiracy we have to prove that the retail chains and brand owners had the criminal intent (to abuse workers) and took part in the act of exploiting workers. Or, to use the language of moral theology, this is a question of whether or not they were in formal (or immediate) material cooperation in the wrongdoing of the Saipan producers.[51]

---

[49] This is not an unrealistic assumption given the press coverage of the Saipan working conditions and given the importance business enterprises accord to doing their due diligence on their major suppliers or customers.

[50] CBS News (1999).

[51] Even if we were to say that retail chains and brand owners were merely material cooperators because they did not intend the exploitation of apparel workers, an argument can nevertheless still be made that they were in immediate material cooperation because of the importance of marketing and distribution in sustaining the Saipan operations.

Proving intent to abuse workers is beyond the scope of this study and we will leave this task to others. For this study, we will simply assume that retail chains and brand owners were merely interested in finding low-cost manufacturers for their clothing lines and not in exploiting workers. We will content ourselves with examining the nature, the basis, and the gravity of their complicity with the violation of human rights in Saipan despite their benign business aims. There are at least three factors that overwhelmingly point to these retail chains' and brand owners' moral responsibility.

First, note the contractual relationship between the Saipan producers, on the one hand, and the retail chains and brand owners, on the other hand. From the latter's viewpoint, they were merely outsourcing functions that were non-essential to their core business of retailing or branded marketing.[52] They could claim that the Saipan apparel producers were autonomous business enterprises completely independent of and distinct from the retail chains and brand owners. Both sides were free to solicit business elsewhere and to transact with other parties. Their relationship with these Saipan manufacturers was a purely arms-length commercial transaction. They were not party to how these Saipan producers ran their factories and were, thus, not morally or legally responsible for their labor practices. It was a purely business-to-business, not an employer–employee, relationship.[53]

Despite these arguments, retail chains and brand owners, on the one hand, and Saipan sweatshop operators, on the other hand, were in a principal–agent relationship. Saipan apparel operators were acting as agents on behalf of the principals (retain chains and brand owners) in contracting the services of workers, producing apparel according to the principals'

[52] Such outsourcing has been longstanding practice in the apparel industry and is not a new phenomenon brought about by contemporary globalization. In the past three decades, other industries have followed a similar path to offshore outsourcing by which firms shed non-essential and non-core activities to subcontractors. This is part of the phenomenon of international vertical specialization.

[53] Many have adopted the same arguments and method to circumvent the law. Apparel subcontractors often further subcontract parts of their operations to smaller jobbers who in turn further "subcontract" with independent workers who are treated as micro-subcontractors in their own right and then paid piece-rate. In this scheme of serial subcontracting, there is no straightforward employer–employee relationship with its attendant burdensome, intrusive moral and legal proscriptions. Instead, sweatshop operators and jobbers rationalize these arrangements as straightforward commercial business-to-business transactions with self-employed people. The person at the bottom of the food chain who does the sewing and cutting is not an employee but a subcontractor in business for herself. Hence, jobbers will claim that they are not legally culpable for the inhumane working conditions. They deny that they are in immediate material cooperation with the exploitation of workers. At best, they are only in mediated remote material cooperation, if at all, because they are simply pursuing business-to-business transactions with other like entrepreneurs. There is no employer–employee relationship in the entire chain of causation that makes them subject to labor laws or subsequent legal claims.

specifications, and then shipping these to the principals' stores. As agents, the Saipan producers could be viewed as managing the entire production process on behalf of their principals. In both philosophical and legal literature, principals are strictly liable for their agents' actions, even if they themselves (the principals) are completely faultless or have no causal contribution to the harm, or both. This is vicarious liability. Principals are morally and legally responsible for the damages caused by agents acting on their behalf.

Moreover, note that retail chains and brand owners themselves were aware of their moral and legal obligations. Many of them had in-house standards and procedures by which subcontractors were carefully vetted for sweatshop conditions. Some even claimed publicly that only subcontractors that subscribed to US labor laws were hired.[54]

Second, retail chains and brand owners were morally responsible by virtue of their functional role in the global apparel market. The United States is the biggest apparel market, and retail chains and brand owners are at the heart of this lucrative, albeit highly competitive, market. Given their buying power and their central role within the US apparel distribution network, the contracts and purchase orders awarded by these retail chains and brand owners determine which subcontractors survive and flourish and which do not. They are, in effect, the "gatekeepers" for who gains access to the large US consumer base. For the year 2000, the top ten retailers alone cumulatively controlled 71.8 percent ($130 billion) of the US apparel market ($182 billion). Thus, retail chains have been called the "eight-hundred-pound gorillas" of the global trade in clothing.[55]

These retail chains and brand owners are not price-takers vis-à-vis their suppliers. They are, in fact, price-makers given their considerable market power. This market share is convincing evidence of these retail chains' and brand owners' significant causal contribution to propping up the Saipan operations. By ignoring the working conditions in these factories, retail chains and brand owners were, in effect, condoning such practices. (After all, they profited from the status quo.) They have thrown their weight around, especially when it comes to setting the prices they pay their subcontractors. They could have just as easily done the same in improving the lot of the Saipan workers producing their apparel. These retail chains

---

[54] CBS News (1999).

[55] The top ten and their respective market shares were Wal-Mart (18.1%), J. C. Penney (12.5%), Federated Department Stores (6.8%), The Gap (6.4%), Target (5.5%), The Limited (5.3%), May (5.3%), Sears (4.5%), Kmart (3.9%), and TJX (3.4%). See Ross (2004, 125, 132).

and brand owners could be properly called indirect employers because they exercised considerable power over the employment practices of their Saipan subcontractors. In fact, empirical evidence confirms that the most effective and quickest way of getting subcontractors to improve their working conditions is to apply pressure on the brand owners.[56]

Related to this market power is the question of voluntariness. Moral responsibility is mitigated in those cases in which there is coercion or compulsion, and the moral choice is not entirely voluntary. Is there any reason to believe that retail chains and brand owners were compelled to source their apparel from Saipan despite the appalling working conditions on the island? Given their sizable market share, the worldwide availability of alternative suppliers, and the intense competition among subcontractors, these retail chains and brand owners enjoyed wide latitude in their merchandising decisions.

Finally, let us examine whether or not the strongest possible moral argument in defense of retail chains and brand owners can stand up against scrutiny and reason. Retail chains and brand owners claim that their commitment is to serve the consuming public by stretching the latter's income through low-priced goods. To carry out this service, retail chains and brand owners search for reliable, efficient, and cost-effective manufacturers who will deliver their orders in the right quantities, the right quality, the right price, and in a timely manner. The maltreatment of Saipan workers was the unfortunate, unintended consequence of their subcontractors' efforts to meet their contractual obligations, or the unintended result of extremely competitive conditions in the global apparel manufacturing business.

Let us examine these claims using the three conditions of the principle of double effect (PDE). Inhumane working conditions that violate human rights are morally unacceptable acts to begin with, regardless of the intention or circumstances surrounding the case (first condition of PDE). Moreover, one cannot achieve the good of the laudable intention (stretching the consuming public's real income) by employing morally unacceptable means (exploiting workers) (second condition of PDE). Furthermore, even if we were to accept, for the sake of argument, that the maltreatment of workers was merely an unintended consequence, the harm inflicted on the Saipan workers simply outweighed whatever benefits may have been produced for the American public (third condition of PDE). Besides, the ill

---

[56] Pines and Meyer (2005). Retailers, in contrast, are said to be not as keen on improving their subcontractors' workplace conditions because of intense price competition.

effects were avertible since there were many alternative manufacturing sites. In addition, note the paradoxical regressive distribution of burdens and benefits in this case. The welfare interests of poor workers in developing nations were sacrificed in favor of well-off consumers in developed nations. In fact, from the standpoint of Christian ethics, the wealthy have an obligation to assist the poor (preferential option for the poor). In this case, far from providing such assistance, economic agents higher up in the food chain were ironically imposing even heavier burdens on the poor and profiting from their desperation. Furthermore, retail chains and brand owners should have exercised due care in ensuring that they had done as much as they could to prevent or minimize the ensuing harms, including exerting moral suasion on their subcontractors. Thus, all three conditions of double-effect reasoning were violated. The contractual relationship between the retail chains/brand owners and Saipan manufacturers cannot be justified by claiming that the Saipan working conditions were merely the unintended consequence of pursuing legitimate ends (serving US consumers).

In sum, retail chains and brand owners had grave moral responsibilities for the Saipan sweatshops because of their functional role and enormous market power in controlling access to the huge US apparel market. Moreover, these subcontractors were working as agents on their behalf. Retail chains and brand owners had a significant, indeed decisive, causal contribution in sustaining the Saipan apparel operations. We can describe their role as an avertible, proximate, and indispensable material cooperation. Some might even go so far as to describe it as immediate material cooperation because of the centrality of marketing in this line of business.

End users of Saipan apparel (consumers)

As a group   Let us examine end users' moral obligations both as a group and as lone consumers. End users had a collective moral obligation because of their significant joint causal contribution. Without their patronage, even the retail chains and brand owners would have been helpless. For this reason, note the sensitivity of retail chains and brand owners to consumer boycotts or to bad press that tarnish the goodwill of their company or brand names. Relatively speaking, the causal contribution of end users taken as a single block was, in fact, much more important compared with retail chains' and brand owners' impact, especially with the recent shift to consumer-centric business models. Going back to our example, it was the revenue stream from consumers that sustained the Saipan operations, the retail chains, and the brand owners. Put in the language of causation, consumers (as a group) completed the circular flow of the Saipan producers. They were jointly a NESS (a necessary element in a set of jointly sufficient conditions) for the harm's occurrence.

Nevertheless, despite their significant causal contribution as a group, we cannot fault end users as *the* cause of the Saipan wrongdoing because between these end users and the harm itself (exploitation of workers) were two intervening moral agents – the factory operators and the retail chains/ brand owners. These end users were merely a condition (albeit an important condition) and not the cause of the harm. This is an important distinction because based on chapter 4's discussion of intervening events, end users (as a group) were less accountable than the retail chains and brand owners, who in turn were less accountable than the Saipan plant operators. This is the case in which accountability diminishes with intervening events (direct causation principle).

US end users, as a group, shared in the moral responsibility for the Saipan wrongdoing because of their capacity to act otherwise. In particular, they had ample economic resources to pay the much higher prices of law-abiding apparel manufacturers. They had a wide range of alternative goods besides Saipan-made clothing; they could have easily shopped at other retail chains. They had easy access to information documenting the abusive employment practices in Saipan. They were educated enough as a group to know that it is immoral to profit from the desperation of others and that they, in fact, had a duty to help those who were poor. Furthermore, US end users were aware that collective actions, such as boycotts, had been effective in the past in correcting unjust practices. And even if they were to argue, as a group, that the Saipan operations were merely the unintended result of their (consumers') legitimate goal and need to satisfy their apparel needs, we can repeat the same exercise we did earlier on double-effect reasoning for the retail chains and come up with same conclusion: the Saipan case does not satisfy any of the three conditions of the principle of double effect, even in the case of end users as a group.

This strong collective responsibility to refrain from patronizing Saipan apparel gives rise to an equally strong derivative moral obligation for NGOs and individuals with the necessary resources to organize collective action. They had the duty to inform the general public of the Saipan wrongdoing, prevent the sale of such apparel within the community, and pressure sweatshop producers and retail outlets to improve working conditions. This is in line with Christian ethics and its principle of socialization and general justice (the duty to work toward the common good according to our means).

As individual end users   The more interesting and more difficult case to consider is the moral obligation, if any, of the lone consumer. We can build on our findings for end users as a group. First, while the lone consumer, say A, was also a part of the circular flow of the Saipan producers, the absence of consumer A would not have disrupted the flow of goods to and from Saipan. Hence, A was not a NESS for the exploitation of Saipan workers. Consumer A was merely part of a very large group of end users who were jointly sufficient for the harm to occur. If enough consumers like A had withdrawn from that circuit, then we would have seen a disruption of the circular flow. As mentioned earlier, Parfit's collective consequentialism (chapter 3) is the proper framework to use for consumer A. Moreover, just like the collective, the lone consumer A was not the cause, but was merely one of a multitude of conditions for the harm to occur. There were many intervening moral agencies between consumer A and the harm itself.

A second important consideration is the extent of both consumer A's causal contribution and moral culpability. The larger the size of the group to which consumer A belonged, the smaller was her share of the causal contribution to the wrongdoing.[57] (Recall the dispersion principle from chapter 4 in which accountability diminishes as the harm or causation is spread among more people or over time.) Thus, there is a *prima facie* case for a correspondingly reduced moral culpability. However, there are other factors to take into account besides causal contribution, such as the consumer's sociohistorical location, goals, and capacity to act. It may, in fact, be possible to have cases in which consumers with larger causal contributions were less culpable than those with much smaller causal contributions but with a greater capacity to avert the harm.

Individual consumers vary widely in their respective personal endowments, societal roles, and access to resources. They differ in their sociohistorical location and, consequently, in their capacity to act. These are important determinants of the "real" prices people face in participating in the marketplace. For example, the poor often pay higher interest on loans, mortgages, and insurance (if they can even obtain them at all) for lack of a good credit history or a well-paid job, or because of their place of residence. Since they have limited mobility and funds, they are unable to buy in bulk from the superstores that provide goods at cheaper per unit costs. Instead, they often shop at more expensive local neighborhood convenience stores.

---

[57] In fact, one can even provide a precise and objective proxy for consumer A's causal contribution by examining the value of her Saipan apparel purchases as a ratio of the sweatshops' entire revenues.

And since they are poor, they eat cheap but extremely unhealthy sources of carbohydrates and proteins (fast foods). Indeed, sociohistorical location matters. Consequently, we cannot make blanket judgments on the culpability of specific consumers without looking at their particular circumstances.

Let us take the hypothetical case of a poor immigrant family who may have had little choice but to purchase Saipan apparel because it was the cheapest available, or because the family may not have had the transportation or the time to look for other stores that provided alternative apparel. Double-effect reasoning will most likely justify or excuse this family's causal contribution to the Saipan wrongdoing. The goal of this poor family was to procure a basic need – clothing. Buying from the neighborhood discount store (which carried inexpensive Saipan apparel) was their only option owing to their lack of mobility or income, or both. Consequently, their causal contribution to sustaining the Saipan work sites was an unintended consequence of satisfying their basic needs. Double-effect reasoning validates the morality of their purchase of Saipan apparel. The importance and immediacy of taking care of this poor family's welfare interests proportionately outweighed the distant harm of their consumer dollars trickling down to the Saipan producers. Using the language of torts from chapter 4, we can call this "remote damage," outside the bounds of this family's moral responsibility. This is an instance in which there is causal contribution to a wrongdoing for which one is not blameworthy. This was a case of invertible, permissible material cooperation that did not even carry a liability to repair the harm. It was an excused material cooperation on the basis of poverty and economic compulsion.

In contrast, a middle-class family had much greater resources to avoid Saipan-made apparel. It had access to more shopping venues and could afford to pay a little more for apparel from other sources. It was also likely to have better access to information. Moreover, given its middle-class status and, consequently, its greater moral obligation to provide assistance to the poor, this family should have taken even greater care to avoid supporting the Saipan abuses and to keep themselves properly informed.[58] The unintended consequence of causally supporting Saipan sweatshops was preventable with minimal effort and reasonable cost.

[58] This obligation to assist the poor can be justified using philosophical or theological arguments. See Rawls (1971) and more recently, Singer (2009). In the case of Christian ethics, we have the preferential option for the poor. Clawson (2009) is a good example of a proactive approach to avoiding complicity in everyday consumption.

Using double-effect reasoning, we can say that the benefit from buying Saipan apparel (greater savings for this middle-class family) was not proportionate to the causal contribution of their consumer dollars trickling down to the Saipan operators and sustaining them in their exploitation of the poor struggling to eke out a living. Double-effect reasoning will not validate this middle-class family's purchase of Saipan apparel given its ample resources to avoid the unintended consequence of supporting the Saipan sweatshops. This was an avertible material cooperation. It was blameworthy.

Of course, we must also have a realistic perspective. This middle-class family's causal contribution and moral obligation were but part of a much larger group's causal contribution and duty. There is a diminution of this obligation as accountability is spread over moral agents and across intervening events (dispersion and direct causation principles from chapter 4).[59] Nonetheless, recall a noteworthy finding from chapter 3: diminished obligations do not disappear completely. Furthermore, note the arguments of that chapter on how these small causal contributions eventually add up to a sizable collective effect. Moreover, even minute moral obligations are significant and consequential because of their impact on the character and virtue of the end user stemming from the reflexive nature of the human act.[60]

In sum, end users as a group were morally culpable for the Saipan working conditions because of their decisive causal contribution, their capacity to do otherwise, and their moral duty to assist the poor. However, we cannot make a similar general statement in the case of each individual consumer. We have to examine the particular situation of each end user, taking into account the agent's sociohistorical location, available resources, and capacity to do otherwise. Each market participant's moral responsibility is unique.

Input markets

Of what little there is in the literature on economic complicity, much of the attention has been focused on the demand side, that is, on the wholesalers and consumers. Not much has been devoted to the input side. Thus, let us examine the moral culpability of the bankers, insurers, bondholders, investors, and suppliers who sustained the Saipan sweatshops from the input side. All these can be covered by a common set of considerations.

---

[59] Some would probably even go so far as to cite the parallel acts principle in which accountability diminishes as others act similarly. Assessing the validity of this principle is beyond the scope of our study.

[60] Kaveny (2000) is emphatic on this point regarding the appropriation of benefits from evildoing.

First, as mentioned earlier, if any of these suppliers intended the exploitation of workers, then they were morally liable for the entirety of the wrongdoing. Recall Kutz's (2000) complicity principle and moral theology's notion of formal cooperation.

Second, in the absence of an intention to exploit workers, these suppliers' causal contribution to supporting the Saipan sweatshops was merely the unintended consequence of pursuing legitimate business interests. Thus, double-effect reasoning will be an important part of our assessment. We have to consider the gravity of the harm and the suppliers' role, resources, and sociohistorical location.

Suppliers of goods and services

Let us first take the case of the sweatshops' bankers, insurers, and suppliers of raw materials (e.g., zippers, buttons, textiles) and services (e.g., accounting, security). They each sustained the operations of the apparel factories but with varying degrees of importance. On the positive side, by transacting with the Saipan apparel producers, these suppliers kept their own respective businesses profitable and viable. The downside, of course, was that they enabled the sweatshop operations. We cannot make a general statement on their moral culpability but must take into account the particular circumstances of each supplier.

There were suppliers whose economic survival depended on the revenues generated from selling supplies or services to the Saipan apparel factories. For example, one could think of the local Saipan bank, insurance broker, or button-zipper suppliers whose major clients were the Saipan apparel producers. In this case, there is reason to believe that the benefits produced by these suppliers (i.e., sustaining their own businesses and providing employment for their workers) outweighed their substantial negative causal contribution to sustaining Saipan sweatshops. It was unfortunately a trade-off between throwing these suppliers' employees out of work and pressuring the sweatshops to cease and desist in their maltreatment of their workers. This was an instance of a clashing set of rights claims: the right to employment (on the part of the suppliers' workers) versus the right to humane working conditions (on the part of the sweatshops' workers). The trade-off should not have arisen in the first place if the Saipan manufacturers, retail chains, brand owners, and end users had only lived up to their moral obligations. But they had not, and these suppliers were, consequently, faced with a hard choice. In this case, improving the sweatshop conditions should come through another route, but not at the expense of the suppliers' workers being thrown out of work. This was an invertible, permissible material cooperation. Depending on the capacity of each supplier, there may have been liabilities to mitigate the resulting harms. Suppliers with a real bargaining or economic power to elicit change in the employment practices of the sweatshops ought to have exercised such leverage by virtue of their obligation to prevent harm (e.g., principle of socialization, scholastic general justice, Kant's person as end). Recall that this is part of the third condition of the principle of double effect calling for due care in averting or mitigating the harm.

However, there might also be suppliers who had a large customer base and whose transactions with the Saipan apparel producers were essential not to their own survival, but only to their profitability (e.g., multinationals). In this case, double-effect reasoning would have required them to cease and desist from dealing with the Saipan manufacturers. The good these suppliers intended (increased revenues and profitability) did not outweigh the consequent harm (sustaining sweatshop operations). Furthermore, they also should have exercised due care in preventing or ameliorating the resulting harms as part of the third condition of the principle of double effect. Otherwise, they were blameworthy parties to the wrongdoing. Moreover, the fact that their survival did not depend on business from the Saipan apparel industry indicates that they had the resources and the capacity to act otherwise. Theirs was an avertible material cooperation. It was blameworthy.

Investors and bondholders

The case of these sweatshops' investors and bondholders is straightforward. In investing capital or lending funds to these sweatshops, investors and bondholders had a significant causal contribution in sustaining the exploitation of the Saipan workers. Financing is an essential prerequisite to any business undertaking. By avoiding such kind of investment or lending, these investors and bondholders would have raised these sweatshops' cost of capital or financing, thereby increasing their cost of production and making it that much more difficult for them to expand, much less thrive. Theirs was an indispensable material cooperation, at the very least.

Furthermore, we can presume that these investors and bondholders had done their due diligence as part of their investment process and were, therefore, well aware of the ethical problems shadowing these apparel manufacturers. Consequently, at worst, we can say that by committing capital or by lending funds to these sweatshops, these investors and bondholders, in effect, endorsed and shared these apparel producers' intention of profiting by exploiting workers. By Kutz's complicity principle, they were morally liable for these sweatshops' misdeeds. In fact, Kutz (2000, 240–253) goes so far as to argue against corporate law's limited liability provisions. He claims that by staying vested in problematic firms, shareholders incur a shared intentionality. Consequently, they should be held *personally* liable for damages arising from corporate malfeasance that the company is unable to cover.

At best, we can claim that their causal contribution to these sweatshops' viability was merely the unintended consequence of a much larger good they pursued – higher returns or diversification for their portfolios. Such an argument fails double-effect reasoning. In the first place, they cannot use immoral means to achieve a laudable goal (second condition of PDE). Second, the fact that they had surplus funds indicates that these investors and bondholders had the necessary resources and capacity to do otherwise. Moreover, if it was only a matter of diversification or higher returns, the global capital market is awash with a vast range of investment instruments to satisfy different investor requirements without such "unethical baggage." Third, the good purportedly pursued (higher returns or portfolio diversification) did not compare with the gravity of the damage inflicted by these sweatshops (violation of human rights, exploitation). The importance and immediacy of the consequent harm far outweighed whatever good these investors may have sought from such investments (third condition of PDE). Thus, we can only conclude that, at best, the sweatshops' shareholders, bondholders, and financiers were gravely complicit in the wrongdoing based on the principle of double effect. Theirs was an avertible material cooperation. In the worst case scenario, they were co-principals to the wrongdoing or were in immediate material cooperation or formal cooperation, depending on their intention and the size or functional importance of their investments or lending in propping up these sweatshops. They fall well within Kutz's (2000) complicity principle.

Special cases: lobbyists, labor recruiters, and government overseers
Before we leave the input market, let us examine the special case of a particular group of service providers. Labor recruiters were instrumental in supplying these sweatshops with workers. Besides duping unsuspecting women from poor countries desperate for work and besides lying to them and often even defrauding them, these labor recruiters were directly aiding sweatshop operators by providing a continuous supply of workers to be exploited. There is a strong case to claim that they were co-conspirators given the central importance of acquiring a pool of workers for sweatshop operations. They had both intent and a key role in the commission of the

wrongful act. It was formal cooperation at the very least. There is no further need to use double-effect reasoning. But even if we give them the benefit of the doubt, they were, at best, in immediate material cooperation with the sweatshop operators, given the importance of obtaining a cheap and docile labor force for this line of business. These labor recruiters were as reprehensible in their evildoing as the sweatshop operators.

Washington lobbyists who had worked to ensure the continued exemption of Saipan from US labor laws and the continued minimal federal oversight of these sweatshop operations must have been aware of the working conditions in these factories. After all, they had been hired to work toward the preservation of the status quo or to loosen federal regulations even further, if possible. These lobbyists were gravely complicit in the wrongdoing because they made it that much easier for the Saipan apparel operators to harm workers' welfare interests. They aided and abetted the apparel industry's immoral and criminal activities. Even if we were to give these lobbyists the benefit of the doubt, they too would be, at best, in immediate material cooperation with the wrongdoing given the importance of keeping government oversight at bay. At worst, they were in formal cooperation given what they knew and what they did (neutralizing the law's safeguards).

Finally, local and federal government officials who turned a blind eye to these factories' working conditions were also gravely complicit on two counts. In the first place, they failed to discharge their duties as officials. Second, they failed to prevent harm by their act of omission or indifference. This included US House and Senate members and their staff who ignored these well-publicized and well-documented abuses and failed to close loopholes in the law. They were even more blameworthy if their indifference or failure to prevent harm stemmed from a quid pro quo, such as campaign contributions. Accountability in this case is made even more serious given their public duty to prevent such harms.

Higher-order moral culpability

In an earlier section under "explanatory query," we examined second- and higher-order causality. In this section, let us complete that assessment by examining the blameworthiness of such higher-order causes (attributive query). In particular, let us evaluate the moral culpability of the following:

- bankers, bondholders, and investors of the culpable retail chains and brand owners;
- shoppers who bought other items (not Saipan apparel) from the morally culpable retail chains and brand-name companies; and
- workers and suppliers of the culpable retail chains and brand owners.

These market participants were not part of the Saipan sweatshops' immediate circular flow sustaining their operations. Instead, these economic agents constituted the immediate circular flow of the retail chains and brand owners that, in turn, were major determinants of the sweatshops' economic viability. Thus, these economic agents could be aptly called second-order causes. Their causal contributions to these sweatshops' wrongdoing, if any, were indirect and were mediated through the retail chains and brand owners.

These higher-order effects are worth examining because of the transitive nature of both causation and moral responsibility. Thus, if A causes B which in turn causes C, we can say that A has causally contributed to C's occurrence. In some cases, moral responsibility can also exhibit such transitivity. For example, parents are morally responsible for their teenagers' misdeeds. Or a principal is morally culpable and liable for its agent's misconduct. In our current case, we want to examine whether or not and to what extent investors, bankers, workers, shoppers, and suppliers of retail chains/brand owners were morally responsible for the wrongdoing of the latter's Saipan subcontractors. After all, by supporting the retail chains and brand owners, these investors and shoppers also indirectly sustained the Saipan sweatshops, one step removed. They were part of the chain of causation, upstream.

Clearly, the indirect support to the Saipan abuses was merely the unintended consequence of these retail chains' investors, suppliers, and shoppers' pursuit of their respective business interests. As a result, double-effect reasoning is an important framework with which to evaluate this issue. We have to weigh the proportion of the good sought relative to the ensuing harms.

Let us, for this discussion, assume that the only wrongdoing was the exploitation of workers in Saipan by apparel subcontractors and that retail chains and brand owners were not engaged in any separate wrongdoing themselves. For ease of exposition, let us pick one retail chain, say Kmart. To what extent were Kmart suppliers and shoppers[61] morally culpable for the wrongdoing of Kmart's subcontractor sweatshop Z?

It is reasonable to note that the causal contribution and culpability of Kmart's suppliers and shoppers to the wrongdoing in sweatshop Z were dependent on (1) the gravity of the harms in sweatshop Z, (2) the proportion of sweatshop Z's output absorbed by Kmart, and (3) the proportion of

---

[61] These were Kmart shoppers buying non-Saipan apparel. They supported Kmart through their patronage, and as a result, also indirectly supported sweatshop Z.

Kmart's sales revenues coming from sweatshop Z. We can make the following claims on the transitive features of causation and moral responsibility:

- At best, Kmart's suppliers and shoppers' causal contribution to and moral responsibility for sweatshop Z's wrongdoing were merely derivative from Kmart's causal contribution to and moral responsibility for sweatshop Z's wrongdoing. In other words, their causal contribution and moral responsibility cannot exceed Kmart's causation and culpability.[62]
- The graver the harm in sweatshop Z, the greater was the moral culpability of Kmart, and the greater was the potential derivative moral culpability of its suppliers and patrons.
- The greater the proportion of sweatshop Z's output absorbed by Kmart, the greater was Kmart's causal contribution to and moral responsibility for the wrongdoing in sweatshop Z, and the greater, too, was the potential derivative causality and culpability of Kmart's investors and patrons.[63]
- The derivative causal contribution and moral culpability of Kmart's suppliers and patrons were directly proportional to their respective functional importance or contribution to sustaining Kmart's operations and profitability. These were also dependent on their capacity to act otherwise.

Given these claims, we can apply double-effect reasoning in weighing the moral responsibility of the aforesaid market participants. On the one hand, let us examine some of the good that emerges as investors, bankers, workers, shoppers, and suppliers supported Kmart's operations:

- lower prices and a wider variety of products for the general public,
- employment generation,
- higher returns and diversification for investors, and
- business opportunities and a distribution network for manufacturers and suppliers.

On the other hand, the harm that ensued was the indirect support accorded to sweatshop Z, Kmart's Saipan apparel subcontractor.[64] How did this harm compare with the preceding list of benefits from Kmart's operations? Using double-effect reasoning in cases of indirect harms, we will tend to have the direct, positive benefits outweigh the ill effects because of the derivative, transitive, and distant nature of these indirect harms. There is greater immediacy and urgency to direct benefits vis-à-vis indirect harms. Moreover, there is a half-life to causation and culpability in the face of

---

[62] Recall the derivative nature of complicity and the diminution of causality and responsibility with intervening events (direct causation principle).

[63] Recall the transitivity of causality and culpability.

[64] Readers are reminded that we are assuming that this is the only wrongdoing for our particular case. In actual practice, we have to weigh all the wrongdoing of both Kmart and its subcontractors.

intervening moral agents (direct causation principle). Between Kmart's suppliers and patrons, on the one hand, and the ensuing indirect harm of worker abuse in Saipan, on the other hand, were two intervening moral agents, namely Kmart management and the Saipan sweatshop owners. Furthermore, recall the metaphors of the cone of causation or the spiral of responsibility. These metaphors accurately capture one critical feature of indirect harms – the circle of people involved widens as we move farther away from the ultimate harm. The number of the second-order causes is much larger than the first-order causes (the cone of causation). Causal contribution and culpability diminish as we move further out in the spiral of responsibility (extended dispersion principle).

Given that we are comparing direct, immediate positive benefits with indirect and attenuated harms, it is much more likely that positive benefits will outweigh the indirect harms in such cases of higher-order causes. The more indirect and the farther removed market participants are from the problematic harm, the more diminished are their causal contribution to and moral culpability for such wrongdoing. Of course, the toxicity of the harm is an important determinant in the half-life of causation and moral culpability as we move farther away from the principal harm in space or time. For example, the Holocaust was so heinous that it still haunts Germany today, more than half a century after the events.

The preceding use of double-effect reasoning is only one of many requisite considerations we have to weigh. The next step is to evaluate whether or not Kmart's suppliers and patrons had alternative venues for pursuing the same positive benefits without incurring the associated indirect harms. Investors, for example, had alternative investment instruments that produced comparable benefits. The same might be said of shoppers, bankers, and suppliers. Did they have alternative shops or clients without these collateral harms downstream? If they did and if these alternatives had no comparable or significant collateral harms, then there was a moral obligation to pursue these alternatives and avoid supporting sweatshop Z altogether, even if only indirectly. Using the available alternatives was a far superior course of action to take. This is part of the due care obligation of the third condition of the principle of double effect. Moreover, appropriating the fruits of evil unnecessarily, whether directly or indirectly, adversely affects the agent's virtue and character.[65] The opposite is also true. The effort and the sacrifice that one undertakes in avoiding such indirect, remote harm build virtue and character.

---

[65] Kaveny (2000).

The case of suppliers is completely different from that of investors or shoppers. Because of Kmart's importance and size in the retail industry, suppliers could not have readily given up their relationship with Kmart merely on account of their indirect support of sweatshop Z. This was particularly true for suppliers who were heavily dependent on Kmart for a good part of their revenues. In these cases, we could repeat the same exercise we did for the local Saipan suppliers and the hard choice they had to face.

In considering the availability of viable alternatives, we are, in effect, weighing the moral agents' resources and their capacity to act otherwise. As in the preceding sections, it is very likely that less-endowed and socio-historically disadvantaged moral agents will not have a robust set of alternatives. For example, the poor may have had little choice but to shop at Kmart to stretch their meager earnings. They may have had to work at Kmart for lack of other employment opportunities. The same may be true for Kmart suppliers. In other words, moral responsibility for indirect harms can only be determined in the specific context faced by the moral agent. Thus, it is the moral agent who is best positioned to make such determination in the internal forum.

Socially responsible investing
As part of higher-order causality and moral culpability, we have to address the problems associated with socially responsible investing (SRI). Given the interlocking nature of business enterprises, especially in our era of globalization, and given the unavoidable adverse externalities that stem from economic life, companies will always produce harmful unintended ripple effects. There will always be winners and losers by the nature of market operations. Remember that price changes are a de facto redistribution of burdens and benefits across affected parties. And most economic decisions will in one way or another ultimately lead to such price changes. Thus, socially responsible investors face the dilemma that there are very few investment instruments, if any, that are completely free of unintended harms, whether direct or indirect.

Given these conditions, how should we go about investing? Keeping our funds in the bank is not harmless either since banks themselves generate their own share of direct and indirect harms. Keeping cash under the mattress also has its ill effects. Besides being impractical, it is not morally right to do so because of the societal opportunity cost of such conduct. These savings could have been put to good use by small- and medium-sized businesses that need to borrow funds from the banking system. Hoarding such funds raises the cost of capital for everyone.

It would seem, therefore, that the best that could be done is to minimize, but not completely eliminate, the harms that we will be indirectly supporting through our investments. Thus, a variety of socially responsible investment funds screen and exclude particularly problematic industries from their portfolios. The industries most commonly excluded are alcohol, tobacco, defense, gambling, pornography, and those with poor environmental and human rights records. Unfortunately, this is not a simple exercise in practice. The corporate world is bound by a complicated web of interconnected ownership and formal or informal alliances. In other words, even companies that seem harmless on the surface are, in fact, directly or indirectly associated with problem industries.[66] SRI fund managers have dealt with these complications by employing subjective standards in screening out companies that are "significantly" or "primarily" engaged in these excluded products or services. Others use quantitative measures in permitting such business transactions up to a certain threshold, generally a maximum of 5 or 10 percent of the revenues.[67] Even these latter seemingly more objective approaches are still unsatisfactory. In particular, why 5 or 10 percent? Why not less, or more? Furthermore, what are the ethical grounds for setting the thresholds where we put them?

At the very least, three factors must be considered in weighing whether or not one should invest in a particular firm with its collateral harms. First, we have to consider the nature of the harms: their toxicity, their scope, whether or not they are avertible, and the firm's causal contribution and functional role in facilitating or sustaining such ills. Second, we have to evaluate the firms' capacity to avoid or to attenuate such direct or indirect harms. Third, if such damage is unavoidable, we must weigh it relative to the benefits produced using double-effect reasoning. We have to consider the remoteness of the injury, the causal contribution, and the gravity of the wrongdoing.

SUMMARY AND CONCLUSIONS

As readers can tell from the length of this chapter, the issue of benefitting from and enabling wrongdoing is a complex matter. Consider the three requisite tasks. First, we have to establish what constitutes economic wrongdoing (object of accountability). This depends on the moral standards we

---

[66] For example, Altria (formerly known as Philip Morris, a major global tobacco producer) once owned Kraft Foods, which in turn held Nabisco and many other billion-dollar food brands.

[67] Sparkes (2002, 27–28, 89–115).

use. Moreover, it is complicated by the difficulty of isolating harms from benefits. Most economic activities produce a mix of both.

Second, the discipline of economics is important in establishing the factual grounds of complicity (basis for accountability). Economics helps us understand the causal role of the different parties involved. Third, we have to identify the limits of complicity (subject of accountability). This last issue requires context and can only be satisfactorily addressed on an individual basis given the importance of considering the gravity of the harm, the economic agents' distance from the harm, and their capacity to act otherwise. We have to make choices on how far back or forward we go in the attribution of individual responsibility for market harms.

Of these three tasks, the most difficult ones are those of establishing the object and the subject of accountability. For the object of accountability, the contribution of Christian ethics is its moral thinking on what constitutes economic misconduct to begin with. For the subject of accountability, it offers the principles of double effect and legitimate material cooperation. Choosing the larger moral backdrop to use is important because it defines the standards employed in evaluating the morality of certain economic activities. This is where disagreements will be fiercest because people differ in their respective visions of the good. Christian ethics will most likely have a much broader range of activities that would be considered morally problematic compared with secular standards.

Occasioning harm (such as the leaving of doors unlocked that leads to a burglary) is properly called a cause (but not the cause) of the harm.[68] One lesson we can draw from this study's examination of the dynamics of economic complicity is the need for ordinary, average economic agents (e.g., consumers, suppliers, etc.) to be conscious of their impact on market processes and outcomes both as individuals and as a group. They may unwittingly sustain deplorable activities. Their economic choices become an occasion for others' wrongdoing. Thus, consumers have an obligation to inform themselves of the conditions under which the goods and services they enjoy are supplied. Legally, they are not considered indirect employers. However, from a moral point of view, especially from Christian ethics, they are indirect employers with attendant obligations to these workers. Indeed, markets can turn us into unwitting "enablers" of wrongdoers.

---

[68] Hart and Honoré (1985).

CHAPTER 6

Hard complicity II: Precipitating gratuitous accumulative harms

Some accumulative harms are unavoidable, while others are unnecessary and avertible. For example, most people require more health care as they grow older. Consequently, we expect to see a general rise in the cost of medicine and health services in an aging population, *ceteris paribus*. This rise in the price of health care affects even the younger and healthier members of the community. This is an example of an unavoidable accumulative effect. We will examine this kind of market outcome in chapters 7 and 8 under "soft complicity." In contrast, the spending binge of many US residents who live beyond their means through credit card debt or home-equity loans causes a much faster rise in global interest rates than should otherwise be the case. Businesses and first-time home buyers are thus forced to pay more for their loans. This is an example of a gratuitous harm. This chapter is about complicity in this latter kind of harm.

OBJECT OF ACCOUNTABILITY (COMPLICITY IN WHAT?)

Nature of externalities

To appreciate the last three types of complicity we examine in this study, it is important to understand the nature of externalities. Our economic decisions are never purely private because they have spillover effects on the rest of the community. There are two types that are relevant for our study: technical and pecuniary externalities. Common to both kinds of externalities are the following characteristics:

- they are the incidental by-products of our economic choices;
- they inflict losses on unsuspecting third parties, even as they endow others with windfall gains;
- their consequent social costs are not reflected in the market prices that guide people in their economic decisions; and

- left unattended, they turn into a redistribution of resources from those who are adversely affected to those who benefit from such ripple effects.

For as long as we are not paying the cost of dealing with these externalities (technical or pecuniary), we have no incentive to change our economic choices. Moreover, the market itself will not correct these spillover effects. Extra-market interventions are needed to rectify such unintended consequences.

Pecuniary externalities

Pecuniary externalities are important for our study because they often create occasions for economic complicity. For our purposes, we can distinguish two kinds of pecuniary externalities – those that are unavoidable and those that are unwarranted. The first is the most common type. Economic transactions ultimately lead to price changes. For instance, globalization has lifted hundreds of millions of Chinese and Indians from living below $1 per day.[1] As a result, they have increased their demand for food, which in turn has led to a rise in global food prices. The same is true regarding their increased consumption of oil and many other basic commodities like iron ore, copper, and cement. These are all examples of unavoidable pecuniary externalities – price and quantity changes in the marketplace as a consequence of economic transactions to satisfy basic needs.

The second type of pecuniary externalities is what I would call the gratuitous kind. These are the harmful unintended ripple effects in the marketplace caused by greed or by overindulgence. There are different variants of such disexternalities: consumption, investment, and production. It is best to explain these through examples.

Gratuitous pecuniary externalities

Consumption disexternalities
US energy use is an example of a consumption disexternality. The nation constitutes only 5 percent of the global population but accounts for 23 percent of its energy usage. One of every ten barrels of crude oil extracted globally ends up in US gasoline tanks.[2] Lax gas mileage standards, lower

---

[1] World Bank (2005).
[2] Data are taken from http://worldpopulationbalance.org/population_energy (last accessed June 21, 2009) and from Gold and Campoy (2009) respectively.

fossil fuel taxes, waste, and inefficiencies in the USA have driven up global energy prices, to the benefit of energy-exporting nations, but to the great detriment of oil-importing poor nations. Inordinate US energy use is an example of a consumption disexternality that has precipitated a much faster rise in oil and food[3] prices than would have otherwise been the case. Obviously, the overindulgent part of such consumption is unnecessary. It is not associated with satisfying vital needs for human survival and growth, especially when viewed in relation to many poor nations that are "crowded out" of energy and food markets. Besides having to pay much higher prices for fuel and food, poor nations have had to divert what little foreign exchange they have from other vital imports. In contrast, the increase in food and commodity prices due to a growing Chinese and Indian middle class emerging from poverty is, for the most part, an instance of unavoidable pecuniary externalities because these are driven by the imperative to satisfy basic needs.

To give one an idea of what is at stake, consider the following. As part of its program for greater energy independence at the height of the rise in oil prices, the USA pushed for greater ethanol use and inadvertently caused a corresponding rise in the price of corn and other food crops. The price of tortillas, a staple in the Mexican diet, jumped by 40 percent in just three months soon after the ethanol initiative.[4] This price jump is significant because a disproportionate part of the poor's household budget goes to expenditures on food.

In theory, an increase in food prices should benefit food growers in poor developing nations, even as net food consumers suffer. However, many World Bank studies find that in the case of Africa, recent food price increases have not led to positive gains. In fact, an additional thirty million have become poor in what is already a continent in poverty.[5] A study that examined data from a sampling of nine low-income countries from Latin America, Africa, and Asia reached the same conclusion. Despite their large agricultural sectors, poor nations will not reap positive gains from an increase in food prices. In fact, a rise in food prices will result in a 4.5 percent increase in poverty rates. If this sampling of nine low-income countries is truly representative of poor nations worldwide, this 4.5 percent increase in poverty rates translates to an additional 105 million people driven to live below $1 a day.[6]

---

[3] Food prices are also affected because of the use of plant crops for ethanol production. Moreover, fertilizer production depends heavily on petroleum as does farm equipment.
[4] Malkin (2007).   [5] World Bank (2008).   [6] Ivanic and Martin (2008).

Commentators, academics, and lawmakers have long warned that the excessive US appetite for oil and its consumption binge are not sustainable. Not only do these cause an imbalance in global capital markets (the USA siphoning huge sums for its borrowing) and not only do they lead to an improper use of capital (US consumption crowding out poor nations from such funds), but they also deplete non-renewable resources that eventually show up as higher commodity prices for poor developing nations. The same can be said of many other developed nations. The moral responsibilities of developed nations become even more significant in light of their premier role in the global economy, their obligations to poor nations, and their extensive financial, human, and material resources relative to the countries they adversely affect. The capacity to act otherwise is an important determinant of culpability for gratuitous harms.

In sum, we define these consumption disexternalities as the adverse unintended consequences of overindulgence by some. Such behavior is morally blameworthy on account of the damage it spawns, in addition to the reflexive harm to the offending moral agents themselves. Those who persist in such conduct can be said to be complicit in precipitating the resulting collective harms.

Investment disexternalities

Investment disexternalities are also best explained in terms of examples. Untold millions in Asia suffered in the aftermath of the 1997–1998 Asian financial crisis. Portfolio investments[7] that had flowed readily into the region during the heady days leading up to the crisis suddenly ran for the exits en masse. Private capital inflows to the region were nearly $50 billion in 1994, and doubled to more than $100 billion in 1996. This was completely reversed during the crisis. There was a net outflow of nearly $100 billion from the region in 1998 alone, the equivalent of 5 percent of the region's GDP. What started out as a currency crisis in Thailand turned into a full-fledged regional financial crisis and an economic downturn. A painful lesson learned from this entire episode is the unreliability of portfolio investments. These are extremely fickle and can set off or at least aggravate economic crises. Many even refer to them as "hot money." Not surprisingly, empirical data show that there have been minimal gains, if at all, for developing countries from capital market liberalization. If anything, such liberalization has, in fact, hurt the long-term growth of poor countries

---

[7] These are investments in stocks, bonds, and other financial instruments.

because of the resulting macroeconomic volatility.[8] To give one an idea of the prevalence of speculation in global financial markets, note that the daily turnover in the market for foreign currencies as of April 2007 is $3.2 trillion – five times the amount of trade and capital flows.[9]

The yen-carry trade is an even more recent example of just how harmful speculative capital flows can be. Japan's $15 trillion in personal savings make it a cheap source of capital. In the yen-carry trade, arbitrageurs borrow in yen at low interest rates and then invest these funds all over the world in non-yen denominated instruments that pay much higher interest rates (usually currency options and derivatives trading). Estimates of the volume of such arbitrage on the eve of the 2008 banking crisis ranged from a few hundred billion dollars to over half a trillion dollars. After the global financial market plunged into turmoil, the interest rate differential between Japan and the rest of the world narrowed as central banks cut interest rates to fight the downturn. There was also a flight out of risky investments. Thus, just as the crisis was worsening in the fall of 2008, these arbitrageurs were unwinding their yen-carry trade, leading to a huge demand for yen to settle yen-denominated debts. The result was a massive strengthening of the Japanese yen against the euro (34 percent in one month) and the US dollar (10 percent in one week).[10] This wreaked havoc on the Japanese stock markets and ruined Japanese export markets at a time when its economy was already suffering deep distress.[11]

Financial speculation inflicted much damage in the lives of ordinary people and workers on Main Street. In the wake of the subprime fiasco, credit froze and caused a domino effect of insolvency or illiquidity among business enterprises, large and small. Industry could not secure vital loans because the banking system itself had been engaged in massive speculative investments that had suddenly gone sour. Tens of millions joined the ranks of the unemployed.[12]

Commodity investors (e.g., hedge funds, investment banks) are believed to have been partly responsible for the surge in oil prices in 2007–2008, which doubled in a span of only a year from $69 a barrel to nearly $150.[13]

---

[8] Prasad et al. (2003). Data are from King (2001, 439) and Kim (2007).
[9] Data are from Bank of International Settlements (2007, Graph B.1, p. 5).   [10] Fackler (2008).
[11] A strong yen means higher prices for Japanese products in global markets.
[12] Unemployment in member states of the Organization for Economic Co-operation and Development (OECD) alone will have risen by 25.5 million by 2010 since the start of the 2008 global financial meltdown (Cox 2009, 13).
[13] Dugan and MacDonald (2009). In the week ending June 30, 2009, it is estimated that non-commercial traders (non-end users) accounted for as much as a fifth of major oil and gas trading (Andrews 2009). These are believed to be predominantly speculators. See also Kroft (2009).

Anticipating a continued rise in oil prices, speculators were buying massive amounts of oil in global markets, not for their own use, but as a form of investment. Such oil supplies were kept in storage and then sold later at a profit when prices had risen high enough to provide profits. Thus, end users with legitimate needs had to pay much higher prices than actual market conditions warranted. What is even worse is that by unduly raising market demand through their buying binge and hoarding, these speculators were, in effect, making their anticipated rise in oil prices self-fulfilling. All this is not even to mention the instability they precipitate because of greater volatility and uncertainty in the marketplace.

Or take the case of the 2005–2008 housing bubble. Speculative buyers were picking up huge swaths of the housing market as investment vehicles in the belief that real estate prices would keep rising. The consequent increase in housing prices meant that first-time home buyers were being "crowded out" by these speculators and forced to pay much higher prices than ought to have been the case.

Thus far, we have only dealt with examples at a generalized macro-economic level. The near-collapse of Morgan Stanley is a vivid anecdotal reminder of the potency of speculative investments. Two days after the bankruptcy of Lehman Brothers, Morgan Stanley itself was on the verge of failure caused by the bearish bets[14] taken by speculative investors against the firm's stock.[15] Rumors were flying that Deutsche Bank had withdrawn a $25 billion credit line for Morgan Stanley. The rumor turned out to be unfounded, but the damage had already been done. Word was out on the street that Morgan Stanley was in trouble. The price for credit default swaps (insurance to guard against Morgan Stanley defaulting on its debts) quickly rose. A year's protection for $10 million worth of Morgan Stanley debt, priced at $221,000 just a week earlier, jumped to $750,000 at 7 a.m. of that fateful day and was up to as much as $2 million before noon (a tenfold increase). Credit default swaps on Morgan Stanley debt were bought by investors holding their debt, but they were also purchased by speculators who were out to make profits by betting against the firm, thereby worsening its market outlook even further. In addition, investors were short-selling[16]

---

[14] "Bears" are investors who, anticipating a drop in overall market conditions, sell their securities today and lock in their profits. They will get back into the market when prices have reached near bottom and buy cheap.

[15] I take the following brief account from Pulliam et al. (2008).

[16] Short-selling means that investors anticipate a drop in the price of the targeted security. In anticipation of this decline, they borrow and sell the security today with a promise to return the security at some future time when it could be bought at a much cheaper price.

Morgan Stanley's stocks, betting that it would drop. This became a self-fulfilling bet with the bank's stock falling by as much as 24 percent by the end of the day.

The steep drop in Morgan Stanley's stock price and the increased cost of insurance for its debt only added credence to the rumors. Spooked investors took their funds out of Morgan Stanley, thereby aggravating the bank's already precarious balance sheet. Hedge funds were actively involved in short-selling the firm, withdrawing their funds from Morgan Stanley, and bidding up the price of insuring its debt (credit default swaps). What was shocking about this incident was that Morgan Stanley's fellow investment banks were among those actively involved in betting against it: Merrill Lynch, Citigroup, Deutsche Bank, and UBS, among others. One would have thought that these investment firms would have been empathetic when it came to speculative attacks on a fellow financial institution. Soon after, the Securities and Exchange Commission (SEC) temporarily banned the short sale of financial stocks.

These are but a few examples of investment disexternalities – the harmful unintended consequences in financial markets inflicted on innocent third parties on account of the irresponsibility and avarice of some. Both the Great Depression of 1929 and the 2008 global economic meltdown underscore the central role of the financial system in facilitating market activity. However, these crises also illustrate how perfectly legal market activities can be easily abused by some, to the detriment of everybody else. Such abuse is an object of accountability. Those who engage in these indefensible investment activities are complicit in precipitating the ensuing harms.

Production disexternalities
Production decisions can also inflict needless unintended harms on innocent third parties. For example, industrial farms have been heavily using antibiotics in animal feed to promote faster growth. Preliminary estimates for the late 1990s indicate that in the USA, eight times more antimicrobials were used for non-therapeutic purposes for hogs, cattle, and poultry (24.6 million lb) than for humans (3 million lb). Moreover, many of the antibiotics used in animal feed, such as penicillin and tetracycline, are vital for human medical therapies. It is estimated that agriculture accounts for as much as 84 percent of all antimicrobial use in the United States.[17] Scientists and medical researchers are concerned that such casual use and abuse of antimicrobials are contributing to the increasing resistance of bacteria to

---

[17] Even the lowest estimates put agricultural use at 40 percent.

many of the key antibiotics used for human therapy. In fact, the EU has banned the non-therapeutic agricultural use of antimicrobials critical for humans.[18]

The use of antimicrobials has clearly improved US industrial farms' output and profits, but at the expense of jeopardizing the effectiveness of the world's antimicrobials through overuse. Their production methods are inflicting a cost on everyone else in the world, including EU residents who have been restrained in the non-therapeutic agricultural use of these human medicines. US industrial farms can be said to be complicit in giving rise to increasingly drug-resistant bacteria.

Other examples of production disexternalities include services with well-known long-term ill effects, such as tanning salons with their heightened risk of skin cancer. Obesity has become epidemic in the USA, and this has been partly due to poor or uninformed eating habits. The heavy promotion and marketing of fast foods and sugary drinks have causally contributed to this harm. Trans fats have been documented to be extremely damaging to the human cardiovascular system. The high sodium content in processed foods aggravates many health problems. While there have been legislative attempts to curtail the use of these ingredients, only the voluntary cooperation and restraint of food manufacturers can make an effective dent in the health problems they spawn. And, of course, even segments of the population that are careful and disciplined in their eating habits are not spared the ensuing harms. They, too, will end up paying higher medical bills because of the increased demand for health care in a population that is sicker than ought to have been the case. Thus, these manufacturers are complicit in both the direct and the accumulative harms they cause on account of their products or their production methods.[19] It is the same story for alcohol and tobacco products. Similarly, retailers of cigarettes, liquor, foods heavily laden with trans fat, pornography, guns, violent video games, and many other harmful products are morally culpable for the disexternalities of the products they carry on their shelves.

Consider a more recent example that can be aptly described as a genuine "race to the bottom": the competitive paring back of lending standards

[18] Of the 24.6 million lb used in the USA, 13.5 million lb were prohibited for non-therapeutic agricultural use in the EU. All data are taken from Mellon et al. (2001). See also Gilchrist et al. (2007). On July 13, 2009, the Obama administration announced that it would seek a ban on the non-therapeutic use of antibiotics in animals (Harris 2009).
[19] See Kenner (2009) and Weber (2009) for other examples of production externalities in the food industry.

throughout the financial system, from the subprime mortgage lenders, all the way up to the insurance firms issuing credit default swaps. Some lenders and brokers were criminal in their activities by deceiving borrowers or by encouraging unqualified home buyers to falsify their income or assets on loan application forms. This is an outright wrongdoing and not the kind of economic misconduct we are dealing with in this chapter. Instead, we are interested in the many other instances in which no fraud was involved. Borrowers who would have otherwise been ineligible were nonetheless provided mortgages by simply adjusting the standards downwards (e.g., lower cutoff for credit scores). Banks, rating agencies, and other related institutions followed suit in scaling back their own standards and due diligence in an effort to make their share of the profits from a booming housing market. Banks that had been traditionally conservative made huge bets on risky housing-related instruments. Rating agencies were keen to rate securitized mortgages even without the necessary empirical data; they did not want to miss out on the fees to be obtained.[20] The "race to the bottom" was on. This herd behavior in not wanting to miss the gravy boat led to a collective lowering of standards that ended with the 2008 financial implosion. Taken individually, many of these separate instances of loosened institutional standards were imprudent and foolish, but not illegal. Collectively, they inflicted grievous damage on the global financial system, the cost of which was ultimately borne by the millions on Main Street who lost their jobs. All these are examples of production disexternalities – reckless business practices that collectively leave a wake of harmful unintended consequences.

And, of course, we have the case of air pollution. Coal-burning utility companies scrimp on investing in cleaner burning processes and equipment. Local consumers enjoy cheaper electricity, but at the expense of communities downwind who have to endure acid rain and foul air. The same is true with garbage incinerators. China's growing affluence has also meant growing mounds of garbage that have to be buried, burned, or processed. Some communities have opted to build trash incinerators that minimize air pollutants, but at enormous capital cost. Other communities, however, build trash incinerators at only one-tenth the cost, but at the expense of dioxin, mercury, and other pollutants spewing into the air and making their way to the USA and across the world.[21] These and many other ecology-related issues, such as overfishing, global warming, or deforestation,

---

[20] Lowenstein (2008).   [21] Bradsher (2009).

are other common examples of production disexternalities we take for granted and accept.

Common features

We can distill common features in the preceding examples of consumption, investment, and production disexternalities and list some of the formal characteristics of a gratuitous accumulative harm. First, the preceding cases inflict unintended harms on innocent third parties. They are all properly called disexternalities. Second, the harm they cause entails raising the risk of injury to others, as individuals (personal risk) or as an entire community (systemic risk). Wasteful gas usage increases the likelihood of higher oil prices for all. Commodity and housing speculation "crowds out" legitimate end users. Production disexternalities raise the risks of drug-resistant bacteria, severe cardiovascular diseases, and systemic financial insolvency. Indeed, individual economic behavior can causally increase the likelihood of injury for others downstream.

Third, unlike the conduct of Saipan sweatshops that was clearly unlawful, the preceding examples of disexternalities are not illegal. Their harmful consequences to the community are well known, but these activities are tolerated and even widely practiced. They are deemed imprudent or reckless, but permissible. A liberal, secular society would find it paternalistic to legislate against many of these economic activities. It would be too intrusive and entail a significant curtailment of the individual's sphere of autonomy or of national sovereignty.[22] This is where we see once again the role and importance of the moral standards employed by the evaluator. As we well know, what is legal is not necessarily moral. For example, communitarians and virtue theorists will find the aforesaid economic conduct to be morally deficient and definitely not what one would expect from people of high character. While not illegal, such activities are nevertheless morally blameworthy given their foreseen harmful effects on others and on the character and virtue of the perpetrators themselves. Libertarians, on the other hand, will find such behavior to be morally acceptable.

A final common feature of these disexternalities is the indirect and roundabout nature of their harms. Their damaging ripple effects become apparent only after a certain critical mass of like actions has been reached or after a time lag. They have the same cumulative feature described in chapter 2: benign at the individual level, but harmful when taken in conjunction with many others acting similarly.

---

[22] This issue is beyond the topic of our study. See Feinberg (1986; 1988) for an in-depth discussion.

Difference from complicity as enabling evildoing
Before proceeding any further, let us examine how this chapter's misdeed (needlessly precipitating accumulative harms) is different from the misconduct in chapter 5 (enabling wrongdoing). In the preceding chapter's case of the Saipan apparel sweatshops, the principal wrongdoer was a clearly identifiable economic agent: the sweatshop operator. In our current case of inexcusable accumulative harms, the principal wrongdoer is a collective – the group of irresponsible consumers, producers, and investors who jointly bring about these adverse externalities. The principal wrongdoing is a collective ill.

In the preceding chapter's case of the Saipan apparel sweatshops, the complicit economic agents were the market participants who sustained the sweatshops' viability as a business. In our current case of unnecessary accumulative harms, the complicit economic agents are each member of the aforesaid collective – each of the irresponsible consumers, producers, and investors who contributed to the cumulative harm. We are, in effect, talking of a "contributory group fault: collective and distributive"[23] with the following characteristics:

1 the collective harm is the result of the contributory fault of each member of the group held responsible;
2 the collective responsibility (and liability) is merely the sum of the individuals' responsibility;[24]
3 the group liability is distributive, that is, we can divide it among the members of the collective held responsible;[25]
4 we are dealing with fault liability rather than vicarious liability because of each member's contributory fault; and
5 those who occasion such accumulative harms are the subject of accountability (i.e., those who are complicit).

Difference from soft complicity

Let us examine the differences between this chapter's complicity and the "soft" complicity of chapters 7 and 8. Both have a similar cumulative dynamic wherein seemingly insignificant acts at the individual level become

---

[23] Feinberg (1970, 243). This is the third of Feinberg's four different types of collective responsibility.
[24] This could also be a synergy in which the whole is greater than the sum of its individual parts.
[25] Since we are dealing with the marketplace, dividing group liability will not be as difficult as in non-economic cases (e.g., bioethics or politics) because we can measure the monetary benefits reaped by each member of the collective at fault. We can impute liabilities according to the benefits reaped.

potent or harmful when combined with other similar actions. As we have seen in chapter 2, the acts comprising accumulative harms are benign in themselves at the individual level and become injurious only when taken together with others' similar acts. In contrast, the constituent acts we examine in this chapter are "generally-but-not-necessarily-harmful activities" to begin with.[26] However, we cannot make the general claim that these individual acts taken by themselves are intrinsically evil per se.

For accumulative harms, the moral character of an individual act cannot be fully gauged until after we have examined it within its larger collective context. For example, buying houses as an investment is not morally wrong when viewed as an isolated act. However, if we evaluate that same act within the larger context of a housing bubble gone awry, then such speculative investing is a morally deficient act given the harm it inflicts on first-time home buyers. Recall Isaacs's (2006) point that murder takes on a different moral quality in the context of genocide. We have to examine a moral act in the context of the whole to which it contributes and of which it is a part.

Or consider another example. Person B is a breadwinner, who has to drive back and forth between three jobs to make ends meet. The air pollution caused by B's driving can be absorbed and processed by the environment. However, a million other people like B with similar driving requirements will collectively cause serious damage to the ecology. Furthermore, these million drivers taken as a group will cause price and quantity changes in the global market for gasoline and oil, thereby causing corresponding changes in the welfare of others around the world. Both the ensuing pollution and the rise in gas prices are examples of accumulative harms we deal with in chapters 7 and 8.

In contrast, person A's choice of a gas-guzzling Hummer is a harmful act at the individual level because the incremental air pollution from the fuel inefficiency of the Hummer is unnecessary. The same can be said for its causal contribution in raising global oil prices. Driving to and from work is not what makes A's driving problematic. Rather, it is the choice of a wasteful Hummer that is morally objectionable. There are alternative vehicles A could have chosen that would have been less damaging to the environment and not improvident in the use of scarce fossil fuels. In this

---

[26] Feinberg (1984, 193–198 at 194). Feinberg calls these aggregative harms to distinguish them from the harmless individual acts that constitute accumulative harms. Lichtenberg (2008) does not make such a distinction in her use of "aggregative" harms. For simplicity, we will not make such a distinction in this study.

case, A and other similar Hummer owners cause an indefensible gratuitous harm, the subject of this chapter.

Recall, too, our earlier distinction between the consumption of the Indian and Chinese middle class emerging from poverty (non-gratuitous accumulative impact) and the inordinate part of US energy consumption (unwarranted accumulative impact). This distinction is critical in the ascription of moral culpability. Cooperators in a gratuitous harm are in an avertible material cooperation. This is always blameworthy material cooperation. In contrast, chapters 7 and 8 deal with an invertible, permissible material cooperation that may or may not entail a liability depending on the circumstances of each cooperator. For example, the legitimate rise in the consumption of the Chinese and Indian middle classes does not excuse them from doing their share in mitigating global warming. Their additional consumption may not be blameworthy, but they nonetheless still have liabilities from such increased consumption and production.

BASIS FOR ACCOUNTABILITY (WHY CULPABLE?)

What are the grounds for holding accountable those who cause such disexternalities? To begin with, the philosophical and theological insights presented in chapter 3 on the problem of overdetermination apply just as well to our current chapter. After all, the moral wrong from these gratuitous accumulative harms stems not only from the individual acts, but also from their joint impact. Readers will recall that the key question in cases of overdetermination is "Will my act be one of a set of acts that will *together* harm other people?"[27] This question applies just as well to our current case.

In addition to the arguments of chapter 3, the principle of double effect can also be used to establish grounds for accountability. In particular, the severity of the resulting accumulative harm outweighs whatever individual or collective benefits are produced. In the sections that follow, we examine additional theological and philosophical arguments on why precipitating gratuitous accumulative harms is blameworthy conduct.

Establishing causal contribution

Consumption, production, and investment disexternalities are instances of foreseen but unintended harm to others. They are clearly foreseen or should be foreseeable to the ordinary person (objective foreseeability) because

---

[27] Parfit (1984, 86, emphasis original).

the causal link between excessive consumption, problematic production methods, and speculative investments, on the one hand, and their subsequent ill effects in the marketplace, on the other hand, is well established.

There is no need to trace the precise path of how consumer A's wasteful gas consumption eventually leads to an increase in global oil prices, or how a specific speculative investment in the housing market raises prices beyond the reach of first-time home buyers. To establish culpability in both cases, it is sufficient to know that empirical evidence clearly shows a causal link between such economic behavior and the subsequent rise in prices. It is the simple law of supply and demand. Recall from chapter 4 that mere empirical causal link is accepted in jurisprudence as causation.

Christian ethics

Consumption disexternalities
The just-use obligation and its superfluous income criterion are important theological warrants for why inflicting needless disexternalities is morally blameworthy conduct. Both insights come from *Rerum Novarum*[28] and are also evident in the social teachings and pronouncements of the various Christian traditions we examined in chapter 2. The goods of the earth are meant for the benefit of all. We find the spirit of this moral duty as far back as the Old Testament. For example, note the gleaning law[29] and the mandate to lend food or money to fellow Hebrews without any interest.[30]

People are obligated to use what is superfluous in their income or wealth for the benefit of the poor. Following Thomas Aquinas, Leo XIII defines superfluity as that which is not needed to maintain the family's social standing within the community. However, John XXIII changes this to a standard that better conforms to Sacred Scripture. He defines superfluity in terms of the relative unmet needs of one's neighbor.[31]

Clearly, overindulgent consumption is unacceptable conduct under the just-use obligation and the superfluous income criterion. In the first place, there is no justification for inordinate consumption in a finite earth in which resources are scarce and vast numbers of people are destitute. These resources should have been used instead to alleviate the plight of those

---

[28] Leo XIII (1891).
[29] Landowners were not supposed to be so thorough in harvesting their field. They had to leave some on the vine or on the ground for the benefit of the aliens, widows, orphans, the poor, and the landless (Dt 24:19–21; Lev 19:9–10; 23:22; Ruth 2).
[30] Ex 22: 25; Dt 23:19–20; Lev 25: 36–37.
[31] Leo XIII (1891, no. 36) and Vatican II (1965, II, chap. 3, fn 10) respectively.

with unmet needs. This is clearly superfluous income or wealth. Unlike neoclassical economic theory, which does not differentiate needs from mere wants, Christian ethics makes this distinction. Needs always trump wants. Moreover, there are varying degrees of needs that ought to be satisfied in a hierarchy of urgency and importance for human survival, development, and flourishing. Such distinction between needs and wants is not a modern phenomenon. The prophetic literature and the Patristic Fathers forcefully condemn avaricious consumption and wealth accumulation, especially in light of others' destitution.[32]

Of course, in addition to the harm that people inflict on others because of their overindulgent consumption, there is also the harm that they bring down upon themselves because of the reflexive dynamic of the human act.[33] Thus, besides the just-use obligation and the superfluous income criterion, the virtue of temperance is another relevant moral consideration that applies to consumption disexternalities.[34]

Production disexternalities

There is much in Christian ethics on production disexternalities. In particular, Christian churches have increasingly been alarmed over the ecological impact of our economic conduct and have joined the worldwide clamor for systemic change in the global economy toward one that respects the environment. This literature is vast and requires a separate volume of its own.[35] It is sufficient for our purposes to note that in Christian theology and ethics, all creation is deemed to be a gift from God. Humans have merely been entrusted the care of the earth, from which God also provides for our needs. The wanton destruction of the ecosystem as a collateral effect of economic growth and development is a sin. It goes against the divine order of creation and reflects human cupidity and avarice. There is enough in God's creation to supply the needs of all including future generations. But such divine providence is marred by the overindulgence and the abusive use of the goods of the earth by many.

John Chrysostom (1971, nos. 110–111) is emphatic that an appropriate trade or occupation is one that is not injurious to the soul and produces goods or services that are truly useful. Thus, he has an antipathy toward those trades that pander to the wealthy's demand for luxuries. John Wesley

---

[32] See, for example, Amos 6:1–7 and Phan (1984).   [33] Cessario (1991); Porter (1995).

[34] See Clawson (2009) for a recent theological reflection on the disexternalities of even our most ordinary daily consumption choices (e.g., clothing, food, garbage).

[35] See, for example, the official statements and declarations of the various Christian churches on economic justice (chapter 3).

(1872, nos. 4–6) encourages his congregants to be diligent in putting their God-given talents and material resources to full use in gaining as much as they can. However, he is quick to add certain conditions. Among these are two that he underscores passionately.

> Neither may we gain by hurting our neighbour *in his body*. Therefore we may not sell anything which tends to impair health. Such is, eminently, all that liquid fire, commonly called drams or spirituous liquors … This is dear-bought gain. And so is whatever is procured by hurting our neighbour *in his soul*; by ministering, suppose, either directly or indirectly, to his unchastity, or intemperance, which certainly none can do, who has any fear of God, or any real desire of pleasing Him. It nearly concerns all those to consider this, who have anything to do with taverns, victualling-houses, opera-houses, play-houses, or any other places of public, fashionable diversion. If these profit the souls of men, you are clear; your employment is good, and your gain innocent; but if they are either sinful in themselves, or natural inlets to sin of various kinds, then, it is to be feared, you have a sad account to make. (Wesley 1872, #4, #6, emphasis original)

In other words, producers are morally responsible for the injurious impact of their goods or services on the physical and spiritual well-being of the community. As we have seen in chapter 2, as a rule of thumb, any economic activity that harms or impedes integral human development is blameworthy.

Investment disexternalities

The Christian tradition's earlier antipathy toward merchants and the charging of interest for loans provides important insights on adverse investment externalities. The Patristic Fathers did not look kindly on merchants who were deemed to be greedy and driven by a desire to accumulate profits as ends in themselves. Trading was viewed as a danger to the soul because it encouraged avarice. Furthermore, it was commonly believed that the only way of succeeding in this profession was to lie, be deceitful, and engage in fraud. Moreover, the merchant class was seen as manipulative in creating artificial shortages and monopolies in an effort to raise prices and reap more gains. Such practices were particularly contemptible when they involved vital necessities such as staples. Indeed, a wide range of Patristic writers, such as Tertullian, Ambrose of Milan, Basil the Great, Gregory of Nazianzus, and Augustine, disapproved of merchants and their profession.

To be sure, there were occasional acknowledgments of the value of the services provided by merchants as they shipped in goods from afar and made them available to the local community. However, for the most part, the presumption was that trade was harmful for one's virtue and salvation.

Ill-gotten profits were the norm and honest profits the exception. Merchants were viewed as an unsavory, sinful lot, lumped together with usurers.[36] It was this antipathy toward merchants that the Scholastics inherited.

Over time, this aversion toward merchants changed, especially during the late Scholastic era. Roover (1974) describes this process well. People began to appreciate the value of their services. Bernardino of Siena, for example, acknowledged three types of merchants who promoted the commonweal through their activities: the importers-exporters, who took the effort, trouble, and risk of shipping in goods from abroad that would not have been available locally otherwise; the storekeepers whose services kept the entire community reliably supplied with the necessary daily provisions at great convenience for the people; and manufacturers who bought raw materials and turned them into finished goods. Thus, by the fifteenth century, theologians had changed their position regarding the morality of trading. Nonetheless, the Scholastic Doctors were adamant in still condemning monopolists, pawn-brokers, those who engaged in price discrimination and price-gouging, those who took advantage of the ignorance or need of their buyers, those who engaged in deceptive merchandising, and those who manipulated prices. For the purposes of our current case, it is interesting to note that included among these are the "speculators, who tried to make profits by rigging the market without serving any useful purpose."[37]

In sum, despite the changing scholastic attitude from antipathy to eventual acceptance of merchants, there is an unequivocal and unchanging condemnation of two types of conduct: exploiting others and seeking profits as ends in themselves. Scholastic writers like Thomas Aquinas and Bernardino of Siena acknowledged that gains from trade were not immoral per se. In light of the real service merchants provided the rest of the community, gains from trading were merely a recompense for their efforts and for the risks they undertook. Moreover, such gains were sought to support their families or to supply the needs of the poor. But profits driven by avarice and a "love of money" and profits that were pursued as ends in themselves were roundly and uniformly censured in the strongest possible terms.[38]

The Christian tradition's teaching on lending money takes a similar path, although one that has taken much longer to traverse. The tradition's prohibition against the charging of interest dates back to Old Testament loan legislation. It is important to understand the socioeconomic context of

[36] Baldwin (1959, 12–16).   [37] Roover (1974, 340).   [38] Roover (1974).

these Hebrew loans. Unlike the modern era, most of the loans in the Ancient Near East were hardship loans of grain or money (to buy grain) rather than commercial loans for trading. An agrarian economy, by its nature, is extremely volatile and uncertain given the vagaries of weather. Moreover, it was a pre-modern economy of precarious subsistence; there was little surplus. Consequently, a bad harvest could be catastrophic for a family, and borrowing from neighbors was the only recourse for survival. Under such conditions, it is understandable why lending at no interest to a fellow Hebrew was a moral obligation for the Chosen People.[39]

Until the Industrial Revolution, the world economy was predominantly agrarian. Thus, the proscription against charging interest for loans carried over through the New Testament, Patristic, and Scholastic eras. Besides, the presumption was that money was sterile, it provided no service, and, consequently, it did not need recompense for its use. It was usurious to gain a return (interest) without having provided any service and, more importantly, it was usurious to profit from the need of others. Thus, the restrictions against charging interest remained in place until the medieval era.

All this, of course, began to change with the emergence of a more commercial economy. Over time, commercial loans became more important, and people began to realize that money was not sterile. It provided vital services in a commercial society where capital was important for trading. Hence, just like the antipathy toward merchants that turned into gradual acceptance, there was a shift in attitudes and teachings regarding the charging of interest within the Christian tradition. The teachings on usury changed in line with the requirements of an emerging commercial and, subsequently, modern industrialized economy.[40] Again, just like the censure of unscrupulous merchants, what was condemned as usurious in the charging of interest for loans was the desire for profit as an end in itself, and not as a recompense for a genuine service provided in exchange.

Both the just-use obligation and the superfluous income criterion are also relevant for the issue of harmful speculative investments. Capitalists are required to use their private properties to create gainful and humane employment for the propertyless. This is the duty to use capital judiciously to create productive activities that are truly beneficial for society. Thus, harmful speculative investments have three strikes against them: they are

---

[39] Gnuse (1985, 19); Lang (1985, 99); Maloney (1974); Neufeld (1953–1954, 194, 197); de Vaux (1965, 170–173).
[40] See Noonan (1957) for an exposition on this development.

not necessary, they injure others' welfare interests, and they do not create productive economic activities for the community.

Philosophical warrants

Locke

The spirit of the Lockean proviso can be used to argue against inflicting these disexternalities. Locke (1690 [1960], II, 27) justifies private property ownership on the basis of people's effort, work, and initiative in making the goods of the earth more productive than would have otherwise been the case. However, there are limits to such appropriation – only to the extent that they can productively put them to good use. Furthermore, "enough and as good" resources will have to be left so that others might have the same opportunity to appropriate property for themselves.[41] Locke's proviso clearly acknowledges scarcity and its zero-sum dynamic as a constraint. Not only is there need to share and to allocate, but, more importantly, there is an implicit acknowledgment of the need to prioritize claims based on some hierarchy of needs.

While Locke refers only to original acquisition, the spirit of his proviso is nevertheless relevant for our assessment of unnecessary externalities. No doubt, the economic agents responsible for such disexternalities are interested primarily in furthering their own interests through mutually beneficial market exchanges. Thus, speculators advance their portfolio strategy even as their counterparties also benefit and advance their own plans. However, these commercial transactions between consenting parties are not merely private in nature because they have adverse ripple effects on the rest of the community. These injurious by-products are not trivial and retard vital welfare interests, as in the turmoil in global financial markets with dire ramifications for ordinary people. Unwarranted externalities fall under the *spirit of the Lockean proviso*[42] because they do not leave "enough and as good" resources for third parties whose interests are damaged by such unintended consequences.

Rawls

Rawls's (1971) well-known lexical rules in his theory of justice as fairness are helpful for our case. In the first rule, Rawls argues that the presumption is to

---

[41] See also Tomasi (1998) and Waldron (1979).
[42] It is the spirit of the Lockean proviso and not the Lockean proviso itself that is useful for our study because the Lockean proviso pertains to original acquisition.

grant maximum individual liberties consistent with everyone else enjoying the same set of freedoms. This rule recognizes the inevitable clash of claims arising from everyone exercising the same guaranteed liberties. Limiting the scope of such liberties may be necessary to head off such conflicts. In the second rule, Rawls argues that inequalities are to be permitted only to the extent that they advance the interests of the most disadvantaged and that the offices that precipitate such inequalities are open to all.

Rawls's lexical rules can be used to argue against needless externalities. In the first place, the consumption, production, and investment excesses of some people severely restrict the life prospects of many others. In our earlier examples, oil-importing poor nations expend valuable foreign exchange earnings to pay for more expensive fuel and food. They end up curtailing their budgets elsewhere, most likely their social services. It is a de facto curtailment of their freedom of action. The second lexical rule is also incompatible with these unwarranted externalities. Far from benefitting from such unintended consequences, it is in fact the poor and the disadvantaged who are most severely affected by such behavior as we have seen in the empirical examples cited earlier.

Mill and Feinberg

We can also argue against unnecessary externalities using Mill's (1859 [1974], 68) liberty-limiting principle of harm to others and Feinberg's (1984, 31–64) three conditions on what constitutes a liberty-limiting harm (chapter 2). Clearly, gratuitous consumption, production, and investment disexternalities are instances of harm to others. In the first place, these externalities set back people's welfare interests. The rise in oil and food prices is, in effect, a sharp cut in the real incomes of non-oil-exporting populations. Or recall how the excesses in the housing and financial markets ultimately inflicted suffering in the lives of untold millions in 2008–2009.

The ripple effects of these indefensible disexternalities impinge on some of the most basic rights that include the right to life and liberty. The liberties of adversely affected people are greatly diminished because of the hurdles added to what is already a formidable set of obstacles. It is the poor and the disadvantaged, after all, who bear the brunt of the ill effects of these disexternalities. They are severely affected because they are the ones with resources too meager to be able to ride out the ensuing shocks or disequilibria precipitated by these consumption and investment disexternalities. The well-off and the middle class are also affected by these price and quantity changes, but they have more and better personal and material resources with which to weather this volatility. In fact, in many cases, they turn these shocks into opportunities allowing them to come out even stronger and ahead of everybody else.

Insights from legal philosophy

Occasioning harm

The legal philosophy and case law on torts also provide many useful insights into why inflicting unwarranted consumption, production, and investment disexternalities is a blameworthy act. Recall that occasioning harm is among the four types of causation (chapter 4). A house-sitter who leaves the door unlocked is aptly described as having causally contributed to the house's subsequent burglary. The inattentive house-sitter can be said to have occasioned the harm through her negligence. This type of causation is about creating the key conditions for the later occurrence of the harm.[43]

Furthermore, in some cases, those who provided the occasion for subsequent harms are also responsible for the ulterior harms even if there had been intervening causes. Take the case of person D who drives recklessly and negligently knocks person G on the side of the highway with a fractured skull. A second driver E runs over G lying on the highway and breaks G's leg. Person D will be culpable for both injuries. And if G were to receive derelict care in the hospital emergency room, D would also be liable for the injury from the doctor's neglect. On the other hand, person E and the slovenly doctor will not be liable for the earlier injuries of G, only those they had inflicted because of their own carelessness.[44] Despite the intervening events, D is held responsible for occasioning the subsequent harms to G that D should and could have foreseen with her reckless driving.

Or take the case of someone who negligently leaves petrol on a barge that is subsequently hit by lightning, thereby setting the entire barge aflame. Under normal conditions, the lightning strike would have been considered *force majeure* or an "act of God" and no one would have been held liable for the damage. However, in this case, someone had carelessly left petrol on the barge and occasioned the subsequent burning of the barge after it was struck by lightning.[45] The person is liable for the ulterior harm (the burning of the barge) because he was at fault in leaving the petrol on the barge, and such faulty action became the occasion for the subsequent harm.

---

[43] See also Hart and Honoré (1985, xlv). For a critique of this view, see Stapleton (1988, 117–122).
[44] This example is taken from Prosser (1971, 320–321). See also Stapleton (1988, 117).
[45] Hart and Honoré (1985, xlv).

This notion of occasioning harm and its attendant responsibility for ulterior harms can be usefully adapted for our current case. Clearly, those who engage in consumption, production, and investment excesses occasion the subsequent adverse ripple effects of such conduct, especially since the resulting ill effects are foreseeable. For example, despite the many intervening events and moral agents in the chain of causation, we can still claim that oil speculators and Hummer drivers are nonetheless partly morally responsible for those who are grievously affected by the needless rise in oil and food prices.

Risk creation

The treatment of undue risk creation as tortious conduct is another insight from law that can be usefully adapted for economic complicity.[46] People living in community impose a certain amount of risk on each other. Consider the following example of mutual risk creation. Every driver who goes on the road creates some risk of causing an accident that injures life or property. Such risks are considered reciprocal and acceptable if every person makes the effort to drive carefully and takes the necessary precautions to ensure that the vehicle is roadworthy. However, such risks are considered beyond the bounds of what is reasonable if a person drives recklessly or drives while intoxicated (or while text-messaging). Such behavior greatly raises the risk of injury to self or to others and is consequently deemed to be tortious conduct.[47] Undue risk creation is an important consideration in the ascription of liability in tort law.

[T]he risk theory of responsibility ... casts on individuals liability for introducing or increasing social risks ... The theory is causal in the sense that the tortfeasor is regarded as intervening in the existing state of society and making a difference to the existing level of danger. This he may do in one of two ways: (1) by increasing or decreasing a risk to the injured party of the same general character as already exists; (2) by exposing the injured party to a risk of a different type from that to which he would otherwise be exposed. (Honoré 1973, no. 81, [7–81], 50)[48]

---

[46] "Creating a dangerous situation" is deemed to be tortious conduct (Beale 1920; Edgerton 1924a, 212). In the traditional corrective-justice view of tort law, "creating an ultrahazardous situation" is tortious (Wright 1988, nos. 1004–1005). Similarly, among legal economists (Law and Economics proponents), the creation of an increased risk of harm constitutes causation of harm. For an extended discussion of risk-exposure in torts, see Wright (1988, nos. 1067–1072). Among the tests of proximate cause is the "harm within the risk test" which takes its name from the concern over risk creation by the tortfeasor (Moore 2002, 153).

[47] This example is from Coleman (1988, 193–194) who describes this as the principle of the non-reciprocity of risk in which injured parties can recover damages from the defendant for the latter's non-reciprocal risk-taking.

[48] See also Honoré (1973, [7–93 to 7–97], 58–60) on risk theory.

Undue risk creation is exactly what gratuitous consumption, production, and investment disexternalities are all about. Market transactions ultimately lead to price changes, which in turn redistribute burdens and benefits within the community. There is a similar reciprocity of risks or mutual risk creation among market participants. We can easily see this in the area of investments. One's decision to invest in New York instead of Frankfurt is eventually reflected in a greater demand for US dollars and a stronger US dollar exchange rate vis-à-vis the euro. The opposite is true for those who prefer to invest in euro-denominated instruments. In either scenario, these decisions create or mitigate risks for other market participants in terms of fluctuating stock prices or currency exchange rates. There is a reciprocity of risks people impose on one another under normal market operations. People will not find fault for such incremental risks because it is part and parcel of normal global capital market operations.

However, there is an undefined and often blurred threshold beyond which certain behaviors are well outside the bounds of normal risk creation. For example, we now know, with the benefit of hindsight, that banks, institutional investors, and hedge funds were creating unusually large risks for the entire global financial system by being so highly leveraged, by trading heavily in credit-default swaps, and by lending so freely without doing their due diligence. Or take the case of subprime mortgage lenders, brokers, and borrowers. In an effort to generate sales volume, subprime loans were dispensed liberally, even with every indication and foreknowledge that many borrowers did not have the income to cover future payments. Most of the economic actors along the entire chain of causation in the subprime mortgage fiasco were not only taking great risks for themselves but also inflicting even greater risks on others, such as the hapless investors in these subprime mortgages after they had been securitized. The 2008–2009 global financial meltdown is an illustration of blameworthy risk creation. The same is true for the many other financial and banking crises and bubbles in economic history. Behind these crises and bubbles are the undue risks generated by irresponsible economic agents eager for windfall profits.

The notion of undue risk creation can also be adapted for consumption disexternalities. One's purchase of a Camry ultimately redounds to the benefit of Toyota workers, at the expense of their GM, Ford, or Chrysler counterparts. In the same way, GM's, Ford's, or Chrysler's decision to outsource parts production to Mexico means that Mexican workers ultimately gain, at the expense of US labor. These are examples of risk creation we accept as the norm in the marketplace. However, past a certain point, such risks are beyond the bounds of normal market operations. Again, with the benefit of hindsight, we find an example of this in the consumption binge of US consumers. Their savings rate plunged to a record low at the turn of the millennium, thereby leading to enormous dollar balances held outside the USA, particularly in China and Japan. Such a consumption binge has made it more likely that the US dollar will eventually lose its value relative to other currencies. This creates greater risks than would have otherwise been the case for countries whose reserves are held largely in US dollar-denominated instruments. This is not even to mention the greater likelihood of a much diminished purchasing power for future generations of US residents. In other words, inordinate US consumption has created higher than normal risks for holders of US currency and financial instruments.

We can also describe our earlier examples of excessive US oil consumption in terms of undue risk creation. Poor nations have had to endure greater risks of debt default, depleted foreign exchange reserves, macroeconomic shocks, and contractionary recessions on account of more expensive oil and greater volatility in global energy and food prices.

It is understandable why those who create non-reciprocal risks or undue risks are held liable for the damages that result from such risk creation. Reckless drivers are held culpable for the damages that result from their risky behavior. Even if they do not cause an accident, these drivers are nevertheless still held liable because of the greater likelihood of injury or death that they inflict on other drivers on the road.[49] This is intuitively appealing to our commonsensical notions of justice and fairness. Moreover, it deters similar behavior in the future. We adopt this insight and claim that those who spawn uncalled-for consumption, production, and investment disexternalities are blameworthy for creating greater than normal risks for everybody else.

Foreseeability

Foreseeability is another useful insight from tort jurisprudence that can be adapted to good effect for our study. In tort law, defendants are even more liable for the ensuing damages if they should have foreseen the harm or if reasonable, prudent people would have foreseen the harm and taken the necessary precautions to avert the injury.[50] Some would even go so far as to

---

[49] Thus, these drivers can still be fined for reckless driving even if they do not cause accidents.
[50] Carpenter (1932b, 398).

define a proximate cause as a "tortious cause that results in a *reasonably foreseeable* injury to a *reasonably foreseeable* plaintiff."[51]

Foreseeability magnifies culpability. Negligence is amplified in the face of foreseeability; undue risk creation becomes even more blameworthy in the face of foreseeability. Moreover, occasioning harm that could or should have been foreseen by the defendant or by the reasonable-person standard makes the defendant's causal contribution to the ensuing injury that much more culpable.

Foreseeability is also at the heart of the question of overdetermination. Recall the grounds for why the individual is held liable for accumulative harms in tort law:

> [T]he standard of reasonable conduct applicable to each defendant is governed by the surrounding circumstances, *including the activities of the other defendants ... The single act itself becomes wrongful because of what others are doing.* (Prosser, 1971, 322–323, emphasis added)

This is precisely the same argument we have seen earlier from Parfit (1984) in his exposition on the five mistakes of moral mathematics. Individual market participants cannot excuse themselves from responsibility for accumulative harms because they can or should have foreseen the joint consequences of their actions with others' like acts. Parfit arrives at the same conclusion as Prosser:

> When ... (2) each of the members of some group could act in a certain way, and (3) they would cause other people to suffer if *enough* of them act in this way ... and (5) each of them both knows these facts and believes that enough of them will act in this way, then (6) each would be acting wrongly if he acts in this way. (Parfit 1984, 81, original emphasis)[52]

Common to the aforesaid views and applications of foreseeability is the notion that predictable harms make their causes that much more responsible for the ensuing damages. These are avertible to begin with. For example, in tort law, responsibility for ulterior harms becomes much easier

---

[51] Fumerton and Kress (2001, 87, emphasis added). Among the tests for proximate/legal cause is the "probable consequence" test. Carpenter (1932a, 238–241) examines the arguments for and against this test.

[52] Carpenter (1932a, 241) makes a similar argument but not in the context of other agents acting similarly. In examining the probable consequence test, he notes that the defendant is liable if any reasonable person would have foreseen how his earlier actions will cooperate with a subsequent superseding or intervening cause to produce the ulterior harm. The defendant should have foreseen the causal contribution of his action in facilitating the occurrence of the harm even if there were intervening causes. Carpenter's observation is similar to Prosser's and Parfit's point if we treat the other agents acting similarly as intervening causes.

to establish if the ulterior harm is foreseeable. Thus, by leaving an open street manhole improperly blocked off or, worse, unattended, workers are responsible for the death or injuries of pedestrians who fall into the manhole. Such deaths or injuries are clearly foreseeable by any reasonable standard, thereby strengthening the case for holding those who had opened the manhole responsible for the subsequent damages.

These commonsensical insights apply just as well to economic complicity. Economic literature has ample empirical evidence establishing the causal link between excessive consumption, inappropriate production methods, and irresponsible investments, on the one hand, and their dire ripple effects, on the other hand. This strengthens the case even further against those responsible for these foreseeable gratuitous disexternalities.

SUBJECT OF ACCOUNTABILITY (WHO IS COMPLICIT?)

A final issue we have to examine is that of who is morally responsible in cases of gratuitous accumulative harms. This is a question that is both easy and difficult to answer. It is easy to answer because anyone who knowingly contributes to these disexternalities, despite having the means to act otherwise, is culpable. One key factor in establishing culpability is the moral agent's awareness of the ensuing harms. The capacity to foresee harm is critical. As a criterion, we could use either subjective or objective foreseeability. Subjective foreseeability refers to what moral agents should have foreseen at the time of their action given what resources and information were available. Objective foreseeability pertains to what a reasonable person would have foreseen in such circumstances.[53] In either case, foreseeability is a straightforward criterion in determining who is morally culpable.

However, the question of who is complicit also poses difficulties because of its many gray areas. We have so far dealt only with the more egregious examples of irresponsible conduct in consumption, investment, and production. In practice, there are many ambiguities that require much further conceptual and empirical work.

Consumption disexternalities

In the case of consumption disexternalities, note the most obvious problems: What are the criteria to be used in determining what constitutes

---

[53] See Fumerton and Kress (2001, 88, fn 17) for an illustration of a difference in the use of such subjective and objective standards in imputing tort liability.

excessive consumption? Who determines these standards? What are their grounds? Are we going to aim for a strict, absolute mathematical equality in the way we divide the earth's resources? How do we deal with intergenerational distribution? Many would most likely accept the claim that there are legitimate inequalities in the manner by which the scarce goods of the earth ought to be divided. Having said this, however, most people would nonetheless also say that there is a limit to how far such legitimate inequalities ought to be permitted given their deleterious consequences for social cohesion. And yet the obvious difficulty is in identifying where we draw the limits to such inequalities and then justifying why we set them at such levels. This will be a problem of interpretation: is the glass half empty or half full?

Production disexternalities

In the case of production disexternalities, what do we do in cases in which the problem lies not with the product itself but with the abuse of the product? For example, sugary drinks and alcoholic beverages consumed in moderation may not adversely affect health. Bottled water has its uses, particularly in developing nations or in areas with inadequate water filtration systems. Plastic shopping bags often have their proper uses. Guns for recreational purposes, such as hunting or personal protection, can arguably be justified. In all these cases, are manufacturers morally liable for the irresponsibility of consumers? How far should they go in ensuring that their products are not misused? Where do we draw the limits of their moral obligations? At what point do manufacturers and service providers cross the line into the realm of disexternalities? We deal with this question at the end of this section.

A second issue is the question of whether or not the failure to prevent harm constitutes an instance of production disexternality by omission. (Recall from chapter 4 that failure by omission is an admissible cause.) This is not an idle academic question nor is it overstretching the issue. Wal-Mart's turn to "green products and methods" has had wide ripple effects in the rest of the economy. Since it is the nation's foremost distribution outlet, it has considerable clout in pushing its suppliers toward "greener" products and production processes. What it carries on its shelves also shapes consumer choices. For example, Wal-Mart's sale of energy-efficient compact fluorescent light bulbs is said to have saved the equivalent of three coal-fired power plants to date.[54] These are three power plants that

[54] Barbaro (2008).

can be foregone. And this is just for one "green" item the company decided to push.

In fact, keenly aware that it has substantial sway in what becomes industry standard, Wal-Mart is creating a universal rating system that assesses products on their environmental and social impact. Similar to the nutrition labels currently required by law, this proposed sustainability index will grade products according to their environmental damage, climate impact, air and water pollution, carbon footprint, and usage of water, energy, and pesticide. Its goal is to have such a label for every item it markets.[55] Manufacturers will find the data-collection requirements of such an index to be onerous and intrusive, but they have no choice since Wal-Mart is the world's biggest retailer. This is an example of a positive production externality.

Indeed, key distribution outlets have heavy moral obligations, just like manufacturers, when it comes to averting aggregative harms. Not surprisingly, MacDonald's has taken steps to include healthier meals in its menu. The problem, of course, is in identifying where to draw the limits of this moral obligation for manufacturers, retailers, and everybody else in the production-distribution chain. Was Wal-Mart's push for energy-efficient light bulbs and a sustainability product label supererogatory or a duty on its part? What are the obligations, if any, of mom-and-pop stores?

To repeat, are instances of failure to prevent harm in the case of the major economic actors a case of production disexternality by omission? I believe they are, based on a standard we have been using all along: moral culpability is a function of one's capacity to act. We contribute to the common good according to our means (scholastic general justice and principle of socialization).

Investment externalities

The question of what constitutes irresponsible investment behavior is even more difficult and even more contentious. Let us take the case of short-selling. When the global financial system teetered on the brink of collapse, the US government imposed restrictions on the short-selling of more than eight hundred stocks, mostly from the financial sector, because of concerns that such short-sales were in fact touching off a self-fulfilling decline in stock prices.[56] Short-selling was putting even financially sound banks

---

[55] Rosenbloom (2009).
[56] Hulbert (2008). In the summer of 2009, the Securities and Exchange Commission (SEC) eventually issued new rules on short-selling that require greater transparency (Scannell 2009).

and institutions at greater risk of collapse. Some were even calling for a permanent restriction on short-selling, while others were quick to point out the importance of short-selling for market efficiency. Ironically, when there was need to relieve banks of their toxic assets so they could start lending again to the general public, the US government turned to these "vulture" investors for their expertise in pricing assets, for their funds, and for their entrepreneurial initiative and risk-taking.[57] Indeed, short-selling, hedging, and other forms of arbitrage can produce positive benefits for the economy.[58]

Or take the case of credit default swaps. These were abused by many as a vehicle for quick returns and pure speculation. They nearly brought down the global financial system in 2008.[59] And yet, it is important to remember that credit default swaps perform a useful service in diffusing risk, thereby laying the groundwork for an even more efficient market. The same can be said of foreign-exchange arbitrage, financial derivatives, commodities trading, and hedging instruments. In many cases, it is difficult to separate predatory from beneficial uses of investment instruments.

Dealing with mixed harms and benefits

We are once again faced with a tangled web of unintended harms and benefits inseparable from each other. The principle of double effect will be useful in determining whether or not certain production and investment activities are justified. Double-effect reasoning will have to balance the clashing interests of beneficiaries and the disadvantaged. Three criteria will be helpful in weighing their competing claims, to wit: how vital are the interests at risk, what other private or public interests are dependent on the interests at risk, and what is the inherent moral worth of the interests at risk?[60]

As we have seen above, the problem often lies not with the product or the service itself, but with irresponsible end users. Feinberg (1984, 193–194)

---

[57] Merced and Kouwe (2009).

[58] Besides entrepreneurial risk-taking, there are other positive benefits from speculative trading. It can dampen price volatility. Speculators buy when commodities are plentiful and cheap (thereby preventing a further or deeper drop in prices), and they sell later as prices rise (thereby dampening a much higher rise in prices than would have otherwise been the case). Arbitrageurs are said to perform a real service by moving the market toward greater efficiency. However, separating beneficial from deleterious speculative trading requires much empirical work.

[59] The size of the credit default swap market on the eve of the global financial meltdown (June 2008) was $57 trillion, slightly larger than global GDP, or four times the size of US GDP (*The Economist* 2009).

[60] Feinberg (1984, 202–206).

suggests that a proper policy response to this dilemma is through "selective permissions and prohibitions" as a middle ground between a permissive blanket permission for such activities, on one end of the spectrum, to the "blunt coercion" of a blanket prohibition, on the other end of the spectrum. Losses will be incurred if legitimate uses and actions are prohibited. It is akin to "throwing the baby out with the bath water."

We already have such a middle-ground approach in the case of prescription drugs, the medical use of marijuana, restrictions in the sale and advertising of alcohol and tobacco, and licensing for guns in certain states. In the financial sector, an example is the proposed Tobin tax as an alternative either to outright capital controls or to unrestrained speculative short-term portfolio flows. Under the Tobin tax, short-term capital flows will be taxed to discourage speculation.

SUMMARY AND CONCLUSIONS

A second type of economic complicity is the conduct that may seem innocuous at the individual level but is deleterious when combined with like action from others. Unlike the accumulative harms of chapters 7 and 8, the preceding harms are gratuitous in the sense that they are unnecessary and avertible, if only market participants refrained from consumption, production, and investment excesses that are known to give rise to extremely adverse externalities. These activities are not illegal, but they are nonetheless immoral because of their ulterior harms.

Many of these problematic market behaviors are readily identifiable and, in fact, governments often step in whenever the resulting accumulative harms become extremely damaging. At some point, the presumptive case for individual autonomy is overshadowed by the need to protect people's vital interests. Thus, note the US financial regulatory reform in the wake of the near global financial meltdown in 2008. It is the most radical tightening of rules since the Great Depression. Hedge funds and many derivatives, heretofore not subject to government oversight, will now be monitored. A new consumer financial product protection agency will head off abusive and predatory practices.[61] Even restrictions on short-sales and oil speculation are being considered.[62] A ban has also been proposed on the routine, non-therapeutic use of antibiotics in livestock and poultry.[63]

Nevertheless, there are still many gray areas that legislation alone will not resolve. In particular, many economic activities produce a mix of

---

[61] Smith and Lucchetti (2009).   [62] Andrews (2009).   [63] Harris (2009).

inseparable harms and benefits. Moreover, it is often very difficult to distinguish beneficial from damaging economic transactions. This is particularly true in the case of investment disexternalities. Just as the Industrial Revolution inaugurated an era of mass consumption, globalization has democratized financial markets in the sense that investing in capital markets is no longer reserved only for the wealthy. More households own various financial instruments through 401(k) plans, college education savings plans, and mutual funds. One upside to the 2008–2009 financial fiasco is the teaching moment it provided in opening our eyes to how damaging many investment practices can be. People ought to take an active interest not only in the rates of return they are earning, but also in how these returns are being generated by their fund managers. They ought to take greater responsibility for the harmful unintended consequences of their investments, especially those they entrust with mutual, index, or hedge funds. Thus, besides overindulgent consumption, another area that calls for a more vigilant and active response from the general public is the case of investment disexternalities.

In many of the gray areas we encounter in consumption, production, and investments, we have to resort to the principle of double effect. And because these are highly context dependent and can be dealt with only on a case-by-case basis, we have to rely on people's goodwill and honesty in their evaluation of their own economic choices. At the end of the day, we are back to the internal forum. In these gray areas, the issues of who is complicit in gratuitous harms and to what extent they are culpable will ultimately have to be answered by individual economic agents themselves. Herein lies a challenge for the community, namely, to instill in everyone a genuine concern for the common good. It is also an occasion for individuals to be prophetic witnesses and virtuous in their economic conduct.

CHAPTER 7

Soft complicity I: Leaving severe pecuniary externalities unattended

The market's much-touted ability to allocate scarce resources to their most valued uses is largely due to its price system. By paying attention to price signals, economic actors are alerted to shifts in the economic terrain that require a corresponding redeployment of their resources and endowments. Unfortunately, these constant price changes create gains for some and unintended losses for others. Some of these ripple effects can be so severe as to warrant extra-market ameliorative action from the community. Thus, the third instance of economic complicity is the failure to live up to the moral duty of attending to the more damaging consequences of such price changes.

OBJECT OF ACCOUNTABILITY (COMPLICITY IN WHAT?)

Nature of pecuniary externalities

The market is a remarkable social institution in the manner by which it orchestrates the production and distribution of goods and services in the right quantity and quality, at the right time, in the right place, and with the right inputs. And it accomplishes this by coordinating the economic decisions of billions of economic agents spread over a wide geographic area. All this is possible because of the market's lifeblood – its price system. Market prices convey huge amounts of ever changing information to disparate economic agents in a timely and cost-effective manner. These price signals inform market participants as to when and how they ought to change the disposition of their resources in an optimal manner. Consequently, among the market's strengths are its dynamism, its agility and responsiveness to changing conditions, and its ability to allocate scarce resources to their best uses (allocative efficiency). In fact, the 1989 collapse of the heavily regimented, centralized Soviet-style economies can be attributed largely to their lack of a functioning price system. Not surprisingly, nations increasingly moved toward more market-oriented economies in the last quarter of the twentieth century with the onset of globalization.[1]

The market's price system, however, has a significant downside to it. Besides the aforesaid allocative function in which price is instrumental in putting scarce resources to their most valued uses, price also has a distributive function. After all, these price changes also determine what people receive for selling their goods in the product market (revenues) or their services (wages, salaries) or capital (interest, dividends) in the input markets. Furthermore, these prices also determine people's real purchasing power. The lower the prices, the bigger is the basket of goods and services consumers are able to afford with their incomes.

Thus, the allocative and distributive functions of the price system are two sides of the same coin. Price movements do not merely move the allocation of scarce resources to their best uses, but they also alter the division of incomes. In other words, price changes are a de facto redistribution of burdens and benefits within the community. For example, people's decision to shop at a newly opened Wal-Mart and avail of its wider selection of goods at lower prices means less revenues for local mom-and-pop stores. Obviously, shoppers and Wal-Mart (including its shareholders, workers, and suppliers) gain from such a decision at the expense of smaller neighborhood stores. But this is just the immediate impact. There are both beneficial and harmful ripple effects as well. Because many Wal-Mart goods are imported from abroad, domestic manufacturing workers will ultimately see a deterioration in their wage earnings, if not lose their jobs outright. The negative effect on neighborhood mom-and-pop stores and on domestic manufacturing workers is an example of an adverse pecuniary externality. In contrast, overseas manufacturers supplying Wal-Mart reap positive pecuniary externalities.

According to economic theory, displaced domestic manufacturing workers and small neighborhood stores ought to look for other types of productive activity because their comparative advantage has changed. They are no longer competitive in their line of work and, according to allocative efficiency, they have to move on to another part of the economy. Of course, this is easier said than done because economic theory assumes that there is perfect knowledge, goods and factor inputs are homogeneous, and it is a frictionless economy. These assumptions mean that displaced economic actors instantaneously know where their services are needed, there is no cost to moving from one job to another, and there is no cost to learning a new

[1] Yergin and Stanislaw (1998).

trade or a new skill. These are obviously unrealistic assumptions. In actual practice, looking for information for a new job or business is not straight-forward, not even in the age of the Internet. Moreover, acquisition of a completely different set of skills is often required for displaced market participants, which is not always easy depending on one's age. This is not even to mention the cost of moving one's domicile across the country. Indeed, contrary to economic theory's assumptions, people have to expend enormous amounts of time, effort, and money in identifying and then switching to their new comparative advantage. The transaction and search costs are sizable, and many economic actors are unable to afford them. This is particularly true for the less skilled and less educated, and for those who do not have a financial cushion. Not surprisingly, developed nations are increasingly wary of economic globalization, even those that until recently had been its most vigorous advocates, like the United States where there are now second thoughts on the wisdom of open markets.[2] Unions have been adamantly opposed to offshore outsourcing. National governments, eager to embrace globalization, have had to "bribe" their own citizens with social safety nets and trade adjustment assistance programs to soften the ensuing career adjustments precipitated by freer trade.[3]

From the preceding brief description and examples of adverse spillover effects, we can readily see the need for extra-market assistance for displaced market participants. In the heuristic model of perfect competition, markets are self-healing and can be left on their own to correct their imbalances and disequilibria. In practice, we know that the adjustment toward the much-desired allocative efficiency can be extremely difficult, and governments have to be actively involved in correcting injurious market processes and outcomes. We have ample empirical evidence of this especially in the wake of the 2008–2009 global financial debacle. And we also have the theoretical justification for such an activist government role in Keynesian economics.[4]

Unlike the preceding chapter on gratuitous ills, most harms from pecu-niary externalities are unavoidable. After all, as mentioned earlier, market transactions inevitably lead to price changes, which in turn cause a redis-tribution of burdens and benefits within the community. There will always be people who gain or lose from such price changes by the nature of market operations. Such shifts are the collateral effects of moving toward allocative efficiency.

The economic wrongdoing in this chapter is not in contributing to these unavoidable third-party effects. There is no fault in being party to these

---

[2] Wessell and Davis (2007).   [3] Rodrik (1998).   [4] Keynes (1936).

adverse unintended consequences. Rather, *the wrongdoing is in the failure to live up to the liability of ameliorating the more severe instances of these pecuniary externalities.* This is in line with the third condition of the principle of double effect regarding due care.

The redistribution of burdens and benefits within the community as a result of price changes is uneven and depends on market participants' sociohistorical location, their human capital, and sheer luck. In many cases, the redistribution is regressive: those who have more will have even more, while those who have little or are vulnerable to begin with will end up having even less. The benefits are widely enjoyed by the public, while the costs are borne only by a few, and often by those who are least prepared to do so.[5] Consequently, we have to deal with a wide variety of people within the community, from those who gain enormously, on the one hand, to those who are severely affected, on the other hand. The object of accountability (the wrongdoing) in this chapter is the failure to attenuate the plight of the latter. This is a case of an invertible, permissible material cooperation that entails liability for mitigating the ensuing harms.[6]

BASIS FOR ACCOUNTABILITY (WHY CULPABLE?)

Prices are in a perennial flux and, consequently, we have an unending stream of economic agents gaining or losing welfare. Do those who have been adversely affected have claim rights to recompense for their losses? Is there a moral obligation to alleviate inimical market outcomes? If so, why? To assess these issues, we first limit the scope of our query by examining which deleterious ripple effects ought to be redressed. We then weigh the arguments for or against such a moral obligation.

What constitutes severe adverse pecuniary externalities?

Not all adverse spillover effects merit ameliorative assistance. That would be an impractical goal because it would overwhelm the community's resources. Furthermore, to rectify all the market's adverse unintended consequences

---

[5] See Barrera (2005a, 43–74).

[6] In Feinberg's (1970, 248–251) typology, this is a "contributory group fault: collective but not distributive," his fourth type of collective responsibility. After all, individual action will not be able to correct this harm on its own; only collective action will be able to do so. Moreover, unlike the preceding chapter's gratuitous harms, we cannot divide the collective fault into its individual components. For example, how do we impute individual responsibility for the demise of the US apparel industry as a result of free trade? Hence, this is a non-distributive group fault.

(assuming this were even possible) is to undo completely the economy's move toward its allocative efficiency. The whole point of price changes is to push market participants to reposition their resources in response to changed circumstances, such as technological advances, population growth, or shifting tastes. Consequently, a relatively free market is extremely responsive and dynamic in allocating scarce resources to their most valued uses. This is not to say that it does not have flaws, but compared with a heavily regimented, centralized economy (e.g., Soviet Union), the market has proved itself to be far superior. Twentieth-century history and our contemporary globalization attest to this claim. Thus, to mitigate every inadvertent market outcome is to reverse the work of the price system. To do so would be to cause more harm than good, if it were even possible to begin with.

Only the most injurious cases of pecuniary externalities merit attention. In fact, this is what is already done today, even in the most capitalist nations. We have unemployment insurance, food stamps, trade adjustment assistance programs, etc. that together form a social safety net. The key points of contention, however, are in identifying when assistance is provided, for how long, how much, under what conditions, and by whom. Moreover, what counts as severe? How serious should the third-party effect be before the community provides relief? Or, in the language of Mill and Feinberg from chapter 2, how extreme does the harm to others have to be before we restrict the scope of individual liberties? What is the threshold for invoking the liberty-limiting principle of "harm to others"?

The easy and obvious answer to this is to say that "harm to others" will be measured in terms of the welfare interests that are put at risk. In particular, recall Feinberg's (1984, 202–206) three criteria from the preceding chapter: how vital are the interests at risk, what other private or public interests are dependent on the interests at risk, and what is the inherent moral worth of the interests at risk? Nations and communities will answer these questions differently depending on their value commitments and their economic resources. The EU, for example, is far more communitarian and opts for a social economy compared with the more individualistic and market-oriented approach of the United States. These issues are related to the even larger and more contentious debate on whether or not economic rights exist. Once again, we encounter the importance of the moral standard employed by the evaluator and by the community. We have a wide diversity of positions from libertarians, who oppose the necessary taxes to fund such programs; to communitarians, who wholeheartedly embrace a generous threshold in providing such assistance; to radical egalitarians, who call for near-absolute equality in the distribution of resources.

In the end, it is probably best simply to view this as a continuum from the trivial to the most severe adverse externalities. And then, depending on the question on hand, one can draw the line that identifies cases that deserve intervention or relief. Such a threshold will vary depending on the context (e.g., available resources, population affected, interests at risk).

The following sections examine the philosophical and theological warrants for the duty to mitigate grievous pecuniary externalities. They serve a second function of determining how generously or how strictly to set the threshold of assistance.

The case against a moral obligation to ameliorate severe pecuniary externalities

"To the consenting, no injury is done"

What are the grounds for requiring market participants to rectify deleterious market processes and outcomes? It is best to begin our evaluation by examining the best arguments that can be made for the opposite position – that there is in fact no such moral obligation. Again, we find a useful insight from law: "To the consenting, no injury is done."[7] People cannot seek redress for injuries sustained from activities they pursued out of their own free will. They have no one to blame but themselves. The presumption is that they voluntarily and knowingly assumed the risks.

"To the consenting, no injury is done" is the starting point for any discussion of rectifying damages incurred in the marketplace. In the first place, it would seem that, on the whole, market participation is purely voluntary; no one is forced to consummate transactions in the marketplace. The presumption is that people know what is in their best interest, they are rational, and they will participate in market exchange only if they believe it will improve their pre-trade welfare.

Second, even in those cases when such belief is erroneous and their post-trade welfare actually worsens, these economic agents were fully aware of such contingencies *ex ante*, but nonetheless still pursued the exchange. These risks are well-known and well-established features of the marketplace, and economic agents are cognizant of these as they trade with each other. In fact, borrowing the language of tort jurisprudence, we can say that market

---

[7] *Volenti non fit injuria* (Feinberg 1984, 215): http://legal-dictionary.thefreedictionary.com (date accessed April 18, 2009).

participants impose a "reciprocity of risk" on each other as they engage in mutually beneficial exchanges. Besides, economic agents can always take protective measures against such contingencies.

Adverse pecuniary externalities are merely part of such "reciprocity of risk" in participating in the marketplace. For example, many college graduates choose a career in Wall Street because of its generous bonuses, its glamor, and its six-figure salaries. In exchange for this, they are fully aware that their continued employment is a function of the health of the economy and the public's bullish investment outlook, among other factors. They have no one to blame but themselves nor should they expect any recompense should there be massive layoffs in the financial industry as did happen in the 2008–2009 financial crisis. It is part of the professional hazards of working in an extremely volatile and competitive sector. Moreover, they have had their returns in good times. Furthermore, they should have gone into a more stable and less unpredictable career if they are so risk averse. The same can be said of business entrepreneurs, indeed, of anyone who participates in the marketplace. People who purchase an airline ticket today are fully aware of the risk that they have just overpaid because of the possibility that the same ticket may sell cheaper in the following weeks, or vice versa, in which case they have gained. People are aware that economic life is fraught with chance and contingencies.

In sum, the legal maxim "To the consenting, no injury is done" is descriptive of market participation. Market exchange has no residual obligations. Parties to the exchange owe no further obligations to one another beyond those stipulated by the contract. Any further gains or losses after the consummation of transactions are theirs alone to enjoy or to bear, as the case may be, as part of the risks they knowingly and willingly undertook. Thus, there is no case for mitigating adverse pecuniary externalities.

Contributory negligence

A second argument against the duty to attend to the market's inimical spillover effects is the notion of contributory negligence. As mentioned earlier, people gain or lose from the constant reshuffling of burdens and benefits within the community according to their sociohistorical location, their human capital, or plain luck. The first two factors are partly shaped by people's choices in the earlier rounds of economic activity. And so, families who have been frugal and have saved a substantial nest egg are in a much better position to weather an economic downturn compared with those who saved little and lived high on the hog when the economy was good. People who worked hard, sacrificed, and invested in an education or vocational training have much better prospects than those who did not bother to make such an effort. Those with a better work ethic who have nurtured good social skills stand a better chance of obtaining and keeping well-paying jobs compared with those with poor work habits or atrocious people skills. In other words, adverse pecuniary externalities are not purely exogenous. There is an endogenous element to them because the opportunities we face in the marketplace (or lack thereof) are partly a function of the opportunities that we have created for ourselves. We could call this the problem of endogeneity. Contributory negligence on the part of the victims weakens and perhaps even negates others' duty to redress such malign results.

Having said this, we should also note, however, that there are limits to how much people can create opportunities for themselves. Economic theory and empirical evidence validate the phenomenon of poverty traps whereby people, through no fault of their own, are caught in a vicious cycle of chronic destitution. The case of malnourished children or those who have to work to supplement their family's income instead of going to school comes to mind. Thus, note the cash-assistance programs in many Latin American countries in which poor households are paid to send their children to school or to bring them to health clinics. The cash-assistance component is in part to compensate the family for the loss of the children's income.[8] These are excellent examples of extra-market interventions to break the poverty trap.

Obviously, the difficult part of the issue is the *ex post* determination of whether or not adversely affected people could have done more in their past to prepare themselves for today's economic shocks and disequilibria. The policy dilemma entails coming up with measures that ensure a fair, if not uniform, treatment of all, should there be an assistance program.

The case for attending to grievous pecuniary externalities

Despite the intuitive appeal of the legal maxim "To the consenting, no injury is done," there are limits to its application, and a strong case can nevertheless still be made in favor of a moral obligation to rectify the market's injurious third-party effects. We examine the arguments for such a moral duty in what follows.

Moral duty to prevent harm

We can, at a minimum, claim that the moral obligation to address harmful market outcomes stems from the moral duty to prevent harm if we can do so

---

[8] Rawlings and Rubio (2003).

at little cost or danger to ourselves. In his four-volume work examining the moral limits of criminal law, Feinberg (1984, 126–186) weighs the question of whether or not we can legislate bad Samaritan statutes and penalize people for failing to prevent harms that they could have easily accomplished with minimal effort or risk to themselves. He challenges the claim that the failure to prevent harm is blameworthy only if there is an obligation to do so, and that such duty originates solely in the case of prior agreements or in the case of special relationships. Feinberg (1984, 160–161) notes that in addition to prior agreements or special relationships, the duty to prevent harm also arises whenever (1) there are the ability and a plausible opportunity to do so, and (2) there is a reasonable expectation that people act in such circumstances to prevent these harms from occurring.[9] The failure to prevent harm falls well within Mill's notion of "harm to others" as a legitimate principle that imposes limits on people's freedom of action.

> The presumptive case for bad samaritan statutes rests on the social importance of avoiding, at reasonable cost, serious harms to personal interests, and the plausibility of the moral claim that imperiled individuals have a right to be saved by those who can do so without unreasonable risk, cost, or inconvenience. (Feinberg 1984, 185)

This position is supported by longstanding European legal tradition and practice dating back to the mid-nineteenth century in which people have the legal obligation to perform "easy rescues."[10] Even Anglo-Saxon common law has similar, albeit less stringent, duties. Resolving the debate on whether bad Samaritan statutes are legitimate or not is beyond the scope of this study. It is sufficient for us merely to note that both legal theory and practice call for sanctions for failing to prevent harm. If acts of omission are in fact penalized, then how much easier it is to argue for a moral (rather than a legal) duty to prevent harm?

As mentioned earlier, adverse pecuniary externalities are often severe in setting back the welfare interests of many, especially those who are vulnerable to begin with. Furthermore, redressing serious spillover effects does not usually impose great inconvenience or sacrifice on market participants because the cost of the requisite ameliorative action is spread across a large number of economic actors. Thus, we can claim that there is a moral obligation to rectify detrimental ripple effects, if only on the basis of the moral duty to prevent grave harms at little cost or danger to the obligation

[9] Of course, we are talking only of grave harms. Furthermore, note the importance of public morality in determining what we may expect from one another.
[10] Rudzinski (1966) provides an appendix that excerpts such provisions from sixteen countries' bad Samaritan statutes.

holder. The unspoken presumption here is that there is a special bond that ties people to each other – their common humanity. However, we can make an even stronger case for such a moral obligation beyond the requirements of common human decency. We can justify this duty on the basis of corrective justice and the nature of the market. We examine both in the next section.

Corrective justice

The true social cost of allocative efficiency: underpriced benefits

The formal characteristic of an externality in economics is the inability to incorporate the cost of a good or service's unintended consequences in its price. The classic example of this is pollution as a technical externality. In the USA, the price consumers pay for gasoline does not include the social cost imposed on others, such as global warming and its attendant ill effects on health, meteorological disturbances, and weather-related economic disruptions. Thus, US consumers' private cost of driving is less than the true social cost of burning the fossil fuels they use. Allocative efficiency requires that the gasoline be taxed to the point at which the private cost of using gas is equal to its social cost. Alternatively, people could voluntarily opt to use carbon offset programs. Only by internalizing the social cost will private economic decisions match what is required by allocative efficiency.

Very little attention has been devoted to the other kind of externality – pecuniary externalities. Unlike its technical variant, a pecuniary externality's inadvertent outcomes are mediated entirely in the marketplace itself. Take the case of freer cross-border trade. Global markets provide nations with cheaper imports and better prices for their exports. The gains from international trade include higher real incomes for consumers, better earnings for exporters, a shift toward nations' comparative advantage, and better prospects for technological change because of the specialization brought about by trade. Moreover, even future generations will benefit from such freer trade today because they will inherit a far more efficient and technically superior economy than would have otherwise been the case in the absence of cross-border exchange. Indeed, the gains are enormous, according to economic theory, and, thus, it is not surprising that the positive value of cross-border trade is one of the rare issues on which there is near-consensus among economists. The theoretical overall gains outweigh the costs of freer trade. Among these costs are workers whose jobs are lost to cheaper imports and who would now have to find another line of productive work in the economy.

Note two important observations that underscore the need to redress severe pecuniary externalities. First, the benefits are enjoyed by a broad spectrum of the economy and across generations, while the costs fall on relatively few, such as displaced manufacturing workers or the less skilled. Second, the prices consumers pay for their cheaper imports do not reflect the total societal costs incurred, such as the opportunity costs of unemployment or underemployment for furloughed workers, skills retraining, search costs, and other frictional expenses in shifting people and resources between industries or across regions. Unless public assistance is provided, these costs will be absorbed principally by the people who are dislocated or who have to undertake painful adjustments. They are paying disproportionately more than their share of the communal cost of moving the economy toward allocative efficiency, to the benefit of the winners who "gain" a second time by not having to share in these social costs.[11]

During major economic disruptions, assistance from the public coffers is more forthcoming, as in the case of activist fiscal and monetary policies to stimulate an economy in a downturn. Taxpayers are much more willing to foot the bill for such expenditures, including other social safety nets such as extended unemployment insurance. After all, these taxpayers themselves benefit more from a booming economy than from one mired in a recession.

Unfortunately, such readiness to address inimical market outcomes does not extend much beyond downturns in a regular business cycle or in an obvious emergency such as the 2008–2009 slowdown. Unlike technical externalities, little has been done to correct severe ordinary pecuniary externalities on an ongoing basis. One possible reason for this asymmetric treatment of technical and pecuniary externalities in both economic theory and policy is that technical externalities are impediments to reaching allocative efficiency. In contrast, pecuniary externalities are the means to attain allocative efficiency by providing people the incentives to reallocate factors and resources to their most valued uses.

We have seen recent grassroots initiatives to correct pernicious market processes. The Fair Trade movement is one such example in which consumers voluntarily pay a higher price for coffee or chocolate to ensure a living wage for coffee or cocoa growers who are often at the mercy of the vagaries of market prices or the greed of middlemen. Longstanding examples, albeit at a multilateral level, are the price stabilization programs that even out the earnings of farmers despite market volatility. Extending such

---

[11] Thus, one could view the Kaldor–Hicks compensation scheme in economic theory as a means of ensuring that everyone internalizes and shares in the true cost of allocative efficiency.

concern beyond agricultural commodities to other ordinary goods or services would be a major leap forward in our mutual solicitude for one another's well-being.

In sum, market prices understate the true social cost of moving the economy toward allocative efficiency. This includes the severe pecuniary externalities that are often privately borne by a narrow segment of the population. People work vigorously to mitigate the ill effects of price changes in the marketplace only during grave emergencies, such as a downturn or a financial crisis.[12] Other than that, harmful market outcomes are left unattended, to be endured by the people on whom they fall.

Thus, mom-and-pop stores that are no longer viable because of mega-discount stores are on their own. US households that are unable to keep up with health care inflation are on their own. Indian cotton farmers who could not repay their loans (for seeds, fertilizer, etc.) because of a drop in global cotton prices are on their own. There were around 100,000 debt-driven farmer suicides in India between 1993 and 2003, an average of 10,000 a year.[13] As the demand for recyclables slackens as a result of the global downturn, rag pickers in New Delhi and Manila are on their own. Fishermen in their flimsy boats from small villages on the northwestern African coast find their catch dwindling because of overfishing by the subsidized industrial trawlers from developed countries. They are on their own.[14]

We could go on to describe the plight of ordinary market participants in both formal and informal markets around the world, and we will find a common indifference to the quandary of those who find themselves suddenly having to bear distressing economic ripple effects on their own. Indeed, market prices understate the true social cost of allocative efficiency. The benefits of allocative efficiency are widely dispersed and enjoyed, but its costs are absorbed by a hapless few, and often by those who are least able to bear them.

Benefitting at the expense of others

There is a mirror image to the problem of underpricing in both technical and pecuniary externalities: the problem of equity. Let us first take the easier case of technical externalities. Besides the failure to reach allocative

---

[12] Thus, note the mega-stimulus packages passed by the major industrialized nations in response to the 2008–2009 crisis. Note, too, their record-breaking $1 trillion additional commitment to the IMF to shore up nations in the throes of a currency crisis (BBC 2009).

[13] Newman (2007).

[14] Many eventually migrate illegally to the EU in search of jobs (Lafraniere 2008).

efficiency, the other issue with pollution as a technical externality is the inequity of imposing the cost of one's conduct on someone else. In unfettered market operations, polluters do not foot the bill for their activities. Instead, the cost is borne by those who suffer health problems downstream and by the whole community, which eventually pays for the clean-up. The inequity is obvious: polluters reap the benefits while dumping the cost on everybody else. It is a free ride for them. This is a transfer of real resources that is unfair and unwarranted by any standard of morality.

There is a similar inequity in the case of pecuniary externalities. In our earlier example, cross-border trade confers enormous benefits on the general public in terms of cheaper goods and services, more vibrant technological change, better comparative advantage, and a closer approximation of allocative efficiency. A continuous stream of both tangible and intangible benefits flows from these gains from trade. However, we also know that these gains come at the expense of the burdens borne by a small segment of the economy.[15] Winners have gained much from international trade's spillover effects, while leaving those adversely affected to bear the cost on their own. Put in Kant's language, we could say that instead of treating those who had been adversely affected as ends in themselves, they have been used as means to move the economy to its point of allocative efficiency. No doubt, detrimental third-party effects are unavoidable by the nature of markets, but leaving unredressed those that are particularly injurious is not. The case for a moral obligation is made even stronger by the benefits reaped as a result of such harms. Corrective-compensatory justice calls for ameliorative action in such cases.

Skeptics may nevertheless still argue that market participants are well aware that inadvertent effects are a normal part of economic life and that it is incumbent upon individual actors to prepare accordingly. These harmful market outcomes may be unintended, but they are foreseeable, and any reasonable person ought to be taking precautions on their own (e.g., insurance or hedging strategies). Thus, skeptics will argue that adverse pecuniary externalities are a matter of prudential preparation rather than an issue of corrective justice. In response to these skeptics, we must point out that these precautions are often expensive and beyond the knowledge,

---

[15] Even neoclassical trade theory acknowledges that while free trade may confer benefits on all participants in absolute terms, there will nonetheless still be relative losses since the growth will not be distribution neutral. In other words, even while the size of the pie increases, the relative size of each participant's slice of the pie will most likely change. Thus, recall the Stolper–Samuelson theorem in the Hechsher–Ohlin model in which the abundant factor gains relative to the scarce factor of production in the aftermath of trade.

means, or skills of most people. Moreover, despite the foreseen nature of these unintended consequences, the marketplace is not a level playing field. It is to this aspect of corrective justice that we now turn our attention.

Non-reciprocal risks

As we have seen in chapter 6, people are liable for subjecting others to undue, above-normal risks in tort jurisprudence. Recall the reciprocity of risks we impose on one another whenever we drive on public roads. We go well beyond the normal bounds of what is considered mutual risk creation whenever we drive recklessly or while intoxicated (or text-messaging). These are subject to severe liabilities.

We adopted this insight on the reciprocity of risk and used it in the case of gratuitous harms in the preceding chapter. I propose that we can adopt the same insight in our current case on what to do with invertible market ripple effects. In particular, we can say that in an ideal market, there should also be a similar reciprocity of risk that we impose on one another in our economic decisions. If so, then corrective justice requires that damages from non-reciprocal risks be rectified. Let us take an example each from macro-economics and microeconomics to illustrate systemic, non-reciprocal risk creation in the marketplace.

Financial globalization has been beneficial for developed countries because it provides them access to cheaper capital and a much wider variety of investment instruments. It facilitates better risk diversification. Empirical data confirm these theoretical benefits. In contrast, less developed countries have generally not benefitted as much and, in fact, have even been harmed on numerous occasions by global financial integration. These developing nations have had to endure greater volatility from large and unpredictable capital inflows and outflows. The output losses from such macroeconomic disruptions have been enormous, as in the 1997–1998 Asian financial crisis. And this is not even to mention the huge social costs (higher poverty rates, etc.) incurred because governments have had to pursue restrictive fiscal or monetary policies in response to the accompanying currency crises.

A key reason behind this differential impact of financial globalization is the absence of essential preconditions in less developed countries: depth in financial resources, well-established institutions, a reliable macroeconomic infrastructure, a robust banking system, strong foreign exchange position, and sound economic policies. Take the case of short-term portfolio flows ("hot money") that dart in and out of global capital markets in search of the best investment opportunities. Developed countries are in a much better position to absorb these sudden lurches in capital inflows and outflows because of the size and stability of their economies. In contrast, less developed countries' economies that are already fragile to begin with are easily disrupted by such massive and sudden capital flows. As we have seen in the debt, banking, and currency crises of the past thirty years, poor and wealthy nations face asymmetric risks when it comes to financial globalization.[16]

We can argue similarly when it comes to the cross-border trade in goods and services. Wealthier countries are in a much better position than emerging nations to ride out unavoidable turbulence from international trade. What may simply be an economic hiccup for developed countries may be completely ruinous for less developed nations given their lack of financial depth. The 2008–2009 global downturn is an example of such non-reciprocal risk creation. It is an illustration of how macroeconomic crises that originate from developed nations are readily transmitted to the poor nations. However, economic events in poor nations hardly make a dent in the developed nations' economies.[17] This is understandable given the differing global roles and sizes of these nations. Nonetheless, it brings home the point that there is non-reciprocity in the economic risks that poor and wealthy nations impose on each other.

We observe the same dynamic at a microeconomic level. The well-off and the middle class hold the bulk of most nations' economic wealth, income, and purchasing power. Consequently, their lifestyles and economic choices have a much larger impact on the poor than vice versa. For example, a shift in preference among the upper and middle classes for imported fruits and vegetables imposes risks of less work or lower wages for California farm workers. In contrast, these California farmhands' economic choices would most likely have minimal impact, if at all, on the lives of most people on Main Street. Obviously, there is a disparity in the mutual risks these two groups impose on one another given their differing relative weights in the economy.

Consider the following common features in the preceding macroeconomic and microeconomic examples. First, in a market economy in which purchasing power means everything, a poor nation's or person's impact on social processes or outcomes is far less than that of a wealthy nation or person. They are non-reciprocal in the risks they create for one another. Second, the ability to deal with, and perhaps even profit from, the market's

[16] Prasad *et al.* (2003).
[17] Of course, the exceptions here are the key oil-exporting poor nations like Iraq, Iran, Nigeria, Mexico, and Venezuela. They can rattle global oil markets.

rapid changes is a function of people's sociohistorical location and resources. Not all market participants are equal in their ability to cope with an extremely fluid market. The same economic event will pose very different sets of risks for market participants depending on their human capital and relative position within the community. In other words, market changes or disruptions pose relatively greater risks for those with less human capital and for those from a disadvantaged sociohistorical location.

Recall that market exchange, by its nature, ultimately leads to a reshuffling of burdens and benefits across the community. These reallocations are inescapable and stem from the distributive dimension of price changes. In effect, market participants create risks for one another through their buying and selling behavior. These are socially necessary risks as part of regular market operations.

As seen in the above examples, the risks created in regular market exchange are not reciprocal or uniform across the economy. Since the risks from adverse pecuniary externalities are socially necessary but uneven and non-reciprocal, we can make a case that there is a moral duty to mitigate excessive non-reciprocal risks. In earlier chapters, we saw that tort law imposed liabilities on those responsible for unduly increasing the risk of harm to others. In our current case, no particular market participant can be identified as solely or even chiefly responsible for these uneven, non-reciprocal risks.[18] They are simply the outcome of normal market operations. Thus, it is a collective responsibility contingent upon all market participants. In other words, the community has an obligation to assist those who have been grievously harmed by such heightened non-reciprocal risks from normal market operations. After all, the entire community has reaped benefits from the market's operations.[19]

Finally, these observations on non-reciprocal risks refute the earlier legal maxim "To the consenting, no injury is done." Even if we were to assume

---

[18] Thus, from Feinberg's (1970, 248–251) typology, this is a "contributory group fault: collective but not distributive," his fourth type of collective responsibility.

[19] The problem of endogeneity cannot be ignored as we examine these non-reciprocal risks. Some market risks are made more severe by people's failure to prepare for these expected contingencies in the marketplace. For example, we have the case of improvident families who did not care to save for a rainy day, thereby making themselves even more vulnerable to market vagaries than would have otherwise been the case. Consequently, we can say that these market risks have at least two components: those that are due to the failure of the economic actor (the problem of endogeneity) and those that are systemic by the nature of the market. Empirically separating these two components from one another is extremely hard, if at all possible. Thus, note the difficulty of putting together the "bail-out" packages for the housing foreclosure crisis and for the banks during the 2008–2009 financial meltdown. The boundaries between personal moral failure and systemic causes were blurred in many cases.

that this legal maxim is valid, for the sake of argument, it applies less and less to market participants in ever more disadvantaged sociohistorical locations. With underdeveloped human capital, these economic agents will find their options to be extremely limited and will be compelled to accept or make do with whatever spillover effects may come their way no matter how unpalatable or how severe they might be. They simply have no choice but to live with whatever the marketplace offers them. In other words, these are the people subjected to economic compulsion; they forgo significant interests in an effort to protect and hold on to even more vital interests.[20] Consequently, we cannot use the legal maxim "To the consenting, no injury is done" to absolve ourselves of the moral obligation to attenuate malign results in the marketplace. There is no genuine consent on the part of many adversely affected economic actors to begin with. In the same fashion, we can also say that contributory negligence (the problem of endogeneity) is not as important in these cases because of the self-reinforcing nature of poverty traps. We cannot excuse ourselves from the moral duty of ameliorating severe market outcomes by making a blanket claim that those who are hurt had contributed to their own injuries by not having prepared themselves adequately for these foreseen market disruptions. This is simply not true of all market participants.

Risk distribution
Torts provide us another justification for the moral obligation to mitigate injurious market outcomes. Tort jurisprudence often assigns liability for harm with an eye toward spreading the cost or imputing it to the party that is best able to pay for such damages.

If, in general, a lump sum burden is more onerous when borne by one person than it would be if divided among many, then one function of tort law may be to ensure that . . . injury burdens are spread. Moreover, if even heavy burdens are less onerous when borne by certain wealth categories rather than others, then another function of tort law . . . may be to allocate injury burdens to those wealth categories able to bear them with relative ease. (Calabresi 1975, 73)

As we can see, two functions of torts are identified in this quote: spreading the burden and distributing wealth. Both insights can be adapted for our current case. As mentioned earlier, one feature of market operations,

---

[20] Thus, Filipina, Sri Lankan, and Indonesian women, many with college and professional degrees, find themselves leaving their children and husbands to work overseas as domestic helpers in order to feed and clothe their own and their extended families. For a more in-depth discussion of the nature and dynamics of economic compulsion, see Barrera (2005a, 3–74).

especially of international trade, is how the benefits are enjoyed by many at the expense of a few. In this case, spreading the cost of the harm is intuitively appealing and is consistent with the notion of corrective justice, especially in light of the gains reaped by the many who benefit from market exchange. Commonsense morality would judge the few to be deserving of some assistance from the many who have gained.

The second function of torts is much more controversial because it is unabashedly about wealth distribution and sticking the cost of the harm to the "deeper pockets." Depending on one's philosophical convictions, some will find such blatant wealth distribution to be beyond the scope of corrective justice. This is not so in our current case, however. We can still adapt this second function of torts for our purposes because these grievous spillover effects are often borne by the very people who, through no fault of their own, are in the most disadvantaged sociohistorical locations.

In his second rule, Rawls suggests that justice as fairness requires that inequalities be permitted only to the extent that the most disadvantaged benefit. Far from reaping benefits, the poor are in fact saddled with the burdens rather than the benefits of community life. Thus, we can invoke Rawls's (1971) justice as fairness as another warrant for why there are moral obligations to rectify pernicious economic processes and outcomes. Since these unavoidable market ripple effects produce enormous gains for their beneficiaries, requiring them to ameliorate the resulting market harms is a matter not of wealth distribution but of corrective justice.

In sum, the notion of corrective justice can be used as a basis for the moral obligation to alleviate the ill effects of market operations for at least four reasons. First, market prices, by their nature, do not include the social cost of attaining allocative efficiency, thereby giving market beneficiaries far more gains than they deserve. Second, if neglected, wide disparities in the resulting redistribution of burdens and benefits from price changes will mean that many gain at the expense of a few. Third, such disparities become even more serious when the few who bear the brunt are most likely the ones in the most disadvantaged sociohistorical locations to begin with. Finally, the risks of participating in the marketplace, while unavoidable, are uneven and non-reciprocal across economic agents, depending on their human capital and sociohistorical location. All these are properly subject to corrective justice and require remedial extra-market action.

Instrumental reasons

We can use neoclassical economics itself to make the case for addressing the market's pernicious third-party effects. In particular, we can argue that allocative efficiency requires that we rectify the market's severe ill effects for at least two reasons: the central role of human capital development for long-term allocative efficiency and the need for efficiency in risk avoidance.

Human capital development

Allocative efficiency is dependent on human capital development. Economic history is replete with empirical proof that technological and organizational innovations hold the key to economic growth and development. Thus, three-field crop rotation, the wheeled plow, and the horse collar were pivotal in the Agricultural Revolution on the eve of the modern era. Breakthroughs in ship construction that permitted larger and lighter ships opened the New World to exploration. The steam engine and inexpensive steel spearheaded the Industrial Revolution. Fordist mass production techniques in organizing the factory floor inaugurated the age of mass consumption.[21] The Digital Age has led to a fundamental reorganization of the global economy as a single, giant workshop within a networked society.[22] Indeed, on the surface, science and technology are the proximate causes of major economic advances in human history. But at a deeper level, it is, in fact, human capital development that laid the groundwork for such innovations and inventions. Nowhere else is this better seen than in our current period of global economic integration.

Globalization is distinctive because it is fueled by an emerging knowledge economy. The source of value creation is no longer land (as it was in the premodern agrarian era) or natural resources and industrial capital (as it was in the nineteenth and twentieth centuries). Instead, human capital is the primary engine for value creation in this Information Age. Companies like Microsoft, Google, Intel, and Infosys have overshadowed traditional industrial firms.

An even more vivid description of this shift in the center of gravity is the ladder of comparative advantage. The ladder used to be based on natural comparative advantage. Labor-abundant countries traded with natural-resource-rich or capital-rich nations, and vice versa. In other words, a nation's production bundle was determined by its endowment of natural resources. As nations moved up higher on the ladder, they handed down their aging industries to the next-tier countries. For example, the manufacture of steel passed from the first-tier countries like the USA and the UK to Japan, then to South Korea and Taiwan, and currently to China, India,

---

[21] Freeman and Perez (1988); Jones (1987); Mokyr (1990, 31–38).   [22] Castells (1996).

Brazil, and Ukraine. Nations climbed the ladder of comparative advantage in an orderly pecking order.

This is no longer the case in our contemporary era. The ladder of natural comparative advantage has been replaced by the ladder of created comparative advantage.[23] Nations have been freed from the shackles of natural-resource constraints. Those with meager natural resources can now leapfrog ahead of traditionally more advanced nations as they climb this new ladder. The most notable example of this phenomenon has been Bangalore, India and its lead in computer-related engineering, programming, and design. Nations can now create their own comparative advantage, and there are no limits to how far or how fast they choose to ascend this ladder. The major constraint to climbing the ladder of created comparative advantage is the depth, breadth, and quality of the nation's human capital.

The central importance of human capital in the knowledge economy is the strongest instrumental argument that can be made for redressing injurious pecuniary externalities. Adverse market outcomes are likely to fall on the less skilled, the less educated, and the more vulnerable who are already living a precarious subsistence to begin with.[24] Moreover, the necessary adjustments in an increasingly knowledge-based economy may require skills and social networking that are far beyond their means. In other words, those who bear the brunt of the downside of freer trade may not have the personal resources to absorb these costs by themselves. If so, they may altogether be shut out of meaningful and productive participation in the economy, with consequent loss not only for themselves but for the entire community. The economy's full capacity is underutilized because its most valuable resource, human capital, is underdeveloped and underutilized.[25] Thus, while the private cost borne by these displaced workers is great, the community's social cost is even greater in terms of the opportunity loss of current and future streams of output and a diminished growth trajectory. Damage to vital welfare interests may irreversibly remove large segments of the population from participating productively in the knowledge economy. Nowhere else is this danger better illustrated than in the case of children from impoverished families.

Poor families are generally the most vulnerable to bearing the brunt of severe market ripple effects. To begin with, these families are most likely

---

[23] Meier (1995, 456–458).   [24] See Alini and Lahart (2009) for a recent example.
[25] In economic terms, the community is well inside its production possibilities frontier. Please note that people are more than just "human capital." I am presenting this instrumental argument only for the sake of making the point that even by using neoclassical economics itself, we can still argue in favor of rectifying grievous inadvertent outcomes.

poor because they have minimal skills, little education, no property, no secure employment, or all of the above. They are the ones trapped in jobs that are subject to volatile market swings. They are the ones who are fired first. They have very few savings, if any, and as a consequence, they have no cushion for any emergencies, such as a family illness.

But this is not the end of the story. Within these poor families, it is the very young who suffer the most. If the family is left to fend for itself and is mired in poverty, it is very likely that the children will grow up as adults also poor and disadvantaged, with little education or skills. This is particularly true in developing countries because malnutrition at a young age leads to permanent intellectual and physical impairment. The opportunities for the child are immediately narrowed down early on, and we have a poverty trap in which destitution is handed down from generation to generation. This state of affairs is self-defeating in a knowledge economy.

From a purely moral standpoint, these children and their impoverished families deserve relief from and assistance against severe spillover effects on the basis of our common humanity. This, by itself, is reason enough to warrant extending aid. Their intrinsic worth as human beings alone is sufficient to merit assistance. However, for this section, all I am emphasizing is that neoclassical economics itself and its goal of allocative efficiency present a strong case for our duty of mutual help. It is an instrumental reason. Tomorrow's allocative efficiency is dependent on today's equity. Or, put in another way, self-sustaining economic development (long-term allocative efficiency) is a function of human capital development in the short term. The East Asian miracles – Japan, Taiwan, South Korea, Singapore, and China – are examples of the critical role of investing in human capital.[26]

Because the social cost of adjusting to allocative efficiency is borne only by a small or unseen group of people, the public does not realize that it is in its own self-interest to assist those who have been seriously hurt by the market's unintended consequences. In the language of externalities, this is a case in which the perceived private benefit (of assisting the displaced) is less than the real total societal benefit of bringing these dislocated workers back

---

[26] The problem with a purely instrumental, utilitarian argument is that policymakers might pursue a perverse strategy of selectively assisting only those segments of the population that are important for future economic growth. For example, children will receive assistance because of their future potential contribution, but not the elderly, the sick, or the disabled. An instrumental argument is severely flawed in this regard. Thus, a position based on the intrinsic worth of every person is still the best argument to make.

into the workforce. Thus, extra-market intervention is needed either from the public purse or from NGOs.[27]

The importance of human capital development today for tomorrow's (long-term) allocative efficiency is again another illustration of a point from the preceding section: market prices do not reflect the true social cost of attaining allocative efficiency. The gains reaped from the marketplace are "underpriced" in that beneficiaries do not have to pay for some of the social costs incurred in producing these benefits.

Risk avoidance

The field of Law and Economics provides us with an additional instrumental reason for why it is in the self-interest of the economy to mitigate terribly damaging ripple effects. Besides the preceding two aforementioned functions of torts (spreading the risk and wealth distribution), we also have deterrence as another aim of tort jurisprudence.[28] This goal can be said to be forward-leaning in the sense that it does not aim to rectify past injuries. It is not retrospective like corrective justice, but prospective. It is concerned with heading off future damage by encouraging people to take appropriate harm-avoidance measures. Thus, liability for damages is assigned on the basis of which parties were in the best position to have foreseen the harm and to have taken preemptive action against it. Proponents of the field of Law and Economics argue that such a social arrangement is efficient because rational economic actors will incur the cost of taking precautions up to the point of potential tort damages. It is a least-cost method of minimizing harms.

We can adapt this notion of minimizing future harms for our current case. As we have seen in the preceding section, the failure to address the market's severe unintended consequences in the short term leads to even greater future harms in terms of lost economic output, especially in a globalized, knowledge economy. In order to minimize these potential harms (for the sake of long-term growth and a future larger economic pie), it is necessary to take preemptive measures today that ensure continued human capital development even in the face of injurious market processes and outcomes. The most effective way of accomplishing this is to provide

---

[27] This is an example of a public good. Other examples are public health and education. The social benefits of having an educated and healthy population exceed the benefits privately reaped by individuals because of the synergy produced. Thus, governments often provide incentives or assistance so that people do not underinvest in their own health or education. Alternatively, governments use taxes and subsidies to provide these critical investments directly as in the case of free universal education.

[28] Calabresi (1975, 77–91).

assistance to market participants whose human capital development is jeopardized by market conditions. This entails redressing the market's severe third-party effects. It is a least-cost method for minimizing injury to long-term allocative efficiency. Such risk- or harm-avoidance measures are best pursued by those able to pay for them – those who have gained the most from market operations. Besides, by ensuring the continued vibrancy of their future economy, the well-off are ultimately promoting their own long-term interest as a group.

In sum, we can adapt insights from social philosophy and tort jurisprudence to argue for a moral duty to ameliorate pernicious market spillover effects. First, we have the moral obligation to prevent grievous harm especially if we have the ability and the opportunity to do so, or when the costs and risks to ourselves are minimal. Second, it is a matter of corrective justice. Third, mitigating the market's severe unintended consequences is necessary for the economy's long-term allocative efficiency. It is in the self-interest of the market's principal beneficiaries to do so.

Christian ethics

Why is there a moral obligation to attend to severe pecuniary externalities from a theological perspective? I propose that we can use the notion of economic security as a divine gift and the principle of restoration as theological warrants for this moral duty.[29]

Due care

The third condition of the principle of double effect calls for due care in ensuring that every reasonable effort had been made to avoid the unintended evil or to mitigate its ill effects. An excellent example of such due care is one of John Wesley's caveats in his sermon *The Use of Money*.

Wesley argues that there is a three-step economic obligation that can be summarized as (1) gain all you can, (2) save all you can, and, then, (3) give all you can. In other words, economic life is about diligently putting our talents and material gifts to their full productive use, being frugal and prudent in the use of what we obtain, and then sharing generously with others all that we have produced or acquired. However, Wesley qualifies what it means to

---

[29] See Birch (1991, 172–182), Brueggemann (1994), Lohfink (1987; 1991), Miller (1985), and Wright (1990). Economic security as a divine gift and the principle of restoration are discussed in greater depth in Barrera (2005a, 77–138).

gain as much as we can. One of his cautionary notes is to ensure that we do not harm others in the pursuit of gain.

We are. Thirdly, to gain all we can without hurting our neighbour. But this we may not, cannot do, if we love our neighbour as ourselves. We cannot, if we love everyone as ourselves, hurt anyone *in his substance* ... We cannot, consistent with brotherly love, sell our goods below the market price; we cannot study to ruin our neighbour's trade, in order to advance our own; much less can we entice away or receive any of his servants or workmen whom he has need of. None can gain by swallowing up his neighbour's substance, without gaining the damnation of hell! (Wesley 1872, no. 3, emphasis original)

The phrase "in his substance" refers to the economic resources and livelihood of others. Wesley is keenly aware of how the market works, the intense competition it engenders, and the various devices employed by people in such an unforgiving environment. Clearly, he is critical of predatory trade practices and not of ordinary business activity. Even more important for our study, by "neighbour," Wesley is most likely referring only to one's immediate neighbors in a local community and not to more distant participants in the entire marketplace, given the limited scope of markets and economic life in the nineteenth century.

However, Wesley's caveat takes new life in our current period of globalization in which the whole world operates as a single workshop. Wesley's point poses a new challenge if we are to take seriously the response of Jesus when queried "Who is my neighbor?" Just as the Good Samaritan did not allow ethnic or religious differences to come between him and the man who fell in with the robbers, Christians today ought to be concerned for humans as fellow children of God wherever they may be. In other words, Wesley's concern for respecting a neighbor's substance can be adapted for our own time. As we have seen earlier, the market produces winners and losers by its nature, and we ought to treat those adversely affected as neighbors. This is all the more reason for us to attenuate the severe unintended consequences we inflict on others' substance as we pursue our own economic well-being. Following Wesley, we ought to be sensitive to the impact of our economic conduct on the livelihood of our neighbors.

Economic security as a divine gift

Using either faith or reason, we can arrive at the conclusion that God provides us with material sufficiency. In the creation accounts of Genesis, the earth is entrusted to humanity's stewardship, and we are supposed to satisfy our needs from the fruits of the earth. It is a mandate of stewardship that entailed collaborative work right from the start. In the formation of the nation Israel, the Chosen People of God were liberated from slavery and given a land of their own – the Promised Land, a land flowing with milk and honey. Their tenure on the land was secure to the degree that they lived according to the Law. Israel was called to be a nation like no other nation; there was supposed to be no poor in her midst. It was to be a nation in which everyone treated one another as an equal, with mutual respect and dignity. As a result, they were to take responsibility for each other's well-being and not allow their fellow Hebrews to wallow in destitution.

The Hebrew covenant is important in another respect. Note that there is disagreement in contemporary political discourse on whether or not economic rights exist. Trimiew (2000) shows that God's covenant with the Chosen People may in fact be used as a paradigm for the debate on economic rights. In particular, the economic duties expected of the Hebrews (e.g., care for one another) has a mirror image – rights. This is consistent with modern Christian social thought which views rights only in the context of their correlative duties, unlike liberalism, which views rights as standing on their own. Not surprisingly, many of the official statements of the Christian churches (chapter 2) call for economic rights.

We find the same Old Testament ideal of material sufficiency in the New Testament. In the Gospels of Luke and Matthew, the invitation is extended to all to let their lives center on the reign of God. There is no need to be anxious for what we are to eat or drink, for God provides for us (Mt 6:25–34; Lk 12:22–32). In the early Church, they held property in common. Some who had property sold it and gave the proceeds to the Church. People gave according to what they had and took only according to what they needed. They shared everything in common. And no one was said to be in want (Acts 4:32–37).

Consider three points from this very brief sketch of relevant insights from the Old and the New Testament. In the first place, we find the constant reassurance that our God is a loving, provident God who provides for our needs. Second, note how such divine provision of material sufficiency cannot be used as an excuse for indolence. Thus, the Hebrews still had to labor, even in the land flowing with milk and honey. Paul was emphatic on fulfilling mundane obligations, such as daily labor for one's own keep, even with an imminent *Parousia* (2 Thes 3:6–12). Third, God provides for humans within the context of community – the nation Israel and the extended Hebrew family in the Old Testament and the community of believers in the New Testament. In other words, God provides for us through each other. Thus, there are two gifts in the divine benefaction of economic security: material sufficiency and the privilege of our participation in God's creative act by providing for one another.

Principle of restoration

Among the Hebrew laws on economic life were the debt and slave legislation, the gleaning law, and the Jubilee Law. In the debt legislation, Hebrews were not to charge their fellow Hebrews any interest for any loans for which interest was usually paid (Ex 22:25; Dt 23:19–20; Lv 25:36–37). Moreover, they could not take collateral from the poor or secure any pledge that was vital for the person's livelihood or survival, such as a millstone to grind grain or a cloak (Ex 22:26; Dt 24:10–13). Furthermore, debts were to be forgiven after six years (Dt 15:1–3). In addition, Hebrews were morally obligated to lend to each other if they had the resources to do so (Dt 15:7–10; Lv 25:35–37).

Similarly, there were laws on the proper treatment of slaves. They were freed after six years of bondage and, on their release, laden by their former masters with goods and gifts (Ex 21:2–6; Dt 15:12–18). Eventually, the Hebrews were urged to welcome into their households their fellow Hebrews who had fallen on hard times. They were to take them in as tenants or hired hands and not as slaves (Lv 25:39–41). In the gleaning law, owners of the fields let the poor, the landless, widows, orphans, and aliens forage on the land (Dt 24:19–21; Lv 19:9–10; 23:22; Ru 2). And in the Jubilee Law, all those held in bondage were released, all debts were forgiven, and ancestral lands were returned to their original owners (Lv 25).

Many of these laws, particularly those that were demanding, ended with motive clauses, in which a reason was provided as to why YHWH was asking them to do that which was difficult (e.g., Lv 25:38, 42–43). God could ask the Hebrews to live up to these demanding statutes because they were merely extending to others the same favors they themselves had received from God in their own moment of need. Thus, the motive clauses often alluded to their liberation from slavery in Egypt.[30]

We can distill an important principle from Hebrew legislation on economic life. Amidst the economy's surprises and its harsh chance and contingencies, these laws conveyed a message of hope to the Hebrews – that no matter how badly they may fall, they can always rely on their fellow Hebrews for a helping hand. More than that, there will be a day of restoration. Thus, they had slave release, debt release, and the return of land to its original owners. If the laws were truly observed, then all Hebrews

---

[30] See Doron (1978) and Gemser (1953).

would be assured of being restored as free men and women living on their own ancestral land, the Promised Land flowing with milk and honey. In the face of life's vicissitudes, Hebrews restored one another to their rightful place in the nation as God's Chosen People.

Contemporary appropriation

No doubt, there is a wide difference between the modern economy and the agrarian culture of the Hebrews. Thus, there are numerous methodological disagreements on how to use Sacred Scripture for contemporary ethical reflection. Skeptics are quick to raise the question of its relevance for modern problems. Resolving these debates is beyond our topic. For this study, I subscribe to the approach that stresses the principle or the spirit underlying biblical norms. Some call this the rules of principle and analogy in biblical hermeneutics.[31] For example, most people would readily accept the continued force and applicability of the two greatest commandments and the Ten Commandments.

The notion of economic security as a twofold divine gift still applies to us today and obliges us to remedy pecuniary externalities that are particularly grievous or regressive in their impact. We, too, are supposed to be a family, a community of God's children where no one should be in want. We are responsible for one another's welfare, and we cannot turn our backs on those who have been severely affected by the market's unintended consequences. Furthermore, just as the Hebrews restored one another to full participation in the life of their nation, we, too, are obliged to restore those who have fallen on hard times in our midst to full participation in our common socioeconomic life, to the extent possible. And just as in the case of the Hebrews, God can ask us to do that which is difficult because we are merely invited to extend to others the same favors we ourselves had enjoyed from God in our own moment of need. Indeed, the notion of economic security as a twofold gift and the principle of restoration provide strong theological warrants for why it is a moral obligation to ameliorate the market's deleterious ripple effects.

SUBJECT OF ACCOUNTABILITY (WHO IS COMPLICIT?)

The preceding sections have sketched philosophical and theological arguments to support the claim that there is, in fact, a moral obligation to assist those who have been seriously harmed by market processes and outcomes.

---

[31] Cosgrove (2002).

But who are the addressees of such a duty? It is to this that we now turn our attention.

Economic theory's compensation principle is a good starting point in assessing who ought to mitigate the severe ripple effects of the marketplace. Specialization and the division of labor mean that economic agents have to trade in the marketplace. Given such flux, it is important to have a measure of whether a particular economic change is beneficial or not. Pareto optimality is a good conceptual tool for such a task because it describes a situation in which we cannot improve anybody's welfare without making someone else worse off. We have reached that point whereby any further reallocation of our scarce resources will cause someone else to suffer. It is a useful economic concept in alerting us to those instances in which we are inefficiently using our endowments. However, there are severe limits to the utility of Pareto optimality or Pareto efficiency. These concepts work only for a small group of economic agents whose welfare gains or losses can be easily monitored, not a realistic option in an actual economy.

An even better and more general concept that can deal with a multitude of economic agents is the compensation principle. This principle allows us to compare easily two states of affairs. A proposed change is welfare improving if beneficiaries gain enough so as to be able potentially to compensate those who lose from the change. Note that it does not matter whether or not actual compensation is given to those who have been adversely affected. The important point is that winners are able to do so potentially. All that is needed is to ascertain that the total benefits far exceed, or at least are equal to, the total losses.[32] Positive economics does not address whether or not winners should actually compensate those who have been disadvantaged. It is interested only in assessing whether or not a particular economic change produces net gains.

Obviously, the compensation principle is very helpful for our study because it already suggests who are the most logical obligation holders – those who have benefitted from the adverse pecuniary externalities. They have the necessary economic surplus to pursue or fund costly extra-market ameliorative action.

SUMMARY AND CONCLUSIONS

Market transactions inevitably lead to price changes, which in turn precipitate a constant reshuffling of burdens and benefits within the

---

[32] Henderson and Quandt (1971, 279–280).

community. This constant adjustment is necessary if the community is to be responsive to changing economic conditions and if it is to attain its point of allocative efficiency, that is, the allotment of its scarce resources to their most valued uses. Thus, the allocative and distributive dimensions of price are mirror images to each other. Furthermore, this constant reshuffling of gains and burdens within the community produces unintended consequences – beneficial for some, but harmful for others.

This chapter has been about our moral obligation to attend to the more serious cases of harmful economic ripple effects. There is a long list of philosophical and theological arguments to justify this moral duty (basis for accountability). The economic wrongdoing lies not in causally contributing to the market's inadvertent harms. There is nothing blameworthy in this because such ill effects are unavoidable by the nature of market transactions. We cannot be faulted for these. However, we are nonetheless morally liable, as a community, to ameliorate the plight of those who have to bear these severe spillover effects. The economic wrongdoing (object of accountability) is in the personal and collective failure to alleviate the more grievous instances of these third-party effects. Those who have benefitted more from the market bear a larger share of this collective moral duty (subject of accountability).

Thus, the third type of economic complicity pertains to individual market participants who do not do their share in redressing the more serious adverse pecuniary externalities of the marketplace. The blameworthy material cooperation here is in leaving untended the market's terribly injurious unintended consequences, despite our capacity to prevent or to ease such harms. This is an invertible, permissible material cooperation that carries liabilities for rectifying the ensuing market ills.

CHAPTER 8

Soft complicity II: Reinforcing injurious socioeconomic structures

The market does not operate in a vacuum. It is governed by formal and informal rules. It is undergirded by a web of institutions painstakingly built up over time. Because of the dynamism and fluidity of the marketplace, its underlying structures are marked by both continuity and change, shaped by the economic choices of market participants. Thus, a fourth instance of economic complicity pertains to the harmful or unjust market practices and institutions that market participants unavoidably perpetuate and reinforce, but unfortunately leave uncorrected.

OBJECT OF ACCOUNTABILITY (COMPLICITY IN WHAT?)

In the preceding chapter, we saw that leaving grievous pecuniary externalities unattended is common in market exchange. Left on its own, the market will not mitigate its severe unintended consequences, and people are simply left to fend for themselves. This is the norm in the modern market economy. After all, such pecuniary externalities are the mechanisms that compel people to redeploy their resources in line with the economy's allocative efficiency. In this chapter, we extend the analysis and consider harmful unintended consequences that are non-pecuniary in nature.

In economics, recall that externalities are unintended consequences the costs of which are not included in the price calculations of economic agents. Technical externalities (e.g., pollution) are the best known of these. The preceding chapter was about pecuniary externalities (e.g., price and income changes). Some have suggested an additional category – "moral externalities" – as a way of alerting people to the unintended effects of their economic choices on morality and the quality of human life and relationships.[1] We are all too familiar with the metaphor of how our carbon

---

[1] Gowri (2004) proposes this term. For example, Sedgwick (1999) examines the market economy's impact on the person's self-understanding. Sennett (1998) finds sociological evidence of a corrosion of

footprint impacts the ecology. Similarly, we could say that the "moral externalities" of our economic choices leave an imprint on the market's moral ecology.[2] This chapter addresses our obligations to attend to the "moral externalities" of our economic conduct.

By its nature, the marketplace is "amoral" in that it does not make value judgments about the morality, propriety, or equity of the activities that transpire within its domain. This means that individuals are free to pursue their own preferences for as long as they stay within the formal and informal rules of the community. The market's requirements for consummating economic exchanges are minimal: the availability of purchasing power and tradable commodities. Put another way, all it needs are buyers and sellers with something of value to trade. Furthermore, the parties to such exchanges do not even have to be adults nor do these exchanges even have to be completely voluntary. As a consequence, the market, as a social institution, can and does perpetrate harmful or unjust processes and outcomes. Consider the following examples of injurious marketplace practices that many would most likely find unsatisfactory, if not disturbing.

1 *In markets, purchasing power is often the only way for most people to access goods and services, even for the most fundamental human needs.*

Thus, hundreds of millions are left to wallow in illness, poverty, and hunger for lack of such purchasing power. Economics Nobel laureate A. K. Sen (1983) argues that modern-day famines have been caused not by supply failures, but by the lack of income or entitlements on the part of the victims. People starve even as there are ample food supplies for all. This market deficiency is evident even in the USA where many suffer chronic hunger and tens of millions of residents have no health insurance or are underinsured.

2 *Left on their own, market processes are often regressive in dispensing burdens and benefits.*

Thus, the poor pay more for credit because they are deemed to be risky borrowers, if they could even obtain such loans to begin with. There is the problem of redlining in the provision of banking, insurance, and mortgage services. The poor also expend more time and money to gain access to water and fuel.[3] In the USA, the uninsured are believed to pay as

---

personal character in the loss of trust and loyalty as a result of changes in the labor market toward temporary work and short-term contracts. George (2001) argues that markets can have damaging effects on the preferences of people (e.g., fast foods).

[2] See Finn (2006) for an exposition on the moral ecology of the market.

[3] Even the right to police protection is often beyond the reach of impoverished communities. In fact, the poor are most often the victims of crimes. Bearak (2009) describes the plight of Diepsloot, South Africa. The closest police station to this destitute community with a population of 150,000 people is ten miles away.

much as three times more for the same health care services than those who have health insurance or are part of a health maintenance organization (HMO) able to negotiate discount prices.[4]

3 *Despite its much-touted ability to allocate scarce resources to their most valued uses, the market does not deal with the equity of such allocation.*

Thus, it is fairly common to have deepening impoverishment for segments of the population and ever widening income and wealth inequality even in the midst of vibrant economic growth. As we have seen in the preceding chapter, market processes do not mitigate adverse pecuniary externalities no matter how injurious they might be.

4 *There is an intergenerational inequity in the use of the goods of the earth because many market participants are susceptible to the problem of the commons[5] or are short-sighted in their conduct.*

Thus, note the serious problem of overfishing and greenhouse gas emission. Future generations will be saddled with depleted fish stocks, a severely damaged ecology, and exhausted natural resources. This is not even to mention this generation's excessive consumer borrowing and massive public debt.

5 *The market does not distinguish needs from wants; it only recognizes purchasing power and the highest bidder.*

Thus, legitimate first-time home buyers are crowded out of the housing market by speculators. Similarly, poor developing countries have to pay more for vital oil and food supplies because of commodity speculators. Wealthy nations divert corn and other scarce agricultural resources, such as land and water, to ethanol production while the poor are burdened with higher food prices.

6 *The market does not distinguish between price and intrinsic value.*

The market only deals with the price at which individual buyers and sellers consummate mutually beneficial exchanges. These prices reflect only the private gains individuals derive from these goods or services, but not the true social benefits that the larger community reaps from these goods.[6] For example, there is a jarring disparity in the pay of teachers, who form the hearts and minds of the young and the country's future, compared with many other professions.

[4] Armour (2007).   [5] Hardin (1968).
[6] Moreover, market prices are based on relative scarcity. Thus, we have the well-known water–diamond paradox in introductory economics courses. We know that water is vital for life and yet its market price is far below that of a diamond. The explanation is the relative scarcity of these goods.

7 *Market outcomes are determined by the relative bargaining power of market participants, thereby making exploitation fairly common in a market setting.*

The poor sell their kidneys. Credit card companies, pay-day lenders, and subprime creditors engage in predatory lending practices. Banks boost their revenues through punitive late fees and high interest rates. Moreover, they target segments of the population who are most likely to fall behind in their payments. Since the earliest days of the Industrial Revolution, we have had the perennial problem of sweatshops. And, then, of course, we also have excessive entitlements, as in the case of CEO pay and bank bonuses.

8 *Left on their own, markets will facilitate the exchange of any good or service regardless of its ill effects.*

The market does not second guess the decisions of economic agents. The latter are sovereign in their choices. Thus, we have the phenomenon of commodification in which non-economic facets of social life are governed by market rules. Some goods or services that have never been bought or sold in the marketplace are now routinely traded, such as human sperm and ova, kidneys, and commercial surrogacy.[7] Genetic engineering opens possibilities for the commercialization of custom-made babies with specific qualities pertaining to gender, physical attributes, genetic make-up, and potential mental aptitude. And of course, in another era, we had slavery, with its unfortunate modern counterpart today in human trafficking. Indeed, the market accommodates trade in any good or service.

Likewise, the market makes no distinction between harmful and beneficial products or services. It is not designed to weigh the impact of goods and services on human development. Thus, pornography, gambling, drugs, violent videos, etc. are routinely traded like ordinary commodities. Prostitution is the proverbial oldest profession. Child labor is rampant. Trans fats, fast foods, tanning salons, cigarettes, and many other goods and services have been documented to be extremely deleterious to long-term health. Tobacco firms have been pushing and profiting handsomely from cigarette sales in less developed countries that have minimal restrictions on tobacco sales or advertising. US credit card companies encourage consumer overspending and debt, even

---

[7] Many have questioned the morality of wage-labor contracts because they treat labor no differently from a commodity that can be traded. See, for example, John Paul II (1981) in his encyclical *Laborem Exercens*.

among vulnerable college students. Advertisers promote an ethos of consumerism, sensualism, and hedonism.

The market has no built-in safeguards that screen out questionable practices, goods, or services. Gowri's (2004) "ethics of artefacts" addresses these issues well. As part of his notion of "moral externalities," he suggests that we examine both the good and ill effects of products or services supplied in the marketplace. We should not focus our moral reflection solely on the nature of acts and the moral agents, but we should also consider the goods and services that we individually and collectively produce and value in the marketplace. The market price of these goods and services often does not reflect their true value for human flourishing. Price and true value rarely coincide because of the "amoral" nature of the market.

9 *While the marketplace does not discriminate between needs and wants or between harmful and beneficial goods or services, it does permit discrimination on the basis of productivity and cost.*

Thus, firms downsize middle-aged and more expensive workers who have served them for twenty to thirty years in favor of younger and cheaper labor from domestic or overseas sources. Women who choose to bear children are penalized with lower pay, slower promotion, or inferior job postings.

10 *By the nature and logic of competition, market processes run the risk of precipitating a "race to the bottom" when it comes to labor, environmental, and tax policies.*

The empirical evidence is mixed. Available data both confirm and invalidate the existence of such a "race to the bottom." Nevertheless, that there are even anecdotal cases of such a race is suggestive of the market's deficiencies.

11 *Left on their own, market processes can trap the poor in a cycle of poverty.*

As we have seen in the last chapter, economic agents' human capital and sociohistorical location determine the difficulty or the ease with which they can participate meaningfully in the marketplace. In the past thirty years, the market has raised hundreds of millions out of poverty.[8] Nevertheless, it can and does exclude large swaths of the population from productively contributing to and benefitting from socioeconomic life.

12 *By their internal logic of "survival of the fittest," market processes are self-destructive in that vibrant competition is ultimately replaced by monopolies or by a handful of economic players at best.*

[8] Chen and Ravallion (2004).

This phenomenon is particularly true in those areas in which economies of scale are huge and important. Thus, note the mergers and acquisitions of major conglomerates across a broad range of industries: airlines, media, steel, auto and aircraft manufacturing, electronics, software, and many others. US agriculture is now dominated by a handful of mega-corporations. Not surprisingly, even the most market-oriented nations, such as the USA and those of the EU, rely on intrusive anti-trust legislation to safeguard genuine competition.

13 *Of course, we have the well-known and well-studied instances of market failures.*

Examples of such market failures include technical externalities (e.g., pollution), the underprovision of merit goods (e.g., education), and missing public goods (e.g., reliable and affordable mass transportation). The market is deficient even by the standards of neoclassical economics and its overriding goal of allocative efficiency. Thus, governments and NGOs have had to step in and make up for what the market is unable to accomplish because of collective-action problems.

This is not an exhaustive listing but just a sampling of deficiencies in market processes and outcomes. This brief sketch merely underscores the point that the market cannot be left to operate on its own without oversight or without clearly defined boundaries.

So, wherein lies the object of accountability? The market is not a moral agent in itself but a collective of market participants. To make matters worse, it is not an organized group of moral agents, but a random aggregation of individuals in search of welfare-improving exchanges with one another. It is thus subject to severe collective-action problems.[9] Furthermore, its de facto goal is allocative efficiency, to the exclusion of everything else. Under such conditions, the market is an amorphous, but highly malleable, social institution that takes its shape and direction from the overarching political economy and public morality that together define its limits and its underlying values.[10]

The market has to rely on extra-market interventions to block or to alter its injurious processes and outcomes. Thus, government agencies and private non-profit groups have had to ameliorate the ill effects of the marketplace. For example, in the case of access to basic needs, governments

---

[9] Recall the prisoners' dilemma and the problem of the commons.
[10] Note the contrast between the more market-oriented approach of the USA and the social economy of the EU. See Zak (2008) for an interdisciplinary examination of the central importance of values in the modern capitalist economy.

provide safety nets, such as unemployment benefits, food stamps, and social security insurance, while NGOs run non-profit social service centers. In the case of the regressive market pricing of credit, we have the Community Reinvestment Act that mandates banks to funnel part of their resources and lending to impoverished communities. And, of course, we now have the private sector and multilateral agencies, such as the World Bank, pouring resources into micro-credit programs following the Grameen Bank's success.

Governments have addressed the skewed distribution of incomes and wealth through progressive taxation and targeted subsidies. Nations have worked hard to address the problem of the commons through multilateral agreements (e.g., on climate change). Even the United States, long a champion of free trade and minimal market oversight, has had to rethink its position on globalization and has had to intervene in limiting CEO pay, at least for the financial institutions receiving a taxpayer bailout. The market's uneven playing field when it comes to bargaining power has led to laws that set minimum wage levels and protect labor unions.

The problem of commodification has been addressed through blocked exchanges: it is illegal to sell votes, public offices, kidneys, babies, children for adoption, sexual services, and drugs in most nations. Moreover, media and video game companies have been ordered to provide ratings for the content of their movies, music, and games. Laws have been passed restricting the use of trans fats and sodium. There is a minimum age for drinking and smoking, in addition to the prohibitive taxes imposed on alcohol and tobacco in an effort to shape private choices.

Laws against gender, age, race, or other kinds of discrimination curtail workplace abuses that treat people as expendable factors of production. Market competition's logic and dynamic of ever greater consolidation and ever larger market shares are checked by anti-trust oversight. Less developed countries have tackled poverty traps through public health and education intervention programs. In the USA, affirmative action provisions in college admissions and in awarding state and federal contracts give disadvantaged groups a chance to rise above systemic obstacles and participate in the marketplace.

Many of these public and private interventions are common practice in many nations. Their widespread use only serves to highlight the widely held belief that the marketplace has significant deficiencies that have to be corrected through extra-market ameliorative action. There is little debate on this, if any at all. Instead, the disagreements are about the thresholds that trigger such interventions; the scope, duration, and degree of such assistance; and the appropriate obligation holders. Responses to these issues vary enormously because different political economies and public moralities espouse dissimilar and often competing visions of the good. Once again, we encounter the central importance of the underlying moral standards employed.

By virtue of their participation in the marketplace, economic actors sustain and even strengthen harmful market processes and outcomes. There are both personal and collective moral duties to alter or, at least, to mitigate these injurious or unjust market practices and institutions by the third condition (due care) of the principle of double effect. To leave them unattended is to be complicit in the harms they perpetrate. This is the object of complicity.

BASIS FOR ACCOUNTABILITY (WHY CULPABLE?)

The philosophical and theological warrants in the preceding chapter's section on the basis for accountability apply just as well to this chapter's more general treatment of harmful market structures. However, there is much more that we can add in making the case for why market participants are bound by a moral duty to alter or, at least, to ameliorate pernicious economic processes and outcomes.

Economics: the nature and dynamics of the market

It is best to begin by carefully examining the causal contribution of the ordinary market participant in sustaining deleterious marketplace practices. Three concepts descriptive of the nature and dynamics of the marketplace will be helpful in this regard: bounded rationality, network externality, and path dependence.

Bounded rationality

Neoclassical economic theory presents *Homo oeconomicus* as a utility-maximizing consumer or a profit-maximizing producer. The appropriate calculations are made by *Homo oeconomicus* prior to every economic decision, given all the relevant information provided by prices and given the resources on hand. Such maximizing calculations ensure that endowments and resources are allocated in an optimum manner so as to produce the best possible stream of utility or profits. These calculations are reevaluated as new information becomes available, as prices change, or as economic conditions shift. This process is called instrumental rationality.

In practice, economic actors do not employ instrumental rationality. Typical market participants are similar to neoclassical economic theory's *Homo oeconomicus* in the sense that they desire the best possible stream of utility and profits for themselves. Moreover, they do make calculations in choosing the best course of action given the constraints and opportunities they face. Nevertheless, there are important differences between theory and practice. To begin with, the economy is extremely dynamic with constantly changing conditions, a steady stream of new information that must be digested, and endless price changes. All these require recalculations as the optimum solutions keep shifting. Thus, if economic actors behaved exactly like *Homo oeconomicus*, there would have been little time left for anything else. Market participants would be preoccupied with redoing their calculations constantly. After all, one must remember that economic theory assumes perfect information and a frictionless economy. It costs little, if anything, for *Homo oeconomicus* to make all these calculations in search of the optimum solution.

In contrast, calculations in real life are costly because they are information-intensive and time-consuming processes. Thus, in practice, economic agents simply use rules of thumb. Instead of maximizing, they "satisfice," that is, they simply settle for outcomes that are not necessarily the optimum but are satisfactory enough given their previous experience and given available empirical evidence. These rules of thumb have been tried and tested, and they evolve as they are tweaked to take into account changing economic conditions. This process is called bounded rationality.[11]

Contrary to the common perception that an unfettered market is an unstructured grouping of economic actors that spontaneously emerges, we, in fact, have an embedded economy that is critically dependent on underlying morals, preexisting relationships, values, and trust for its smooth operations.[12] In this socially embedded marketplace, institutional structures and processes determine outcomes, and culture matters enormously for long-term economic performance.[13] All these underscore the central role of formal and informal rules of thumb in the marketplace. These rules of thumb are accumulated and refined over time by social convention, public morality, empirical data, and politics, among other things.

---

[11] See Heap (1989) for an in-depth examination of the difference between instrumental and bounded rationality.

[12] Polanyi (1944).

[13] For example, see Schultz (2001) and Sen (1995). See also the economic literature on social capital.

Consider some examples of such marketplace rules of thumb. Most shoppers go to their favorite warehouse discount store without having to scour Sunday newspaper ads for the best deals for everything they have to purchase. For most people, the time and effort expended are not worth the savings. Based on their experience, these shoppers are more or less familiar with the kind of service and prices they can expect from their favorite stores.

Merchandisers and retailers routinely accept customer returns. Major-ticket items come with year-long product warranties; multi-year warranties are available for purchase. Restaurant and taxi tips of 15 percent are common in the USA but not in Europe. At least thirty-day credits are expected in most business transactions. Sales commissions are an important part of compensation schemes in the field of marketing. Family health care coverage, paid vacation and sick days, and maternity leave are routinely provided by firms even without being compelled to do so by law.

In all these cases, market participants do not have to calculate whether each of the above practices will maximize their utility or profits. Most of these are standard or are considered industry best practices. In other words, many economic decisions are based on custom, law, and usage, and are not the outcome of maximizing exercises. Understanding the formation of these formal and informal rules of thumb is important. It is to this that we now turn our attention.

Network externality
The notion of network externality partly explains the dynamic behind the formation of the aforesaid rules of thumb. The best examples of network externalities are currencies and languages. The US dollar has been weakening and its future prospects have been dimmed in the past decade given the gargantuan US fiscal and trade deficits. Nonetheless, despite flaws in US economic policies, there is still a vibrant demand for US dollar-denominated instruments because of the dominance and function of the US dollar as the de facto international currency. It is attractive to hold, despite the availability of other stronger and more stable currencies, because the US dollar offers ready and easy liquidity. It is widely accepted and is the standard currency used in international trade. The more people use the US dollar, the stronger is its position as the international currency of choice.

The same phenomenon is true for the English language. No international accord was reached that made English the de facto working language of the Internet. But because of its widespread use, people have an incentive to learn and to use it in order to broaden their access to various people and e-resources. Not surprisingly, many nations require their school children to study English as a second language. And even adults take the initiative of voluntarily learning the language. Even EU members rely heavily on English to communicate with one another.

Network externality also explains much of what we see in the technological arena. Microsoft cornered the PC operating system market because MS-DOS established an early dominance and became the standard for the desktop computer industry. Apple has had to provide compatibility programs so that Microsoft software and files can also work on its computers. The fierce battles between Betamax and VHS and latterly between high-definition DVD and Blue-Ray are about becoming the industry standard. The same is true in the competition between WordPerfect and Word. Adobe (pdf files), Powerpoint, Excel, and many other types of office software have become quasi-industry standards because of their widespread use. And, of course, an excellent example of a network externality is QWERTY, that is the arrangement of the letters on the keyboard. We have long known that there are alternative ways of arranging the letters that are more efficient and less prone to errors. However, given the ubiquity of QWERTY keyboards and given the enormous investment of time and effort in relearning a new keyboard configuration, QWERTY will most likely be the standard for the foreseeable future.

In all these cases, a network externality is about a self-reinforcing critical mass. The more people employ a particular standard, the more firmly is that standard set in place. Moreover, new adopters and subsequent users reinforce the position of the standard even further, thereby attracting even more people to use it. The cost for both new and early adopters is continually lowered as the network externality becomes even more firmly entrenched. In economic terms, one could think of network externalities in terms of increasing returns to scale. The usefulness of the standard is enhanced even further with new adopters.

Marketplace rules of thumb are governed by the same dynamic. There is an operative network externality in the custom, law, and usage that undergirds the bounded rationality of economic life. Market processes are strengthened even further as more people subscribe to them. Thus, manufacturers are compelled to issue discount coupons as more people rely on them and as their competitors employ them. Supermarkets, department stores, and electronics retailers have had to take out large ads or provide inserts in the weekend papers. Newspapers have had to bolster their online platforms, and those that initially charged subscription fees to access their websites quickly abandoned such an effort when it became clear that web users were not going to put up with it. Thus, note, too, how airlines are very tentative in changing their policies to save costs until they see their competitors follow suit (e.g., fees for checked-in bags, reduced in-flight meal and beverage services, and expiring frequent flyer miles). Brand-name owners and major retail chains have voluntarily monitored their subcontractors' workshop conditions. Starbucks and other similar enterprises tout their use of Fair Trade suppliers, while other businesses pledge to give part of their revenues to charity. Talk of corporate social responsibility and in-house corporate ethics committees are *de rigueur*. In all these cases, there is a herd effect in embracing marketplace practices that have become widespread or routinely expected by the public. And in embracing these practices themselves, new adopters contribute toward making these the norm for everybody else.

The upshot of network externalities for our study is that individual market participants causally contribute to sustaining and even further strengthening marketplace practices. The coffee connoisseur who patronizes only Fair Trade coffee contributes to making this the standard behavior in the marketplace – the expected behavior both for other coffee drinkers and for coffee brewers. Students who refuse to purchase sweatshop college apparel contribute their share in curtailing exploitative work conditions. The household that boycotted Nestlé products for its unethical marketing of baby formula in developing nations causally contributed to changing Nestlé's predatory practices. We could go on with many other examples, such as the recent sensitivity to the carbon footprint of our individual economic choices and the organic food movement that supports locally grown produce and less harmful production methods.

Path dependency

Path dependency is a related concept to network externality. In simple terms, path dependency means that past economic outcomes shape current economic processes. In the perfectly competitive model of neoclassical economic theory, the economy is assumed to be frictionless and there is perfect information. This means that there is ease of entry or exit, and it is costless to move goods and factors of production to different parts of the economy. Of course, we know that these are heroic assumptions because, in practice, there are enormous transaction, transportation, and other frictional costs in moving goods and factors of production from one sector to another. Moreover, it takes time to acquire, process, and disseminate information. Thus, entrepreneurs are careful in their decisions on the kind of business enterprise they establish, when and where they operate, and how much capital they risk. After all, it will most likely be difficult to unwind these brick-and-mortar investment choices once they are made.

The importance of prior decisions is also underscored by the roundabout nature of economic activity. Take the case of something that we easily take for granted – our daily supply of bread. Households rely on supermarkets and grocery stores, which in turn depend on bakeries upstream. Further up the chain, food manufacturers have to supply bakeries with flour, and even further upstream, farmers have to plant and harvest the wheat. Along this entire chain, machine tool manufacturers and other ancillary suppliers have to provide tools and equipment for farmers, flour millers, bakers, and stores. These manufacturers and suppliers will require inputs themselves. In other words, behind a simple product, such as a slice of bread, lies a complex web of market infrastructure that required a chain of prior investment decisions. Indeed, where we are today in the economy is largely, but not entirely, dependent on where we have been and how far we have traveled in the past.[14] It is best to illustrate this phenomenon with examples.

The poverty trap described in the preceding chapter is one such example. Or consider Detroit's Big Three automotive firms. The previous decades of oil costing $10 to $20 per barrel lulled them into pouring their efforts and resources into producing large and gas-inefficient vehicles. After all, they were merely providing what US consumers demanded. The lessons from the dual oil embargoes of the 1970s had not been learned. Moreover, the United Auto Workers (UAW) saddled the industry with huge legacy health and pension costs, in addition to onerous and less flexible workplace rules. Thus, unlike firms such as Toyota, which invested instead in gas-efficient hybrids, the Big Three were not agile or strong enough to deal with the 2007–2008 oil price hikes and the 2008–2009 economic slowdown. Indeed, the past decisions of all parties involved – the Big Three, the UAW, and US consumers – severely restricted the US automotive industry's ability to respond to these twin crises.

Or consider the case of mass transportation. Unlike many European nations, the USA has lagged in investing in reliable and cost-effective mass transport systems. The automotive industry was partly built on the US reliance on the car as its primary mode of transportation. This was an era of cheap and plentiful gas. Given the current geopolitics of oil, climate change, and population growth, mass transport has attracted greater attention and

---

[14] I am not saying that the past determines present processes and outcomes. All I am claiming is that the past influences where we are today, although we are not necessarily or completely determined by our past. Such would be economic determinism.

funding from the US federal government. However, developing a mass transport network for the major US population centers will be that much more difficult and expensive because of the nature and design of the US transport infrastructure built around the automotive industry.

Past economic choices and outcomes shape the opportunities available for subsequent periods. However, as we will see in the next section, even long-established and widely adopted market practices are subject to change. Nonetheless, the phenomenon of path dependency accentuates the difficulty and expense of making such changes. The more deeply embedded market practices are, the longer it will take and the more difficult it will be to effect change. Thus, for example, it will take much effort to alter some harmful practices that have become deeply rooted in the modern economy, more so in some countries than in others: wasteful gas consumption from needless driving, brand-name consumption, overconsumption and inordinate credit card debt, a winner-take-all mentality, agricultural subsidies, tobacco marketing, unrestricted gun sales, Internet pornography, sports gambling, unrestricted CEO pay and perks, and unaccountable multinationals. The more individual economic actors participate in these activities, the more they support and strengthen these harmful market practices as acceptable norms, and the more difficult it will be to alter them. People may be desensitized and merely accept market harms as inevitable, or an immutable fact of economic life, or a necessary trade-off for the innumerable, impressive benefits provided by the marketplace. Eventually, injurious economic processes and outcomes are socially accepted or ignored. Market participants may be unwittingly dragged into a cumulative circular causation.

In sum, recall how we began in chapter 1 with a description of Kutz's three means by which economic complicity arises: through a significant causal contribution to the harm ("but for" causation), through participatory intent in a structured collective action (e.g., Dresden bombing, corporations), or through a quasi-participatory intent in an unstructured setting such as the marketplace. Bounded rationality, network externality, and path dependency further validate Kutz's (2000, 166–203) claim that quasi-participatory intent in unstructured harms constitutes complicity. After all, individual economic actors causally contribute to sustaining harmful marketplace practices and institutions through their buying and selling activities. In conforming to market custom, law, and usage, these economic agents further strengthen marketplace formal and informal rules of thumb (bounded rationality), thereby establishing them even further as the expected behavior for everybody else (network externality and path dependency). As we have seen in chapter 3, the moral quality of individual acts is partly determined by the moral quality of the collective act to which they contribute and of which they are a part.

Obligation to initiate change

The phenomena of bounded rationality, network externality, and path dependency do not mean that market rules and processes are immutable. No market practice or institution, no matter how deeply entrenched in public morality or widely adopted, is immune to change. (Think of slavery, medieval guilds, and workplace minority and gender discrimination.) The modern marketplace is extremely dynamic in engendering technological and organizational innovations. We have seen this from the Industrial Revolution to the current emerging globalized knowledge economy. The modern marketplace has proved itself to be extremely responsive to changing conditions. In fact, some of the organizational innovations in the past three hundred years have been about setting moral boundaries in limiting excesses in market processes and outcomes. Note the social legislation that emerged in response to the abuses during the Industrial Revolution. Consider, too, the current struggle to set new public moral standards in response to globalization. In other words, altering harmful marketplace practices and institutions is very much part and parcel of market participation.

Many harmful marketplace practices and institutions have been rejected and changed down through history via grassroots action. Recall Wilberforce and the abolitionist movement, apartheid divestment, and Nestlé's marketing of baby formula. Such successful reforms make individual market participants that much more responsible for doing their share to mitigate injurious market processes and outcomes.

Moreover, the better communication infrastructure provided by the Digital Age magnifies this moral duty even further. We can easily obtain and disseminate information, and we live in an ever more interconnected world. With such vastly improved access to information and to each other, we are now in an even better position, more than at any time in history, to see the adverse ripple effects of our economic choices on others, even on people halfway across the world. Consequently, we have even greater obligations to mitigate the harmful unintended consequences of our actions. Equally importantly, the microelectronics revolution has made it so much easier to initiate or to participate in collective action today, including lobbying government for appropriate action. Indeed, far from discouraging change, bounded rationality, network externality, and path dependency strengthen our personal and collective responsibility to rectify harmful or unjust market processes and outcomes. Some would even go so far as to call the omission to do so complicity by tolerating evil.[15]

Christian ethics

Christian theology's notion of "social sin" is directly relevant to the issue of complicity in reinforcing harmful social structures. In his *City of God*, Augustine (1958) already highlights the problems we have created for ourselves in the temporal city. In his Christian realism, Niebuhr (1932) is critical of unjust social structures that urgently need to be changed. Most authors attribute the specific notion of "social sin" to liberation theology, the Latin American Medellin Bishops' conference, and the Synod of Bishops' (1971, no. 51, 5, 3) document *Justice in the World*. These mark a clear break in terms of their explicit use and understanding of "sinful social structures." This has been called the "de-privatization" of sin, which has heretofore been viewed primarily and solely in personal, and not social, terms.[16]

At a minimum, social sin consists of (1) social structures and institutions that debase human dignity, (2) situations that serve as catalysts for personal sin, and (3) the acquiescence of people who tolerate such evils.[17] There are four schools of thought regarding the nature and dynamic of social sin: as merely the social effects of personal sin, as the embodiment of personal sin, as co-essential with personal sin, and as the primary phenomenon.[18] While there are those who would go so far as to argue that social sin has an independent existence of its own separate from personal sin, the predominant view is still the traditional position that treats personal sin as the primary analogue. Social sin is sin by analogy; it has a secondary sense of sin. Social sin is merely derivative.[19] This is an issue similar to the philosophical debate on whether or not there is such a thing as collective fault or collective responsibility. After all, the collective does not have an intention of its own.

Personal sins unavoidably affect social structures. Recall the earlier model of the common good proposed in chapter 2. The common good is relational by its nature (God to the person, person to other people, the community to each member within its ranks, individuals and the community to the

---

[15] Kissell (1996).
[16] Baum (2003). See Nelson (2009) for a recent assessment of the literature on social sin.
[17] O'Keefe (1990, 29).   [18] O'Keefe (1990, 17–25).
[19] Sacred Congregation for the Doctrine of the Faith (1986, no. 75); John Paul II (1987, no. 36); O'Keefe (1990, 19).

marginalized, and the stewardship of the earth). What we do or fail to do affects not only us, but others as well. Many philosophers agree that the person is social by nature. We need each other for everything – from survival to growth and development. In theological language, we are family, all belonging to the one Body of Christ. What happens to a member of the Body affects all (Eph 4). Thus, social sin is not merely the effect of personal sin; it is the collective embodiment of personal sins. History provides ample evidence of how personal sin corrupts and eventually erodes even the very best of social institutions. We find this from Solomon's paganization of Israel[20] because of his personal sins, all the way to the twentieth century, in the likes of people such as Hitler, Stalin, Pol Pot, and company.

But there is a two-way interaction. While personal sin engenders social sin, social sin in its own turn becomes the occasion for even more personal sins. The person flourishes only in community. Social life is the womb that nurtures the character of moral agents. And while the community does not determine personal virtue and character, it nonetheless has a tremendous influence on the kind of person people choose to be.[21] Social life has a large role in the ease or difficulty with which human flourishing is attained.

An unfortunate consequence of personal sin is the loss of a sense of sin that eventually dulls the conscience and paves the way for even more subsequent sins.[22] Thus, social sin manifests itself and wreaks further havoc of its own by creating a false consciousness among people, by perverting the community's self-understanding, and by creating a momentum of institutionalized wrongdoing – all the necessary ingredients that make it very likely that later collective decisions will add further to earlier injustices.[23] There is a self-reinforcing dynamic to social sin. Not surprisingly, some are led to conclude that social sin has a life of its own separate from personal sin, or that the two (personal and social sin) are co-essential.

Just like tort jurisprudence and social philosophy, moral theology has struggled to provide a satisfactory answer to the question of individual responsibility for social sin or collective wrongs. Some have suggested that the ascription of such individual responsibility depends on people's role in the collective wrong, their causal contribution, and the voluntariness of the cooperation with evil.[24] What is clear in the tradition, however, is that there is a moral duty to correct or to work toward the elimination of social sin if one has the resources or the opportunity to do so. Besides, it is part of the due care provision (third condition) of the principle of double effect.

---

[20] Birch (1991).   [21] Birch and Rasmussen (1989, 77–99); Hauerwas (1981).   [22] Ragazzi (2004, 365).
[23] Baum (1975, 200–203).   [24] Himes (1986). See also O'Keefe (1990, 69–75).

Thus, it has been suggested that contemporary almsgiving and philanthropy that leave unjust social structures unaddressed as root causes of destitution are as hollow and reprehensible as an unjust Israel in the Old Testament offering sacrifices and holocausts.[25] Referring to social sin in US economic life, Catholic bishops note, "Acquiescence in them or failure to correct them when it is possible to do so is a sinful dereliction of Christian duty."[26] Referring to an international economic order that benefits rich nations at the expense of the poor and reflecting on the implications of this for Christians in the United States, the Presbyterian Church passionately asserts:

There is no way any of us can escape these structures or these benefits ... Our single choice is whether we will collaborate with the powers that be or seek to change the situation, whether we will accept the status quo or commit our lives to the construction of a more just global society. *To do nothing* in today's struggle is not to assume neutrality; it is to support the status quo. *To remain silent* is not to withdraw from the battle; it *is to give consent to the way things are.* (Presbyterian Church 1984, no. 29.339, emphasis added)

This is a sentiment that is echoed in the declarations on contemporary economic justice from the different Christian traditions that we reviewed in the preceding chapters. They call for both personal conversion and collective action in redressing the root causes of economic ills.

Human accomplishments in the modern era have been long and impressive, especially in harnessing science and technology for the improvement of human welfare. Nonetheless, it is likewise a feature of modern life that these signal human accomplishments have been turned against humanity itself, from the abuse of the environment and natural resources, to the misuse of science and technology in waging even deadlier war and destruction. Consequently, we should be vigilant in constantly asking ourselves whether or not our accomplishments lead to greater love or to selfishness, to a fuller life or to death.[27]

This paradox applies just as well to the marketplace. The market is a remarkable social institution, the hallmark of the modern economy. For all its ills, the modern market economy has to be given credit for supporting the largest population base ever in human history and at the highest per capita income at that. Moreover, the market is also responsible for integrating the whole world as one functional entity. More than at any time, people all over the world are truly working together as a single economy. Much

[25] Perkins (1994, 45).   [26] National Conference of Catholic Bishops (1986, no. 77).
[27] John Paul II (1979, no. 15).

good can be wrought from the market, as we have seen in the reduction of the absolute numbers of people in poverty since 1980.[28] Nonetheless, like everything else, the marketplace as a human accomplishment can be corrupted as we have seen in the many preceding examples of wrongdoing. Only the vigilance and the moral courage of individual moral agents will ensure that the market does not end up like many other human accomplishments – as instruments of destruction, exploitation, greed, mistrust, and hatred.

Philosophical warrants

Locke

The spirit of Locke's (1690) "enough and as good" proviso on the original acquisition of private property is relevant for our current issue. Whether we are dealing with unmitigated grievous pecuniary externalities (previous chapter) or with uncorrected harmful market practices, we are dealing with the damage market processes and outcomes inflict on people's vital welfare interests. In all the examples from this and the preceding chapter, we find people's welfare interests set back and their rights violated. In particular, they are unable to access critical market goods and services to meet their basic needs. Often, they can do so only with great effort and extreme hardship, and sometimes at the expense of their other vital interests.

There is always a cost incurred in producing economic gains given the scarcity of economic resources. Some enjoy the gains while others end up having to bear the cost, or a combination of both. Given these conditions, we can adapt the spirit of Locke's "enough and as good" proviso for our own use.[29] Economic agents who benefit from market operations must ensure that they do not reap or keep so much of the gains as to leave little else for others, especially those who bear more of the costs or receive little of the gains. The latter are those who will not have "enough and as good" increments to their welfare at the end of the day. Consequently, it is incumbent on those who have gained much to pay the cost of altering market structures and institutions for a less extreme distribution of burdens and benefits in the next rounds of economic activity.

---

[28] Chen and Ravallion (2004).
[29] Locke's proviso pertains to original acquisition. Thus, we are merely using the underlying spirit of his proviso and not the proviso itself.

Human rights

Human rights can also be used as a basis for the moral obligation to attend to harmful socioeconomic structures. Thomas Pogge's (2002) book *World Poverty and Human Rights* is an illustration of the main point of this chapter. He argues that contrary to popular belief, wealthy nations' moral duty to assist destitute countries does not arise solely from the positive obligation to aid those who are in need. In fact, the moral duty stems from the even stronger negative moral obligation not to cause harm to others.

To appreciate fully his arguments, recall the difference between positive and negative rights. Satisfying negative rights merely entails not interfering with the exercise of people's rights. Thus, all we have to do to fulfill civil and political rights (e.g., freedoms of speech, movement, and religion) is not to interfere with other people's exercise of these rights. On the other hand, to meet positive rights (e.g., socioeconomic right to food, clothing, shelter, and medical care), the community has to expend real resources to assist those who are unable to procure these for themselves. Proponents of positive rights argue that there is a moral floor beneath which we will not allow people to sink. Shue (1980, 18) calls this the "morality of the depths." Thus, the community has a moral obligation to ensure that people are able to satisfy their basic needs. This positive moral duty includes removing institutional obstacles (such as harmful market practices) that prevent people from enjoying these rights. One such widely acknowledged positive moral obligation is the duty to assist the poor. Failure to discharge this duty is, in effect, an omission to prevent harm. The problem with relying on positive rights is that there is still a fierce debate over whether or not socioeconomic rights exist to begin with.[30] Besides, satisfying positive rights will most likely require tough political choices because they entail taxation and a de facto redistribution of community resources.

Let us now go back to Pogge's thesis. In his view, poor nations have been impoverished by the global socio-political-economic order in which international economic rules have been skewed in favor of the developed world. He argues that developed nations have, in fact, enriched themselves at the expense of poor nations. The latter are compelled to subscribe strictly to intellectual property rights (to the benefit of wealthy nations), even as the rich countries in their own turn restrict access to their own markets and subsidize agricultural goods, to the great detriment of poor nations. Moreover, wealthy nations exploit developing countries' natural resources, collude with these poor countries' autocrats, and even saddle them with

---

[30] See Trimiew (1997) for this debate.

unsustainable loans. The funds from these sovereign debts are ultimately either wasted or stolen by these autocratic governments, with the citizens of these poor nations eventually burdened with having to pay back these loans. He also points out that even the multilateral agencies, such as the World Bank, the IMF, and the WTO, have been coopted by wealthy nations for their own ends at the expense of developing countries.

In light of all this, Pogge argues that the moral failure of wealthy nations vis-à-vis poor countries is not merely a failure of omission, such as the failure to assist the poor. It is, in fact, a much more serious offense of hurting these impoverished populations through the rich nations' ruinous self-serving policies. Recall that some would claim that inflicting harm is much more blameworthy than failing to prevent harm. This is the positive acts principle from chapter 4.[31]

Pogge notes that rich nations are complicit in causing global poverty through their actions and the global institutional order they have imposed. Consequently, they have a negative obligation to cease disadvantaging poor nations and to rectify the damages they have already inflicted (corrective-compensatory justice). Such moral obligations are made even stronger since wealthy nations profited handsomely from their wrongdoing.[32]

In sum, human rights can be used in two ways to justify the moral duty to rectify harmful market practices and institutions. First, we could claim that there are positive rights, that is, socioeconomic rights, such as the right to food, clothing, medical care, and shelter. These rights give rise to a correlative duty to provide assistance to those who are unable to satisfy these claim-rights on their own. Of course, the problem with this method of justification is that many do not believe that positive, socioeconomic rights exist. The second route is a much stronger justification because the moral duty to address harmful market practices is based not on the obligation to assist the poor, but on the duty not to inflict harm. Failing to assist the poor is a mere omission (the failure to prevent harm), while inflicting harm is much more serious as it entails an actual causal contribution to the harm itself. Skeptics will find it much more difficult to dismiss the latter.[33]

---

[31] See, for example, Moore (1999, 31–34; 2002, 150–151).   [32] Pogge (2005, 69–74).

[33] The Achilles heel of Pogge's (2002; 2005) thesis is not his philosophical arguments but his interpretation of the empirical data that he uses as his starting point. For example, many will dispute his claims by pointing to the self-inflicted problems of many poor nations, such as corruption, political instability, and undisciplined economic policies. There is contributory negligence on the part of poor nations. It is very likely that both sides have a point. There are both exogenous and endogenous causes behind the plight of many poor countries.

Distributive justice
An appeal to distributive justice is another way of justifying the moral duty
to rectify harmful market practices and institutions. In fact, different
schools of thought can be used to argue for such a moral responsibility.
Given our space constraint, we can only provide a non-exhaustive illustration of how one might use the requirements of distributive justice as
grounds for the moral duty of mitigating grievous pecuniary externalities
and attending to harmful market practices and institutions.

A. K. Sen (1992) argues that the goal of political economy is to assist
members of the community to build up their capacity to work toward their
respective goals and to function as self-actualizing economic agents. To
implement his "capabilities and functionings" approach to distributive
justice, we would have to remove systemic impediments that prevent
economic actors from acquiring the aforesaid capacity. This would, of
course, include mitigating injurious pecuniary externalities and rectifying
harmful market practices and institutions.

In his theory of justice as fairness, Rawls (1971) proposes in his second
lexical rule that inequalities be permitted only to the degree that these
benefit the most disadvantaged and only if the public offices that generate
such inequalities are open to all. As we have seen earlier, the harms from
severe pecuniary externalities or injurious socioeconomic structures are
often borne by those who are least able to bear these burdens. Thus,
correcting both of these is a prerequisite to satisfying Rawls's second
lexical rule.

Of the various proponents of egalitarianism, Dworkin (1981) argues in
favor of an "equality of resources" as the best path to justice within the
community. Implementing this type of egalitarianism, however, is not
possible without first correcting the market's structural flaws. We have to
attenuate the market's pernicious unintended consequences that cause or
magnify inequalities in the distribution of burdens and benefits across the
community.

Marx (1867) critiques capitalism for its intrinsic imbalance in power and
its unfair outcomes. There is a need to transform socioeconomic processes
that perpetrate such imbalances and exploitation. These obviously require
corrective action.

This is just a sampling of how wildly dissimilar schools of thought on
distributive justice nevertheless converge on the need to attend to severe
pecuniary externalities and to remedy baleful marketplace practices and
institutions. Distributive justice can provide a robust justification for
the moral obligations proposed for this and the preceding chapter's soft

complicity. It also illustrates once again the importance of the moral standards employed in dealing with the issue of economic complicity.

Identifying obligation holders

Identifying who has the moral obligation to correct harmful market practices and institutions should be a fairly straightforward exercise. To begin with, those who have benefitted from the status quo have the duty to shoulder the cost of rectifying its flaws that have unduly burdened other market participants. The greater the proportion of benefits reaped, the heavier are the obligations.

Likewise, market participants who are in a much better sociohistorical location or who hold critical public offices or who possess unique or vital resources for improving market processes and outcomes also have a more significant share of this moral duty. In fact, these are also likely to be the people who ought to take the lead in organizing the requisite collective action for change.

We are not ascribing moral responsibility to these individuals simply on the basis of group membership. We are still basing their duties on their likely causal contribution to sustaining and reinforcing harmful market processes and outcomes. These are likely the ones who have benefitted the most from the status quo or the ones with the best sociohistorical location.[34] Establishing the extent of these individual causal contributions is an empirical matter that can only be determined in their particular context.

Establishing degree of individual liability

Far more difficult than identifying who is morally culpable is the issue of determining the degree of liability for the obligation holders. It was collective action that produced such accumulative socioeconomic harms, and it will also be collective action that can rectify them effectively.[35] Unfortunately, there is an asymmetry in this dynamic. On the one hand,

---

[34] We are dealing not with vicarious liability, but with fault liability.

[35] Based on Feinberg's (1970, 248–251) typology of collective responsibility, this is a "contributory group fault: collective but not distributive." This means that the fault or liability for the wrongdoing can be imputed not to any single individual but to a collective.

giving rise to the accumulative harm does not require deliberate effort on the part of anyone. The harm simply emerges spontaneously without the need for organized activity or collective intent (e.g., overfishing, global warming). It just materializes as part of the "invisible hand."

On the other hand, undoing the accumulative damage requires deliberate collective effort, for a number of reasons. First, typical individual market participants will most likely not voluntarily incur the additional cost of doing their share in rectifying the accumulative harm unless others do likewise. After all, unscrupulous market participants will simply free-ride on their efforts. This is the classic prisoners' dilemma and the problem of the commons. Second, setting an accumulative harm aright often requires coordination if it is to be effective. For example, in the case of harmful pecuniary externalities, one would first have to decide on the threshold of severity that merits assistance and then identify those who deserve such relief. In both cases there is a need for organized action at the level of the community.

In effect, what we have in these past two chapters is a case in which individuals can best discharge their moral responsibilities through collective action. This gives rise to a second set of moral duties – the moral obligation to initiate and to lead the requisite ameliorative collective action. To whom should we ascribe such responsibility of leadership and initiative? Perhaps the easiest way of responding to this question is to go around it and to resolve another issue that is relatively less demanding to answer at an abstract level: what are the grounds for such a duty of organizing the requisite remedial collective action? Consider the following.

First, we have the obligation to prevent harm, especially if it can be done at minimal cost or risk to ourselves.[36] Second, we have the scholastic notion of general justice by which individuals voluntarily shoulder their share of burdens in community life according to their means. Third, the various Christian traditions consistently call on those who are in key social positions or who have the resources to provide relief to those who are no longer able to function for the common good (principle of socialization). Fourth, we could also cite the superfluous income criterion by which people are obliged to use whatever is superfluous in their resources for the benefit of others. Superfluity is measured in terms of the relative unmet needs of one's neighbor. Related to this, of course, is the just-use obligation of our personal gifts and resources. Fifth, using the Christian understanding that we are made in the image and likeness of God, we can argue that selflessness and the requirements of charity call on us to serve the common good by

---

[36] Feinberg (1984, 126–186).

rectifying these harmful structures according to our means. Sixth, recall how tort jurisprudence often assigns liability on the basis of the capacity to absorb the damages or to forestall harms.

Indeed, the greater the capacity to act or to contribute on the part of the economic actor, the greater is the obligation. Note that this is often enforceable not in the external forum, but in the internal forum of the mind and heart. On a side note, the importance of collective action underscores the role of private voluntary groups, the NGOs, besides governmental action.

One final mention must also be made of the strength of individual obligations. The ordinary market participant is only one out of billions of other economic actors. Thus, the individual's causal contribution to perpetrating and reinforcing harmful market processes and outcomes is infinitesimal. Consequently, some might even argue that the individual's moral responsibility for such flawed economic processes is trivial at best. As we saw earlier, we can turn such a claim on its head. That the market participant is merely one out of billions of other economic actors makes the individual's moral obligation that much stronger, not weaker. After all, with so many other market participants, the individual's share in the requisite ameliorative action would be correspondingly much smaller and, therefore, that much easier to fulfill.

SUMMARY AND CONCLUSIONS

The first impression one gains of the marketplace is that it is a spontaneous gathering of people trading with each other and improving their welfare in the process. In fact, the market is undergirded by a web of formal and informal rules accumulated over time through custom, law, and usage. Economic agents reinforce these underlying practices and institutions through their participation in the marketplace.

Unfortunately, some of these are harmful or unjust social practices and institutions. In these cases, there is a collective moral obligation to alter or, at least, to attenuate these injurious market processes and structures. This is called for by the due care provision (third condition) of the principle of double effect. This is an invertible, permissible material cooperation that carries a collective and personal liability to ameliorate the harm. It is the failure to live up to this liability that constitutes economic wrongdoing (object of accountability). Complicity arises if individuals fail to do their share in discharging this collective liability. The critical contribution of Christian ethics for this fourth type of complicity is its notion of social sin, the scholastic notion of legal justice, the principle of socialization, and the selflessness of charity that works for the promotion of the common good.

PART III

Synthesis and conclusions

CHAPTER 9

Toward a theology of economic responsibility

Economic responsibility is the corollary of economic complicity. After all, the issue of complicity is ultimately a question of responsibility. But why be responsible? Why take responsibility for distant harms whose causes are either ill-defined or unidentified, or both? Why hold oneself to account when the community itself does not hold us legally or morally culpable? Any theological reflection on economic complicity must necessarily articulate a corresponding ethics of economic responsibility. In what follows, we examine the foundations of a theology of responsibility for economic harms using the literature on the nature of responsibility, Sacred Scripture, and the official statements of the various Christian churches on economic justice.

FITTING IN WITHIN THE LITERATURE

Let us begin by clarifying the type of economic responsibility we examine in this chapter. There are at least three types of economic responsibility according to the object of the duty. First, we have the positive obligations, such as our responsibility for helping those who are in need. There is much in both the philosophical and theological literature on this kind of economic responsibility. The second type pertains to stewardship for the gifts that we hold in trust, such as our skills and our possessions. The third deals with negative obligations, such as not hurting others or rectifying the unintended ills that we cause. This last type of economic responsibility is the topic of our study and of this chapter.

The philosophical literature on responsibility is extensive. Schweiker (1995) suggests two sets of distinctions that are helpful in describing various theories of responsibility. With respect to first principles, we have what he calls strong and weak theories. With respect to moral focus, we have agential, social, and dialogical theories.[1]

---

[1] The following typology and description of theories of responsibility are drawn from Schweiker (1995).

A strong theory of responsibility is one in which the first principle and the foundation that gives moral life intelligibility are responsibility and its demands. The primary lens with which we view life and evaluate the rightness or wrongness of human acts is responsibility (not utility, end, happiness, or fairness). A weak theory of responsibility is one in which responsibility is merely a secondary consideration or auxiliary lens. It supports an even more basic principle (e.g., the good, duty). Responsibility is not the benchmark against which moral choices are evaluated, but it is nevertheless still a relevant criterion.[2]

Regarding moral focus, we have agential theories. These revolve around moral agents and their deeds. The focus is on agents' moral choices. However, agential theories differ in the criteria they use in evaluating the rightness or wrongness of a human act. Thus, Immanuel Kant (1785 [1990]) has his categorical imperative in which an act is moral only if the principle of such an act can be generalized for everybody else without exception. Schweiker considers Kant's to be the most important agential theory of responsibility in contemporary thought. It is also an example of a strong theory of responsibility.

Paul Tillich's work is an example of a weak agential theory of responsibility. In his moral theory, morality is about self-actualization. He notes that, "The moral imperative is the command to become what one potentially is, a *person* within a community of persons."[3] *Agape* holds the key to such self-actualization. It is the root principle of this morality.

Social theories of responsibility are concerned with moral agents' place, role, contributions, and interactions within the community. Marion Smiley (1992) is an example of a strong social theory of responsibility. For Smiley, responsibility is part of and, in fact, flows from social and political practice. People's self-understanding develops through living, communicating, and interacting within the community. As individuals and as a collective, moral agents take responsibility for the suffering of others and for other external harms.

Stanley Haeurwas (1984) is an example of a weak social theory of responsibility. For Hauerwas, responsibility is important, but it is not the ultimate principle. Rather, God's action in the person of Jesus Christ is the first principle of morality. It is God's initiative and action that animate the community of faith as its members mutually form one another's Christian identity. The community of faith is the womb that forms and nurtures the person's character.

[2] Schweiker (1995, 42).   [3] Tillich (1963, 19, emphasis original).

Dialogical theories of responsibility focus on moral agency as an encounter with the other and as a response to the other. Responsibility is relational; it is about response. H. Richard Niebuhr (1963) is an example of a strong dialogical theory in that he sees responsibility as the first principle of ethics. Life and moral agency are about responsiveness. Moral agents relate to one another within a complex web of mutual responsiveness. The human person is distinctive not so much as an artificer ("man-the-maker") or as a member of a community ("man-the-citizen"), but for his capacity for purposeful action and responsiveness ("man-the-answerer"). Karl Barth (1985–1986) is an example of a weak dialogical theory of responsibility. No doubt, responsibility is still central to his ethics because the moral agent is charged with obeying the command of God. But it is God's divine command, not responsibility, that is the ultimate principle of morality.

Having reviewed the different theories of responsibility, Schweiker (1995, 41–42) proposes his own ethics of responsibility because he finds the above-mentioned accounts of morality to be inadequate. They concentrate on particular facets of moral life, often to the exclusion of other important dimensions. Schweiker gleans key moral insights from the preceding theories and integrates them into his own account of responsibility. Thus, he avoids their shortcomings while building on their strengths. He calls his imperative of responsibility an "integrated ethic." We will examine more of his ethics later in this chapter.

Schweiker's integrated approach is ideal for the problem of economic complicity. Besides, agential, social, and relational-dialogical theories mutually enrich each other and present a much more complete view of what is, in reality, a complex moral life. The term "complicity" is from the Latin word *complicitās*, which means being in a state of complexity or being involved. And, indeed, as we have seen in the preceding chapters, there is nothing simple about the phenomenon of economic complicity. Only the most egregious instances of clearly immoral acts present cut-and-dried cases, such as human trafficking and exploitation. The vast majority of cases, however, ultimately require prudential judgment that weighs numerous relevant factors, such as the nature and gravity of the harm, the social location and role of the moral agent, and personal capability. For example, in the case of the Saipan sweatshops, recall the challenge of assessing the moral responsibility of suppliers, consumers, bankers, shippers, etc. (chapter 5). Even tort jurisprudence has had to resort to a convenient legal device called proximate cause in view of the difficulty of establishing individual causality or culpability (chapter 4). Economic life is complex and dynamic, and so too are its ills. Consequently, no single theory of responsibility suffices in our efforts to impute personal culpability for complex economic harms. Different cases will require their own respective moral foci.

For example, for hard complicity, the moral focus should clearly be on the moral act of the agent. (Think of sweatshop operators and their labor recruiters.) Kant's agential theory explains why there is a duty not to harm others. His categorical imperative is invaluable in making the case for why moral agents should cease and desist from activities with severe disexternalities (e.g., speculative investments, overuse of microbials, inordinate consumption). The nature of the act or the intention of the moral agent, or both, are critical in cases of hard complicity. These should be the proper moral foci, and agential theories are better suited to assessing this type of blameworthy material cooperation.

This is not so for soft complicity. In these cases, the problem lies not with the intention of the moral agent or with the initial moral act, but in the failure to mitigate the ensuing ill effects. And even with this duty to attenuate the consequent injury, the individual can do so effectively only through collaborative work with others. Collective-action problems are the major obstacles to resolving problems of soft complicity. It is difficult to initiate and sustain such concerted action in the absence of critical social mechanisms. Moreover, even if we are able to get some form of collective action going, it is often ineffective because of free-riders.

The social theories of responsibility are clearly helpful in dealing with such collective-action problems because the community has the power to mandate or facilitate remedial action. These theories can be instrumental in shaping a community ethos that institutionalizes the practice of helping those adversely affected by market outcomes. We have repeatedly seen how market activity always leaves a trail of both burdens and benefits that are often difficult to disentangle or change. There are always winners and losers in market exchange. The community can make it common practice for winners to compensate or assist those who are severely disadvantaged.

In these cases, the proper moral focus should be on community institutions vis-à-vis the moral agent. Social and political institutions are vital channels through which individuals can contribute toward redressing collective harms. Moreover, the community can apply moral suasion by praising or criticizing particular acts (e.g., shaming free-riders). Thus, social theories of responsibility are relatively more important for dealing with soft complicity compared with agential theories.

When it comes to remote complicity (e.g., consumers of sweatshop apparel), the lines and the degree of individual moral responsibility are blurred. We often find ourselves unable to establish with precision the nature of the agent's personal moral obligation. In these cases, the agential and the social theories are of limited use. Instead, personal responsibility based on an appreciation of I–Thou encounters can fill the gaps left by agential or social theories of responsibility. Recall that the moral focus of dialogic-relational theories of responsibility is on responsiveness. They are better suited to moving moral agents to internalize a deep sense of responsibility and concern for others. For most people, laws, social mandates, or community pressure to take responsibility will most likely not be compelling in cases of remote material cooperation. Rather, it will be moral agents' internal moral compass that will provide the impetus.

For most cases, it is very likely that we can and should combine all three moral foci. For example, Kant's categorical imperative is also useful in demonstrating why it is in everyone's interest that we mitigate the harmful unintended consequences of market transactions (chapters 7 and 8). Attending to instances of soft complicity (harmful pecuniary externalities and unjust social structures) is not only fair, but it also ensures peace of mind for all – that no one will be left alone to shoulder burdens that are properly communal in nature.

Or take the case of consumption, production, and investment disexternalities (chapter 6). The ordinary market participant is unable singlehandedly to change harmful market processes and outcomes. The social approach to responsibility gets around this problem by making the requisite ameliorative action a community undertaking. For example, using Smiley's (1992) pragmatic framework of responsibility, we can justify social policies that severely restrict damaging speculative investments, curtail injurious production methods, or discourage excessive consumption.

Dialogical theories of responsibility are helpful in dealing with a wide variety of market-mediated complicity. To begin with, they ensure that power is not misused. They are also critical for addressing a particularly pernicious effect of market operations – the twin dangers of impersonalism and individualism. As the size of communities and markets expands, economic exchange becomes ever more anonymous. We do not know (and often do not care to know) who produced the clothes we wear, the food we eat, and the electronic gadgets we use. Our obligations to these workers end at the point of sale when we hand over our payment for our purchases. There are no residual obligations, economic or otherwise, owed to these workers. The cut-and-thrust of competitive market operations breeds an ethos of survival of the fittest, and with it, a hardened competitive individualism. Such a hostile environment makes it even more unlikely for the ordinary economic agent to attenuate voluntarily the ill effects of market operations or to contribute to such a communal effort (e.g., Fair Trade). Very few of the points made in this book will find resonance in hearts and minds that are steeped in the market's impersonal and individualistic ethos.

The I–Thou relationship, with its notion of mutual responsiveness and its implicit mutual respect, bridges the widening separation between moral agents that comes with ever larger markets. Dialogical theories of responsibility prevent us from using spatial or temporal distance as an excuse to walk away from our duties to one another. We care for the people with whom we exchange in this grand division of labor, even if we do not see them, or know them, or are far away from them. We do not treat them merely as trading partners or as suppliers or as potential customers; rather, we treat them as persons. We never view them as factors of production, but instead as fellow human beings struggling to eke out a livelihood to support loved ones. The problem of economic complicity would be greatly diminished, if only there were a better appreciation for the dialogical theories' view of human life as one of I–Thou encounters. Responsibility is essentially about genuine responsiveness.

In sum, economic complicity requires nothing less than an integrated approach to responsibility. Economic life is far too complicated and dynamic, as is the notion and praxis of responsibility. Given these twin complexities, we need a correspondingly robust theory and practice of economic responsibility.

BUILDING BLOCKS FOR A THEOLOGY OF ECONOMIC RESPONSIBILITY

In what follows, we examine the grounds for a theology of responsibility for economic harms using three different sources: ontology, Sacred Scripture, and tradition.

Ontology

Jonas–Schweiker ontology

Schweiker (1995) builds on the earlier work of Hans Jonas (1984), *The Imperative of Responsibility*. In this much-celebrated work, Jonas claims that there is a need to overhaul radically our entire way of going about ethics because technological progress has undermined the axioms of traditional moral thinking, to wit:

- *Techne* is ethically neutral with respect to both its subject and object.
- Ethics is anthropocentric, concerned primarily with interpersonal relationships.
- The human person is "considered constant in essence and not itself an object of reshaping *techne*."
- The good or evil with which the moral agent is concerned is proximate and not remote.

(Jonas 1984, 4)

Our technological age has rendered these premises untenable. Since 1984 when the English translation of Jonas's work was published, we have amassed even more unimaginable technological powers that have often outpaced our capacity for moral discourse. Thus, embryonic stem cell research, genetic engineering, the possibility of human cloning, global warming, and, of course, the old familiar specter of nuclear annihilation, have demonstrated how:

- *Techne* can no longer be assumed to be ethically neutral with respect to its subject or object (e.g., embryonic stem cell research for those who believe that life begins at conception).
- Ethics has to be inclusive in weighing the impact of moral action on non-human beings as well (e.g., the earth, animal, and plant life).
- The essence of what it is to be a human person is not immutable after all (e.g., those who do not see anything immoral in human cloning, or even in experimenting with it in the interest of pushing the frontiers of science).
- Moral action can produce accumulative harms that become apparent only after a time lag or after a certain critical mass, or both (e.g., climate change).[4]

There is a need for a complete rethinking of ethics given the potency of technology that now threatens human existence and, indeed, nature itself. Ethics will have to be reformulated in the face of greatly expanded human powers. Given the ripple effects of our technologies and how we often misuse them, we are now even more responsible for the future.

In the face of a much more potent and often misdirected human agency, Jonas proposes a new set of moral imperatives as a rational response to the changed and precarious state of the human condition.

"Act so that the effects of your action are compatible with the permanence of genuine human life"; or expressed negatively: "Act so that the effects of your action are not destructive of the future possibility of such life"; or simply "Do not compromise the conditions for the indefinite continuation of humanity on

---

[4] These are my illustrations and not from the original work of Jonas.

earth"; or again turned positive: "In our present choice, include the future wholeness of Man among the objects of your will." (Jonas 1984, 11)[5]

Unfortunately, this new ethics of responsibility is merely an assertion. It still
has to be justified. Jonas knows that there is a need to provide grounding for
his new ethics. This is a difficult task because of the loss of traditional
metaphysics and theism as legitimate foundations for public norms in the
wake of the Enlightenment. Nonetheless, Jonas believes that there must be
an ontological foundation to ethics. Ethics cannot be separated from
ontology.

   Jonas grounds his ethics in his ontology of nature. He argues that there is
a self-affirming quality, indeed, a self-affirming purposiveness to every
being, to wit: the opposition of being with non-being, of life with death.
"Life is the explicit confrontation of being with non-being."[6] The ontology
behind his ethics is the preservation of existence over non-existence, of
being over non-being.

   Schweiker (1995, 207) takes this a step further by noting that in understanding the difference between being and non-being, and in desiring
existence over non-existence, the human person is conscious that there is
value to a state of being over non-being, to a state of existence over non-
existence. In other words, the human person knows that goodness comes
with being, rather than with non-being. Schweiker pushes Jonas's ontology
further by raising even more foundational questions.

> But the question is whether or not this point about purposiveness can be rendered
> intelligible without something like a theological claim ... Can we make sense of
> the immanent claim of a being to realization which resonates with our sense of
> being agents without articulating that claim in theological terms? ... [C]an the
> goodness of existence endemic to our consciousness as agents be conceived without
> endorsing the reality of an unconditional good, that is God? (Schweiker 1995, 207)

In other words, moral agents discern that the self-affirming purposive
orientation and dynamic intrinsic to beings are good. But where did this
consciousness of goodness and desire for "being over non-being, reality over
destruction" come from? What are their basis and measure? What are the
grounds for this self-affirming purposiveness? Schweiker (1995, 207) concludes that there is irony to Jonas's ethics in that it is "the self-limitation of

[5] Bernstein (1994, 846–847) notes that it is ironic that even as Jonas laments the anthropocentrism of
  traditional ethics, he himself is anthropocentric in his new ethics. He questions why Jonas gives
  precedence to human life over other forms of organic life. After all, the self-affirming purposiveness of
  beings (versus non-beings) applies not only to human life but to other organic life as well.
[6] Jonas (1984, 81).

God that creates the unlimited space of human responsibility." It is the divine mode of being that gives rise to the grounds and the moral space for a responsibility and morality that seek to preserve the integrity of life.

Schweiker provides a new understanding of moral agency, power, and value: "Every human act endorses the reality of God in the affirmation of being against its negation and fragmentation" (1995, 208). True value comes from the proper exercise of power as it affirms and ennobles life and its orientation toward self-preservation. In other words, any exercise of power that debases or destroys life is self-defeating and hollow. With this new understanding of moral agency, power, and value, Schweiker proposes an integrated ethics of responsibility in which *moral agents face the imperative of respecting and enhancing persons, the common good, and the community of life before God in all their actions and relations.* This "community of life" includes all non-living entities that are critical for the preservation of life, such as the ecology.[7] This is an ethics that calls for the respect of all creation given the interrelatedness of all creatures. In living up to this imperative of responsibility, moral agents attain a unique good – moral integrity – that enhances and brings their life to a much higher level of existence.

In effect, Schweiker provides a moral-ontological proof of God. His ethics of responsibility is clearly similar to Jonas's imperatives. However, unlike Jonas, Schweiker insists that moral agents can discharge this ethics of responsibility only *before God.* Power is about the pursuit of the good in affirming and enhancing the integrity of the community of life. And all this transpires before God who is the unconditional good providing the moral space and the means for the exercise of responsibility. Note, too, the implicit but central assumption in both Jonas's and Schweiker's imperatives on the affirmation and preservation of the integrity of life: *We have to take ownership and responsibility for the harmful, unintended consequences of our moral acts!* The enhancement of the community of life is the end for which power is exercised. This strikes at the heart of why economic complicity is blameworthy.

Aristotelean–Thomistic metaphysics
Since ontology is important for ethics, it is worth examining an alternative ontological foundation for the imperative of responsibility. Besides Jonas's and Schweiker's ontology, we could also use Aristotelean–Thomistic metaphysics to undergird a theological ethics of economic responsibility. Given

---

[7] Schweiker (1995, 209, 244).

our space constraint, I can only sketch an outline of such an ontological foundation.

God has necessary existence since, by definition, any being who is God could not be dependent on anything or anyone for existence. Existence is in the very nature of God. Creatures, however, are merely contingent in their existence because they cannot guarantee their own continuance as beings. They decay, die, and are destructible.

Contingent existence is possible only by participation in the existence of a necessary being. After all, there is no other source of existence but necessary beings. Thus, creatures merely participate in the necessary existence of God. Similarly, the goodness and perfections we find in creatures are merely a participation in the supreme goodness and perfection of God. In other words, creatures merely reflect a particular dimension of the goodness and perfection of God. They communicate these particular dimensions of God's perfection and goodness according to their mode of being and operation.[8] In the case of human beings, they do so through their rational faculties, that is, through the reasoned use of their freedom. Moral goodness is the distinctive manner by which human beings reflect their participated perfections and goodness from God.

The entire ensemble of creatures (the universe) has its final end in God.[9] Moreover, every creature is part of the order of the universe and also has its final end in God. Every creature is also oriented toward fulfilling the end (*telos*) of the universe of which it is a part and to which it contributes. They individually contribute to attaining the *telos* of the universe according to the mode of their being and operation. For example, a tree produces fruit, absorbs carbon dioxide, and fulfills many other functions as part of a delicate biosphere. Every creature has its own *telos*, an end or a purpose for which it exists.

In the case of humans, they contribute to maintaining the order and attaining the end of the universe through their moral agency. For example, in caring for the ecology, in preserving harmony among themselves, in discovering truth, and in creating works of art, human beings contribute in their unique way to the order and advancement of the universe to its final end in God.

There is a *telos* to economic life (e.g., provision of basic needs, community building, outlet for human creativity, venue for inventiveness and

---

[8] Since God's goodness and perfection are unequaled (by the nature of God), not even the entire ensemble of creatures (the whole universe) can fully communicate together the perfection and supreme goodness of God.

[9] After all, theirs is merely a participated existence and a participated goodness in God.

personal growth). Responsibility entails the use of the person's moral agency and other personal gifts to move creatures and the human community toward their respective ends. Taking responsibility for the harms we cause is an important part of this moral goodness.[10] To use the language of Jonas and Schweiker, moral agents are charged with respecting and enhancing the integrity of the community of life that envelops them. Thus, using Aristotelean–Thomistic metaphysics, we arrive at the same imperative of responsibility that Jonas and Schweiker propose.[11]

Sacred Scripture

Sacred Scripture has a privileged role in Christian theology.[12] Thus, it is also important for us to examine the scriptural foundations of a theology of responsibility for economic harms. Both the Old and the New Testament have much to teach on economic life. Foremost among these are the many admonitions concerning the care of the poor. These are positive obligations (first type of responsibility) and we will not deal with them in this section since we are concerned merely with teachings related to economic complicity. Recall that complicity entails causing harm either directly (e.g., hard complicity) or indirectly (soft complicity) through our market choices. They entail negative obligations (e.g., ceasing and desisting from the injury-causing activity) or corrective positive obligations (e.g., restitution for the injuries inflicted). Thus, we will focus only on a very small subset of biblical economic teachings.

Individual responsibility

We will first establish the basis for individual responsibility. Taking responsibility for the consequences of our actions is a longstanding teaching in both the Old and the New Testament. Genesis provides numerous examples, as in the cases of Adam and Eve in Eden, Cain for the killing of his brother Abel, and the contemporaries of Noah, to name a few. Even as collective responsibility-punishment (e.g., Ex 20:5) and collective identity are important in the Ancient Near East and for the Chosen People of God,[13] there is nonetheless a keen appreciation for individual accountability. As early as the Old Testament, we already find many passages in which

---

[10] Schweiker calls this moral integrity or the ethical good, his fourth kind of goods.
[11] See Wright (1957) and Barrera (2005b, 19–40, 209–237) for a more in-depth presentation.
[12] I subscribe to Cosgrove's (2002) rules of principle and analogy in using Sacred Scripture for contemporary ethics.
[13] Robinson (1936).

individual responsibility is stressed in Israel (e.g., Dt 24:6; Ez 14:20, 18:2; Jer 31:30; Prv 24:12; Sir 16:14). The New Testament brings this focus on individual accountability to a whole new level with its repeated call for personal conversion, repentance, and discipleship and with its frequent reminders of an eventual eschatological judgment for every person (e.g., Mt 25:31–46). Thus, from Genesis to Revelation, individual responsibility is a constitutive feature of moral life alongside collective responsibility. The two are not mutually exclusive, but neither do they substitute for one another. There is a proper role for each.

Torts and restitution

Individuals are obligated to take responsibility for the injuries they cause to life, limb, or property. Consider, for example the tort laws in the Old Testament (Ex 21:12, 18, 22, 26–36; 22:1–15; Dt 22:8, 13–19, 28–29; Lv 6:1–7; 24:18). In these cases, wrongdoing or negligence that causes harm constitutes sufficient grounds for punishment or fines, or both. Those who harm life or property have to provide restitution, even if the injuries caused are unintended. Clearly, justice requires a cessation to the wrongdoing, restoration to the victim, compensation for that which cannot be recovered or returned in whole, and additional punitive penalties in cases of intentional harm.

In the New Testament, we find Zacchaeus promising to pay back fourfold anyone whom he may have defrauded (Lk 19:1–10). In paying back fourfold what was unjustly taken, Zacchaeus is not merely restoring that which he had taken from others; he is also imposing on himself additional punitive damages as atonement (retribution) for his wrongdoing. We see in this case both corrective and retributive justice at work.

A common theme running through the Old Testament tort laws and the Zacchaeus narrative is the principle that moral agents are liable for the injuries they inflict on others as a result of their wrongdoing or negligence, whether intended or unintended. Restitution or punitive damages, or both, are a necessary part of such accountability, in addition to whatever other non-pecuniary penalties may be imposed by the community.

Prophetic literature

The Old Testament prophets vehemently condemn economic injustice and urge Israel to turn away from its sinful ways and to revert to its covenant relationship with God. After the Hebrews' liberation from Egyptian slavery, God had formed them into a nation in a land flowing with milk and honey. As the Chosen People of God, they were to be a nation different from all other nations in the manner by which they cared for one another in an economy of mutual respect and a politics of service. Unfortunately, Israel fails to live up to its election of responsibility and chooses instead to emulate the economics and politics of the surrounding nations. By the time of the monarchs, the nation has turned to an economics of privilege and a politics of power. Many are driven into debt, poverty, and, eventually, slavery on account of the heavy impositions of the royal court and the elites.[14] Pharaonic subjugation is replaced by oppression from their fellow Hebrews. Thus, we see the harsh denunciations of the prophets who plead, cajole, and denounce the royal court and the privileged class for having spurned the stipulations of the Covenant.

Part of the prophetic preaching is against economic misdeeds. Thus, Isaiah (10:1–3) condemns those who subvert the laws in order to rob widows and orphans. Amos (4:1–2; 6:1–7; 8:4–6) warns of a forthcoming day of punishment for the rich who wallow in their indulgent consumption and maltreat the poor. Jeremiah (22:13–14, 13–17) indicts those who exploit workers and withhold their pay. Micah (6:8) reminds people of the importance of love, humility, and justice before the Lord. Ezekiel (22:29–30) laments the widespread extortion, robbery, and mistreatment of the vulnerable. Indeed, the prophets preach mightily against the economic injustice that marred the Promised Land given by God to Israel, warning the Chosen People that they were about to lose this divine gift.

These are but a sampling of the prophetic passages relevant for our study. It is sufficient for us to note that underlying these prophetic indictments is the understanding that wrongdoing, including that of an economic nature, is abhorrent in the eyes of God. These malfeasors bring down evil consequences on themselves and on the people who depend on them. But there is also a hopeful message behind these harsh prophetic passages. There is hope for forgiveness and renewal, if only malefactors cease and desist in their wrongdoing, take responsibility for their actions, and repent.

Biblical hostility to wealth

Scripture scholarship has brought new light to the interpretation of biblical passages dealing with wealth. There is a strong undercurrent of hostility to wealth running through the Old Testament, Ancient Near Eastern literature, and the Synoptic Gospels.[15] Social scientific criticism attributes such hostility

---

[14] Birch (1991).
[15] For example, see Mk 10:23–25 and Lk 6:23–26. See Schmidt (1987) for an extended discussion of this phenomenon. See Nickelsburg (1978–1979) for parallels between the Gospel of Luke and Enoch on the disparagement of wealth.

to the limited-goods nature of the ancient economy. This is the phenomenon in pre-modern societies in which people believed that communal resources were limited. There is only a finite amount to go around. In other words, one's consumption or use of resources necessarily leaves that much less for others. Economic activity has a zero-sum dynamic. The implication of this is that the rich are immediately suspect, indeed, guilty of wrongdoing. After all, they are able to accumulate so much wealth only by depriving everybody else of such resources. How the rich gained so much wealth (even if through honest work or shrewd investing, or good fortune) is irrelevant. The presumption is that the rich, by amassing so much of the communal resources, are impoverishing or inflicting injury on everybody else. Thus, we have the many scripture passages that harshly condemn the rich. No distinction is made between those who enriched themselves through wrongdoing and those who toiled and worked legitimately to acquire their fortune.

Let us examine the latter case. It seems unfair and counter-intuitive to the modern mind to hold the rich morally culpable even if their wealth was acquired through virtue (e.g., hard work, frugality, prudence) or laudable activity (e.g., entrepreneurship), or both. However, it is important to remember that for people who believe that they live in a limited-goods society, what is deemed morally blameworthy in such cases of honestly acquired wealth is the hoarding of scarce community resources. The rich are held liable not for their virtuous, hard work, but for their failure to mitigate its harmful unintended consequences even as they have the means to do so. The continued possession of such wealth by the rich means that they are not doing enough to ameliorate the unintended injurious ripple effects of their legitimate activities. The presumption is that the continued possession of such wealth in a limited-goods society is *prima facie* evidence of a failure to redress the ill effects of their having acquired so much of the community's finite resources. It is this that is morally problematic. There is a presumed duty to share with others. They should have been engaged in almsgiving on a scale that would have put communal resources back in circulation within the community, even as they help the destitute – the proverbial two birds with one stone. And in doing so, they would have reduced their holdings of wealth (the public's finite resources). Thus, wealth becomes an indictment that the rich have not been engaged in genuine, substantive almsgiving.[16]

[16] Perkins (1994, 50–51) arrives at the same conclusion and notes that inequality in the distribution of wealth was not the issue in the New Testament. Rather, it was the failure of the rich to recirculate the wealth back into the economy in terms of debt relief or almsgiving because they were preoccupied with their own consumption and comfort. In accumulating wealth, the rich were leaving that much less for others.

This argument upends the commonly held view that almsgiving is a supererogatory act or that it stems from the positive obligation to provide assistance and relief to the destitute. Based on the aforementioned limited-goods-society framework, almsgiving becomes a negative obligation, that is, an obligation not to harm others. Almsgiving in this case stems from the duty to keep the community's limited resources circulating within the economy. It is not supererogatory but a requirement of justice. The deeper underlying axiom in the limited-goods-society worldview is the under-standing that the goods of the community are meant for the benefit of all regardless of how titles of ownership are assigned.[17]

We find this interpretation and understanding of Sacred Scripture affirmed in Patristic writings. Despite the many admonitions in the New Testament on voluntary divestment, the Fathers of the Church do not advocate complete dispossession. In fact, they accept the right to private property ownership as having a legitimate function in God's order of creation. However, unlike the Greek and Roman interpretation and practice of private property ownership, the Patristic teachings underscore the obli-gations that come with such right to ownership – almsgiving and sharing with the destitute. This is based on the biblical understanding that God gave the earth for the use of all. The Patristic Fathers distinguish between own-ership and usufruct. They are scathing in their condemnation of the wealthy for their failure to live up to the duties that come with their riches.

Tertullian describes alms as "trust funds of piety" that resulted from wealth that was not spent "upon banquets or drinking-parties not thankless eating-houses, but to feed the poor and bury them, for boys and girls who lack property and parents, and then for slaves grown old and shipwrecked mariners." Ambrose even goes so far as to address the wealthy: "You are not making a gift of your possessions to the poor person. You are handing over to him what is his."[18] Almsgiving is, in effect, merely restitution for what was stolen to begin with. Hoarded wealth is theft from the poor. We see in Patristic literature a similar vehement hostility to wealth based on the implicit premises of a limited-goods society: that the fruits of creation are finite and that they are a gift for all, thereby creating the duty of almsgiving.[19]

This biblical and Patristic view of wealth and almsgiving as mirror images of each other is directly relevant for the two cases of soft complicity we have

---

[17] In our own time, this has been called the principle of the universal destination of the goods of the earth. See Vatican II (1965).
[18] Phan (1984, 38).   [19] Gonzalez (1990); Phan (1984, 35–41).

examined. Chapters 7 and 8 concluded that market participants have a moral responsibility to bear their share of the communal obligation to attend to the harmful pecuniary externalities or the unjust social structures that emerge out of regular market operations. These harms are completely unintended and result from laudable work. Nevertheless, market participants are morally culpable, not for the harmful unintended consequences of their legitimate activities, but for their failure to attenuate these injurious collateral effects even as they have the means to do so. This is part of the due care provision (third condition) of the principle of double effect.

In sum, scripture scholarship concerning wealth gives us a principle that is relevant for the problem of complicity, to wit: there is a moral obligation to rectify the harmful unintended consequences of even ethical activities, if we have the means to do so. The blameworthiness arises in leaving these injurious ripple effects unattended. This moral obligation is made even stronger if we have reaped benefits from such activities.

Exploitative almsgiving

Another helpful finding of social scientific criticism in biblical scholarship is the admonition in the Gospel of Luke against the Greco-Roman practice of patronage. In Luke 14:12–14, Jesus calls on his dinner host not to invite his friends or kin or the wealthy or the powerful, but the poor, the lame, the blind, and the maimed – people whom the host would never have associated with and people who could not reciprocate his favor (cf. Lk 6:27–35).

As mentioned earlier, in a limited-goods society, the rich are expected to share their wealth with the rest of the community. The rich reinject their wealth back into the community through their benefactions or through their social spending, such as underwriting public games and entertainment, monuments, and building projects. The idea is to ensure that the community's finite wealth and resources are kept circulating in the economy. In return for such spending, the rich garner public adulation, honors, goodwill, and prestige within the community. Such sharing is not altruistic because the wealthy are interested in enhancing their own social status and influence. The accumulation of power is their primary goal.

In addition to such public spending, giving people favors is another means by which the rich recirculate wealth back into the community while accumulating power and status for themselves. In the Greco-Roman world, having a powerful benefactor is essential for protection, political access, favors, or financial assistance. It is a form of social and political insurance for the ordinary citizen. In return for these, clients accord their patrons respect, loyalty, services, or favors. The larger the number of clients that are beholden to them, the greater is the prestige and power of the patron within the community.

In such a hierarchical, status-conscious society, people from different classes do not associate with one another. They move around only with their own kind. And in holding banquets or meals, they invite only their social peers or people who would be able to return the favor and reciprocate with a similar invitation in the future. Luke (14:12–14; 6:27–35) is critical of such an ethics of reciprocity.

There are at least two concerns regarding this practice. First, it is an impediment to building a genuine community. There is no mutual respect for one another and no appreciation for their equality as human beings. Rather, wealthy and powerful benefactors deem themselves superior to their clients. Thus, note that an important ethical theme in Luke-Acts is *koinōnia*, that is, fellowship, community, and communion. Luke presents the early Church as a fellowship of equals, as a people of "one heart and one mind." They concretely manifest this by holding their goods in common (Acts 4:32–35). Scripture scholars point to Luke's use of the Greek notion of friendship in which friends share everything in common.[20] Equal and respectful regard and affection for one another are at the root of *koinōnia*, the exact opposite of patron–client relationships criticized in Luke 14:12–14.

A second problem with the Greco-Roman practice of patronage has to do with the improper use of wealth to hold clients in subservience, fear, and dependence. Benefactions are, in fact, exploitative because the rich are taking advantage of the clients' vulnerability to enhance their own prestige, power, status, and influence. In other words, clients are used as means to further the patrons' own ends. Far from assisting the needy, the Greco-Roman practice of patronage uses wealth to dominate others and to amass even more power. Patrons are merely changing their wealth from one form of tangible power (material affluence) to other forms of power (influence and social standing). One could call this exploitative, self-serving, or negative almsgiving.

Patronage goes against the end (the *telos*) for which the fruits of the earth have been given by God. God entrusted the earth to humanity, not that they might dominate or hold others in subservience, but that all may be well provisioned. Genuine almsgiving is indiscriminate and prodigal in the way it assists the destitute, without expecting anything in return. Thus, in Luke 14:12–14, it is the poor, the lame, the blind, and the maimed who are honored with an invitation, the people whom the host would have never

---

[20] Johnson (2004).

associated with, much less share a meal with and invite to enjoy the hospitality of his home. The host would have never moved in such circles beneath his social status. He would have been ridiculed in the Greco-Roman community for such folly.

This indictment of patronage is relevant for our study because it addresses the same underlying moral problem as hard complicity in which the powerful view their neighbors not as equals, but as inferiors to be dominated, exploited, and used for their own ends. It is the same problem of the powerful taking advantage of the plight of the poor and the needy and using them for profit and personal gain (e.g., sweatshop operations). In the case of unconscionable consumption, production, or investments (chapter 6), we have people who exhibit a similar indifference to their neighbors' well-being. A common moral flaw we find in cases of hard complicity is the lack of respect for the dignity of others who are viewed merely as objects or as opportunities for profit and advantage. For perpetrators of hard complicity, wealth and power are to be used to press their own advantage to the fullest extent.

In sum, the underlying moral principle behind the Lucan teaching against patronage illustrates what genuine economic responsibility for harms entails – never treating the poor or the vulnerable as expendable means or opportunities for personal gain. It is a call to *koinōnia*, a genuine fellowship of care and friendship with others. This is the antithesis of both Greco-Roman patron–client relationships and the cases of hard complicity we examined. Power, privilege, and wealth ought not to be used for wrong ends (e.g., self-aggrandizement). The requisite immediate response is to cease and desist from such wrongdoing.

Sensus fidei: *official church declarations on economic justice*

The official statements of the various Christian traditions on economic justice provide a wealth of insights for a theology of responsibility for economic harms. These documents converge in many of their social teachings on economic justice despite their deep disagreements over unfettered market operations and despite wide differences in their theology and ecclesiology. We have conservative evangelicals and fundamentalists, on the one hand, and the more liberal mainline Protestant and Roman Catholic churches, on the other hand, arriving at the same conclusions regarding the minimum conditions that a just economy must exhibit.

This agreement is probably due to their common biblical and theological starting point: a firm belief in a loving God who created the heavens and the earth, who sent us His only Son Jesus Christ to die and to save us from sin, and who adopted us as His own children. Thus, as family, we are meant to live in mutual love and care for one another. The goal is to live in co-humanity and to bring God's purposes to reality by affirming and helping people realize their God-given potential. As Christians, we have been invited to live in a community of faith in which the sanctity of life is actively protected and promoted.

These core beliefs have a material impact on the kind of economic life we ought to have. God provides for the spiritual and material needs of all; indeed, God provides an abundance for all. We are called to value all of God's creatures. Ours is an economy of mutual respect and equal worth for all as brothers and sisters. As disciples, we have the privilege of continuing the work of Christ, especially among the poor, and of participating in God's ongoing creation. Our care and love for the poor are a measure of our love of God. All is grace, and far from having an inflated sense of human accomplishment, we are grateful and humbly acknowledge our mere stewardship of the wondrous gifts entrusted to our care. In fact, our moral choices in economic life affect our relationships with God and our neighbor. Consequently, economic justice is an imperative of the Christian faith. The Christian churches keenly appreciate the unmerited divine gifts we have received and the consequent high expectations God has for us – high expectations that we ought to have for ourselves and for one another.

Given these shared theological premises, many of these Christian traditions also converge in some of their views on what has gone awry in our economic life: great and increasing inequality in economic wealth and political power; pervasive job insecurity; chronic unemployment and underemployment; the erosion of worker rights and protection; hunger and homelessness; disease, malnutrition, and death for children; the feminization of poverty; diversion of scarce resources for excessive military spending; racism and discrimination; environmental degradation; lack of the most basic needs such as health care, education, clean water, and sanitation for many; materialism and consumerism; the loss of meaning and purpose of life for the rich; and the loss of hope for the destitute.

In the pain of having to name the ills that afflict us today, these disparate Christian traditions arrive at another uncanny convergence: their shared conclusion that Christians cannot walk away and be indifferent to the economic ills and suffering we witness around us. Our faith will not permit us to do so. Moreover, some of these traditions even go so far as to admit openly their role in directly or indirectly perpetuating these social problems.

But in all these traditions, there is an unequivocal acknowledgment of human failure and sinfulness and our need for God's redeeming grace.

It is stunning to read the frank admission of the churches that are bold and honest enough to admit their complicity and share of the fault. No summary or paraphrasing can do justice to the eloquence and sincerity of their admission, and I present a sampling of these.

As North American Christians in the United Church of Christ, *we must boldly confess the inequity and injustice in the economic system of the United States*, at the same time *we admit our involvement with injustices in the global economy*. This confession requires both naming the structural problems inherent in our economic system and confronting the effects of racism, sexism, materialism and militarism. *The church cannot be truly prophetic without honest confession.* (United Church of Christ, 1989, 132–133, emphasis added)

Accepting the need to face up to the clear mandate and expression of the will of God on how we ought to treat one another, the Church goes further and admits:

We shrink from this acknowledgment, however, because we are afraid to bear the suffering love of Christ in our lives. We resist because we find our own vested interests challenged if we are faithful to God's covenant. We hesitate, for to acknowledge the reign of God and justice is to expose our loyalty to mammon and we are unmasked as idolaters. (United Church of Christ, 1989, 136)

The entire section on the "Statement of Christian conviction" (section VI) is a confession and repentance for their individual and collective roles in sustaining economic injustice with an honest admission, "Our silence and complicity contribute to the economic oppression of persons whom God loves."[21]

The official statement of the General Synod of the Church notes that "commitment to economic justice becomes a profound human responsibility" since the necessary resources are available to eradicate poverty. The Church, by its own account, has done little to play its part in mitigating economic injustices both in the USA and abroad.[22]

The United Methodist Church (2000) also recognizes the need to work more assiduously in reforming sinful social structures. It urges its membership to be proactive at the local level in working for economic justice. The Church also calls for vigilance in ensuring that its investments do not abet wrongdoing, but are put to work instead in promoting justice. Most telling

---

[21] United Church of Christ (1989, 147).   [22] United Church of Christ (1989, 131).

of all is how the Church ends its statement by reminding local churches and individuals "to live a simpler, more modest lifestyle."

The Lutheran Church in America (1980) observes that our individual and collective economic choices "reflect what a society is and influence what it is becoming." Moreover, it notes that the requirements of justice are not revealed but are gradually discerned and discovered in our daily interactions in the different realms of life. But they can be discerned only by a truly reflective people who heed their conscience and who make the effort to inform and nurture that conscience.

In the lead paragraph of its official statement, the American Lutheran Church (1980) admits that it has done little as a church to do its part in shaping socioeconomic structures to be more in line with God's will. Hence, its document is entitled "The Reformation is unfinished!" As individuals and as a church, they accept their participation in the social structures of society. Consequently, they bear obligations to bring the economy more in line with God's order of creation. And since they are both sinners and saints, they hold that their social involvement must be doctrinally balanced to entail both faith and works.

A theological commentary on the Episcopalians' *Taking Action for Economic Justice* is emphatic that the statement is not meant to be a precursor to a "fund drive." Rather, it is a wake-up call to the affluent members of the congregation to be more engaged with the poor in the latter's struggles and quest for "equal opportunity within an insensitive system."[23] This entails a difficult passage from "mere condescension toward the poor to genuine partnership with them."

"Church" is that human geography in which the rich own and live out their need for the poor and the poor discover and live out their gifts for the rich in the name of Jesus Christ. *The fact that bifurcation rather than amalgamation characterizes the social make-up not only of society, but of the Church itself, highlights the need for conversion and pilgrimage on the part of the People of God.* (Perkinson 1988, A-9, emphasis added)

The Presbyterian Church (1984, no. 29.338–339) concludes its theological reflection on Christian faith and economic justice with an impassioned plea against inaction and indifference. To do nothing is to be complicit in the economic wrongs from which rich nations benefit enormously. They recognize that they are middle class and that they enjoy advantages many others can only dream of. They admit being part of a jarring disparity in

---

[23] Perkinson (1988, A-88).

which great wealth is accumulated, hoarded, or misused even as millions lack the most basic needs. They concede that they face as yet an unfulfilled obligation to share with others the same advantages they enjoy and to turn a harsh economy into one that is caring.[24]

The Reformed Church in America (1984, 52) calls for humble repentance in those instances in which their economic conduct is not in conformity with the witness of Sacred Scripture. They, too, readily admit that they are middle class and must, consequently, address their obligations toward the poor. Sacred Scripture has already clearly taught how to deal with poverty in the midst of a high-income society. The Church reminds its membership of Calvin's admonition to the rich of how wealth and power can impede growth in their spiritual lives.[25]

The evangelicals gathered in Oxford declare, "We acknowledge that all too often we have allowed society to shape our views and actions and have failed to apply scriptural teaching in this crucial area of our lives [economics], and *we repent.*"[26] Five years later, they affirm that they should not be party to unjust socioeconomic divisions because as a community of faith they should reflect the unity of the Triune God.[27]

In their 1971 Synodal document *Justice in the World*, Roman Catholic bishops note that the Church must live in its own life the justice that it preaches. Otherwise, it loses credibility. Moreover, the bishops conclude the section on the Church's witness with a frank declaration:

Our examination of conscience now comes to the life style [*sic*] of all: bishops, priests, religious and lay people ... In societies enjoying a higher level of consumer spending, it must be asked whether our life style [*sic*] exemplifies that sparingness with regard to consumption which we preach to others as necessary in order that so many millions of hungry people throughout the world may be fed. (Synod of Bishops 1971, no. 48)

The US Catholic Bishops in their 1986 Pastoral Letter *Economic Justice for All* (no. 347–358) echo the same concerns on the importance of witness within the Church itself as an economic actor.

These churches' reflections on economic justice are relevant for a theology of responsibility for economic harms because of the unusual convergence of their conclusions and resolutions. That they come to a common

---

[24] De Vries (1998, 225). Recall our earlier discussion of patron–client relationships and the invitation to the rich and the powerful to share their resources with the poor without thought of return.
[25] De Vries (1998, 227).
[26] Second International Conference on Christian Faith and Economics (1990, emphasis added).
[27] Third International Conference on Christian Faith and Economics (1995, no. 22).

admission and repentance, despite their theological, philosophical, and ecclesiological differences, encompassing both conservatives and liberals, is reflective of the Holy Spirit at work. One cannot help but be reminded of the *sensus fidei* in Roman Catholic theology.

> The holy People of God shares also in Christ's prophetic office: it spreads abroad a loving witness to Him, especially by a life of faith and love ... The whole body of the faithful who have an anointing that comes from the holy one (cf. 1 Jn 2:20 and 27) cannot err in matters of belief. This characteristic is shown in the supernatural appreciation of the faith (*sensus fidei*) of the whole people, when, "from the bishops to the last of the faithful" (Augustine, *De Praed. Sanct.* 14, 27) they manifest a universal assent in matters of faith and morals. (Vatican II 1964, no. 12)

The Holy Spirit worked through the Chosen People of the Old Testament. It is the same Holy Spirit that animated the apostles and the early Church in continuing the work of Christ. And it is still the same Holy Spirit that works to this day in the faithful believers who seek only to do the will of God and to be witnesses to the Gospel. It is the yearning and hunger for God that have led these churches to their conclusion that there is something wrong in our shared economic life, that we contribute to it, and most important, that we are ultimately responsible for such flawed or unjust market processes and outcomes.

TOWARD A THEOLOGY OF RESPONSIBILITY FOR ECONOMIC HARMS

The preceding sections have laid out ontological, scriptural, theological, and experiential grounds for our moral obligation to take responsibility for the harms we directly or indirectly cause. A theology of responsibility for economic harms has to show the relationship between power, responsibility, and freedom. Power is the reality we confront, responsibility pertains to our response, and freedom is the outcome we reap. We examine each in the following sections.

Power

Economic processes and outcomes are shaped by the relative bargaining power of market participants. Such power can be misused or abused, but it can also be used for good. Thus, it is important to understand the nature of economic power.

The conditions that prompted Jonas to propose a new ethics and our own difficulties in dealing with the issue of economic complicity are strikingly similar. Recall his account of the four premises of traditional ethical thinking that have been upended by modern technology. Contemporary globalization can be likened to modern technology in the manner by which it has undermined the same longstanding axioms of traditional market ethics.

1 *Techne* (or market processes and institutions) cannot be assumed to be ethically neutral with respect to its subject or object (e.g., the treatment of labor as a factor of production no different from capital, equipment, or raw materials).
2 Economic ethics can no longer be anthropocentric but has to weigh the impact of economic activity on the biosphere (e.g., pollution, depletion of non-renewable resources, global warming).
3 The essence of what it is to be a human person is not immutable after all (e.g., commercial surrogacy, commodification of ova and sperm, commodification of vital human organs, human trafficking).
4 Individual economic acts produce accumulative harms that become apparent only after a time lag or after a certain critical mass is reached, or both (e.g., consumption, production, and investment disexternalities in chapter 6).[28]

The technological conditions described by Jonas bear a striking similarity to how market processes have also rendered untenable the premises undergirding traditional economic ethics. Perhaps this should not surprise us at all. To begin with, innovations in contemporary market exchange are heavily and directly reliant on technology (e.g., the Internet and the microelectronics revolution). Hence, if we talk of modern technology, we necessarily have to talk of economic activity as well. Moreover, technological progress does not merely entail tangible assets like computers or new equipment. Technological progress can also come in the form of organizational innovations, that is, improvements in the manner by which we organize ourselves so as to be even more efficient in our collective endeavors. An excellent example of this is offshore outsourcing in which the whole world is integrated as a single workshop. Parts coming from different

---

[28] These are my illustrations and not from the original work of Jonas. Furthermore, note that some of these concerns are not new. For example, some have questioned the morality of wage-labor contracts that in effect commodify labor. Furthermore, many have long criticized the claim that the market is a value-neutral institution or process. Nonetheless, globalization has exacerbated many of these problems and has highlighted the flaws in these premises.

continents are assembled at a single site (e.g., consumer electronics, Boeing and Airbus planes, cars).[29]

How is all this relevant for the study of economic complicity? Recall that the more intractable cases of economic complicity are those that stem from the greatly expanded reach of economic agency. The ripple effects of our actions spread much farther and are even more disruptive. Economic complicity becomes a major and widespread phenomenon as consumers all over the globe become unwitting parties to the inhumane working conditions in the factories and farms that produce their goods. Economic complicity becomes a real concern because the predatory and dishonest mortgage lending of some brokers in California can wipe out the hard-earned savings of retirees in Iceland. In other words, market participation entails some form and degree of power. Some have it more than others. Technological-organizational innovations and the new wealth created by globalization have greatly expanded the reach and potency of our individual and collective economic agency. There is a corresponding need to rethink economic ethics in the wake of our greater economic power to affect others and to shape the future – the very same concerns of Jonas over modern technology.

Responsibility

An adequate theology of responsibility for economic harms would most likely be characterized by a sweeping, all-encompassing imperative and by a moral realism that acknowledges the trade-offs that come with everyday choices. We examine each in the following sections.

A sweeping imperative

Jonas and Schweiker propose a rethinking of ethics because people today can easily ennoble or destroy future lives through their proper use or abuse of technology. Moral agency has acquired a new potency and, consequently, it has to be presented with a correspondingly more demanding ethic – the respect and preservation of the integrity of life in whichever time period it may be found. The "extensification and intensification" of power must be matched by a corresponding "extensification and intensification" of responsibility.[30] In other words, an expansion in the scope and impact of our

---

[29] Other recent examples are research networking and just-in-time inventory production methods. An example of an organizational innovation from an earlier era is Fordist mass production in the early twentieth century.
[30] Lüpke (2009, 464–466).

power leads to a like expansion in the scope and demands of our moral duties. The two are mirror images of one another.

There are no temporal limits to such responsibility, save that of the limits of the reach and power of technology. On top of this, note that we are unable to pinpoint specifically who will be the victims and the perpetrators, and when, where, and to what degree these various parties will be involved or affected. These are all unknown variables because of the unpredictable ripple effects of a more potent technology. Hence, Jonas's and Schweiker's imperatives are correspondingly general and all-encompassing: respect and enhance the community of life under all circumstances.

We are faced with the same dynamic and need in the phenomenon of economic complicity. Since market processes and organizational innovations have greatly expanded the reach of economic agents across both space and time, we are unable to pinpoint *ex ante* all the parties who will be involved or adversely affected. We know that there will be economic ills down the road, but we do not know ahead of time who specifically will be disadvantaged, where, when, and to what degree. It is the familiar problem of establishing causality (chapters 2 and 4).[31] Furthermore, recall that many economic harms are accumulative in nature and have a lag. Moreover, market activity creates many unintended consequences. How then ought we to change economic ethics in the face of such uncertainties and unknowns? By binding ourselves to a correspondingly far-reaching and all-encompassing new imperative.

Building on the new imperatives of Jonas and Schweiker, we can say that economic agents also face the same ethics of responsibility to respect and preserve the integrity of the community of life in all their economic choices, actions, and relations. The spatial and temporal reach of these duties are as extensive as the spatial and temporal limits of the ripple effects of our economic choices. And following the additional twist in Schweiker's ethics of imperative, we will also claim that economic agents face a new ethics of responsibility that respects and ennobles the community of life in all their actions *before God*, the One whose self-limitation provides the moral space and grounds for such expansive moral choices to begin with.

In practical terms, this means that people are morally responsible for accumulative harms, no matter how remote they might be from the injury or how minuscule their contributory fault or causal contribution to the injury. They are bound by a *prima facie* obligation to respect and enhance the integrity of life wherever it may be and in whatever generation it may be

---

[31] The most that we can do *ex ante* is to rely on forecasts using known causal correlations.

found. In other words, Jonas's and Schweiker's new imperatives of responsibility turn out to be just as applicable to cases of economic complicity in
which unintended but foreseen ill effects ripple through both space and
time inflicting injury on unsuspecting third parties (disexternalities). We
have obligations for the harms we directly or indirectly inflict, even if
unintended, *ceteris paribus.*[32] The more wide-ranging and potent the ripple
effects of our actions, the greater are the scope and requirements of our duty
to respect and enhance the integrity of life. The demands of this imperative
of responsibility are co-extensive with the enhanced reach and power of our
economic agency – the "extensification and intensification" of economic
responsibility.

Moral ambiguities

Schweiker's moral realism is useful for the issue of economic complicity.
There are trade-offs in the preservation of the integrity of the community of
life. This is important for market ethics because economic choices, by their
nature, entail opportunity costs.

In Schweiker's (1995, 209, 244) imperative, his "community of life"
includes the human person, the common good, all life forms, and all
inanimate entities such as rocks, oxygen, and many others. It is an all-
inclusive notion of community encompassing the ecosphere. Following
Thomas Aquinas, he notes that human beings are rational social animals.
Thus, they require and value different types of goods. Schweiker (1995, 119–
120) proposes three types of goods, to wit:

1 pre-moral goods (e.g., biological needs, food, clothing, shelter, bodily
   health, etc.),
2 social goods (e.g., customs, law, practices, beliefs, etc.), and
3 reflective goods (e.g., personal beliefs, values, self-understanding).[33]

There are values attached to each of these goods, and human life is about
acquiring and balancing these various goods with the goal of attaining
integrity of life. This comes about only as the person enjoys the unity
(wholeness) of values that come from these goods.

Schweiker (1995, 121) is realistic and acknowledges that there are trade-
offs in the pursuit of these three goods and their corresponding values.
Human beings cannot escape from hard choices. Sometimes, these are even

---

[32] Readers are reminded that such duties can be mitigated or intensified by the many other factors that
are also relevant in the ascription of moral culpability for market harms, such as gravity of harm,
personal capability, and sociohistorical location.
[33] His fourth good is moral integrity or the ethical good.

tragic choices. He calls this the moral ambiguities that shadow moral life. Some goods and their values often have to be sacrificed for other goods. Moreover, these burdens and benefits are unevenly distributed across people. Not surprisingly, Schweiker employs the principle of double effect in securing and maintaining the integrity of life even as human choices produce both values and disvalues.

This moral ambiguity is descriptive of economic complicity. There are unintended disvalues that come in the wake of our pursuit of values. But this realism is not the only reason why Schweiker's ethics is suitable for our current study. Even more important is the conviction that *despite these moral ambiguities, despite these hard, even tragic, choices, moral agents will nevertheless still have to respect and enhance the integrity of the community of life.* Moral ambiguities do not excuse us from the imperative of responsibility. How then do we satisfy simultaneously these two seemingly incompatible claims of upholding the integrity of life even in the face of moral ambiguities?

We find many instances in economic life in which these two competing claims are reconciled. Take the case of soft complicity. Our market activities produce unintended, often severe, adverse consequences for other market participants. In addition, we may be unwittingly reinforcing unjust market structures and processes. Such malign market effects and institutions surely create disvalues and even violate the integrity of life for other market participants (e.g., manufacturing workers laid-off in consequence of freer trade). But in economic life, this is not necessarily the end of the story. It has long been recognized that winners can compensate the disadvantaged even while preserving the social gains from market activity. In other words, while specific instances of market choices can lead to disvalues, we can attenuate these disvalues through extra-market mechanisms. Thus, the integrity of the community of life can still be preserved and even enhanced at the end of the day despite the moral ambiguities that confront us. Concrete examples include the carbon offset programs, Fair Trade, and, of course, the trade adjustment assistance programs for workers adversely affected by international trade. Unfortunately, as we have seen in the preceding two chapters, the moral problem of economic complicity arises when people choose not to trouble themselves with such extra-market remedial measures. Often, they simply walk away from these disvalues that they could easily ameliorate.

In sum, despite the hard, even tragic, opportunity costs we face in life, moral agents are nonetheless still bound to respect and enhance the integrity of the community of life through remedial action. This is particularly important for the cases of soft complicity we examined. Mitigating the unintended harms we spawn in the market is relatively easy compared with other ethical realms like bioethics or war because, in economic life, we can often restore the good that has been lost through compensation or subsequent preferential treatment (e.g., affirmative action).

Freedom

Jesus Christ is the paradigm of responsibility. He is the unavoidable reference point in responding to two questions: to whom and for what are we responsible?[34]

To whom are we responsible?

Responsibility is said to be forensic in nature. After all, to be responsible is to be accountable for a trust or a duty. Sacred Scripture is fundamentally forensic in its understanding of responsibility. We see this succinctly encapsulated in 2 Corinthians 5:10. We will all individually stand before the judgment seat of Christ one day and receive our just deserts.[35] We will have to account for how well we have used the manifold gifts in our lives to reflect the goodness and perfection of God. At a minimum, such stewardship entails not harming or impeding others' integral human development and making right whatever injuries we may have caused that mar God's order of creation. Naturally, this includes economic life. The parable of the final judgment (Mt 25:31–46) is about the failure to discharge our positive obligations for one another's well-being: feeding the hungry, clothing the naked, and visiting the sick and imprisoned. If the final judgment is exacting when it comes to failures of omission, how much more demanding will it be when it comes to our failures of commission in which we inflict injury to others? On the day of reckoning, we will be held responsible for the harms we could have prevented but chose not to avert, and we will also be held to account for the injuries we have unavoidably caused, but failed to mitigate.

For what are we responsible?

There is more for which we are responsible besides how we have treated our neighbors. On that day of judgment, we will have the benefit of eschatological hindsight. On that day, we will be our own harshest judge when we realize the heights of freedom and perfection to which we could have soared,

---

[34] Lüpke (2009).   [35] Lüpke (2009, 466–467).

but did not, and the plenitude of graces we could have availed of for such a purpose, but did not. This includes our economic agency.

Economic growth and development are generally defined in terms of the expansion of people's range of choices. Economic growth and development are about having the means and the opportunities for greater freedom of action. This greatly enhanced power has created a dilemma similar to that described by Jonas who laments the difficulty of grounding his new ethics in the modern milieu: "Now we shiver in the nakedness of a nihilism in which near-omnipotence is paired with near-emptiness, *greatest capacity with knowing least for what ends to use it*" (Jonas 1984, 23, emphasis added). Jonas notes the paradox of how technology has increasingly imbued the modern person with ever greater powers, even as the modern moral agent has been increasingly diminished in knowing to what end such powers ought to be exercised.

It is the same sad irony in economic life. People have amassed great wealth and power because of technological progress and globalization. At the same time, however, they are increasingly unable or unwilling to discern the end for which such powers ought to be used. The ostentatious and self-indulgent consumption of the super-rich or the nouveau riche or even of ordinary people in the face of widespread global poverty is a case in point.

Economic life entails unavoidable trade-offs that often require hard choices and self-sacrifice, but these are also the occasions for rising to new heights in our moral integrity. The numerous instances of complicity in the preceding chapters are foregone opportunities by which power can be used to enhance the integrity of the community of life. The market produces accumulative harms (e.g., pollution), but it can also bring forth accumulative benefits (e.g., knowledge economy, Internet, easier networking, greater interdependence). Much good can be accomplished (including putting an end to poverty), but only if we work together and set aside our myopic self-interest. We can mitigate many of the harmful ripple effects of our economic choices, but only if we willingly accept great personal sacrifice. There are endless promising possibilities by which economic wealth and its attendant power can be used to ennoble life.[36]

People cannot be compelled to work for the good or to use power wisely. Social legislation and community shaming mechanisms can prevent people from misusing power, but these social institutions cannot force people into positive action. Such can only come from the heart and the mind. After all, remember that the vast majority of cases of economic complicity can be

---

[36] Warren Buffett and the Gates Foundation come to mind.

addressed only in the internal forum. Thus, it is all the more important for moral agents to understand, appreciate, and internalize the ontology underlying their power and their moral choices. In particular, economic agents should realize that they themselves are diminished to the degree that they are morally complicit in economic harms, no matter how remote or minuscule their causal contribution might be. Or, to put it another way, as moral agents struggle to rectify harmful market ills, often at great cost to themselves, they are not only ennobling others but enhancing their own moral integrity as well.

According to Jonas's and Schweiker's imperative of responsibility, the moral agent experiences a new and higher level of self-affirmation and life by pursuing the good. Thus, responsibility is central to human authenticity, advancement, goodness, and moral agency.[37] In the process of affirming the integrity of life around them, moral agents also affirm and enhance their own integrity of life.

Herein lies what we may call the paradox of responsibility. We are freest only after we wholeheartedly embrace our responsibilities. Ontologically speaking, responsibility gives rise to a freedom that can be defined as "the self-affirmation of life against its negation."[38] In Aristotelean–Thomistic terms, people attain moral goodness to the degree they reflect the goodness and perfection of God according to the mode of their being and operation – the reasoned use of their freedom. In Sacred Scripture, both the old and the new Chosen People of God are invited to live up to their duties to one another as part of their election of responsibility so that they might live a full life. Zacchaeus is an example of one who takes this to heart. The various Christian churches seek to do the same as they confront the economic injustices of our day and confess to their complicity. Indeed, for the followers of Christ, genuine freedom requires that we wholeheartedly embrace our responsibilities. Living up to our responsibilities with alacrity is a necessary condition for genuine freedom.

To most secular minds, this is odd because responsibility entails burdens and constraints to our freedom of action. This only serves to expose a key difference between the secular and the Christian understanding of freedom. For many in a liberal, secular society, freedom is understood as autonomy, that is, freedom of action. In contrast, Christians understand freedom as the power to do good. It is a rational freedom that brings about a union of hearts and minds as it serves the common good. It is a freedom that seeks and finds

---

[37] Jonas (1984, 85); Schweiker (1995, 199).   [38] Schweiker (1995, 198).

its end only in union with God.[39] The Cross stands for death, defeat, and folly to the secular mind. In contrast, the Cross stands for genuine freedom and victory for Christians (1 Cor 1:18).

SUMMARY AND CONCLUSIONS

In this chapter, we examined the foundations for a theology of responsibility for economic harms. From ontology, we can use Jonas's ontology of nature, which Schweiker extends further into a moral-ontological proof of the existence of God. In both cases, we arrive at a new ethics of responsibility that calls for the respect and enhancement of the integrity of the community of life. Aristotelean–Thomistic metaphysics can be used to arrive at the same imperative.

The scriptural grounds for a theology of responsibility for economic harms include the biblical teachings on the importance of individual responsibility, Old Testament torts, and the prophetic indictments against economic misdeeds. We also have the call for ameliorative generosity behind the Synoptic hostility to wealth and the Lucan admonition against exploitative almsgiving in the Greco-Roman practice of patronage.

The official declarations of the various Christian traditions on contemporary economic injustice reflect the continued work of the Holy Spirit in our own time. Despite their theological differences and deep disagreements over unfettered market operations, these disparate Christian churches nonetheless converge in their acknowledgment that we are sinful, we have contributed to contemporary market ills, we have not done enough to address these wrongs, and we are in need of God's redeeming grace.

An adequate theology of responsibility for economic harms requires an understanding of the proper relationship between economic power, economic responsibility, and freedom. Why take responsibility for economic harms whose causes are either ill-defined or unidentified, or both? Why hold oneself to account when the community itself does not hold us legally or morally culpable? What are the theological grounds for taking responsibility for the direct and indirect harms of our economic choices? Why be responsible?

The response to all this is simple: to be true to who we are. To be truly free. After all, we cannot disengage genuine love of self from what ultimately enriches and completes it – love of neighbor and love of God. This is the bedrock foundation for a theology of taking responsibility for the harms we

---

[39] Sacred Congregation for the Doctrine of the Faith (1986).

directly or indirectly cause through our market activity. The enhanced economic powers brought about by technology and globalization are double-edged. They can be employed to accumulate even more power by dominating others and debasing life in the process. Or they can be used to ennoble life and, in the process, stumble on to the unimaginable powers that come with authentic freedom – the power to love and be loved. Indeed, economic power can go a long way. Responsibility is a necessary way station as we move from economic power to authentic freedom. It is a threefold movement of power–responsibility–freedom.

CHAPTER 10

Synthesis: Christian ethics and blameworthy material cooperation

While Christian moral theology has much to offer on questions of material cooperation in bioethics or war, it has done little when it comes to economic life. To my knowledge, there is no extended treatment in Christian ethics to date on the problem of blameworthy material cooperation in economic wrongdoing or in accumulative harms. This disparity in treatment is not due to a lack of awareness of the problem of economic complicity. As mentioned earlier, John Chrysostom (1971, nos. 110–112) and John Wesley (1872) were concerned that their congregants not engage in trades or occupations that were injurious to the well-being of others. St. Elizabeth of Hungary abstained from food and drink that were unjustly acquired from peasants. Abolitionists were keenly aware that to patronize slave-grown sugar was to be tainted with the evils of the slave trade.

In appealing to the First World to be more solicitous of the poor countries in his social encyclical *Populorum Progressio*, Paul VI (1967, no. 47) alluded to the wealthy nations' duty to provide a fair, if higher, price for the exports of Third World nations. In effect, he was arguing that First World consumers are morally responsible for the work and pay conditions of laborers in developing countries who supply their needs. Later, John Paul II (1981, nos. 77–81) spoke of the indirect employer in *Laborem Exercens*. Unfortunately, he did not develop in greater depth who precisely is an indirect employer and why. All he did was to define the indirect employer as anyone who is in any way responsible for sustaining or enabling the relationship between the direct employer and workers.

Paul VI's and John Paul II's concerns are, of course, neither original nor unique. Patristic economic teachings argue that economic conduct is never merely personal but is always social in its impact and in its obligations. Thus, the rich man's hoarded affluence is theft from the poor.[1] And, of course, we have the prophetic indictment of opulent lifestyles in a doomed

---

[1] See, for example, Phan (1984).

Israel (Amos 6:1–7). Scripture scholars believe that the biblical attitudes toward wealth and possessions had been shaped by a limited-goods society with its characteristic zero-sum dynamic in which our use of scarce goods necessarily leaves that much less for others.[2]

Despite this longstanding appreciation of the deleterious spillover effects of our economic conduct, Christian moral theology has yet to provide a more thorough examination of blameworthy material cooperation in economic wrongdoing or in market harms. We must address this deficiency in the literature because globalization has made the ripple effects of our market transactions that much more powerful in their impact and reach. Economic complicity has become an even more significant problem in light of global economic integration. There is a need for people to understand how and why they can unwittingly enable or perpetrate pernicious market processes and outcomes.

As mentioned in the Introduction, this book has two goals: (1) to examine the contributions and deficiencies of Christian ethics in dealing with the issue of economic complicity and how it can be supplemented by social philosophy and law, and (2) to study the nature of economic complicity, its attendant moral issues, and the most common instances of such blameworthy material cooperation. In this concluding chapter, we synthesize what we have learned about the morality of economic complicity.

CONTRIBUTIONS SPECIFIC TO CHRISTIAN ETHICS

How does this study advance Christian ethics? What new insights does it provide moral theologians? How can Christian ethics advance the literature on economic complicity? The following sections list seven contributions of this study specific to Christian ethics.

Conceptual framework of analysis

The most obvious resources for dealing with economic complicity from within Christian ethics are the scholastic principles of legitimate cooperation with evil and double effect. These are the most logical starting points. However, these principles are nothing more than methods. They need to be supplemented with an anthropology and an overarching moral framework that distinguishes right from wrong, good from evil. After all,

---

[2] See, for example, Lohfink (1986, 224–225). See Foster (1967) and Gregory (1975) for the limited-goods society.

note that in the first conditions of both principles, there is a need to determine whether or not the act in question is intrinsically evil. Moreover, as part of the third conditions of both principles, we have to weigh whether or not intended beneficial goals justify incurring the unintended but foreseen harms. Thus, both principles can be applied only within a much larger moral backdrop.

Christian ethics provides such a theological-moral framework from its extensive teachings on economic morality that stretch all the way from the Old Testament to contemporary church social teachings. Thus, note its notion of the *telos* (end) of economic life and creatures; the twofold order of creation; the common good and its concomitant social principles; the familial nature of community; the notion of evil as a privation of the good; the just-use obligation and its superfluous income criterion; economic security as a twofold divine gift; the principle of restoration; social sin; and many more. Indeed, the Christian moral tradition has a wide array of tried and tested conceptual tools and teachings that can be brought to bear on market morality. Christian ethics has much to contribute. However, these insights and methods have yet to be put together into a single framework of analysis tailored for the issue of economic complicity.

This study advances Christian ethics by embedding the principles of cooperation with evil and double effect within a much larger analytical framework (Part I). The first four chapters provide both a moral account of economic complicity and diagnostic tools that can be used to deal with actual cases.

Interdisciplinary cross-fertilization

A second contribution of this study is its engagement with other disciplines in exploring how Christian ethics can be enriched by non-theological sources of moral reflection and vice versa. Moral theology's signature contributions to the issue of complicity – its principles of legitimate material cooperation and double effect – are insufficient. For example, in spite of the importance of causal proximity in distinguishing proximate from remote material cooperation, Christian ethics does not have a theory of causation.

Moreover, these two scholastic principles need finer distinctions suited for economic issues. We do, of course, already have the different types of material cooperation: immediate versus mediate, proximate versus remote, and necessary versus contingent. Each of these pairs of distinctions has its own specific set of criteria. Nonetheless, these distinctions are still too broad and subject to ambiguities. Since material cooperation is thinly and abstractly specified, it can be arbitrarily interpreted to suit the evaluator's interests. Unscrupulous people can easily misuse it to rationalize their wrongdoing.

Furthermore, as we have seen in chapter 2, economic harms present complications. Market ills are cumulative, overdetermined, synergistic, interlocking, and heavily mediated. The traditional distinctions of material cooperation and the principle of double effect are inadequate in dealing with the complexity of economic problems.

In addition, the attribution of individual responsibility for collective harms needs to be precise. Charity requires justice as a necessary condition. The latter is principally about giving people their due. In the case of economic complicity, this entails being able to grade varying degrees of culpability with consistency and accuracy, to the extent possible.

This study has adopted insights and methods from social philosophy, economics, and law that can make the scholastic principles of cooperation with evil and double effect much more robust and easier to apply to contemporary issues in the marketplace. The final section of chapter 4 summarizes how other disciplines augment Christian ethics as a framework of analysis. They provide greater specificity and more refined rules for implementation. Social philosophy, tort jurisprudence, and economics supply a much richer lexicon and an expanded set of critical factors to consider. In particular, we cannot overemphasize the value of the theory of causation as a supplement. Christian ethics has nothing comparable to the legal theory of causation in terms of its practical utility for real-life issues. The proposed augmented framework of analysis makes the scholastic principles of legitimate material cooperation and double effect even more potent and useful in evaluating market ills.

Faith and reason

A third contribution is this study's illustration of a hallmark of Christian theology – the interaction of faith and reason. The biggest surprise finding in this study is the remarkable degree of agreement and complementarity in the insights and methods of tort jurisprudence and some liberal social philosophies, on the one hand, and Christian ethics, on the other hand. Consider some of the points of convergence: contributory negligence as a factor in imputing culpability in torts (cf., principle of subsidiarity);[3]

---

[3] To facilitate comparison, I have put moral theology's insights in parentheses.

greater fault for parties in the best position to have foreseen and averted the ensuing harm (cf., principle of socialization, scholastic general justice); risk avoidance and wealth redistribution as functions of torts (cf., principles of socialization, relative equality, and just-use); omission or the failure to prevent harm as causation (cf., principle of socialization); inducing and occasioning harm as causation (cf., principle of solidarity); the importance of individual example in eliciting collective action to mitigate harm (cf., scandal as a consideration in cooperation with evil); the importance of non-causal factors such as justice, equity, need, and capabilities in weighing moral responsibility (cf., biblical *sedeq*); the critical role of knowledge, intention, and the capacity of the moral agent to avert harm (cf., Christian anthropology, principles of socialization and double effect); attention to injurious or unjust bounded rationality and path dependency (cf., social sin); Lockean "enough and as good" proviso in the original appropriation of private property (cf., economic security as a divine gift); Kantian respect for the person as an end and never as a means (cf., intrinsic human dignity); Rawlsian justice as fairness (cf., principles of restoration and relative equality).

These many points of intersection should probably not come as a surprise considering that, on the one hand, tort jurisprudence and liberal social philosophy often reflect people's intuitive moral sensibilities, while Christian moral theology, on the other hand, relies on natural law. The principle of double effect is said to be nothing but the "codification of ethical common sense, not the arcane, logic-chopping invention of philosophers as it has so often been portrayed."[4] Commonsense morality serves as a basis for conversation between these disciplines. Economists can assist theologians and ethicists improve their theoretical work through a better understanding of the nature of the marketplace – an important terrain of moral decision-making (e.g., chapter 2). For their part, theologians and philosophers can alert economists to the normative implications of economic theory and policy (e.g., chapter 9). This exchange promotes conversation and carves out a niche for Christian ethics in the secular, pluralistic public arena of ideas. It also pushes Christian ethicists to reach out beyond the confines of theology. Besides, the use of the sciences, philosophy, and empirical evidence to complement Sacred Scripture and theology in ethical reflection has been very much a part of Christian theological methods.[5]

---

[4] Oderberg (2004, 215)
[5] Note, for example, the use of social scientific criticism in biblical studies (e.g., Carter 2001; Meeks 1983).

Highlighting Christian anthropology

A fourth contribution of this study is its illustration of what is distinctive about Christian ethics. If tort jurisprudence, liberal social philosophy, economics, and Christian ethics converge on the same conclusions and policy proposals, then what is the need for Christian ethics? After all, many in the secular, pluralistic public arena claim that its requirement of faith is an impediment to conversation rather than a help.

The many overlapping points noted earlier should not obscure these disciplines' fundamental differences. Nowhere is this better seen than in the case of overdetermination in chapter 3. Recall that a peculiar feature of accumulative harms is the superfluity of individual causal contributions. Furthermore, these individual contributions are minute compared with the total harm.

Both moral theology and the secular philosophies we examined agree that causal contributions to accumulative harms are never morally insignificant, no matter how redundant or minuscule they might be. For the secular philosophies we studied, rule utilitarianism is particularly helpful for this issue. An important consideration in weighing the morality of an individual act is the larger context and collective outcome of which it is a part and to which it contributes. In contrast, Christian ethics justifies its position by appealing to the nature of the human person. To begin with, people shape their own character through their moral choices, even if these acts may have insignificant external consequences. No moral act is ever too small or redundant for a virtuous life.

Equally important is the Christian view of the nature of the human community. Consider the various schools of thought on the nature of the human person. At one end of the spectrum is radical individualism with communitarianism at the other end. Christians view the human community, not as contractual, but as familial in nature. Such a familial view of community goes beyond even the most communitarian approaches in secular philosophy in terms of the gravity and the scope of obligations that people owe one another. We are not merely people living in community; we are in fact family in the truest sense of the word. As family, we are animated not merely by civic virtue, but by love for one another. As a result, our mutual duties are neither synthetic nor contractual that can be abrogated or renegotiated. These obligations come with human nature and personhood. We cannot just walk away from them or remake them according to our liking.[6] Ties and

---

[6] Thus, social justice and charity have to be rooted in truth if they are to be genuine and effective (Benedict XVI 2009).

bonds and their concomitant duties are vital, perhaps even preeminent, considerations in Christian thought.[7] Thus, individual acts, no matter how superfluous or minute in contributing to harms, are never morally insignificant. Every moral act matters regardless of how unimportant the consequences might appear. Moreover, from Aristotelean–Thomistic metaphysics, every creature reflects some unique dimension of the goodness and perfection of God. No creature is ever redundant or minuscule in the order of God's creation. Thus, while both moral theology and various secular approaches arrive at the same conclusion on the question of overdetermination, they start from a different understanding of the nature of the human person and the human community.

This contrast is just a glimpse of many other differences in the axioms of Christian moral theology, on the one hand, and law, liberal social philosophy, and economic policy, on the other hand. Unlike secular approaches, Christian ethics finds its completion not in justice or in the attainment of a juridic order alone in which tolerance is the critical social virtue. Instead, for Christian ethics, justice is a necessary though not a sufficient condition for a full life. Justice must find its perfection in charity, in the attainment of a union of hearts and minds. It reaches beyond a juridic order and seeks the common good.

Unlike liberal thought, whose concern is the provision of as wide a personal sphere of autonomy as possible that is consistent with everyone else enjoying the same, Christian thought is concerned with rational freedom, defined not as autonomy of action, but as growth in the love of God and neighbor. It is about the reasoned use of freedom in reaching the fullness of what it is to be truly and fully human. Unlike liberalism which asserts claims on the basis of rights, Christian ethics situates rights only within their larger context of obligations. Rights and duties are inseparable.

Christian thought goes beyond the Kantian call for the treatment of human beings as ends in themselves and never as a means. It goes further to seek integral human development, that is, the development of body, mind, and spirit. Human flourishing entails the development of the whole person and of every person. Christian thought goes further than the Kantian respect for the human person by anchoring such intrinsic worth in God's providential love and care for every creature, but especially for humans who are created for their own sake and in the divine image and likeness. Moreover, every person has been saved by Christ and is invited to an eternal union with God.

---

[7] This is consistent with the centrality of *sedeq* (righteousness) in biblical justice. *Sedeq* entails living up to the particular demands of relationships. See Achtemeier (1962a, 1962b) and Donohue (1977).

These bedrock moral foundations are among the most distinctive contributions of Christian thought to the issue of economic complicity. And given its more demanding anthropology, it is not surprising that Christian ethics has a much more expansive and more demanding set of moral duties relative to most secular philosophies, normative economics, or law. Two quick examples should illustrate this point.

First, recall our earlier examination of what constitutes economic wrongdoing in chapter 5. Because of its relatively "thick" and more defined notion of the good, Christian moral theology would have a much longer list of economic activities that would be considered wrongdoing compared with law, economic policy, or most secular philosophies. There are many more instances of blameworthy material cooperation according to Christian ethics compared with secular thought and practice. In fact, it would consider most of the harmful but tolerated economic activities we listed to be morally unacceptable.

A second contrast pertains to the relatively large number of positive obligations in Christian thought compared with liberalism's greater reliance on negative duties. For example, Christian ethics imposes much more urgent and more binding obligations to ameliorate severe pecuniary externalities (chapter 7) and to rectify injurious social structures (chapter 8) than would law, economic policy, or most secular philosophies. In addition, Christian ethics strongly advocates socioeconomic rights on the basis of the human person's intrinsic worth. In contrast, many social philosophers contest the existence of such rights.

The radical demands of Christian thought and practice can also be illustrated using the legal categories of liability: fault, strict, and absolute. In Part II of this book, we deliberately limited ourselves to economic complicity that entails contributory fault on the part of those being held responsible. Thus, we are speaking only of fault liability in this study, that is, liability in the wake of a faulty action.

However, fault liability does not fully exhaust all the moral obligations imposed by Christian thought. There are two further sets of duties. The first is that of strict liability, that is, we are morally responsible for rectifying damage even if we are not at fault. The parable of the Good Samaritan is a vivid example of this obligation. The Samaritan's act was not supererogatory from the Christian point of view. He was merely discharging the moral duty that stems from love of God and love of neighbor. Recall, too, the extensive and challenging economic obligations of mutual solicitude in both the Old and the New Testament.

A second, even stronger set of obligations is that of absolute liability. In strict liability, the contributory negligence of the injured party can mitigate or even negate the liability of the person being held responsible. Not so in absolute liability. In the latter, the contributory fault or negligence of the injured party does not mitigate or negate the liability of the defendant. This is relevant for contemporary economic life. Christians have strong obligations to alleviate the plight of those in distress, even if the victims are partly to blame for their condition.[8] No doubt, people should be responsible for working toward their own well-being. Recall how St. Paul sternly admonishes those who had given up work. He was very clear that those who refused to work deserved severe censure (2 Thess 3:9–13). In modern Christian social thought, the principle of subsidiarity asserts that people ought to do for themselves what they are capable of accomplishing. In the principle of integral human development, individuals have the duty to work toward their own flourishing, to the extent possible. In the scholastic understanding of general justice, members of the community have to contribute to the common good according to their means.

Nevertheless, despite these clear obligations to take responsibility for one's own personal well-being, the Christian witness is overwhelmingly one of unqualified aid to those in need, even for those who may be blameworthy for their own distress. The Hebrews were expected to extend to others the same favors that had been given them by God in their own moment of need. Thus, we have the exacting Old Testament laws on economic life with no prior conditions attached: the gleaning law, slave release, debt forgiveness, the return of ancestral lands to their original owners, and mandatory lending at no interest.[9] Jesus Christ unconditionally ministered to and welcomed one and all, including public sinners. We are expected to give the same unconditional mutual assistance. The parable of the sheep and the goats (Mt 25:31–46) is not contingent on determining first whether or not there was contributory negligence involved before we dispense aid to the hungry, thirsty, naked, sick, and imprisoned.

Such categorical positive obligations go beyond Sacred Scripture. Thus, among the Patristic Fathers, wealth is supposed to be used for the poor.[10] Almsgiving has been very much a part of the Christian tradition from its Old Testament roots to our modern era. And then there is the just-use obligation attendant to the right to private ownership and its superfluous

---

[8] Recall the problem of endogeneity from chapter 7.   [9] Lohfink (1987).   [10] Phan (1984).

income criterion whereby the excess in our wealth or income is measured in terms of the relative unmet needs of our neighbors.[11]

Wogaman (1986, 34–35) warns against basing our common economic life on justice alone in which people merely get what is their due. Prior to justice is the even more potent reality of grace: we enjoy whatever it is we have only by the grace of God. Consequently, when we produce and distribute our economic goods, our primary aim is the affirmation of human dignity without "asking first whether people have deserved what they receive." Justice should operate within our acknowledgment of and gratitude for grace in our own lives. Otherwise, in our singular pursuit of justice, we run the risk of self-righteousness and arrogance in our own accomplishments.

As a final example, consider Bernard Häring's (1964, 495–519) list of key principles in evaluating permissible material cooperation in social life. The first principle he cites is the centrality of "love of self and love of neighbor (responsibility for the kingdom of God on earth)" (498) as the bedrock reason for why we should avoid participating in or facilitating others' wrongdoing. His third principle[12] notes that material gain (or fear of material loss) is never a legitimate reason for material cooperation. In addition, Häring observes that the individual must be willing to subsume personal interest for the greater good because "evil affecting a community is always greater than evil inflicted on one individual" (499). In all this, note his strong communitarian, indeed familial, standards for individual conduct, even to the point of sacrificing self for the community and even to the point of disregarding personal material loss. For many secular philosophies and even for some Christian ethicists, the risk of personal material loss is a valid consideration in applying both the principles of legitimate material cooperation and double effect. Not so for Häring.

Clearly, Häring proposes a much tougher set of standards. This is reflected in his economic examples of licit and illicit material cooperation in pharmaceutical stores, taverns, movie houses, merchandising, room rentals, and many other businesses. Activities that would have been tolerated by a secular evaluator are deemed morally reprehensible, such as the sale of indecent clothing, lurid advertising, unseemly dancing and deportment, and many others (502–505, 507–510). The standards of moral theology and secular society are worlds apart.

---

[11] Leo XIII (1891); Vatican Council II (1965: part II, chapter 3, fn 10).
[12] The second principle refers to the usual conditions of the principles of material cooperation and double effect.

Bridging scholastic material cooperation and philosophical complicity

The fifth contribution pertains to how we might relate the scholastic principle of legitimate material cooperation with the legal and philosophical notion of complicity. Complicity requires intention on the part of accomplices to aid or abet the wrongdoing. In contrast, cooperators in material cooperation do not share the intention of the wrongdoer nor do they wish the success of the misdeed. Otherwise, this would be formal, not material, cooperation. Thus, some have gone so far as to claim that no material cooperation is the same as complicity.[13]

Chapter 1 argued that while they are not equivalent concepts, philosophy's "moral complicity" and scholastic "blameworthy material cooperation" do overlap. The key argument that permits us to make this claim is Kutz's (2000, 166–203) notion of quasi-participatory intent in "unstructured" harms. Recall his point that what may appear on the surface to be "unstructured" is in fact undergirded by social norms, custom, law, and informal rules. Chapter 8 explained that the market is an example of such a phenomenon. This means that people can be held to account for their economic conduct that perpetuates the ills of a way of life or of social structures of which they are part or to which they contribute. Consequently, the language of "moral complicity" can be extended even to the unintended but foreseen harmful ripple effects of our economic activities. In other words, moral complicity and blameworthy material cooperation are overlapping concepts.[14]

The implication of this overlap or of Kutz's quasi-participatory intent is not trivial. Many of the economic harms and wrongdoing relevant for our study are collective in nature and are unintended but foreseen market ills. This overlap permits us to draw methods and insights from the legal and philosophical literature on complicity to supplement the scholastic notion of material cooperation.

Normative distinctions for material cooperation

A sixth contribution of this work to Christian ethics is the expansion of the distinctions we use for material cooperation. Since the market produces inseparable harmful and beneficial outcomes, our assessment of complicity in market harms will necessarily involve using the principles of legitimate

---

[13] Oderberg (2004, 217–218).
[14] They are not identical sets because formal cooperation is also part of moral complicity.

material cooperation and double effect in tandem. This joint use leads us to augment the traditional positive, descriptive distinctions of material cooperation (immediate vs. mediate; proximate vs. remote; necessary vs. contingent) with a set of normative distinctions (avertible vs. inavertible; permissible vs. impermissible; liable vs. non-liable). These normative distinctions will be helpful in grading the various degrees of culpability.

Economic responsibility and theological ethics

A seventh contribution is the preceding chapter's examination of the conceptual building blocks of a theology of responsibility for economic harms. We can draw insights from philosophical and theological ethics, metaphysics, Sacred Scripture, and the official statements of the various Christian traditions on economic justice. These support our finding that we ought to take responsibility for the ill effects of our economic activities. Note that these also provide philosophical and theological grounds for the due care provision (third condition) of the principle of double effect, which states that we ought to prevent or at least minimize the unintended harms of our morally permissible actions.

Summary

The issue of complicity can be broken down into three main areas of inquiry: the object of accountability (complicity in what?), the subject of accountability (who is complicit?), and the basis for accountability (why culpable?). Christian ethics has an extensive literature on what constitutes economic wrongdoing (object of accountability). Much has been written in theological circles on the ideal socioeconomic life (chapter 2). After all, the Church has been a longstanding critic of the shortcomings of the market economy.[15]

Christian ethics has relatively less to offer when it comes to determining the subject of accountability (who is complicit?). Its signature contributions to this question, of course, are its principles of legitimate material cooperation with evil and double effect. There are handbooks on moral questions that occasionally include casuistic exercises on specific cases of economic complicity, but these are rare, not systematic or comprehensive in their evaluation or resolution, and not devoted specifically to economic ethical

---

[15] In his book *Everything for Sale*, Kuttner (1996, 54) observes, "The church, of course, is the longest-running counterweight to the dogmas of a pure market."

dilemmas.[16] Chapters 3 and 4, and the cases in Part II, are primarily about the attribution of individual moral responsibility for collective economic harms. They illustrate a more systematic approach to this issue.

Christian ethics has the least to offer when it comes to articulating the basis for accountability (why culpable?). There has been very little in theological ethics on this question. Chapter 9 outlines the philosophical, ontological, and scriptural building blocks for a theology of responsibility for economic harms.

In sum, this book is hopefully a contribution to closing the gap in the ethical literature on blameworthy material cooperation in economic wrongdoing or in market harms. In particular, it has offered insights and methods for the ascription of individual moral responsibility (subject of accountability) and has proposed philosophical and theological grounds for taking responsibility for economic harms (basis for accountability) – two of the three critical dimensions of economic complicity that have received little attention in Christian ethics.

CONTRIBUTIONS TO THE GENERAL LITERATURE

Besides the preceding contributions of this study specific to Christian ethics, we have additional contributions to the general literature. First, this study tackles a much-neglected but consequential subject matter: the nature of market-mediated complicity. The ethics of cooperation is said to be one of the least explored areas of moral philosophy. It is treated as a special topic in ethics. This gap has to be rectified because cooperation in others' good or wrongful action is the norm rather than the exception.[17] This interdependence is particularly true and intense in economic life. Unfortunately, the phenomenon of economic complicity has received even less attention in the literature. This is presumably because it is well beyond the question of allocating scarce resources to their most valued uses or because of the conceptual and practical difficulties posed by accumulative harms in economics. Besides, most people believe that we are bound only by our contractual obligations. After all, market participants are rational; they know and pursue what is in their own best interest. They will not consummate market transactions that do not improve their welfare. Thus, all obligations cease as soon as the terms of contracts are fulfilled. There are no residual obligations and, therefore, there is no such thing as complicity in enabling wrongdoing or in perpetrating collective ills.

[16] See, for example, Grisez (1997).   [17] Oderberg (2004, 204).

Moral philosophy and economic theory have lagged behind grassroots action when it comes to the notion of residual market obligations. Capital markets are often depicted as the den of iniquity and the epitome of greed and unconscionable profit-making. And yet, socially responsible investing (SRI) has ballooned into a major industry of its own within the financial sector.[18] The Fair Trade movement, college students' anti-sweatshop protests, and voluntary carbon offset programs are other recent initiatives that address the unintended consequences of our economic conduct. There has been a constant stream of books and video productions on the dire consequences of our consumption and production decisions in the marketplace.[19] In an earlier generation, we had the push to divest in South Africa for its apartheid policies, the consumer boycott of table grapes initiated by César Chávez, and the pressure to change Nestlé's practices in marketing its infant formula in the developing world. And, of course, even earlier than these were the appeals to the English public at the turn of the nineteenth century to avoid slave-grown sugar as part of the abolitionists' campaign to bring an end to the transatlantic slave trade.

Indeed, popular practice has far outstripped theoretical work on the matter of economic complicity. This is true not only for the discipline of economics, but also for law, social philosophy, and even Christian ethics. This book is a modest contribution toward pushing theory to catch up with praxis. In so doing, we might persuade even more people to be conscientious in attending to the harmful ripple effects of their market transactions. Thus, the first contribution of this book beyond Christian ethics is its examination of the nature of market-mediated complicity, a much-ignored topic in the literature.

Second, this work expands the scope of our traditional understanding of what constitutes complicity. It claims that there are many other ways by which we cooperate in wrongdoing in the marketplace besides the obviously criminal activities. Few would dispute that aiding and abetting illicit economic activities, such as drug running, human trafficking, and arms smuggling, constitutes complicity. Sweatshops are probably the most easily recognizable of these. This study has argued for a more expansive list that

---

[18] While total assets under professional management in the United States grew by 260 percent from $7 trillion in 1995 to $25.1 trillion in 2007, SRI assets rose by 324 percent from $0.64 trillion in 1995 to $2.71 trillion in 2007. In 1995, there were 55 SRI funds with $12 billion in assets. By 2007, it had grown to 260 SRI funds with $201.8 billion. In the United States alone, $1 of every $9 or 11 percent of $25.1 trillion in assets under professional management in 2007 are screened using socially responsible criteria (Social Investment Forum 2007, ii–iii). Sparkes (2002, 356, 389) puts global SRI assets at $2.7 trillion as of 2001.

[19] See, for example, Clawson (2009), Kenner (2009), and Weber (2009).

includes non-traditional forms of economic complicity that involve some of the most ordinary market conduct we take for granted or tolerate: unattended severe pecuniary externalities, overconsumption, speculative investing, production disexternalities, and the reinforcement of unjust social structures and practices. With the exception of consumerism, the theological-philosophical case has yet to be made as to why we have a moral obligation to avoid or to rectify these common market activities. Chapters 6, 7, and 8 devote an enormous amount of attention to making just such a case. These will probably be the most contested and criticized parts of this study given what is at stake – having to change our conduct in the marketplace whether as individuals or as a community. Moreover, these will also be the most likely chapters to strike at the heart of readers' political and philosophical beliefs regarding free market operations. What is at stake in these three chapters is the acknowledgment that we, in fact, have residual market obligations that come with the economic liberties that we have heretofore enjoyed and, unfortunately, occasionally abused. (Think of the excesses that led to the 2008 subprime meltdown.)

Third, the existing literature on complicity has been criticized for not paying attention to the more fundamental issues. In particular, while the manualist tradition and Anglo-Saxon common law have examined various types of complicity, they hardly address why complicity is morally problematic.[20] For this project, we not only examined four types of material cooperation in economic wrongdoing (Part II), but we also carefully presented the reasons why such instances of complicity are morally blameworthy from philosophical, theological, and even economic perspectives. Thus, note the extensive sections entitled "Basis for accountability," especially for the last three cases of complicity.

Fourth, the field of business ethics has long dealt with cases of corporate complicity. This study is a first step toward doing the same for economic ethics. However, the task facing economic ethicists will be neither as easy nor as straightforward as that facing business ethicists, because unlike corporate complicity, economic complicity deals with accumulative harms. The last three types of complicity we examined are examples of accumulative harms. These pose additional analytical difficulties compared with the traditional type of complicity (e.g., criminal activities) because of the need to deal with the remoteness of damage, intervening events, mixed harms and benefits, interlocking agencies, and concurrent causes, among others. Part II is

---

[20] See Kaveny (2003, 24, 26) for this critique.

an illustration of how we might deal with these additional evaluative complications.

Fifth, besides illustrating the value of interdisciplinary work in social ethics, this study is a contribution toward making the case that Christian ethics is a credible conversation partner even in a secular, pluralistic setting. In particular, this study has shown how Christian ethics can provide helpful conceptual tools and methods in sorting through complex social problems. For example, note the wide use of the principle of double effect beyond theological circles. Or consider the usefulness of the proposed normative distinctions[21] for material cooperation for business ethicists in their work on the due care condition of the principle of double effect.[22] The same is true in the case of the principle of subsidiarity. Or note how the positive distinctions[23] on the types of material cooperation are just as descriptive compared with the "substantial factor" or "active force" test of legal causation. We have gained much in having tort law, economics, social philosophy, and theological ethics mutually reinforce each other in dealing with economic complicity. There is no reason why the same could not be replicated as we work through many other social issues.

Finally, this book is a contribution to the ongoing struggle to shape marketplace morality. One finding of this study that clearly stands out is that there is no single, simple, or universal set of principles that can deal with the tough issues raised by economic complicity. What constitutes economic wrongdoing? Why are we morally culpable for distant harms? What are our moral obligations and how strong are their claims? These questions cannot be resolved in cookbook fashion. It is the same finding of legal scholars in their longstanding quest for a single overarching moral theory of torts. Thus, we ultimately have to depend on the prudential judgment of those who make the decisions. In our case, since most questions of moral complicity are addressed in the internal forum, it is every market participant's prudential judgment that will matter in the end.

Far too often, the individualistic, competitive, and impersonal ethos of the marketplace seeps into personal behavior and attitudes. Consider, for example, the erosion of the traditional Confucian values of community and family in China and East Asia as a result of this region's economic

---

[21] Avertible vs. inavertible material cooperation; permissible vs. impermissible material cooperation; liable vs. non-liable material cooperation.

[22] See, for example, Bomann-Larsen and Wiggen (2004).

[23] Immediate vs. mediate material cooperation; proximate vs. remote material cooperation; necessary vs. contingent material cooperation.

growth and development in the past three decades.[24] Thus, it is all the more important to make a convincing case that we have residual obligations in the marketplace. Having a well-reasoned conceptual framework helps in making such a case. If successful in advancing our understanding of economic complicity, this book should also sensitize people to the harmful ripple effects of their market transactions. This is where Christian ethics can make its most significant impact in the public arena of ideas. Over and above the methods it provides with its principles of legitimate material cooperation and double effect, Christian ethics has an even more important contribution to make: its articulation of what it is to be truly and fully human and its understanding of what a human community is all about.

LOOKING AHEAD

Whether we like it or not, we affect the lives of many others in positive or negative ways through the incidental by-products of our actions. This is especially true in economic life where even our most laudable activities inflict unintended harms on others. These spillover effects are unavoidable given the circular flow of economic life. We are inextricably bound to one another in an interlocking chain of causes and effects.

> [T]he bald fact is that we do wrong together even when we neither intend anything in particular, nor have any sense of togetherness. Because our actions reach beyond our intentions, and because their effects may damagingly overlap with those caused by agents we neither know nor care about, we are always already complicit with others, and incur responsibilities we never could have guessed at.
>   ... [O]ur activities involve us in the lives of others, and we can no more wash our hands of this fact than we can live hermetically sealed from others. *'Participation without intention' is a fact of life*. (Williams 2002, 206–207, emphasis added)

Whether we like it or not, our participation in accumulative harms is also a fact of economic life.

Globalization and the Digital Age have not only escalated and accelerated this social phenomenon of "participation without intention," but they have also created new responsibilities. Globalization has made our web of interdependence that much more intense and complicated. We are better informed of the plight of peoples across the globe in the era of microelectronics. Improved communications, better transportation, and

---

[24] See, for example, Song (2002) and Elegant (2007).

higher income levels have expanded our capacity to provide assistance to those in distress. We can no longer plead ignorance or the inability to help in turning a blind eye to economic suffering or injustice elsewhere in the world. Moreover, we are ever more interconnected in our economic activities, exemplified by offshore outsourcing and corporate networking. The whole world is truly becoming a single workshop.

At the same time, however, market rules and thinking are seeping into and reshaping ever larger swaths of social life. Together with the move from the local to the global, the shift to more market-driven lifestyles has resulted in disturbing unintended consequences. There is a diminished sense of community, and we run the risk of feeling less responsible and less empathetic for others given the absence of bonds that tie us together. Personal relationships have increasingly been replaced by anonymous and arms-length commercial transactions.

Furthermore, economic disruptions now spread with lightning speed and across greater distances. Misdeeds from halfway across the globe can adversely affect local communities with little warning. This makes the issue of market-mediated complicity that much more important to address, given the long litany of unintended harms that have arisen in the wake of global economic integration. What makes the situation even more intolerable and urgent is that even as the benefits of market operations are widely enjoyed, their adverse ripple effects are privately borne by people who are least able to bear them, or who are disadvantaged to begin with – the uneducated, the young, the elderly, the unskilled, and the destitute. These burdens are not merely privately borne, but they are also often quietly endured because they happen to fall on people who are voiceless and unseen, living at the fringes of what is supposed to be a human community.

We have the ingredients for a paradoxical, worrisome outcome. Our individual economic choices have ever wider and more consequential ripple effects, even as greater marketization hardens us in a competitive individualism with minimal regard for others. Globalization ironically amplifies our moral obligations for one another's well-being, even as it greatly expands the occasion for our facilitating others' economic wrongdoing. More than ever, we should be wary of the harmful unintended consequences of our market transactions.

Unfortunately, as we have seen repeatedly throughout this book, there are many gray areas when it comes to imputing individual responsibility for injurious market processes and outcomes. Measuring causal contribution, assessing the toxicity of harm, establishing causal links upstream and downstream, weighing harmful and beneficial effects in the principle of double effect, and assigning proper weights to the manifold factors we have to take into account – all these requisite tasks pose significant technical challenges.

Justice requires precision in the attribution of individual culpability for collective wrongs, but the nature and dynamics of the marketplace make this extremely difficult. In particular, accumulative socioeconomic harms are synergistic, heavily mediated, unavoidable, and unintended. They have a superfluity of causes. Moreover, the precise causal paths from particular causes to their respective cumulative outcomes are indiscernible. Furthermore, there is often an intertemporal delay in which the ultimate damage is not immediately visible in the current period. Many wrongs become apparent only after a certain critical mass of individual actions has been reached (they are cumulative by nature after all), and often only after some time has elapsed. Consequently, the costs of collective harms are often ignored by their perpetrators because they can be easily passed on to the next generation, to unsuspecting market participants, or to those who are voiceless, powerless, or unable to resist. It is unusual to see the public anticipate and head off collective harms early on.[25]

Thus, at the end of the day, many problems dealing with blameworthy material cooperation can only be addressed with prudential judgment and a generous spirit of accommodation. Not surprisingly, in writing about moral responsibility, the social philosopher Joel Feinberg (1970, 30–33) concludes that such questions can only be adjudicated "before the tribunal of conscience," that is, in the internal forum. We might as well resign ourselves to the reality that the law and the courts are not the primary venues for dealing with the unaddressed ills and injustices spawned by most cases of market-mediated complicity. The conviction of Unocal for complicity with the Burmese government on forced labor and human rights violation under the Alien Tort Claims Act[26] and the 1999 federal and state lawsuits filed against retail chains and brand owners for complicity with Saipan sweatshops are the exceptions rather than the norm.

Relying solely or heavily on the internal forum is fraught with the obvious problems of moral hazard and self-serving rationalization. Unscrupulous people will simply free-ride on others' self-restraint in

[25] This is why the carbon footprint offset programs, the organic food movement, and Fair Trade are so distinctive. They exemplify a "pay as you go" approach to dealing with communal harms in which people own up to their residual responsibilities and voluntarily bear the cost of repairing the unintended ill effects of their market transactions instead of passing them on to others.
[26] Aceves (1998).

mitigating accumulative harms (e.g., global warming or overfishing). The unprincipled can easily rationalize away their moral obligations. Thus, it becomes even more important to present a case for dealing with economic complicity – a case so clear and so compelling as to win over hearts and minds to voluntarily live up to their duties. In the final analysis, addressing market-mediated complicity will rely on personal initiative in avoiding the enabling of others' economic wrongdoing or in mitigating voluntarily the adverse ripple effects of our economic activities.

These difficulties posed by economic complicity underscore the distinct advantage of Christian ethics compared with law, economic policy, or secular philosophy. Because of its insistence on treating others as family, Christian social ethics can move people to take responsibility for rectifying distant or accumulative harms even if it is unclear as to who is bound by that duty. Unlike justice, which requires precision, charity can afford to be less precise because it is about self-giving and is unmeasured by its nature. Love of God and love of neighbor are Christians' "universal solvents" in dealing with the many gray areas of social problems, including blame-worthy material cooperation in economic wrongdoing or in collective harms.

Kutz (2000, 254) says it well when he notes that "We hold ourselves and each other accountable ... because in responding to one another we foster the relationships that make our lives good." Christian ethics goes further than this and anchors these life-giving relationships in a biblical righteous-ness (*sedeq*) in which we wholeheartedly embrace the particular demands that come with these relationships. For men and women re-created in the new-found liberty in Christ, these obligations are not impositions or burdens but are welcome gifts and signs of love.

References

Aceves, William. 1998. "Doe v. Unocal 963 F. Supp. 880," *The American Journal of International Law* 92: 309–314.

Achtemeier, P. J. 1962a. "Righteousness in the NT," in vol. IV of *The Interpreter's Dictionary of the Bible*. Edited by George Arthur Buttrick. 4 vols. New York: Abingdon Press.

1962b. "Righteousness in the OT," in vol. IV of *The Interpreter's Dictionary of the Bible*. Edited by George Arthur Buttrick. 4 vols. New York: Abingdon Press.

Alini, Erica and Justin Lahart. 2009. "The Less Educated Take the Worst Hit," *Wall Street Journal*. June 6.

American Lutheran Church. 1980. "The Unfinished Reformation, A Statement of the American Lutheran Church." www.elca.org/What-We-Believe/Social-Issues/Journal-of-Lutheran-Ethics/Portfolios/Social-Statements-of-the-ELCA/Predecessor-Church-Body-Documents/American-Lutheran-Church/The-Unfinished-Reformation-A-Statement-of-The-American-Lutheran-Church-1980.aspx (last accessed December 18, 2009).

Andrews, Edmund. 2009. "US Weighs Curbs for Speculators in Energy Trades," *New York Times*. July 8.

Aquinas, Thomas. 1947–1948. *Summa Theologica*. Translated by Fathers of the English Province. 3 vols. New York: Benzinger.

Armour, Stephanie. 2007. "Gap Widens Between What Insurers, Uninsured Pay," *USA Today*. May 7. www.usatoday.com/money/industries/insurance/2007–05–07-uninsured-usat_N.htm (last accessed June 24, 2009).

Aronson, Ronald. 1990. "Responsibility and Complicity," *Philosophical Papers* 19: 53–73.

Associated Press. 2002. "Gap, Penney's Settle Sweatshop Suit," *CBS News*. September 26. www.cbsnews.com/stories/2002/09/26/national/printables523469.shtml (last accessed January 13, 2009).

Augustine. 1958. *City of God*. New York: Doubleday.

1960. *Confessions*. Translated by John Ryan. Garden City, NY: Image.

Baldwin, John W. 1959. *The Medieval Theories of the Just Price: Romanists, Canonists, and Theologians in the Twelfth and Thirteenth Centuries*. Transactions of the American Philosophical Society, Volume 49, Part 4. Philadelphia: American Philosophical Society (series paper).

Bank of International Settlements. 2007. *Triennial Central Bank Survey: Foreign Exchange and Derivatives Market Activity in 2007*. www.bis.org/publ/rpfxf07t. pdf (last accessed June 21, 2009).

Barbaro, Michael. 2008. "Wal-Mart Sets Agenda of Change," *New York Times*. January 24.

Barrera, Albino. 2005a. *Economic Compulsion and Christian Ethics*. Cambridge University Press.

    2005b. *God and the Evil of Scarcity: Moral Foundations of Economic Agency*. University of Notre Dame Press.

    2007. *Globalization and Economic Ethics: Distributive Justice in the Knowledge Economy*. New York: Palgrave-Macmillan.

Barth, Karl. 1985–1986. *Church Dogmatics*. 5 vols. Edinburgh: T&T Clark.

Baum, Gregory. 1975. *Religion and Alienation: A Theological Reading of Sociology*. New York: Paulist Press.

    2003. "Social Sin," in *New Catholic Encyclopedia* XIII. Project Edited by Thomas Carson and Joann Cerrito. Detroit: Gale, pp. 244–246.

BBC. 2003. "Nazi Row Hits Holocaust Memorial." October 27. http://news.bbc. co.uk/2/hi/europe/3219199.stm (last accessed June 7, 2009).

    2004. "Salt Reduction." September 10. http://news.bbc.co.uk/2/hi/programmes/newsnight/3646056.stm (last accessed June 8, 2009).

    2009. "G20 Leaders Seal $1 Tn Global Deal." http://news.bbc.co.uk/2/hi/7979483.stm (last accessed December 31, 2009).

Beale, Joseph. 1920. "The Proximate Consequences of an Act," *Harvard Law Review* 33: 633–658.

Bearak, Barry. 2009. "Constant Fear and Mob Rule in South Africa Slum," *New York Times*. June 29.

Benedict XVI. 2009. *Caritas in Veritate*. Vatican City. www.vatican.va/holy_father/benedict_xvi/encyclicals/documents/hf_ben-xvi_enc_20090629_caritas-in-veritate_en.html (last accessed July 7, 2009).

Bennett, Jonathan. 2001. "Foreseen Side Effects versus Intended Consequences?" in *The Doctrine of Double Effect: Philosophers Debate a Controversial Moral Principle*. Edited by P. A. Woodward. University of Notre Dame Press.

Bernstein, Richard. 1994. "Rethinking Responsibility," *Social Research* 61: 833–852.

Birch, Bruce. 1991. *Let Justice Roll Down: The Old Testament, Ethics, and Christian Life*. Louisville, KY: Westminster John Knox Press.

Birch, Bruce and Larry Rasmussen. 1989. *Bible and Ethics in the Christian Life*. Revised edition. Minneapolis: Augsburg.

Black, Jane. 2008. "California Becomes 1st State to Enact Trans Fat Ban," *Washington Post*. July 26.

Bomann-Larsen, Lene. 2004. "Reconstructing the Principle of Double Effect: Towards Fixing the Goalposts of Corporate Responsibility," in *Responsibility in World Business: Managing the Harmful Side-effects of Corporate Activity*. Edited by Lene Bomann-Larsen and Oddny Wiggen. Tokyo and New York: United Nations University Press, pp. 82–98.

Bomann-Larsen, Lene and Oddny Wiggen. *Responsibility in World Business: Managing the Harmful Side-effects of Corporate Activity.* Edited by Lene Bomann-Larsen and Oddny Wiggen. Tokyo and New York: United Nations University Press.

    2004. "The Principle of Double Effect, Revised for the Business Context," in *Responsibility in World Business: Managing the Harmful Side-effects of Corporate Activity.* Edited by Lene Bomann-Larsen and Oddny Wiggen. Tokyo and New York: United Nations University Press, pp. 99–102.

Bonhoeffer, Dietrich. 1964. *Ethics.* Edited by Eberhard Bethge. New York: Macmillan.

Borgo, John. 1979. "Causal Paradigms in Tort Law," *Journal of Legal Studies* 8: 419–455.

Bradsher, Keith. 2009. "China's Trash Problem May Also Be the World's," *New York Times.* August 12.

Brueggemann, Walter. 1994. "Justice: The Earthly Form of God's Holiness," *Reformed World* 44: 13–27.

Burridge, Richard. 2007. *Imitating Jesus: An Inclusive Approach to New Testament Ethics.* Grand Rapids, MI: B.W. Eerdmans.

Calabresi, Guido. 1975. "Concerning Cause and the Law of Torts: An Essay for Harry Kalven, Jr.," *The University of Chicago Law Review* 43: 69–108.

Carpenter, Charles. 1932a. "Workable Rules for Determining Proximate Cause: Part I," *California Law Review* 20: 229–259.

    1932b. "Workable Rules for Determining Proximate Cause: Part II," *California Law Review* 20: 396–419.

Carter, Charles. 2001. "Social Scientific Approaches," in *The Blackwell Companion to the Hebrew Bible.* Edited by Leo Purdue. Malden, MA: Blackwell, pp. 36–58.

Castells, Manuel. 1996. *The Rise of the Network Society.* Cambridge, MA: Blackwell.

Cavanaugh, Thomas. 2003. "Review of *The Doctrine of Double Effect: Philosophers Debate a Controversial Moral Principle.* Edited by P. A. Woodward," *The Philosophical Quarterly* 53: 147–149.

    2006. *Double-effect Reasoning: Doing Good and Avoiding Evil.* Oxford Studies in Theological Ethics. Oxford: Clarendon.

CBS News. 1999. "Tagged with a Sweatshop Label," CBS News. January 14. www.cbsnews.com/stories/1999/10/14/archive/printable28419.shtml (last accessed January 13, 2009).

Cessario, Romanus. 1991. *The Moral Virtues and Theological Ethics.* University of Notre Dame Press.

Chan, Sewell. 2008. "A Tax on Many Soft Drinks Sets off Spirited Debate," *New York Times.* December 16. www.nytimes.com/2008/12/17/nyregion/17sugartax.html (last accessed June 8, 2009).

Chen, Shaohua and Martin Ravallion. 2004. *How Have the World's Poorest Fared since the Early 1980s?* World Bank Policy Research Working Paper no. 3341. Washington, DC: World Bank.

Chrysostom, John. 1971. "The Seventh, or Euboean, Discourse," in *Dio Chrysostom*. Translated by J. W. Cohoon. Cambridge, MA: Harvard University Press.

Clawson, Julie. 2009. *Everyday Justice: The Global Impact of Our Daily Choices*. Downers Grove, IL: InterVarsity Press.

Coleman, Jules. 1982. "Moral Theories of Torts: Their Scope and Limits: Part I," *Law and Philosophy* 1: 371–390.

1983. "Moral Theories of Torts: Their Scope and Limits: Part II," *Law and Philosophy* 2: 5–36.

1988. *Markets, Morals and the Law*. Cambridge University Press.

Cosgrove, Charles. 2002. *Appealing to Scripture in Moral Debate: Five Hermeneutical Rules*. Grand Rapids, MI: Eerdmans.

Cox, Simon. 2009. "The Long Climb: A Special Report on the World Economy," *The Economist Special Reports*. October 3.

De Vries, Barend. 1998. *Champions of the Poor: The Economic Consequences of Judeo-Christian Values*. Washington, DC: Georgetown University Press.

Dicken, Peter. 2007. *Global Shift: Reshaping the Global Economic Map in the 21st Century*. Fifth edition. New York and London: Guilford Press.

Donahue, John. 1977. "Biblical Perspectives on Justice," in *The Faith That Does Justice: Examining the Christian Sources for Social Change*. Edited by John Haughey. New York: Paulist Press.

Doron, Pinchas. 1978. "Motive Clauses in the Laws of Deuteronomy: Their Forms, Functions and Contents," *Hebrew Annual Review* 2: 61–77.

Dugan, Ianthe Jeanne and Alistair MacDonald. 2009. "Traders Blamed for Oil Spike," *Wall Street Journal*. July 28.

Dworkin, R. 1981. "What is Equality?" *Philosophy and Public Affairs* 10: 185–246.

The Economist. 2009. "Trade Compression: Number Crunch." July 9.

Edgerton, Henry. 1924a. "Legal Cause, Part I," *University of Pennsylvania Law Review and American Law Register* 72: 211–244.

1924b. "Legal Cause, Part II," *University of Pennsylvania Law Review and American Law Register* 72: 343–375.

Elegant, Simon. 2007. "China's Me Generation," *Time*. November 5.

Essick, Kristi. 2001. "Guns, Money and Cell Phones," *The Industry Standard Magazine*. June 11. www.globalissues.org/article/442/guns-money-and-cell-phones (last accessed June 6, 2009).

Fackler, Martin. 2008. "In Japan, a Robust Yen Undermines the Markets," *New York Times*. October 28.

Fagothey, Austin. 1972. *Right and Reason: Ethics in Theory and Practice*. Fifth edition. St. Louis, MO: C. V. Mosby.

Feinberg, Joel. 1970. "Collective Responsibility," in *Doing and Deserving: Essays in the Theory of Responsibility*. Princeton University Press.

1984. *Harm to Others: the Moral Limits of the Criminal Law*. Oxford University Press.

1986. *Harm to Self: The Moral Limits of the Criminal Law*. Oxford University Press.

1988. *Harmless Wrongdoing: The Moral Limits of the Criminal Law*. Oxford University Press.

Finn, Dan. 2005. "Centesimus Annus," in *Modern Catholic Social Teaching: Commentaries and Interpretations*. Edited by Kenneth Himes. Washington, DC: Georgetown University Press, pp. 436–467.

2006. *The Moral Ecology of Markets: Assessing Claims about Markets and Justice*. Cambridge University Press.

Foster, George. 1967. "Peasant Society and the Image of Limited Good," in *Peasant Society: A Reader*. Edited by Jack Potter, May Diaz, and George Foster. Boston, MA: Little, Brown.

Freeman, Chris and Carlota Perez. 1988. "Structural Crises of Adjustment, Business Cycles and Investment Behaviour," in *Technical Change and Economic Theory*. Edited by Giovanni Dosi, Christopher Freeman, Richard Nelson, Gerald Silverberg, and Luc Soete. London and New York: Pinter.

Fumerton, Richard and Ken Kress. 2001. "Causation and the Law: Preemption, Lawful Sufficiency, and Causal Sufficiency," *Law and Contemporary Problems* 64: 83–105.

Gemser, B. 1953. "The Importance of the Motive Clause in Old Testament Law," in *Congress Volume, Copenhagen, Vetus Testatmentum Supplements*, Vol. I. Leiden: E. J. Brill.

George, David. 2001. *Preference Pollution: How Markets Create the Desires We Dislike*. Ann Arbor: University of Michigan Press.

Gilbert, Margaret. 2002. "Collective Wrongdoing: Moral and Legal Responses," *Social Theory and Practice* 28: 167–187.

Gilchrist, Mary J., Christina Greko, David B. Wallinga, George W. Beran, David G. Riley, and Peter S. Thorne. 2007. "The Potential Role of Concentrated Animal Feeding Operations in Infectious Disease Epidemics and Antibiotic Resistance," *Environmental Health Perspectives* 115: 313–316.

Gillett, Richard. 2005. *The New Globalization: Reclaiming the Lost Ground of Our Christian Social Tradition*. Cleveland, OH: Pilgrim Press.

Gnuse, Robert. 1985. *You Shall Not Steal: Community and Property in the Biblical Tradition*. Maryknoll, NY: Orbis.

Gold, Russell and Ana Campoy. 2009. "Oil Industry Braces for Drop in U.S. Thirst for Gasoline," *Wall Street Journal*. April 13.

Golding, M. P. 1961. "Causation in the Law," *Journal of Philosophy* 59: 85–95.

Gonsalves, Milton. 1990. *Fagothey's Right and Reason: Ethics in Theory and Practice*. Ninth edition. Englewoods, NJ: Prentice Hall.

Gonzalez, Justo. 1990. *Faith and Wealth: A History of Early Christian Ideas on the Origin, Significance, and Use of Money*. San Francisco: Harper & Row.

Gowri, A. 2004. "When Responsibility Can't Do It," *Journal of Business Ethics* 54: 33–50.

Graham, Keith. 2006. "Improving and Embracing Collective Responsibility: Why the Moral Difference?" *Midwest Studies in Philosophy* 30: 256–268.

Gregory, James. 1975. "Image of Limited Good, or Expectation of Reciprocity?" *Current Anthropology* 16: 73–92.

Griese, Orville. 1987. *Catholic Identity in Health Care: Principles and Practice.* Braintree, MA: Pope John Center.

Grisez, Germain. 1997. *The Way of the Lord Jesus, Volume III: Difficult Moral Questions.* Quincy, IL: Franciscan Press.

Hardin, G. 1968. "The Tragedy of the Commons," *Science* 162: 1243–1248.

Häring, Bernard. 1964. *The Law of Christ, Volume II: Special Moral Theology.* Westminster, MD: Newman Press.

Harris, Gardiner. 2009. "Administration Seeks to Restrict Antibiotics in Livestock," *New York Times.* July 14.

Harsanyi, John. 1979. "Bayesian Decision Theory, Rule Utilitarianism, and Arrow's Impossibility Theorem," *Theory and Decision* 11: 289–317.

Hart, H. L. A. and Tony Honoré. 1985. *Causation in the Law.* Second edition. Oxford: Clarendon Press.

Hauerwas, Stanley. 1981. *A Community of Character.* Notre Dame University Press.

  1984. "The Moral Authority of Scripture: The Politics and Ethics of Remembering," in *The Use of Scripture in Moral Theology.* Readings in Moral Theology No. 4. Edited by Charles Curran and Richard McCormick. New York: Paulist Press.

Heap, Shaun Hargreaves. 1989. *Rationality in Economics.* Oxford and New York: Basil Blackwell.

Henderson, James and Richard Quandt. 1971. *Microeconomic Theory: A Mathematical Approach.* Second edition. Tokyo: McGraw-Hill.

Hicks, John. 1979. *Causality in Economics.* New York: Basic Books.

Himes, Kenneth. 1986. "Social Sin and the Role of the Individual," *The Annual of the Society of Christian Ethics*: 183–218.

Honoré, Tony. 1961. "Causation in the Law," in *Freedom and Responsibility.* Edited by Herbert Morris. Stanford University Press. Originally published in *Law Quarterly Review* 72 (1956), Part I: 58–90.

  1973. "Causation and Remoteness of Damage," *International Encyclopedia of Comparative Law.* Vol. 11, Chapter 7. Tubingen and New York: J. C. B. Mohr.

Howarth, David. 1987. "'O Madness of Discourse, That Cause Sets up with and Against Itself.' Book review of *Causation in the Law* by H. L. A. Hart and Tony Honoré," *The Yale Law Review* 96: 1389–1424.

Hulbert, Mark. 2008. "Maybe Short-Selling Isn't so Bad, After All," *New York Times.* September 28.

Isaacs, Tracy. 2006. "Collective Moral Responsibility and Collective Intention," *Midwest Studies in Philosophy* 30: 59–73.

Ivanic, Maros and Will Martin. 2008. *Implications of Higher Global Food Prices for Poverty in Low-Income Countries.* World Bank Policy Research Working Paper no. 4594. Washington, DC: World Bank.

John Paul II. 1979. *Redemptor Hominis (Redeemer of Man).* Vatican City.

  1981. *Laborem Exercens.* Boston: Daughters of St. Paul.

  1987. *Sollicitudo Rei Socialis.* Boston: Daughters of St. Paul.

Johnson, Luke Timothy. 2004. "Making Connections: The Material Expression of Friendship in the New Testament." *Interpretation* 58: 158–171.

Jonas, Hans. 1984. *The Imperative of Responsibility: In Search for an Ethics for the Technological Age*. Translated by Hans Jonas and David Herr. University of Chicago Press.

Jones, E. L. 1987. *The European Miracle: Environments, Economies and Geopolitics in the History of Europe and Asia*. Second edition. Cambridge University Press.

Kadish, Sanford. 1985. "Complicity, Cause and Blame: A Study in the Interpretation of Doctrine," *California Law Review* 73: 323–410.

Kant, Immanuel. 1785 [1990]. *Foundations of the Metaphysics of Morals*. Second edition. Translated by Lewis White Beck. New York: Macmillan.

Kaveny, M. Cathleen. 2000. "Appropriation of Evil: Cooperation's Mirror Image," *Theological Studies* 61: 280–313.

2003. "Complicity with Evil," *Criterion*. Autumn: 20–29.

Keenan, James and Thomas Kopfensteiner. 1995. "The Principle of Cooperation: Theologians Explain Material and Formal Cooperation," *Health Progress* 76: 23–27.

Kenner, Robert, producer. 2009. *Food, Inc.* (videorecording). Los Angeles, CA: Magnolia Home Entertainment.

Kernohan, Andrew. 1993. "Accumulative Harms and the Interpretation of the Harm Principle," *Social Theory and Practice* 19: 51–72.

Keynes, John Maynard. 1936. *The General Theory of Employment, Interest, and Money*. New York: Harcourt Brace.

Kim, Anthony. 2007. "The Asian Financial Crisis 10 Years Later: Time to Reaffirm Economic Freedom," Heritage Foundation, Washington, DC. www.heritage.org/research/asiaandthepacific/bg2054.cfm#_ftn2 (last accessed June 21, 2009).

King, Michael. 2001. "Who Triggered the Asian Financial Crisis," *Review of International Political Economy* 8: 438–466.

Kissell, Judith Lee. 1996. "A Comprehensive View of Complicity as Positive Collaboration and Toleration-of-Evil." Doctoral dissertation, Georgetown University. Ann Arbor, MI: UMI.

1998. "Complicity and Narrative: Insight for the Healthcare Professional," *Medicine, Healthcare and Philosophy* 1: 263–269.

1999. "Complicity in Thought and Language: Toleration of Wrong," *Journal of Medical Humanities* 20: 49–60.

Kristof, Nicholas. 2009. "Striking the Brothels' Bottom Line," *New York Times*. January 11.

Kroft, Steve. 2009. "Did Speculation Fuel Oil Price Swings?" *60 Minutes CBS News*. "The Price of Oil." January 11. www.cbsnews.com/stories/2009/01/08/60minutes/main4707770.shtml (last accessed June 21, 2009).

Kuttner, Robert. 1996. *Everything for Sale: The Virtues and Limits of Markets*. University of Chicago Press.

Kutz, Christopher. 2000. *Complicity: Ethics and Law for a Collective Age*. Cambridge Studies in Philosophy and Law. Cambridge University Press.

Lafraniere, Sharon. 2008. "Europe Takes Africa's Fish and Boatloads of Migrants Follow," *New York Times*. January 14.

Lang, Bernhard. 1985. "The Social Organization of Peasant Poverty in Biblical Israel," in *Anthropological Approaches to the Old Testament*. Edited by Bernhard Lang. Philadelphia, PA: Fortress Press; London: SPCK, pp. 83–99.

Leo XIII. 1891. *Rerum Novarum*. Boston: Daughters of St. Paul.

Lichtenberg, Judith. 2008. "The Demandingness of Negative Duties," unpublished paper. http://web.nmsu.edu/~philosophia/demandingness%20of%20negative%20duties.doc (last accessed June 8, 2009).

Liguori, Alphonsus. 1905–1912. *Theologia Moralis*. Edited by L. Gaudé. 4 vols. Rome: Ex Typographia Vaticana.

Locke, John. 1690 [1960]. *Two Treatises of Government*. Edited by Peter Laslett. Cambridge University Press.

Lohfink, Norbert. 1986. "The Kingdom of God and the Economy in the Bible," *Communio: International Catholic Review* 13: 216–231.

    1987. *Option for the Poor: The Basic Principle of Liberation Theology in Light of the Bible*. Berkeley, CA: Bibal Press.

    1991. "Poverty in the Laws of the Ancient Near East and of the Bible," *Theological Studies* 52: 34–50.

Lowenstein, Roger. 2008. "Triple-A Failure: The Ratings Game," *New York Times Magazine*. April 27. www.nytimes.com/2008/04/27/magazine/27Credit-t.html (last accessed June 21, 2009).

Lüpke, Johannes von. 2009. "Responsibility as Response: Biblical-Theological Remarks on the Concept of Responsibility," *Studies in Christian Ethics* 22: 461–471.

Lutheran Church in America. 1980. "Economic Justice: Stewardship of Creation in the Human Community," Adopted at the Tenth Biennial Convention., Seattle, Washington. www.seminary.wlu.ca/docs/publicpolicy/socialjustice_2.pdf (last accessed December 20, 2009.)

McKinley, James. 2009. "U.S. is Arms Bazaar for Mexican Cartels," *New York Times*. February 26.

Malkin, Elisabeth. 2007. "Thousands in Mexico Protest Rising Food Prices," *New York Times*. February 1.

Maloney, Robert. 1974. "Usury and Restrictions on Interest-Taking in the Ancient Near East," *Catholic Biblical Quarterly* 36: 1–20.

Mangan, Joseph. 1949. "An Historical Analysis of the Principle of Double Effect," *Theological Studies* 10: 41–61.

Maritain, Jacques. 1947. *Person and the Common Good*. Translated by John J. Fitzgerald. New York: Charles Scribner's Sons.

Marx, Karl. 1867 [1906]. *Capital: A Critique of Political Economy*. New York: Modern Library.

Matera, Frank. 1996. *New Testament Ethics: The Legacies of Jesus and Paul*. Louisville, KY: Westminster John Knox Press.

Meeks, Wayne. 1983. *The First Urban Christians: The Social World of the Apostle Paul*. New Haven: Yale University Press.

Meier, Gerald. 1995. *Leading Issues in Economic Development*. Sixth edition. Oxford University Press.

Mellon, Margaret, Charles Benbrook, and Karen Lutz Benbrook 2001. *Hogging It: Estimates of Antimicrobial Abuse in Livestock*. Cambridge, MA: Union of Concerned Scientists. www.ucsusa.org/assets/documents/food_and_agriculture/hog_front.pdf (last accessed June 20, 2009).

Merced, Michael de la and Zachery Kouwe. 2009. "'Vulture' Investors Eye Bad Assets, but Warily," *New York Times*. February 11.

Mill, John Stuart. 1843 [1973]. *A System of Logic, Ratiocinative and Inductive, Being a Connected View of the Principles of Evidence and the Methods of Scientific Investigation*. Vol. VII of *Collected Works of John Stuart Mill*. General editor: J. M. Robson. London: Routledge & Kegan Paul; Toronto: University of Toronto Press.

1859 [1974]. *On Liberty*. Harmandsworth: Penguin.

Miller, Patrick. 1985. "The Human Sabbath: A Study in Deuteronomic Theology," *Princeton Seminary Bulletin* 6: 81–97.

Mokyr, Joel. 1990. *The Lever of Riches: Technological Creativity and Economic Progress*. Oxford University Press.

Moore, Michael. 1999. "Causation and Responsibility," *Social Philosophy and Policy* 16: 1–51.

2002. "Causation," in *Encyclopedia of Crime and Justice*. Edited by Joshua Dressler. Second edition. New York: Macmillan.

Morris, Herbert, ed. 1961. *Freedom and Responsibility: Readings in Philosophy and Law*. Stanford University Press.

National Conference of Catholic Bishops (NCCB). 1986. *Economic Justice for All: Pastoral Letter on Catholic Social Teaching and the US Economy*. Washington, DC: NCCB.

Nelson, Derek. 2009. *What is Wrong with Sin? Sin in Individual and Social Perspective from Schleiermacher to Theologies of Liberation*. Edinburgh: T&T Clark.

Neufeld, Edward. 1953–1954. "The Rate of Interest and the Text of Nehemiah 5:11," *Jewish Quarterly Review* 44: 194–204.

Newman, Bryan. 2007. "Indian Farmer Suicides – A Lesson for Africa's Farmers," *Food First*. Institute for Food and Policy Development. February 16. www.foodfirst.org/node/1626/print (last accessed June 23, 2009).

Nickelsburg, George. 1978–1979. "Riches, the Rich, and God's Judgment in 1 Enoch 92–105 and the Gospel According to Luke," *New Testament Studies* 25: 324–344.

Niebuhr, Reinhold. 1932. *Moral Man and Immoral Society*. New York: C. Scribner's Sons.

Niebuhr, H. Richard. 1963. *The Responsible Self: An Essay in Christian Moral Philosophy*. New York: Harper and Row.

Noonan, John. 1957. *The Scholastic Analysis of Usury*. Cambridge, MA: Harvard University Press.

Nordstrom, Carolyn. 2007. *Global Outlaws: Crime, Money, and Power in the Contemporary World*. Berkeley: University of California Press.

Oderberg, David. 2004. "The Ethics of Co-operation in Wrongdoing," in *Modern Moral Philosophy*. Edited by Anthony O'Hear. Royal Institute of Philosophy Supplement no. 54. Cambridge University Press, pp. 203–228.

OECD. 2006. *OECD in Figures 2006–2007*. Paris: OECD.

O'Keefe, Mark. 1990. *What They are Saying about Social Sin?* New York: Paulist Press.

Parfit, Derek 1984. *Reasons and Persons*. Oxford: Clarendon Press.

Parker, Joseph Clinton. 2003. "Moral Complicity: An Expressivist Account." Doctoral dissertation, Rice University. Ann Arbor, MI: UMI.

Paul VI. 1967. *Populorum Progressio*. Boston: Daughters of St. Paul.

Perkins, Pheme. 1994. "Does the New Testament Have an Economic Message?" in *Wealth in Western Thought: The Case for and Against Riches*. Edited by Paul G. Schervish. Westport, CT: Praeger, pp. 43–64.

Perkinson, James. 1988. "Taking Action for Economic Justice: A Theological Assessment (Summary Statement)." Appendix A, Episcopal General Convention. www.enej.org/pdf/How-to%20Manual/Appendix%20A.PDF (last accessed December 20, 2009.)

Phan, Peter. 1984. *Social Thought*. Message of the Fathers of the Church. Wilimington, DE: Michael Glazier.

Phillips, David Morris. 1982. "The Commercial Culpability Scale," *The Yale Law Journal* 92: 228–290.

Pines, Gina and David Meyer. 2005. "Stopping the Exploitation of Workers: An Analysis of the Effective Application of Consumer or Socio-Political Pressure," *Journal of Business Ethics* 59: 155–162.

Pogge, Thomas. 2002. *World Poverty and Human Rights: Cosmopolitan Responsibilities and Reforms*. Cambridge, UK: Polity Press.

    2005. "Severe Poverty as a Violation of Negative Duties," *Ethics and International Affairs* 19: 55–83.

Polanyi, Karl. 1944. *The Great Transformation*. New York: Farrar and Rinehart.

Pontifical Council for Peace and Justice. 2004. *Compendium of the Social Doctrine of the Church*. Vatican City.

Porter, Jean. 1995. *Moral Action and Christian Ethics*. Cambridge University Press.

    2005. "Virtue," in *Oxford Handbook of Theological Ethics*. Edited by Gilbert Meilaender and William Werpehowski. Oxford University Press, pp. 205–219.

Prasad, Eswar, Kenneth Rogoff, Shang-Jin Wei, and M. Ayhan Kose. 2003. *Effects of Financial Globalization on Developing Countries: Some Empirical Evidence*. International Monetary Fund Occasional Paper no. 220. Washington, DC: International Monetary Fund.

Presbyterian Church (USA). 1984. *Christian Faith and Economic Justice*. Office of the General Assembly. Louisville, KY: Presbyterian Church (USA).

    1985. *Toward a Just, Caring and Dynamic Political Economy*. Advisory Council on Church and Society. New York: Presbyterian Church (USA).

Prosser, William. 1971. *Handbook of the Law of Torts*. Fourth edition. Hornbook series. St. Paul, MN: West Publishing.

Puliam, Susan, Liz Rappaport, Aaron Lucchetti, Jenny Strasburg, and Tom McGinty. 2008. "Anatomy of the Morgan Stanley Panic–Trading Records Tell Tale of How Rivals' Bearish Bets Pounded Stock in September," *Wall Street Journal*. November 24.

Ragazzi, Maurizio. 2004. "The Concept of Social Sin in its Thomistic Roots," *Journal of Markets and Morality* 7: 363–408.

Rawlings, Laura and Gloria Rubio. 2003. *Evaluating the Impact of Conditional Cash Transfer Programs: Lessons from Latin America*. World Bank Policy Research Working Paper no. 3119.

Rawls, John. 1971. *A Theory of Justice*. Cambridge, MA: Harvard University Press.

Raz, Joseph. 1986. *The Morality of Freedom*. New York: Oxford University Press.

Reformed Church in America. 1984. "Biblical Faith and Our Economic Life, Report of the Christian Action Committee," in *Acts and Proceedings of the 1984 General Synod*. Grand Rapids, MI: Reformed Church in America.

  1990. "The Two-tiered Society: Inequality and the Ascendancy of Capitalism, Report of the Christian Action Committee," in *Acts and Proceedings of the 1990 General Synod*. Grand Rapids, MI: Reformed Church in America.

Robeck, Nesta de. 1953. *Saint Elizabeth of Hungary: A Story of Twenty-four Years*. Milwaukee, WI: Bruce.

Robinson, H. W. 1936. "The Hebrew Conception of Corporate Personality," *Beiträge zur Wissenschaft vom Alten (und Neuen) Testament* 66: 49–62.

Rodrik, Dani. 1998. "Why Do More Open Economies Have Bigger Governments?" *Journal of Political Economy* 106: 997–1032.

Roover, Raymond de. 1974. "The Scholastic Attitude toward Trade and Entrepreneurship," in *Business, Banking, and Economic Thought in Late Medieval and Early Modern Europe*. Edited by Julius Kirshner. University of Chicago Press.

Rosenbloom, Stephanie. 2009. "At Wal-Mart, Labeling to Reflect Green Intent," *New York Times*. July 16.

Rosenbloom, Stephanie and Michael Barbaro. 2009. "Green-Light Specials, Now at Wal-Mart," *New York Times*. January 25.

Ross, Robert. 2004. *Slaves to Fashion: Poverty and Abuse in the New Sweatshops*. Ann Arbor, MI: University of Michigan Press.

Rossouw, G. J. (Deon). 2003. "Business is not Just War. Transferring the Principle of Double Effect from War to Business," *South African Journal of Philosophy* 22: 236–246. Reprinted in *Responsibility in World Business: Managing the Harmful Side-effects of Corporate Activity*. Edited by Lene Bomann-Larsen and Oddny Wiggen. Tokyo and New York: United Nations University Press, pp. 39–49.

Rudzinski, Aleksander. 1966. "The Duty to Rescue: A Comparative Analysis," in *The Good Samaritan and the Law*. Edited by James Ratcliffe. Garden City, NY: Anchor.

Sacred Congregation for the Doctrine of the Faith. 1986. *Instruction on Christian Freedom and Liberation*. Boston: Daughters of St. Paul.

Sartre, Jean-Paul. 1948. *The Emotions: Outline of a Theory*. Translated by Bernard Frechtman. New York: Philosophical Library.

Scannell, Kara. 2009. "US Issues New Rules on Short-Selling," *Wall Street Journal.* July 28.

Schendel, Willem van and Itty Abraham. 2005. *Illicit Flows and Criminal Things: States, Borders, and the Other Side of Globalization.* Indianapolis: Indiana University Press.

Schliesser, Christine. 2006. "Accepting Guilt for the Sake of Germany: An Analysis of Bonhoeffer's Concept of Accepting Guilt and its Implications for Bonhoeffer's Political Resistance," *Union Seminary Quarterly Review* 60: 56–68.

    2008. *Everyone Who Acts Responsibly Becomes Guilty: Bonhoeffer's Concept of Accepting Guilt.* Louisville, KY: Westminster John Knox Press.

Schmidt, Thomas. 1987. *Hostility to Wealth in the Synoptic Gospels. Journal for the Study of the New Testament*, Supplement series 15. Sheffield: JSOT Press.

Schrage, Wolfgang. 1988. *The Ethics of the New Testament.* Translated by David E. Green. Philadelphia: Fortress Press.

Schultz, Walter. 2001. *The Moral Conditions of Economic Efficiency.* Cambridge University Press.

Schweiker, William. 1995. *Responsibility and Christian Ethics.* New Studies in Christian Ethics no. 6. Cambridge University Press.

    2009. "Protestant Ethics," in *Handbook of Economics and Ethics.* Edited by Jan Peil, and Irene van Staveren. Northampton, MA: Edward Elgar, pp. 407–415.

Second International Conference on Christian Faith and Economics. 1990. "Oxford Declaration on Christian Faith and Economics," *Transformation* 7: 1–8. Reprinted in *On Moral Business: Classical and Contemporary Resources for Ethics in Economic Life* (1995). Edited by Max Stackhouse, Dennis McCann, and Shirley Roels with Preston Williams. Grand Rapids, MI: Eerdmans, pp. 472–482.

Sedgwick, Peter. 1999. *Market Economy and Christian Ethics.* Cambridge University Press.

Sen, Amartya. 1983. *Poverty and Famines: An Essay on Entitlement and Deprivation.* Oxford University Press.

    1992. *Inequality Reexamined.* Cambridge, MA: Harvard University Press.

    1995. "Moral Codes and Economic Success," in *Market Capitalism and Moral Values: Proceedings of Section f (Economics) of the British Association for the Advancement of Science, Keele 1993.* Edited by Samuel Brittan, and Alan Hamlin. Brookfield, VT: Edward Elgar, pp. 23–34.

Sennett, Richard. 1998. *The Corrosion of Character: The Personal Consequences of Work in the New Capitalism.* New York: W. Norton.

Shavell, Steven. 1980. "An Analysis of Causation and the Scope of Liability in the Law of Torts," *The Journal of Legal Studies* 9: 463–516.

Shue, Henry. 1980. *Basic Rights: Subsistence, Affluence, and US Foreign Policy.* Princeton University Press.

Sider, Ronald. 1977. *Rich Christians in an Age of Hunger: A Biblical Study.* Downers Grove, IL: InterVarsity Press.

Singer, Peter. 2009. *The Life You Can Save: Acting Now to End World Poverty.* New York: Random House.

Smiley, Marion. 1992. *Moral Responsibility and the Boundaries of Community: Power and Accountability from a Pragmatic Point of View.* University of Chicago Press.

Smith, Adam. 1776 [1937]. *The Wealth of Nations.* Edited by Edwin Canaan. New York: Modern Library.

Smith, Jeremiah. 1911–1912. "Legal Cause in Actions of Torts,"(three parts) *Harvard Law Review*: Part I. (1911, 25(2): 103–128); Part II (1911, 25(3): 223–252); Part III (1912, 25(4): 303–327).

Smith, Randall and Aaron Lucchetti. 2009. "Relief and Resignation Spread across Wall Street," *Wall Street Journal.* June 19.

Smock, Audrey Chapman, ed. 1987. *Christian Faith and Economic Life.* New York: United Church Board for World Ministries.

Social Investment Forum. 2007. *2007 Report on Socially Responsible Investing Trends in the United States.* Washington, DC: Social Investment Forum. www.socialinvest.org/pdf/SRI_Trends_ExecSummary_2007.pdf (last accessed February 11, 2010).

Song, Young-Bae. 2002. "Crisis of Cultural Identity in East Asia: On the Meaning of Confucian Values in the Age of Globalisation," *Asian Philosophy* 12: 109–25.

Sparkes, Russell. 2002. *Socially Responsible Investments: A Global Revolution.* Hoboken, NJ: Wiley.

Stapleton, Jane. 1988. "Law, Causation and Common Sense," *Oxford Journal of Legal Studies* 8: 111–131.

Synod of Bishops. 1971. *Justice in the World.* Boston: Daughters of St. Paul.

Third International Conference on Christian Faith and Economics. 1995. "Agra Affirmations on Christian Faith, Market Economics and the Poor," *Transformation* 12: 5–7.

Tillich, Paul. 1963. *Morality and Beyond.* New York: Harper Torchbook.

Tomasi, John. 1998. "The Key to Locke's Proviso," *British Journal of the History of Philosophy* 6: 447–454.

Trimiew, Darryl. 1997. *God Bless the Child that Got its Own: The Economic Rights Debate.* Atlanta, GA: Scholars Press.

2000. "The Renewal of Covenant and the Problem of Economic Rights: The Contributions of Daniel Elazar," *Annual of the Society of Christian Ethics* 20: 105–109.

United Church of Christ. 1989. "A Pronouncement on Christian Faith: Economic Life and Justice," Appendix in *Do Justice: Linking Christian Faith and Modern Economic Life* by Rebecca Blank. www.ucc.org/justice/economic-justice/pdfs/DoJustice.pdf (last accessed December 20, 2009).

United Methodist Church. 2000. "Economic Justice for a New Millennium." http://archives.umc.org/interior.asp?ptid=4&mid=916 (last accessed December 20, 2009).

Vatican II. 1964. "Lumen Gentium (Dogmatic Constitution of the Church)," in *Vatican II: The Conciliar and Post Conciliar Documents.* General Editor: Austin Flannery. Boston: Daughters of St. Paul.

1965. *Gaudium et Spes.* www.vatican.va/archive/hist_councils/ii_vatican_council/documents/vat-ii_const_19651207_gaudium-et-spes_en.html (last accessed February 11, 2010).

Vaux, Roland de. 1965. *Ancient Israel.* 2 vols. New York: McGraw-Hill.

Verhey, Allen. 1984. *The Great Reversal: Ethics and the New Testament.* Grand Rapids, MI: Eerdmans.

Villars Statement on Relief and Development 1991. Reprinted in *On Moral Business: Classical and Contemporary Resources for Ethics in Economic Life.* 1995. Edited by Max Stackhouse, Dennis McCann, and Shirley Roels with Preston Williams. Grand Rapids, MI: Eerdmans.

Waldron, Jeremy. 1979. "Enough and As Good Left for Others," *Philosophical Quarterly* 29: 3190–3228.

Waterman, A. M. C. 2002. "Economics as Theology: Adam Smith's Wealth of Nations," *Southern Economic Journal* 68: 907–921.

Weber, Karl, ed. 2009. *Food Inc.: How Industrial Food is Making us Sicker, Fatter and Poorer – and What You Can Do About it.* New York: Public Affairs.

Wesley, John. 1872. "The Use of Money," Sermon 50 (1872 edition, edited by Thomas Jackson). http://gbgm-umc.org/umw/Wesley/serm-050.stm (last accessed February 8, 2010).

Wessell, David and Bob Davis. 2007. "Pain from Free Trade Spurs Second Thoughts," *Wall Street Journal.* March 28.

Williams, Garrath. 2002. "'No Participation without Implication': Understanding the Wrongs We Do Together," *Res Publica* 8: 201–210.

Williams, Glanville. 1951. *Joint Torts and Contributory Negligence.* London: Stevens.

Wogaman, J. Philip. 1986. *Economics and Ethics: A Christian Inquiry.* Philadelphia: Fortress Press.

World Bank. 2005. *World Development Report 2006: Equity and Development.* Washington, DC: World Bank.

2008. "Food Price Crisis in Africa," *World Bank Research Digest* 3: 1, 8.

Wright, Christopher. 1990. *God's People in God's Land: Family, Land, and Property in the Old Testament.* Grand Rapids, MI: Eerdmans.

Wright, John. 1957. *The Order of the Universe in the Theology of St. Thomas Aquinas.* Analecta Gregoriana 89. Rome: Apud Aedes Universitatis Gregorianae.

Wright, Richard. 1988. "Causation, Responsibility, Risk, Probability, Naked Statistics, and Proof: Pruning the Bramble Bush by Clarifying the Concepts," *Iowa Law Review* 73 (July).

Yergin, Daniel and Joseph Stanislaw. 1998. *The Commanding Heights: The Battle between Government and the Marketplace that is Remaking the Modern World.* New York: Simon & Schuster.

Zak, Paul, ed. 2008. *Moral Markets: The Critical Role of Values in the Economy.* Princeton University Press.

Zanardi, William. 1990. "Consumer Responsibility from a Social Systems Perspective," *International Journal of Applied Philosophy* 8: 57–66.

Index

tort law as means of addressing, 72–75. *See also*
    tort law
typology of, 5, 97–99
unstructured harms, quasi-participatory intent
    in. *See* quasi-participatory intent in
    unstructured harms
wrongdoing. *See* wrongdoing, benefiting from
    and enabling
market failures, 211
market outcomes, distribution of, 43–45
Marx, Karl, 227
mass transit, 57, 218
material cooperation, 12, 25–27, 276–277, 281
Medellin Bishops' Conference, 221
mediate cooperation, 12
merchants and commerce, early Christian
    antipathy toward, 161–162
metaphysics, Aristotelean–Thomistic, 54,
    241–243, 263, 264, 272
Methodists, 252
micro-lending, 65, 108, 212
Microsoft PC operating system, as network
    externality, 216
migrant workers, 63, 65, 116, 191, 279
Mill, John Stuart
    on accumulative harms, 36
    gratuitous accumulative harms, precipitating,
        165–166
    interdependent agencies and, 81–82,
        85, 90
    liberty-limiting principle of harm to others,
        36–37, 165–166
    overdetermination and, 55
    pecuniary externalities, failure to attend to,
        181, 185
    wrongdoing, enabling and benefiting from,
        5, 123
minuscule causal contribution, 48–49,
    60–64. *See also* overdetermination
monopolies, market circumstances encouraging,
    210, 212
moral ambiguity in market economics, 259–261
moral blameworthiness versus legal liability,
    66–67
moral complicity versus material cooperation,
    25–27
moral focus of theories of responsibility, 234–238
moral mathematics and overdetermination,
    56–58, 61
moral responsibility for benefiting from/enabling
    wrongdoing, 126–144
morality of market, ongoing struggle to shape,
    281–282
Morgan Stanley, 151
Morris, Herbert, 75

Nazi Germany, 53, 63, 118
necessary (indispensable) cooperation, 13
"necessary element in a set of jointly sufficient
    conditions" (NESS) test, 55–56, 83,
    122–123, 124, 125, 131–135
necessity of market participation, 43
needs versus wants, failure of market to
    distinguish, 208
negative and positive human rights, 225, 226
negative duty in hard complicity, 99
NESS. *See* "necessary element in a set of jointly
    sufficient conditions" test
Nestlé boycott, 63, 65, 217, 220, 279
network externalities, 215–217
NGOs. *See* non-governmental organizations
Niebuhr, H. Richard, 221, 235
Nike, 111
non-governmental organizations (NGOs), 65, 211,
    212, 230
non-reciprocal risk, 190–193

obesity and dietary abuses, 116, 153, 209, 284
object of accountability
    accumulative harms as. *See* accumulative harms
    Christian ethics on, 277
    in gratuitous accumulative harms, 146–158
    in injurious socioeconomic structures, 206–213
    pecuniary externalities, failure to address,
        177–180
    in theology of economic responsibility,
        261–264
    in wrongdoing. *See under* wrongdoing,
        benefiting from and enabling
occasioning harm, tort law on, 166–167
Oderberg, David, 70
omission as cause of harm, 77
ontology and theology of economic responsibility,
    238–243, 263
organic food movement, 284
output markets. *See* demand side economics
overdetermination, 5, 48–69
    absolute responsibility, concept of, 61
    act versus rule utilitarianism, 57–58, 64
    in Christian ethics, 49–54
    collective context, individual action within, 59
    consequentialism or moral mathematics,
        56–58, 61
    distinction of Christian ethics and secular law
        and philosophy on, 68, 271
    duplicative or redundant causation, 48–49,
        54–60
    in economic theory, 64–66
    human community, Christian understanding
        of, 51–53
    metaphysics, Aristotelean–Thomistic, 54